FR◐

Easy

TO
CHARLESTON, SAVANNAH & ST. AUGUSTINE

By

Stephen Keeling and Lesley Abravanel

Easy Guides are ✦ Quick To Read ✦ Light To Carry
✦ For Expert Advice ✦ In All Price Ranges

FrommerMedia LLC

Published by
FROMMER MEDIA LLC

ISBN 978-1-62887-124-1 (paper), 978-62887-125-8 (e-book)

Editorial Director: Pauline Frommer
Development Editor: Billy Fox
Production Editor: Donna Wright
Cartographer: Andrew Dolan

For information on our other products or services, see www.frommers.com.

Frommer Media LLC also publishes its books in a variety of electronic formats. Some content that
appears in print may not be available in electronic formats.

Manufactured in the United States of America

5 4 3 2 1

CONTENTS

ABOUT THE AUTHOR

Stephen Keeling has been traveling to the American South since 1991 and has lived in New York City since 2006. He worked as a financial journalist for 7 years before writing his first travel guide, and has subsequently worked on numerous guidebooks, including *Frommer's Florence, Tuscany & Umbria* and *Frommer's Complete Guide to Italy*.

Lesley Abravanel, like many native New Yorkers, now resides in Florida where she writes three weekly gossip and nightlife columns, a restaurant gossip column and blog for the *Miami Herald*, pens Florida guidebooks for Frommer's, and, in her spare time, collects hot sauces, raises twin toddlers, and attempts to learn Swedish from her Stockholm-born husband. You can always find her on Twitter, where she has no qualms speaking—er, Tweeting—her mind on everything from reality television to politics.

ABOUT THE FROMMER'S TRAVEL GUIDES

For most of the past 50 years, Frommer's has been the leading series of travel guides in North America, accounting for as many as 24% of all guidebooks sold. I think I know why.

Though we hope our books are entertaining, we nevertheless deal with travel in a serious fashion. Our guidebooks have never looked on such journeys as a mere recreation, but as a far more important human function, a time of learning and introspection, an essential part of a civilized life. We stress the culture, lifestyle, history, and beliefs of the destinations we cover, and urge our readers to seek out people and new ideas as the chief rewards of travel.

We have never shied from controversy. We have, from the beginning, encouraged our authors to be intensely judgmental, critical—both pro and con—in their comments, and wholly independent. Our only clients are our readers, and we have triggered the ire of countless prominent sorts, from a tourist newspaper we called "practically worthless" (it unsuccessfully sued us) to the many rip-offs we've condemned.

And because we believe that travel should be available to everyone regardless of their incomes, we have always been cost-conscious at every level of expenditure. Though we have broadened our recommendations beyond the budget category, we insist that every lodging we include be sensibly priced. We use every form of media to assist our readers, and are particularly proud of our feisty daily website, the award-winning Frommers.com.

I have high hopes for the future of Frommer's. May these guidebooks, in all the years ahead, continue to reflect the joy of travel and the freedom that travel represents. May they always pursue a cost-conscious path, so that people of all incomes can enjoy the rewards of travel. And may they create, for both the traveler and the persons among whom we travel, a community of friends, where all human beings live in harmony and peace.

Arthur Frommer

THE BEST OF CHARLESTON, SAVANNAH & ST. AUGUSTINE

Traveling from Charleston to St. Augustine, via Savannah, is just 265 miles and 4 hours by car, but it is a journey that runs through one of the richest cultural corridors in America. Surrounded by the landscapes of the Deep South—live oaks dripping with Spanish moss, stately antebellum mansions, blossoming magnolia trees, and tranquil sea marshes—you'll take a trip back in time, from the romantic English colonies of South Carolina to the subtropical Spanish roots of Florida.

Charleston remains one of the best-preserved cities in America's Old South, a charming colonial enclave of cobbled streets, horse-drawn carriages, and gorgeous mansions. This is where the Civil War—"The War Between the States"—began in 1861. Crumbling plantation houses still lie on secluded, leafy estates, and the scent of fried shrimp, bubbling gumbo, and she-crab soup waft through the streets. **Savannah,** Charleston's Georgian rival, is similar. Both were founded by English colonists, and possess an abundance of Southern charm, elegant architecture, and heaps of history. Yet there are differences. Savannah's graceful squares are unique, lush gardens spread throughout the city, and the nightlife, free-wheeling spirit, and party-centric culture here is more like Key West that its staid northern cousin. **St. Augustine** is the smallest city of the three, similarly loaded with history, but this time with a Spanish flavor that makes it truly unique in North America. From the legendary "Fountain of Youth" and the old Spanish Castillo San Marcos, to the Mediterranean fantasies of Henry Flagler, there's nothing quite like it.

And there's more. In between the three cities, along the steamy, lush Atlantic coastline of the Deep South, are the pristine beaches of Hilton Head, family-friendly resort of Myrtle Beach, unspoiled barrier islands rich in Gullah culture, some of the best golf courses in the country, and enticing colonial towns such Georgetown and Beaufort.

THE best OLD SOUTH EXPERIENCES

- o **Soaking Up the 19th-Century Elegance:** Charleston, Savannah, and smaller towns such as Beaufort and Georgetown in South Carolina are the top destinations in the Deep South where you can experience what life was like in the 19th century by checking into a B&B in a restored historic building. Live out your Rhett Butler or Scarlett O'Hara fantasies in one of these Victorian parlors, surrounded by wall paintings of bygone belles. Typical of these is the **Eliza Thompson House** (see p. 123), built around 1847 in Savannah's antebellum heyday.

- o **Wandering the Isle of Hope:** Spanish conquistador Hernando de Soto came here 4 centuries ago looking for gold. The island later became a place of refuge for Royalists escaping the guillotine of the French Revolution. Today, the **Isle of Hope,** 10 miles south of Savannah, is an evocative and nostalgic reminder of Savannah's yesteryears. You can go for a stroll in a setting of oaks lining the bluff, plenty of Spanish moss, and Georgia pine, dogwood, magnolia, azalea, and ferns. See p. 145.

- o **Having a Picnic Among Plantation Ruins:** This part of the Deep South is littered with elegant plantation buildings, with perhaps the most evocative ruin within the **Wormsloe State Historic Site** south of Savannah. Nature trails are cut through the property, and there are picnic tables (see p. 145). You can imagine being one of the romantic figures in *Gone With the Wind* at the more preserved **Boone Hall** (p. 77), or venerable **Magnolia Plantation & Gardens** (p. 75).

- o **Pursuing Grits, Game & Gumbo:** All three cities are crammed with fine restaurants, with seafood, Southern cuisine, and especially Lowcountry cooking king. Lavish eating and drinking have long been local customs. The surrounding area was (and is) rich in game and fish, including marsh hen, quail, deer, and crab. Adding to these hunters' trophies is the bounty of local gardens, full of old favorites including collard greens, beets, turnips, peas, okra, and corn. That corn is ground into grits as well, and the okra is used to thicken gumbos, for which everyone down here seems to have a favorite recipe.

- o **Enjoying a Martini in Bonaventure Cemetery:** In *Midnight in the Garden of Good and Evil,* Mary Harty invites John Berendt, the author of The Book, for martinis in this moss-draped Savannah cemetery (see p. 146). It has since become a tradition to partake of this quaint custom. On the former grounds of an oak-shaded plantation, you can enjoy your libation amid the long departed. Of course, the proper way to drink a martini, as in "The Book," is from a silver goblet. Your seat? None other than the bench-gravestone of poet Conrad Aiken.

- o **Going Back to Colonial Days:** At **Charles Towne Landing,** gain insight into how colonists lived 300 years ago when they established the first English settlement in South Carolina. Even the animals the settlers encountered, from bears to bison, still roam about (see p. 75). **St. Augustine's Colonial Quarter** is a fine effort to re-create the oft-forgotten Spanish period of early American history (p. 204).

- o **Retracing Gullah life on Daufuskie Island:** Of all the barrier island's along this stretch of coast, **Daufuskie,** the setting for Pat Conroy's autobiographical book *The Water Is Wide* (1972), is the most evocative of old plantation and Gullah culture. You'll need to take a boat to get here (p. 172).

- o **Tasting She-Crab Soup:** She-crab soup is to the Lowcountry what clam chowder is to New England. This rich delicacy has many permutations, but in most kitchens it

Charleston, Savannah & St. Augustine

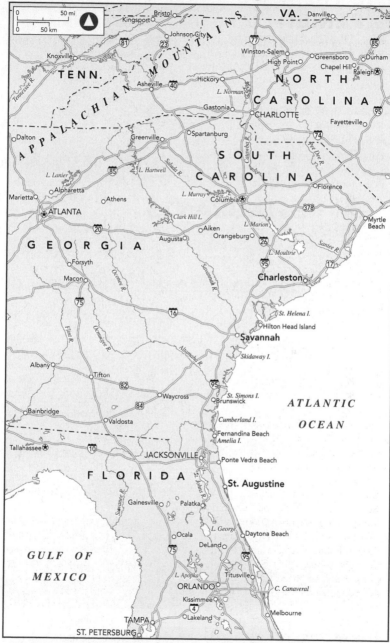

is concocted from butter, milk, heavy cream, sherry, salt, cayenne pepper, crabmeat, and the "secret" ingredient: crab roe. See chapter 5.

o **Seeing Civil War History from the Southern Perspective:** Visit the place where the first shots of the Civil War were fired at **Fort Sumter** on April 12, 1861 (p. 78), or **Fort McAllister State Park** near Savannah, which fell to a bayonet charge that concluded General Sherman's infamous March to the Sea (p. 145). **Old Fort Jackson** (p. 145) served as headquarters for the Confederate river defenses during the Civil War, while the **Confederate Museum in Charleston** (p. 69) preserves the memory of the Boys in Gray.

o **Hiring a Horse & Carriage:** Nothing captures the languid life of the Lowcountry better than a horse-drawn-carriage ride through the semitropical landscape. Most times of year, the heavenly scent of tea olive, jasmine, or wisteria blossoms pervades the streets. You'll feel like you're back in the antebellum South as you slowly clip-clop past sun-dappled verandas and open-air markets selling fruit, vegetables, and straw baskets. For Savannah, see p. 147; for Charleston, see p. 78.

best RESTAURANTS

o **Angel's BBQ, Savannah:** No-frills barbecue joint and minor Savannah institution, thanks to classic pulled pork or BBQ beef brisket sandwiches, accompanied by "angel fries" (fries topped with BBQ-baked beans and cheese), and collard greens with peanuts. See p. 131.

o **A. W. Shuck's, Charleston:** Settles the demands of city dwellers who really know their bivalves. Oysters, perhaps the best in the South, are prepared here in various delightful ways, including, of course, chilled and served on the half shell. See p. 62.

o **Catch 27, St. Augustine:** Fabulous Southern restaurant specializing in fresh seafood. It's a small, cozy place, with a blend of classics like shrimp and grits, gumbo and crab cakes, with more refined dishes such as linguine and clams. See p. 200.

o **Circa 1886 Restaurant, Charleston:** Charleston's most elegant setting for a romantic dinner. That it also serves some of the city's best Lowcountry and French cuisine comes as an added bonus. To get in the right mood, take in the water views from the restaurant's cupola. See p. 56.

o **Elizabeth on 37th, Savannah:** Housed in a palatial neoclassical villa from the turn of the 20th century, it's filled with antique furniture from the *Gone With the Wind* era. The food brings a modern interpretation to the South's cuisine—black-eyed peas are served with cauliflower and roasted shitake mushrooms, and the Savannah red rice is enlivened with shrimp, river clams, grouper, sausage, and okra. See p. 133.

o **Fig, Charleston:** Contemporary, exceedingly creative bistro leading the farm-to-table movement in Charleston, with ingredients sourced from Lowcountry producers. See p. 56.

o **The Floridian, St. Augustine:** Fresh, locally sourced produce and a creative menu, blending Southern classics with lighter options, makes this extra special; think fried grit cakes or marinated chicken topped with sweet potato dumplings. See p. 200.

o **Gary Lee's Market, Brunswick:** Best barbecue on the whole coast, served in an old-school, no-frills shack. Order sandwiches, plate lunches, or cuts of beef and smoked sausages by the pound to take home. Finish off with a slice of pie or cake, all made locally. See p. 180.

- **Hall's Chophouse, Charleston:** Best steakhouse in the South, with 28-day aged steaks, supplied by Allen Brothers of Chicago, a buttery treat that melts in the mouth. See p. 58.
- **Mrs. Wilkes' Dining Room, Savannah:** Another Savannah tradition. Visitors and locals have been standing in line here since the 1940s for real downhome Southern fare. Mrs. Wilkes' time-tested recipes get a workout every day, feeding generations of the local citizenry on barbecued chicken, red rice and sausage, corn on the cob, squash and yams, and plenty of dishes with okra. Don't leave without trying Mrs. Wilkes' cornbread and collard greens. See p. 130.
- **Olde Pink House Restaurant, Savannah:** Seems to put more flavor into its offerings than its competitors do. You don't get just fried fish here, but the likes of black grouper stuffed with blue crab and drenched in a Vidalia onion sauce, or crispy scored flounder with a tangy apricot sauce. The setting is both elegant and romantic, making the Pink House even more appealing. See p. 129.
- **Sundae Café, Tybee Island:** An unlikely gem hidden away in a strip mall off the beach, serving cool, contemporary Southern-style cuisine and an incredible key lime pie. See p. 159.
- **Vine Bistro & Wine Bar, Hilton Head:** Cozy, Italian-style bistro with a farm-to-table menu inspired by the cuisines of the Mediterranean, France, and Italy. Chef Olivier Allain's creations range from salmon pasta and line-caught, crispy black grouper, to an unforgettable osso buco. See p. 168.

best HOTELS

- **Casa Monica, St. Augustine:** By far the most elegant choice in the heart of Old Town, a magnificently restored, Spanish-style 1888 gem with uniquely furnished rooms and an air of royalty. See p. 199.
- **The Cloister, Sea Island:** This hotel has been called the grande dame of all Southern resorts. The Cloister's clubby vibe means formal dinners by night and outdoor activities by day: Think along the lines of the best tennis in Georgia, riding, fishing, and swimming (at the beach or in two inviting pools). See p. 186.
- **Governor's House Inn, Charleston:** Luxurious B&B in a two-story wooden mansion built way back in 1760. Relax like a colonial planter in paneled rooms with canopy beds, fireplaces, antiques, and original hardwood floors. See p. 50.
- **Hamilton-Turner Inn, Savannah:** Dating from 1873, this four-story French Empire house is one of the most upscale B&Bs in Savannah. The building earned notoriety in John Berendt's *Midnight in the Garden of Good and Evil,* but those high-rolling party days are over. It's now a serene oasis. See p. 120.
- **Inn at Middleton Place, Charleston:** Modern luxury hotel secluded among tall pines and live oaks on the grounds of the historic 18th-century Middleton Plantation. See p. 53.
- **Kenwood Inn, St. Augustine:** Enjoying a peaceful location, this 1880s Queen Anne Victorian treasure features gorgeous period rooms, its own pool, and a complimentary cocktail hour every day. See p. 198.
- **Mansion on Forsyth Park, Savannah:** Built in 1888, this is the most spectacular hotel in Savannah and also home to one of the city's top places to eat—700 Drayton Restaurant. See p. 128.

o **Old Village Post House, Mount Pleasant:** Just across the Cooper River from Charleston, this small, charming hotel sits above a lauded restaurant in a quiet historic neighborhood. See p. 54.

o **Rhett House Inn, Beaufort:** A Greek Revival standout built in the 1820s, with the sumptuous rooms blending antiques and oriental rugs with fresh orchids and contemporary style. See p. 177.

o **The Sea Pines Resort, Hilton Head:** This is the oldest and most famous of the island's resort developments. Set on 4,500 thickly wooded acres, with a total of three golf courses, Sea Pines competes for the summer beach traffic as few resorts in the Caribbean ever could. Its focal point is Harbour Town, which is built around one of the most charming marinas in the Carolinas. Luxurious homes and villas open onto the ocean or golf courses. See p. 166.

o **Two Meeting Street Inn, Charleston:** This 1892 Queen Anne mansion harbors one of the city's most enticing B&Bs, with Tiffany stained-glass windows, an attractive wrap-around porch, and carved oak paneling throughout. See p. 51.

o **Wentworth Mansion, Charleston:** An 1886 Second Empire building filled with the kind of architectural details with which America's robber barons decorated their lavish estates: hand-carved marble fireplaces, Tiffany stained-glass windows, and elaborate wood and plasterwork. Built by a rich cotton merchant, the mansion has been successfully converted into one of South Carolina's grandest hotel addresses. See p. 50.

best FOR FAMILIES

o **Colonial Quarter, St. Augustine:** The Colonial Spanish Quarter is a fun reconstruction of life during the Spanish period in Florida, with reconstructed homes and workshops set up circa 1740s, and volunteers dressed like Spaniards. See p. 204.

o **Family Kingdom Amusement Park, Myrtle Beach:** A good, old-fashioned sea-front amusement park, replete with scary wooden roller coasters, carousels, cotton candy, and a Ferris wheel. See also **Splashes Oceanfront Water Park,** just across the street. See p. 102.

o **Patriots Point Naval & Maritime Museum, Charleston:** Explore the USS *Yorktown,* one of America's most famous navy ships, the enlightening Shipyard Museum, the USS *Clamagore,* and even a 1945 submarine. See p. 77.

o **Pirate and Treasure Museum, St. Augustine:** In 2010, this wildly entertaining museum relocated here from Key West, opening a window into the golden age of piracy with a combination of interactive exhibits and rare original documents and artifacts. You even get the chance to fire a cannon (electronically), and a special Hollywood exhibit displays Johnny Depp's actual sword from *Pirates of the Caribbean.* See p. 207.

o **Summer Waves, Jekyll Island:** Kids will love this waterpark with a speed flume, wave pool, and Force 3 slides. For toddlers, there's the Pee Wee Puddle—fun in only a foot of water. See p. 187.

o **WonderWorks, Myrtle Beach:** Kids will delve right into the hands-on learning experiences in this wacky-looking building, with some 100 high-tech games, interactive exhibits, and simulations designed to introduce scientific principles: think hurricanes, optical illusions, and laser tag. See p. 104.

best MUSEUMS

o **Calhoun Mansion, Charleston:** Charleston boasts many house museums but this is the undoubted king of them all, a lavish over-the-top Italianate mansion built in 1876. Tour the house to view the opulent 35 rooms, a grand ballroom, Japanese water gardens with koi ponds, ornate chandeliers, and decorative lighting designed and installed by Louis Comfort Tiffany. See p. 66.

o **Charleston Museum, Charleston:** The best place to learn about Lowcountry history, from the Native Americans who first lived here, to the struggles of the first African American slaves and European settlers, and the American Revolution. See the personal items of Francis Marion—aka the "Swamp Fox"—on display. See p. 67.

o **Lightner Museum, St. Augustine:** Henry Flagler's Spanish Renaissance *Alcazar Hotel* closed in 1931, and now serves as this whimsical museum, containing Victorian cut glass, Tiffany lamps, antique music boxes, an Egyptian mummy, and even a fossilized dinosaur egg. See p. 204.

o **SCAD Museum Of Art, Savannah:** Savannah's top art gallery features a permanent collection of work by Hogarth, Van Dyck, Gainsborough, Salvador Dalí, and Andy Warhol. See p. 143.

o **Patriots Point Naval & Maritime Museum, Charleston:** The region's major museum showstopper contains famed aircraft carrier USS *Yorktown,* a fascinating the Shipyard Museum, the USS *Clamagore,* a 1945 submarine, and the USS *Laffey,* a destroyer commissioned in 1944. See p. 77.

o **Villa Zorayda Museum, St. Augustine:** Built by eccentric Bostonian architect Franklin W. Smith in 1883, the Villa Zorayda was his re-creation of Spain's Alhambra. Today the villa is home to an intriguing collection of Smith's personal belongings and rare antiques, including the "Sacred Cat Rug," a 2,400-year-old carpet made from the hairs of ancient Egyptian cats. See p. 207.

best GOLF COURSES

o **Palmetto Dunes Oceanfront Resort, Hilton Head:** This course, designed by George Fazio, is an 18-hole, 6,534-yard, par-70 course named by Golf Digest as one of the "75 Best American Resort Courses." It has been cited for its combined "length and keen accuracy." See p. 163.

o **Old South Golf Links, Bluffton:** This 18-hole, 6,772-yard, par-72 course has been recognized as one of the "Top 10 Public Courses" by Golf Digest. It has panoramic views and a natural setting that ranges from an oak forest to tidal salt marshes. See p. 163.

o **The Lodge at Sea Island Golf Club, St. Simons Island:** Owned by the Cloister, the most exclusive resort in the South, this widely acclaimed golf course lies at the end of the Avenue of Oaks, the site of a former plantation. Opened in 1927, the club consists of several courses, such as the 18-hole Ocean Forest (7,011 yd., par 72). It has been compared favorably to such golfing meccas as St. Andrews in Scotland and Pebble Beach in California. See p. 184.

best BEACHES

o **Anastasia Island, St. Augustine:** Home to fine beaches just a couple of miles from the Old Town. **St. Augustine Beach** is a family-friendly area, with the wilder Anastasia State Park to the north home to over 1,600 protected acres of dunes, marshes, and a wind-beaten group of live oaks. See p. 209.

o **Hilton Head:** This resort-studded island offers 12 miles of white-sand beaches; still others front the Calibogue and Port Royal sounds. The sand is extremely firm, providing a good surface for biking and many beach games. It's also ideal for walking and jogging—against a backdrop of natural dunes, live oaks, palmettos, and tall Carolina pines. See p. 161.

o **Myrtle Beach & the Grand Strand:** This is the most popular sand strip along the Eastern Seaboard, attracting 12 million visitors a year—more than the state of Hawaii. Sure, it's overdeveloped and crowded in the summer, but what draws visitors to Myrtle Beach is 10 miles of sand, mostly hard packed and the color of brown sugar. See p. 101.

o **Tybee Island, Savannah:** With its golden sands, Tybee makes for a great break from the city. You'll be following the footsteps of Blackbeard, who often took refuge here. See p. 157.

SUGGESTED ITINERARIES

The itineraries that follow take you to some of our favorite places along the enticing coastline between Charleston, Savannah, and St. Augustine. The pace may be a bit breathless for some visitors, so skip a stop occasionally to have some chill-out time—after all, you're on vacation. Of course, you can also use any of these itineraries as a jumping-off point to develop your own custom-made adventure.

If your time is limited, you may want to concentrate on the main attractions, described in "Charleston, Savannah & St. Augustine in 1 Week" tour. If you've been to these cities before, and you have more time, the 2-week itinerary takes in more of the surrounding coastline, often equally fascinating, and littered with old plantations, fine beaches, and historic towns. Families might want to consider the "Charleston, Savannah & St. Augustine for Families" tour.

CHARLESTON, SAVANNAH & ST. AUGUSTINE IN 1 WEEK

Though you could spend months here and still not absorb everything the region has to offer, 1 week of very focused travel will give you a decent taster of the historic and culinary charms of Charleston, Savannah, and St. Augustine. Only 275 miles separate Charleston in South Carolina with St. Augustine in Florida, a distance covered efficiently and relatively quickly by car thanks to I-95 (an interstate that conveniently skirts Savannah about half way along). This weeklong itinerary treads a mix of familiar and less-visited highlights.

Days 1 & 2: Charleston ★★★

Start off at the Battery, aka **White Point Gardens,** to gain a sense of the city's maritime roots and layout. From here you can look out across the harbor and Cooper River to **Fort Sumter,** where the Civil War began—it's an essential first-stop (p. 78). Back in town, take in at least one of Charleston's historic homes: the **Aiken-Rhett House Museum** (p. 66), **Nathaniel Russell House Museum** (p. 71), and **Calhoun Mansion** (p. 66) are the most rewarding for first-timers. Make sure you browse **Charleston City Market** (p. 67), taking in one of the food stalls or restaurants here. To get a dose of history visit the **Charleston Museum** (p. 67) or **Old Slave Mart Museum** (p. 72), and view (from the outside, at least) some of the city's elegant churches: **St. Michael's Episcopal Church** (p. 73) and **Old Bethel United Methodist Church** (p. 72) are the most appealing. End a very exhausting day with a stroll around the languid **College of Charleston** campus before grabbing dinner at one of Charleston's award-winning **restaurants** (p. 68) and seeing a show such as the **Black Fedora** the local "comedy mystery theatre."

For Day 2, you should try to hit one or more of the following four major attractions in the Charleston environs. The most Mercury-footed families manage to see all of them in 1 day. If that's too fast a pace for you, skip one or two. In order of importance, they are **Magnolia Plantation** (p. 75), **Middleton Place** (p. 76), **Cypress Gardens** (p. 91), and **Drayton Hall** (p. 75).

Days 3–5: Savannah ★★★

On the morning of Day 3, leave Charleston, taking U.S. 17 south to I-95 South, which brings you right into Savannah, a distance of 105 miles (2 hr. by car).

You'll be based in Savannah for 3 nights. Set out as soon as you check into a hotel to explore the Historic District and some of Savannah's elegant squares—try and see **Reynolds Square** and **Johnson Square** at least (p. 136). The best way to get acquainted is to take one of the **Old Town Trolley Tours** (p. 147) for orientation purposes, if nothing else. In the afternoon, visit the **Mercer Williams House Museum** (p. 140) and the **Telfair Mansion and Art Museum** (p. 143). Select one of the restaurants along the Savannah riverfront for dinner. On the morning of Day 4, take in the **Owen-Thomas House and Museum** (p. 142) and the **Davenport House Museum** (p. 138). In the afternoon, go on one of the Savannah riverboat cruises operated by the **River Street Riverboat Co.** (p. 147). If you finish in time, browse some of the **shops** of Savannah (our coverage of the possibilities begins on p. 149). On Day 5 you have a choice: There is plenty more to see in Savannah, or you can take in some of the delights in the outskirts. In the city it's worth visiting at least one historic church, such as **Christ Church Episcopal** (p. 136) or **Independent Presbyterian Church** (p. 140), before paying your respects at the **Flannery O'Connor Childhood Home** (p. 138), dedicated to Savannah's greatest writer, and visiting the flamboyant **Green-Meldrim Home** (p. 139). In the afternoon Girl Scouts aficionados may want to check out the **Juliette Gordon Low Birthplace** (p. 141), while the **SCAD Museum Of Art** (p. 143) offers quality art exhibitions and the **Savannah History Museum** (p. 142) is an illuminating introduction to the city's past. End the day with a **ghost tour** of Colonial Park Cemetery (p. 137). If you'd rather get out of the city, spend a day touring bucolic **Isle of Hope** and **Wormsloe Historic Site** (p. 145), or lounge on the beaches at **Tybee Island** (p. 157).

Days 6 & 7: St. Augustine ★★★

On the morning of Day 6, leave Savannah, taking I-95 south all the way to **St. Augustine,** a distance of 175 miles (around 2 hr. 40 min. by car).

Hit the Old Town and stroll along **St. George Street** as soon as you arrive to get a sense of the city's historic roots, though save the **Colonial Spanish Quarter** (p. 192) for the afternoon. While in the area, check out **Peña Peck House** (p. 206), the **Spanish Military Hospital & Museum** (p. 207), or **Ximenez-Fatio House** (p. 208). On Day 7 start with a tour of the breezy battlements at **Castillo de San Marcos** (p. 203), before taking in the **Pirate and Treasure**

Museum (best for families; p. 207) or the **Oldest House** (p. 206). Save the afternoon for some serious museum time: The **Lightner Museum** (p. 204) and **Villa Zorayda Museum** (p. 207) are the best. If you have time, end your adventure with a visit to **The Fountain of Youth** (p. 204).

A 2-WEEK ITINERARY

With 2 weeks to play with it's possible to go beyond the well-trodden (and spectacular) Charleston–Savannah–St. Augustine trail to soak up some of the Lowcountry highlights on route, especially the barrier islands along the coast, littered with untouched forests, crumbling plantations, pristine beaches, and some of the best golf courses in America. Additional stops include the historic town of Beaufort in South Carolina and the Space Coast in Florida, home to America's Space Program.

Days 1 & 2: Charleston ★★★

Follow the itinerary suggested in "Charleston, Savannah & St. Augustine in 1 Week," above.

Day 3: Beaufort ★★

It's a 70-mile drive to our next overnight stopover in **Beaufort,** a small town shaded by huge live oaks, rich in antebellum history and the ambience of the Old South. If you can't make the walking tour by the **Spirit of Old Beaufort** (p. 176), try and visit the **John Mark Verdier House Museum** (p. 176) to get a sense of what life was like here before the Civil War, and pop in to the 18th-century **St. Helena's Episcopal Church** (p. 176). With more time you can drive out to rustic **Hunting Island** (p. 177), and climb the spectacular lighthouse before taking dinner at the **Old Bull Tavern** (p. 178).

Day 4: Hilton Head ★★

It's just 35 miles from Beaufort to **Hilton Head Island,** where you could easily spend the whole day lounging on fabulous **beaches** (p. 161). If history is more your thing, make for the **Coastal Discovery Museum** (p. 161) and try to join a **Gullah Heritage Trail Tour** (p. 161). Hikers and nature lovers will enjoy the numerous trails in the **Audubon-Newhall Preserve** (p. 162), **Sea Pines Forest Preserve** (p. 162), or nearby **Pinckney Island National Wildlife Refuge** (p. 162), while **golfers** are also spoiled for choice (p. 163). Overnight in Hilton Head.

Day 5: Daufuskie Island ★★

For Day 5, pre-arrange a day-trip from Hilton Head to **Daufuskie,** one of the most enigmatic barrier islands on this stretch of coast. Most of the island remains wild and raw live-oak forest, the setting for Pat Conroy's seminal book *The Water Is Wide* (1972), but **tours** (see p. 173) take in all the main sights, and include a meal at the **Old Daufuskie Crab Company Restaurant** (p. 174). Local landmarks include the **Billie Burn Museum** (p. 173), **Bloody Point Lighthouse** (p. 174), several **art galleries,** and the **Mary Fields School** (p. 174) where Conroy taught in the late 1960s. Overnight back on Hilton Head Island.

Days 6–8: Savannah ★★★

Drive 30 miles from Hilton Head to Savannah and follow the itinerary suggested in "Charleston, Savannah & St. Augustine in 1 Week," above.

Days 9 &10: The Golden Isles: St. Simons ★★ & Jekyll ★★

Leave Savannah on the morning of Day 9, heading for the town of **Brunswick,** 75 miles to the south. From Savannah, follow the signs to I-95 to the Brunswick turnoff.

Once at Brunswick, follow the signs to the E. J. Torras Causeway, which leads to **St. Simons Island.** Pick up the makings of a picnic in the village along Mallory Street and enjoy it at the south end of the island at **Neptune Park,** where there's a freshwater swimming pool, a play park for the kiddies, and picnic tables. Instead of driving around, we recommend you take the informative **St. Simons Trolley Island Tour** (p. 181). Make sure you visit **Fort Frederica National Monument** (p. 181) before you leave, a rare remnant of Georgia's early colonial past. If you still have energy, climb up the tower at **St. Simons Island Lighthouse Museum** (p. 182) for scintillating views of the Golden Isles.

On Day 10, drive back over the causeway leading to Brunswick, where you follow Route 17 south for 9 miles to **Jekyll Island;** here you can overnight. Like St. Simons Island, this is mostly an island for play, with its fine beaches and other outdoor pursuits. Drive south on North Beachview Drive to some of the island's 10 miles of public beaches with picnic areas. Try to time your visit to take one of the guided tours of the **Historic District** from the **Jekyll Island Museum** (p. 187) to see the fabled "cottages" of America's Gilded Age millionaires, or visit the injured creatures at the **Georgia Sea Turtle Center** (p. 187).

Day 11: Amelia Island ★★

It's just 62 miles south (mostly on I-95) from Jekyll Island to **Amelia Island** across the Florida state line, so leave early and you'll have a full day here. Start by exploring the shops and cafes in the pretty main town, **Fernandina Beach** (p. 221), whose Victorian heyday is reflected in the array of wooden mansions and turrets along the main drag, Centre Street. The old county jail, now **Amelia Island Museum of History** (p. 224), provides an insight into the island's past, while **Fort Clinch State Park** (p. 222) preserves the remains of an unfinished fortress and several nature trails. **Main Beach** at the eastern end of Fernandina's Atlantic Avenue, a mile from the town center, is the perfect place to spend the afternoon. Make sure you at least take a peek inside the **Florida House Inn** (p. 226), the state's oldest hotel, or grab a drink in the cozy pub, even if not staying here.

Days 12 & 13: St. Augustine ★★★

Drive 71 miles south to St. Augustine and follow the itinerary suggested in "Charleston, Savannah & St. Augustine in 1 Week," above.

Day 14: The Space Coast ★★★

From St. Augustine it's 113 miles south along I-95 to the **Kennedy Space Center** (p. 215), the extraordinary home of NASA's space program. You could easily spend the whole day here, taking the various tours, visiting the exhibitions, watching the IMAX movies, and meeting and talking to a real-life astronaut. Just 6 miles away lies the **Astronaut Hall of Fame** (p. 216), containing the world's largest collection of astronaut memorabilia, as well as stomach-churning simulation rides.

CHARLESTON, SAVANNAH & ST. AUGUSTINE FOR FAMILIES

Coastal South Carolina, Georgia, and northern Florida can't compete with Orlando when it comes to heavy-hitting family attractions, but amongst all the history and Southern elegance are numerous entertainments for kids, not least a string of untrammeled, sandy beaches. This route is anchored by Myrtle Beach and St. Augustine, the two biggest family-friendly cities in the region, combining fun attractions such as the ubiquitous Ripley's with fine beaches, restaurants, and historic attractions. Charleston and Savannah, too, are riddled with attractions popular with kids.

Days 1 & 2: Myrtle Beach & the Grand Strand ★★

At times the entire 60-mile string of beaches around the resort of **Myrtle Beach,** aptly called the Grand Strand, seems to have been designed expressly for children, with kid-friendly facilities and amusements as well as dozens of resorts serving kids' menus. Family rates at many of the hotels are yet another enticement.

The Strand stretches from the border with North Carolina in the north all the way south to Georgetown (see "Day 3," below). At the hub is Myrtle Beach itself. Most families like to organize their time between the beach and man-made amusements. Parents may want to sneak away for some serious golfing (see "Golf," p. 104).

On the first day, allowing time for the beach, families can visit the **Myrtle Waves Water Park** (p. 103) and **Ripley's Aquarium** (p. 103), the most visited attraction in South Carolina, or take a ride on the **SkyWheel Myrtle Beach** (p. 104). Little scientists or just bored kids will love **WonderWorks** (p. 104).

While still based at a hotel along the Grand Strand, you can spend the morning of Day 2 exploring **Myrtle Beach State Park** (p. 101), with its sandy beach and pavilions, picnic tables, and a swimming pool. It's riddled with nature trails. In the afternoon, drive down to **Murrells Inlet** (p. 98), 11 miles south. It's called the Seafood Capital of South Carolina for good reason. While in the area, you can pay a call on the beautiful **Brookgreen Gardens** (p. 99). Back in Myrtle Beach, attend one of the many variety shows in the area, including the **Alabama Theatre** (p. 112) for family fun.

Day 3: Georgetown ★★

On the morning of Day 3, head down the coast along Route 17 until you see the turnoff for **Huntington Beach State Park,** 3 miles south of Murrells Inlet and across from Brookgreen Gardens (see above). The 2,500-acre park offers a completely different experience from the gardens, and it opens onto one of the best sandy beaches along the Grand Strand. Spend the morning here and also enjoy a picnic under one of the shelters and a stroll along the boardwalk.

After lunch, continue the rest of the way to Georgetown, a distance of only 28 miles south of Myrtle Beach. After checking in to a hotel, we suggest one of the river cruises aboard the *Carolina Rover* or the *Jolly Rover* that set sail from Georgetown Harbor. For more details, see "River Cruises" on p. 95. Georgetown has more than 50 historic buildings that date back as far as 1737. For information on tours of Georgetown, see p. 94.

Days 4 & 5: Charleston ★★★

From Georgetown on the morning of Day 4, drive southwest along Route 17 for 62 miles into the historic seaport of Charleston, the highlight of most visits to South Carolina and a very kid-friendly town. Check into a hotel for 2 nights and begin your adventure.

For a lesson in history outside the classroom, kids can see where the Civil War began at the **Fort Sumter National Monument** (p. 78). Later the whole family will be fascinated by the *H. L. Hunley* **Confederate submarine** (p. 74), which sank one fateful day in 1864 but was later raised. A good 2 or 3 hours can be spent at **Charles Towne Landing** (p. 75) enjoying its 663 acres; for kids, this is one of the highlights of a visit to Charleston. Wind down the afternoon with a visit to the **South Carolina Aquarium** (p. 74).

For Day 5, you should try to visit one or more of the major plantations outside of Charleston: **Magnolia Plantation** (p. 75), **Middleton Place** (p. 76), and **Drayton Hall** (p. 75), or just spend the day amongst the battleships at **Patriots Point** (p. 77).

Day 6: Hilton Head ★★

It's a 100-mile drive to our next overnight stopover at Hilton Head, so you should leave as early as you can in the morning. Follow the signs out of Charleston to Route 17, heading southwest until it reaches Route 21 going west to I-95. Follow this until you come to the junction with Route 278, which will take you east into Hilton Head.

Devote the day to romps along the beaches and taking one of the boat cruises (see p. 163). In the afternoon, you can take your kids to the nature preserve of **Sea Pines Forest Preserve** (p. 162) for walks among the wildlife, including white-tailed deer. There are several picnic areas here for lunch. Overnight in Hilton Head.

Day 7: Savannah ★★★

You have a choice. You can stay yet another day on Hilton Head, enjoying its beaches and outdoor activities, or you can drive across the Georgia state line for a visit to Savannah, 120 miles south of Charleston. Should you choose the latter, drive west once again to I-95, which you follow south until you see the exits for Savannah. I-95 lies 10 miles west of Savannah. Just follow the signs leading to the Historic District, where you can overnight.

Savannah is packed with attractions the entire family can enjoy including the **Ships of the Sea Maritime Museum** (p. 143); the **Massie Heritage Interpretation Center** (p. 142), geared to children; a tour of the **Civil War forts** (see p. 145); and **Savannah riverboat cruises** (p. 147).

Day 8 & 9: St. Augustine ★★★

From Savannah it's 175 miles to **St. Augustine,** so try and start early. Kids will love the Colonial Spanish flavor here, with the costumed interpreters and traditional activities inside the **Colonial Spanish Quarter** (p. 192) is one of the highlights. You should be able to squeeze in a visit to the **Castillo de San Marcos** (p. 203) to maintain the Spanish theme. On Day 9 start off with a bang (literally) at the wildly exciting **Pirate and Treasure Museum** (p. 207), before grabbing some sweet treats at the **Whetstone Chocolate Factory** (p. 212). In the afternoon drive up San Marcos Avenue to the northern edge of the city for the family-oriented **Authentic Old Jail** (p. 203), **Oldest Store,** and **Old St. Augustine History Museum** (p. 206).

Day 10: The Space Coast ★★★

Needless to say, kids of all ages tend to be enthralled by the **Kennedy Space Center** (p. 215), 113 miles south of St. Augustine along I-95. Assuming you get here by mid-morning, you'll easily spend the rest of the day at the center (there are food courts and cafes on-site). In addition to the tours, displays of enormous rockets, exhibits on the history of the moon landings, IMAX movies, and a bumpy space shuttle launch simulation are top draws.

CHARLESTON, SAVANNAH & ST. AUGUSTINE IN CONTEXT

3

Hollywood has been reluctant to let go of its love affair with this colorful corner of the Old South, and bestselling novels and Academy Award–winning screenplays continue to mine the mystique of three cities clad in their own complex history. While many of those Southern stereotypes do apply—the amiable drawl, stately homes, the hot-buttered grits, and the famed 'Southern hospitality' are all very much apparent—some things are quite different. St. Augustine, in particular, has a unique history (see p. 192), founded by the Spanish some 40 years before English colonists stumbled ashore in Virginia.

All three cities are incredibly beautiful and very old by American standards, matched in the South perhaps only by New Orleans. There have been battles with Native Americans, British troops, Yankees, and Spaniards throughout their long histories, and though there have been periods of severe slump, Charleston and Savannah, especially, have always been much richer than the surrounding countryside. While none of these cities gained the notoriety of other Southern hotspots during the turbulent Civil Rights era, protests did take place, with plenty of sit-ins at downtown businesses (and "wade-ins" at Tybee Beach). Thanks primarily to tourism, all three cities are booming today, with millions visiting each year, some by cruise ship. Savannah, in particular is often voted one of the coolest cities in America.

In this chapter, we'll take you from St. Augustine's, Savannah's, and Charleston's founding in Colonial days, through their many stages of growth, decline, and rebirth, with special attention paid to their unique art and architecture. We'll also learn about the cities through a tour of Low-country cuisine.

CHARLESTON, SAVANNAH & ST. AUGUSTINE TODAY

The late historian C. Vann Woodward once labeled the **New South** "the Second Reconstruction." As the millennium deepens, he noted that Yankees were coming South, rural life was diminishing, and urbanization was ongoing. "Let's call it the 'Bulldozer Revolution,'" he wrote, adding that, nonetheless, "I don't think it has demolished the South."

Charleston and Savannah have been two of the biggest benefactors of this revolution. **Charleston** boasts the fourth-largest container seaport on the East Coast, and is also the primary medical center for the eastern part of South Carolina, with several major hospitals, including the sixth-oldest continuously operating school of medicine in the United States. Many locals are employed in the information-technology industry (aka the "Charleston Digital Corridor"), at companies such as Blackbaud, Google, and CSS. The U.S. Navy's Space and Naval Warfare Systems Center became the largest employer in the metropolitan area in 2004 (with some 22,000 employees today), trailed by the Medical University of South Carolina. Boeing South Carolina is the largest private sector employer. Yet many historic buildings still remain intact in Charleston, something of a miracle considering that tornadoes, hurricanes, and several wars (including the Civil War) have swept across this low-lying city. In 1886, Charleston was almost destroyed by an earthquake that measured 7.5 on the Richter scale. In 1989, Hurricane Hugo devastated the city, destroying three-quarters of the homes in the Historic District and causing more than $2.8 billion in damage. And let's not leave out urban renewal in the 20th century, which leveled many landmark structures.

In demographics, the population of Charleston is around 67% white and 27% African American (the latter group is declining rapidly), with only a few percent identified as Latino/Hispanic or of Asian descent. The population of Charleston's greater metropolitan area is estimated to be well over half a million. In stark contrast to the rest of South Carolina, Charleston voters are among the most liberal in the state (the current mayor is a Democrat).

Like Charleston, **Savannah** remains an incredibly important port city, lying along the U.S. Intracoastal Waterway. And like New Orleans, Savannah is prone to floods because of its flat topography. Today, the city's population is estimated at approximately 142,000, with over half a million in the greater metropolitan area. Just over half its residents, some 55%, are African American. Unlike many cities of the Southeast, the Hispanic or Latin population is small—some 4%. Savannah is not as rich city as it might seem from the perspective of the Historic District, with some 22% of the population below the poverty line.

The port, along with tourism and the military, is the local economy's mainstay. One of the world's largest paper mills, owned by International Paper, is one of the biggest employers. The Gulfstream Aerospace Company, maker of private jets, and JCB, the third largest producer of construction equipment in the world, also have their home bases in Savannah. The Memorial University Medical Center is also a major employer. Like Charleston, Savannah tends to be a lot more liberal when it comes to politics than its hinterland. In 2012, Democrat Edna Jackson became the city's first female African-American mayor.

St. Augustine is much smaller in comparison, with a population of just over 12,000 in the central core, and around 70,000 in the greater metropolitan area. Though the city serves as the headquarters for the Florida National Guard, its economy is far more dependent on tourism than its northern neighbors, with around 5 million visitors per year. It's a lot less racially mixed too, with over 80% of the population white, and just 15% African American. Founded in 1968, private Flagler College is the major educational institution in the city, with around 2,500 students.

Today, as the cities with the most history and antebellum glamour, Charleston, Savannah, and St. Augustine are three of the main tourist attractions in the South. They both contain some of the most luxurious hotels in the region, and are also known for the quality of their restaurants.

THE MAKING OF CHARLESTON & SAVANNAH

In stark contrast to St. Augustine (covered on p. 192), Charleston and Savannah have much in common—a similar historical background, shared social traditions, and cherished culinary customs. Although they have their own distinct origins, the cities both began life as British colonies. Their settlement by Europeans during the 17th and 18th centuries gave them a similar character, which has lasted to this day.

Colonial Days

It is estimated that some 18,000 Native Americans were living in what is now the state of South Carolina when the first European invaders arrived in the 16th century. The Spanish, sailing from what is now the Dominican Republic and entering South Carolina waters through St. Helena Sound (between Beaufort and Edisto Island), landed ashore on August 18, 1520. The next year, two more Spanish galleons arrived at Winyah Bay (north of Charleston), the site of present-day Georgetown. Native American settlers ran out to greet them—a big mistake. The choicest specimens were taken back to the Dominican Republic as slaves.

The first Spanish settlement in South Carolina was founded by **Lucas Vázquez de Ayllón** of Toledo, a Spanish conquistador, who sailed into South Carolina waters in 1526 with an estimated 500 settlers. The resulting community, **San Miguel de Guadalpe,** predated the English settlement at Jamestown, Virginia, by exactly 81 years. Attacks by hostile natives, widespread disease, and a particularly bad winter forced the settlers to abandon their colony after only 3 months. Only 150 men and women survived to be evacuated.

In 1562, fleeing religious persecution from the French Catholics, **Huguenot** settlers sailed into Port Royal Sound (between Hilton Head and the town of Beaufort). Under their leader, Jean Ribaut, they came ashore at Parris Island to build **Charlesfort,** today the site of a U.S. Marine Corps station. Their little settlement was to last only 1 year, with the starving colonists sailing back to France. In 1566, the conquistador Pedro Menéndez de Avilés established the Spanish settlement of **Santa Elena** and Fort San Felipe on the site of the abandoned French colony. Due to the hostility of local tribes, both were abandoned in 1587.

The British began settling the area in the 1670s. In London, King Charles II awarded the territory of "Carolina," stretching from Virginia to Spanish Florida, to eight so-called "Lord Proprietors."

CHARLESTON: THE LORDS PROPRIETORS GET THEIRS

The English had better luck at Jamestown, Virginia, in 1607. By the mid-1600s, tobacco farmers had drifted south into the Albemarle Sound region of northeastern North Carolina, around Elizabeth City and Edenton. They were the first permanent European settlers in the Carolinas and Georgia.

But real colonization began after the restoration of King Charles II in England. In 1663, strapped for funds and owing financial and political debts to those who had supported his return to the throne, King Charles granted to eight **Lords Proprietors** all of North America between 31 degrees and 36 degrees North latitude—that's all of the

Carolinas and Georgia. The grant was later extended north to 36½ degrees, to make sure that the Albemarle Sound area wasn't in Virginia, and south to 29 degrees. This southern extension infuriated the Spanish because it encompassed nearly half of their colony in Florida.

The proprietors named their possession **Carolina,** in the king's honor. You'll see these men's names throughout the Carolinas: George Monck, duke of Albemarle; Edward Hyde, earl of Clarendon; William Craven, earl of Craven; brothers Lord John Berkeley and Sir William Berkeley (the latter was then governor of Virginia); Sir George Carteret; Anthony Ashley-Cooper, later the first earl of Shaftesbury; and Sir John Colleton.

The proprietors soon recruited rice farmers from Barbados, who arrived on the banks of South Carolina's Ashley River in 1670. Within a decade, they had established **Charles Town.** With slaves producing bumper rice and indigo crops, and with one of the colonies' finest natural harbors, South Carolina soon became the wealthiest of England's American colonies. Charles Town (its name was changed to Charleston in 1783) was America's busiest port until well into the 19th century.

The proprietors appointed a colonial governor to sit in Charles Town, with authority to appoint a deputy for northern Carolina. The great distances involved made this plan unworkable, so in 1710, Edward Hyde (a cousin of Queen Anne, who was then on the throne) was named governor of the north. This arrangement lasted until the proprietors sold their possession to the British crown in 1729, whereupon North and South Carolina became separate British colonies.

SAVANNAH: CONVICTS & CATHOLICS NEED NOT APPLY

Partially to create a buffer between the Spanish in Florida and flourishing South Carolina, the British crown in 1732 granted a charter to a group of investors, headed by **Gen. James Edward Oglethorpe** (1696–1785), to establish a colony in the southern part of the original Lords Proprietors grant, to be called **Georgia,** after the king.

Still in his 30s when he sailed into what would become the port of **Savannah,** Oglethorpe had already served in the military for 21 years, been a member of parliament for 11 years, and served on a committee that uncovered widespread abuse of prisoners in England's jails. He had also spent 5 months in jail for killing a man in a brawl.

Oglethorpe's utopian goal was to create a microcosm of England—but without landownership, slaves, hard liquor, and Catholicism. Contrary to popular belief, he did not recruit convicts for this enterprise, instead, he sought industrious tradesmen, small-business owners, and laborers with promises of free passage, land to farm, and supplies. Hundreds of people in London applied to sail west, but only 114 men and women were chosen, as well as a doctor and a pastor. There would be freedom of worship in this new land on America's southeast coast, providing a settler wasn't a slave, a Roman Catholic, or a lawyer.

Seven months after being granted the charter, the colonists sailed from the port at Gravesend, England, aboard an overcrowded vessel called the *Anne.* They were heading west on a rough, wave-tossed voyage into an uncertain future. The crew and passengers were close to starvation when they landed at the historic bluff above the Savannah River in 1733.

Like Columbus in the Bahamas, Oglethorpe and his colonists did not discover an unoccupied Savannah, but encountered an already inhabited land of Native Americans. The Lowcountry area of Georgia, or so it is believed, had actually been inhabited by nomadic tribes since the end of the Ice Age, when vegetation returned to the land and

A short history OF ST. AUGUSTINE

St. Augustine has radically different origins than Charleston and Savannah. It was founded by Spanish much earlier, in 1565, and remained a Spanish colony (with a short break), until 1821. Indeed, this is the oldest permanent settlement in North America.

The town was founded in 1565 by Spanish general **Pedro Menéndez de Aviles** in response to a French expedition to settle the area. Landing south of the French fort on August 28, 1565, the day of the Spanish Festival of San Augustin, Menéndez named the site **St. Augustine.** Within a few weeks he had destroyed the French settlement (and massacred most of the colonists).

Not much happened in subsequent years. Only the enthusiasm of Menéndez himself held the early colony together, a generally insignificant outpost of the Spanish empire dependent on supplies from Mexico. Unlike the British colonies to the north, St. Augustine was primarily a military outpost, not a plantation settlement, and slaves were rarely imported. Spanish-British rivalry often spilled over to the New World. Thanks to the devastating attacks of Francis Drake in 1586 and the pirate Robert Searle in 1668, nothing survives of that early settlement. Only the stone-built Castillo de San Marcos escaped further destruction wrought by raiding Carolina governor James Moore in 1702. General James Oglethorpe himself (p. 19) led another attack from Savannah in 1740, but failed to take the city.

In 1763, the **Treaty of Paris,** concluding the Seven Years' War in Europe, ceded Florida to the British, and the Spanish gladly deserted St. Augustine for Cuba.

animals roamed its plains. It was a good thing that the Native Americans were friendly, because they could easily have overpowered the weakened colonists.

The **Yamacraws,** a small tribe, had fled the Spanish conquistadors in Florida and had moved north to settle in Georgia. It was this group that was on hand to greet Oglethorpe. Instead of attacking, the Yamacraws were hospitable to these invaders who would change their continent forever. The Native Americans not only lived in peace with Oglethorpe's colonists, but they would also later help them fight off invasions by the Spaniards and other hostile tribes.

SAVANNAH RISES

While in London, Oglethorpe had fantasized about the new place he wanted to found in the Americas. For this dream city, he wanted rectilinear streets that would cross at right angles. The core of town would be filled with squares that would be earmarked as "green lungs," or public parks, so settlers could "breathe the fresh air." Savannah would be laid out in "wards" around these central squares.

Once in Savannah, Oglethorpe also set aside space for markets and public areas. He established a 10-acre **Trustees' Garden,** modeled after the Chelsea Botanical Garden in London. The garden, however, was doomed to fail because many of the plants were not hardy enough for the hard clay soil of coastal Georgia. The mulberry trees died, denying a home to silkworms, and the vines planted in the vineyards didn't bear grapes.

Oglethorpe viewed himself as the spiritual leader of the colony, and indeed he was called "Father Oglethorpe" by the colonists. His new city was founded only 6 months

During the **Revolutionary War** (1776–83), the city served as a haven for British Royalists fleeing the war, many of whom moved on to the Bahamas or Jamaica. In 1783 the Brits handed Florida back to the Spanish. The Spanish, however, did little with their old colony, and after St. Augustine became part of the United States in 1821 (when Florida joined the Union), it gradually became a backwater.

Most of what you see today dates from the late 18th century or the Spanish Revival building boom of the 1880s and 1890s, when tycoon Henry Flagler developed the town as his first Florida winter resort. It was from here that Flagler masterminded his coastal railway, a venture that would take him all the way to Key West. By the early 20th century the city was already attracting tourists to its alligator farms and the "Fountain of Youth" (p. 204).

Sleepy it may have been, St. Augustine woke up during the **Civil Rights** era of the 1960s. From May through July of 1964, local activists led by Dr. Robert B. Hayling organized marches, sit-ins, and other forms of peaceful protest with the backing of Martin Luther King, Jr.; hundreds of black and white civil-rights supporters were arrested, and the KKK responded with violent attacks. St. Augustine was actually the only place in Florida where King was arrested (June 11, 1964). The **"St. Augustine Movement"** was a pivotal component of the national Civil Rights Movement, helping to end segregation in the South.

Today the city is a major tourist destination and a relatively prosperous city, with its Spanish heritage the biggest draw.

before a new set of colonists arrived from Europe, many escaping religious persecution. The ban on Catholics was rescinded. Not just Catholics, but Jews and Protestants also arrived, many coming from Iberia, especially Portugal.

Without slaves (and also without liquor, some wags say), the settlers had a rough go of it initially. Only after the colony's first African slaves arrived in 1750 did rice, indigo, and cotton make the colony economically viable. As in South Carolina, the owners of the large plantations dotting the coastal plain around Savannah grew rich, as did their merchant friends in the city itself. In a few short years, one out of every three persons in the colony was a slave, working the rich plantations that enveloped Savannah to its west.

Politically, the colonists in around Savannah turned back further expansion by the Spanish coming north from Florida. Originally, the Spanish had wanted to make Georgia a colony. Oglethorpe, helped at the time by his Native American friends, thwarted their plans.

The founding father stayed in Savannah until 1743, finally giving up his dream and sailing back to London. The throne felt that Oglethorpe had failed as an administrator, and he was replaced by **William Stephens,** who was sent to govern in his place. The Trustees originally named by the king held onto their charter until 1752 before finally abandoning it. A political movement at the time wanted to turn their Lowcountry area into another royal colony like that enjoyed by South Carolina, centered at prosperous Charleston.

By 1754, a royal colony was established. Savannah became one of the leading ports of the Southeast, although it never overtook its major rival, Charleston. The prosperity of Lowcountry plantations became especially marked when the **French and Indian War** of 1763 came to an end. Britain won Florida, which ended Spain's attempts to forge colonies along the east coast of America. The slaves began to build cotton plantations and Colonial buildings soon came to dominate the landscape in the Lowcountry around Savannah and Charleston.

GIVING CORNWALLIS FITS

People in Charleston and Savannah had mixed feelings about **independence** from Great Britain. The rich planters and merchants saw themselves as being English, but they also chafed at the British import and export taxes, which hurt their businesses.

There were enough go-for-it patriots around, however, to throw things toward the side of freedom. In 1775, a group of revolutionaries tarred and feathered British Loyalists in Charleston, and at least a decade before the American Revolution, the residents of Savannah began to defy their English rulers. British property was being destroyed, and so-called **Liberty Boys** often fought openly with Loyalists. The raucous **Peter Tondee's Tavern** at Whitaker and Broughton streets became the center of a growing rebellion in Savannah led by the Liberty Boys. In defiance of royal authority, they flew a flag, featuring a rattlesnake with 13 rattles. Each of these rattles symbolized a different American colony.

These grog-swilling colonists defiantly wore homemade Liberty stocking caps and went so far as to erect a so-called Liberty Pole in front of Tondee's Tavern. The Declaration of Independence was read in Savannah for the first time in front of this tavern, and it was also at Tondee's Tavern that the Liberty Boys first heard the news of the battles of Lexington and Concord. The die was cast: America's war of freedom had begun, even though there were many Loyalists still residing in Georgia and Carolina.

When the British attacked Charleston in 1776, Revolutionary soldiers quickly built **Fort Moultrie** at the mouth of Charleston Harbor. They used palmetto logs, which proved to be impervious to cannon fire. The fort held out for 4 years, and the palmetto became the new state's symbol. Also in 1776, General William Moultrie defeated an invading fleet of 50 British warships outside Savannah. Although outnumbered and lacking adequate ammunition, the revolutionaries battled the British from a fort hastily assembled on Sullivan's Island. This early victory was followed by disaster. Before Christmas of 1778, the city of Savannah fell to British troops, with Charleston falling in the spring 2 years later.

Lord Cornwallis, the British commander, had decided in 1780 to launch a Southern strategy against George Washington's Continental army. His plan was to take Charleston; march overland through the Carolinas, picking up Loyalist volunteers as he went; and attack George Washington in Virginia. It took him 14 battles to finally capture Charleston, but **Francis Marion** (nicknamed "the Swamp Fox") escaped into the Lowcountry marshes. Marion, a descendant of the Huguenots, was born in a settlement near Georgetown in 1732, and brought up in the South Carolina Up Country, the swamps and thickets that comprise the northwestern corner of the state. What Marion learned about guerilla warfare fighting the Cherokees in the Up Country, he used to his state's advantage against the British. He made periodic raids on British installations, and then disappeared with his men into the swamps, where he could not be routed.

The support of Loyalist hill folk, which Cornwallis had counted on, disappeared when his forces massacred a group of rebels trying to surrender near Lancaster, South Carolina. The locals then pitched in with the patriots to defeat the British army at the **Battle of Kings Mountain,** near Gaffney. Cornwallis was forced to send half his men back to Charleston, significantly weakening his forces.

Cornwallis advanced through North Carolina to meet defeat at Washington's hands at **Yorktown** in 1781. The British troops he had sent back to Charleston held out for a year, but they evacuated when Gen. Nathanael Greene's army advanced to within 14 miles of the city. Charleston was the last British-held city south of Canada ("Mad" Anthony Wayne and his troops had reclaim Savannah earlier in 1782).

After the war, Savannah was made the capital city of Georgia, a position it would lose in 1785 to Augusta, which in time would lose out to Atlanta. A major blow to the prestige of Charleston came in 1786, when the capital of South Carolina was moved to the more centrally located Columbia, a newly created city in the sort of border territory between the Lowcountry and its traditional rival, the Up Country.

Antebellum Triumph & Tragedy

In the years following the American Revolution, commerce in Charleston and Savannah boomed. On the Lowcountry plantations, **cotton** was king, and both cities benefited as the major ports from which to ship it north or abroad.

In 1793, **Eli Whitney** invented the cotton gin on a plantation near Savannah. A former schoolteacher from the North, Whitney created this new device with the aid of a widow, Catherine ("Caty") Greene, who ran the plantation and had been married to Nathanael Greene of Revolutionary War fame. The cotton gin allowed seeds to be removed with far greater speed and efficiency than by existing methods. Thanks to this invention, Lowcountry cotton plantations flourished for the next 6 decades.

Charleston was also profoundly affected by the invention of Whitney's cotton gin. In time, rice barons turned to growing cotton, and Sea Island cotton became highly valued for its long, silky fibers. By the mid-1830s, South Carolina's annual cotton crop was nearing 70 million pounds, accounting for more than half of America's exports to Europe. Cotton would remain king in and around Charleston right up to the advent of the Civil War. Charleston's bankers and shippers constructed canals to export slaves outward from their arrival point at the city's port, and to bring cotton from the interior of South Carolina quickly to the harbor in Charleston, where ships were waiting to take it abroad.

Disaster struck Savannah in 1796 and 1820, when two major fires left half the city in ruins. The famous Savannah City Market was burned in both instances. As if the fire of 1820 didn't devastate Savannah enough, a **yellow fever epidemic** broke out and about one-tenth of the city's population died. Yellow fever struck again and again during the 19th century.

Both Europe and America turned their attention to Savannah in 1819 when the SS *Savannah* became the first steam-powered vessel to cross the Atlantic. The vessel departed Savannah on May 22 of that year, arriving at the port of Liverpool a record 29 days later. Triumphantly, the ship went on to Glasgow, Stockholm, and even to St. Petersburg. But in 1821, the vessel was caught in gale winds and capsized off the shores of Long Island.

The "Best Friend of Charleston," as the new **South Carolina Canal & Railroad Company** was called, opened up newer and faster markets, as rail lines in the 1840s were extended as far as the Carolina Up Country. The emerging spokesperson for South Carolina's interests was the towering **John C. Calhoun,** who was married to a Lowcountry plantation heiress. Resigning as the vice president to Andrew Jackson in 1832, he devoted all his considerable intellect and power to preserving both the cotton industry and slavery. Elected to the U.S. Senate, he fought against federal export taxes on cotton.

Antebellum Charleston and Savannah were at the peak of their prosperity, fueled by cotton and slavery. But ominous clouds were on the horizon as tension between the North and South grew steadily worse.

Threats to secede were issued by South Carolina from 1832 until the actual outbreak of the Civil War. Charleston financiers and Lowcountry planters, more than any other force in the South, took the dangerous steps to divide the nation, especially in the wake of the election of Abraham Lincoln, who swept into the presidency without a single electoral vote south of the Mason-Dixon line.

The Civil War

There was rejoicing on the streets of Savannah as its neighbor South Carolina seceded from the Union on December 20, 1860. The election of President Abraham Lincoln, who was despised in Savannah, had demoralized the city. In 1861, Georgia followed South Carolina in separating itself from the Union.

One of the most portentous days in the history of America came on April 12, 1861, as South Carolina troops began their bombardment of **Fort Sumter** under Union control, in Charleston Harbor. The Union troops held out for 34 hours of shelling before surrendering their citadel. By May 11, President Abraham Lincoln in Washington had declared war against the Confederate States of America. Calling it the **"War of Northern Aggression,"** Southerners hoped for a quick and easy victory.

Within a few months, federal troops occupied much of the coastal lowlands of the Carolinas and Georgia, leaving only the port cities of Wilmington, Charleston, and Savannah in Confederate hands, albeit blockaded by the Union navy.

On April 11, 1862, Union cannons fired on **Fort Pulaski,** 15 miles east of Savannah. They overcame the masonry fortification in just 30 hours, but Savannah itself was months from occupation. With its port blockaded by the Union, Savannah suffered greatly during the war. Goods were hard to come by, as Savannah had always looked to the sea for its livelihood. But the city endured bravely, with both men and women aiding the war effort.

Although the port of Charleston came under heavy bombardment by Union forces, especially in 1863, the city was hardly a major battleground during the Civil War—certainly not in the way it was during the American Revolution. Charleston did play a major role in **blockade running** during the war, however. Amazingly, only 7 months after the surrender of Fort Sumter, Union forces occupied Hilton Head, Beaufort, and St. Helena Island on the doorstep of Charleston and remained in control there throughout the war.

The Carolinas and Georgia otherwise escaped heavy fighting until May 1864, when Union General Ulysses S. Grant told **General William Tecumseh Sherman** to "get into the interior of the enemy's country as far as you can, inflicting all the damage you can against their war resources." Thus began Sherman's infamous **March to the Sea,** the world's first modern example of total war waged against a civilian population. Savannah was the final target.

Leaving Atlanta burning, Sherman departed for the sea on October 17, 1864, cutting a 60-mile path of destruction across central and eastern Georgia. "We have devoured the land, and our animals eat up the wheat and corn fields close," Sherman reported. "All the people retire before us, and desolation is behind. To realize what war is, one should follow our tracks."

Despite his orders, looting and pillaging were rampant, but there were few attacks on civilians and none against women.

Sherman arrived at Savannah on December 10, in time to make the port city a Christmas present to Lincoln. (Fortunately, he did not burn the city.) In January 1865, he turned northward. On April 26, 2 weeks after General Robert E. Lee surrendered to Grant at Appomattox Courthouse in Virginia, General Joseph E. Johnston met Sherman at Durham, North Carolina, and handed over his sword. The war was over.

Reconstruction

Even by 1863, Union forces had begun **land redistribution,** awarding parcels of **Sea Island** and various hunks of plantations to freed slaves. Some 40,000 freedmen took over nearly half a million acres of plantation lands. It was to be only a temporary grant, however. By 1866, President Andrew Johnson had given most of the land back to the former white landowners, the landed gentry.

At the end of the Civil War, victors from the North flooded Charleston and Savannah, filling both cities with **"carpetbaggers,"** the name derisively given to carpetbag-carrying Yankees who flooded the South during Reconstruction, hoping to make a quick buck. The golden age of antebellum life was over.

At first, Confederate war veterans dominated the state legislatures in Georgia and South Carolina. They enacted so-called **black code laws,** which gave some rights to the newly freed slaves but denied them the vote. This and other actions infuriated the Republicans who controlled the U.S. Congress and wanted to see the South punished for its rebellion. In 1867, Congress passed the **Reconstruction Act,** which gave blacks the right to vote and divided the South into five districts, each under a military governor who had near-dictatorial powers. Approximately 20,000 federal troops were sent to the South to enforce the act.

Recalcitrant white officials were removed from state office, and with their new vote, the ex-slaves helped elect Republican legislatures, and many blacks won seats. Despite doing some good work, these legislatures were corrupt. They enacted high taxes to pay for rebuilding and social programs, further alienating the struggling white population.

The animosity led to the formation of two secret white organizations—the Knights of the White Camelia and the Knights of the **Ku Klux Klan**—that engaged in terrorism to keep blacks from voting or exercising their other new rights. The former slaves were also disappointed with the Republicans when it became obvious that they wouldn't receive the promised **"40 acres and a mule."** Those who did vote began to cast them for their former masters.

During Reconstruction, blacks from plantations throughout Georgia flooded into Savannah, living in poverty. For the planters, though, cotton returned as king and would reign supreme until the arrival of the boll weevil.

All this set the stage for whites to regain control of Georgia in 1871. By 1877, **President Rutherford B. Hayes,** a Republican, withdrew federal troops from the South. Reconstruction was over.

During the next 20 years, white governments enacted **Jim Crow laws,** which imposed poll taxes, literacy tests, and other requirements intended to prevent blacks from voting. Whites flocked to the **Democratic Party,** which restricted its primaries—tantamount to elections throughout the South—to white voters. Blacks who did try to vote faced having the Ku Klux Klan burn crosses on their lawns, or even being lynched. Indeed, "strange fruit" hung from many Southern trees during this period.

Racial segregation became a legal fact of life, from the public drinking fountains to the public schools. The U.S. Supreme Court ratified the scheme in its 1896 *Plessy*

In 1923, the Broadway musical *Running Wild* introduced **"The Charleston,"** which quickly became a nationwide craze. Silent movies, such as *Our Dancing Daughters* with Joan Crawford, were particularly fond of depicting the dance. Even the stuffy Duke of Windsor took Charleston lessons. Though the original song and dance was named after the South Carolina city, Charleston actually had little to do with either. The composer of the song, African-American jazz pianist **James P. Johnson,** claimed he'd been inspired by Charleston dockworkers, but was born in New Jersey and spent most of his career in New York.

vs. Ferguson decision, declaring "separate but equal" public schools to be constitutional. Black schools in the South were hardly equal, but they surely were separate.

Throughout the 19th century, Charleston and Savannah remained rigidly segregated. In 1878, the first public school for blacks was opened in Savannah (in 1865, the American Missionary Association had established the **Avery Normal Institute** for African Americans in Charleston, but this was a private secondary school). In 1891 Savannah opened its first public college for blacks. Educational segregation remained in place until well into the 20th century.

On August 31, 1886, Charleston was nearly destroyed by an **earthquake** measuring 7.3 on the Richter scale. Over 2,000 buildings were destroyed causing $6 million worth of damage, a vast amount at the time. It took the city years to recover.

Into the 20th Century

As Charleston and Savannah entered the 20th century, things were looking up (at least, for their white citizens). The cities had regained some economic power, with ships fanning out to take exports such as lumber around the world.

But after World War I, economic devastation set in. A fierce hurricane in 1911 had already destroyed rice production, and in 1922 the **boll weevil** began attacking the cotton fields in Lowcountry plantations. King Cotton was dethroned. If that weren't enough, America entered a grave Depression sparked by the Wall Street Crash in 1929.

Racial segregation remained a way of life. Few suffered more than the region's black populace, who had little chance of making a living in the South. During the first 4 decades of the 20th century, black Southerners began a vast migration to Washington DC, New York, Cleveland, Detroit, and Chicago, among other cities. On the eve of the Japanese attack on Pearl Harbor in 1941, more white people than black were living in Charleston. This had not been true since the dawn of the 18th century.

One positive result of the ongoing poverty was that few in Charleston or Savannah could afford to revamp their homes in the latest styles. "Too poor to paint; too proud to whitewash," went the rallying cry. The result are cities whose collection of antebellum architecture is unsurpassed.

The economy was helped when the **Eighth Air Force** was established outside Savannah, restoring some vigor to a sagging economy in World War II. But by this time Savannah was literally falling apart. Its historic buildings were being torn down or left to rot. Finally, in 1955, a group of determined ladies saved the historic Davenport House from the wrecking ball, and Savannah began to take preservation seriously.

The Gullah Tongue Makes It to Broadway

While he was living in Charleston in the 1920s, **DuBose Heyward** wrote *Porgy*, which in time became a Broadway play. Later, it became even more famous as a folk opera created by **George Gershwin** and retitled *Porgy and Bess*. Living for a time in Charleston, Gershwin incorporated sounds and rhythms he'd experienced in black churches around the Lowcountry. Heyward was inspired by the city's rich heritage, even though the glorious mansions of old had fallen into disrepair and Charlestonians were going through hard times—"too poor to paint, too proud to whitewash." Heyward used not only the byways of Charleston for his setting, but also the Gullah language for his dialogues.

Civil Rights

Charleston and Savannah took a back seat in the civil rights movement of the 1950s. Sit-ins to protest segregated businesses did take place, but the drama, for the most part, was centered in Atlanta, under the leadership of Martin Luther King, Jr. As late as 1959 and 1960, segregation in Charleston and Savannah was firmly entrenched and backed by official state law. Unlike much of the more rural South, however, Savannah had a more progressive attitude regarding race relations. Even before the surge of the civil rights movement, there was relative tolerance between the races, as African Americans slowly integrated themselves into the city's social fabric. Local leaders urged the city to face its problems of race relations with decency and dignity—and without hate. By 1961, Savannah was desegregating its public schools; Charleston followed 2 years later.

Modern Times

The latest trends show a reversal of the great emigration pattern in the early decades of the 20th century that saw some 6½ million blacks uproot themselves and head north. Urban decay and increasing violence in many Northern cities have led to a reverse emigration pattern. At the post-millennium, figures showed a return by thousands of blacks to the South and burgeoning growth in the population figures of Charleston and Savannah.

In 1989, Charleston was devastated by **Hurricane Hugo,** a storm that badly damaged 75% of the homes in the Historic District. The hurricane caused over $2.8 billion in damage, and once again, it took several years for the city to fully recover.

In 2005 the **Arthur Ravenel, Jr., Bridge** (or the New Copper River Bridge) was opened, linking downtown Charleston with the suburb of Mount Pleasant and replacing its dangerously overloaded predecessors. With a main span of 1,546 feet, it is the longest cable-stayed bridge in the Western Hemisphere. The bridge is designed to endure wind gusts in excess of 300 mph and earthquakes of up to 7.4 on the Richter scale. It also includes a shared bicycle-pedestrian path called Wonders' Way.

In Savannah, the **Oglethorpe Mall** opened in 1969, with **Savannah Civic Center** following in 1974, and **Savannah College of Art and Design** founded in 1978. The Savannah Mall opened in 1990, but it was the release of *Midnight in the Garden of Good and Evil* in 1994 that really put the city on the tourist map (see above).

MIDNIGHT IN THE GARDEN OF good & evil

Even though the book was published back in 1994, *Midnight in the Garden of Good and Evil* retains an icy grip on Savannah's popular image, at least where the tourist industry is concerned. To this day, the book is the *New York Times'* longest-standing best seller. What gives **John Berendt**'s work added spice is that it is technically non-fiction, based on events that actually happened.

In May 1981, Savannah antiques dealer **Jim Williams** shot his lover-assistant, a hustler named Danny Hansford, age 21. As a result, through a complicated legal process, Williams became the first person in Georgia to be tried four times for murder before he was finally acquitted. In a bizarre twist, Williams died at age 59 just 6 months after the final trial, from pneumonia and heart failure.

The case could have slipped into history as another gay murder. However, writer John Berendt drifted into town one day, became intrigued by the story, and eventually wrote his mega bestseller. The novel is jazzed up with other colorful Savannah residents, notably **The Lady Chablis,** a local drag queen and entertainer who still lives in the city. Berendt's original agent turned down the story as too bizarre and "too regional." Buyers of books felt otherwise, and, in 1997, Clint Eastwood even directed the movie version.

Berendt's book put Savannah on the tourist map, and millions began to visit. Through the interest created by what is locally called "The Book," the city became a tourist attraction that started to compete with its northern neighbor, Charleston. **Mercer House,** where the murder took place, remains one of the biggest draws.

ARCHITECTURE & ART

The grandest architecture of the antebellum South is centered around Charleston and Savannah, which survived the Civil War a lot better than Atlanta (which, of course, General Sherman burned to the ground).

Many of these once-elegant structures still stand today to enchant us, although they are in varying states of preservation, some no more than ruins. From churches to gardens, chapels to memorable homes, plantation houses to graceful frame structures, Charleston and Savannah have it all.

Charleston's Art & Architecture

All you need to do is walk down Broad Street in the center of Charleston to see three-dozen ornately decorated and historic structures on the block between East Bay and Church streets. Much of what has been saved was because of an ordinance passed in 1931 that preserved whole sectors of town. Charleston was the first city in the world to adopt such a preservation law.

The historic core of the city lies **south of Broad Street.** This sector is certainly one of the great districts of architecture in the Deep South. But the landed gentry in the heyday of the plantation era also built many superb homes and mansions in other sections of the city, such as **Harleston Village** and **Radcliffeborough.** Harleston Village lies west of the Historic District. Directly north of Harleston is the neighborhood of Radcliffeborough, beginning north of Calhoun Street. Some of the grandest Victorian manses stand around **Colonial Lake.** These neighborhoods deserve at least an hour of your time to walk around. Lacy iron gates, 19th-century ornaments, towering old trees, and private gardens make it worthwhile, even if you're not particularly interested in architecture.

The **Georgian-Palladian** style reigned supreme in historic Charleston, lasting over the centuries, and surely there are more columns in Charleston today than in a small Greek city in classical days. One of the finest Georgian mansions in America stands at **64 S. Battery St.,** dating from 1772 when it was built by William Gibbes, a successful ship owner and planter. He modeled it after English designs but was also inspired by Palladio. The house is not pure Georgian, however, as **Adamesque** features, such as wrought-iron railings, were added later.

The **columned single house** prevailed for 250 years—there are some 3,000 such houses standing in Charleston today. Its most defining feature is its single-room width, and it is also set at right angles to the street. One of the most evocative examples of a Charleston single house is the **Colonel Robert Brewton House** at 71 Church St. The domestic structure of the single house is one of Charleston's greatest contributions to city architecture in America.

Some were more lavish than others, but even less-expensive dwellings were adorned with wrought-iron balconies or two-columned porches. Although much great architecture is gone, what remains is nearly 75 buildings from the colonial period, approximately 135 from the 18th century, and more than 600 built during the antebellum heyday.

COLONIAL TO ADAMESQUE

In the beginning, roughly from 1690 to 1740, there was the colonial style, with such defining features as clapboard wooden siding, low foundations, and steeply pitched roofs. The **John Lining House** at 106 Broad St. is the most evocative building of that period. Coexisting for a certain time with colonial architecture was Georgian, a style that flourished between 1700 and 1800. Its defining features are box chimneys, hipped roofs, flattened columns, and raised basements. Nowhere is this style better exemplified than in the **Miles Brewton House** at 27 King St.

As colonial and Georgian faded, another style of architecture appeared, especially during a 3-decade span beginning in 1790. Although it was called Federalist architecture in the North, most Charlestonians referred to the structures of this era as "Adamesque" or "the Adam period," a reference to what Scottish brothers James and Robert Adam were creating in the British Isles. The best example of Federalist/ Adamesque architecture in Charleston is the **Nathaniel Russell House** at 51 Meeting St., which is open to the public (see p. 71).

Constructed around the same time as the Nathaniel Russell House, the **James Moultrie House,** at 20 Montagu St., is an Adamesque treasure of delicate proportions. Although it was built by a planter, Daniel Cobia, it became more famous as the address of the Moultrie family in 1834. Dr. Moultrie, related to the Revolutionary War hero Gen. William Moultrie, was one of South Carolina's early physicians, founding its first medical school.

A magnificent Adamesque mansion, built around 1802, was constructed at 60 Montagu St. The restored **Gaillard-Bennett House,** constructed by a rice planter, Theodore Gaillard, is famous for its fluted columns with "tower-of-the-winds" capitals, along with an elliptically shaped window in its portico gable and a modillion cornice, with other Palladian architectural motifs. In 1870, 5 years after the end of the Civil War, Robert E. Lee was a guest of the Bennett family, and he spoke to admiring well-wishers from the second-floor balcony.

CHARLESTON, SAVANNAH & ST. AUGUSTINE IN CONTEXT

Architecture & Art

cuisine IN THE LOWCOUNTRY

A Southern-style **breakfast** may consist of the following: homemade biscuits, country (very salty) ham, red-eye gravy, and grits swimming in butter. If a fellow were still hungry, he might cook up some Jimmy Dean sausage, toss a few buckwheat pancakes with cane syrup (or molasses), and fry a mess of eggs with the yolk cooked hard. Healthy? Hardly. But it's easy to eat very well (and very nutritiously) in the South, given the region's bounty of local vegetables and fruits, farm-raised meats, and fresh-off-the-boat seafood.

Southern cuisine is a blend of the Old World (meaning Europe) and the New World (meaning North America). Necessity forced early settlers to find ways to integrate New World foods, like wild turkey and corn, into their bland diet of dumplings and boiled chicken. Many of the most important elements of the cuisine came from African slaves, who championed such exotica as okra and peanuts, and who turned the vitamin-rich black-eyed peas, used by plantation owners to fertilize fields, into a Southern classic. These influences came together to create Southern cuisine, an amalgam that embraces such favorites as sweet-potato pie, pecan pie, buttermilk biscuits, sweetened iced tea, long-cooked greens, sweet creek shrimp, fried green tomatoes, pan gravy, and peanuts (preferably boiled).

Virtual culinary wars have broken out over how to make **Southern fried chicken.** Even Colonel Sanders once denounced the way that his chain franchise fried chicken. One old-time cook who had a reputation for serving the best fried chicken in Georgia confided that her secret was bacon grease and a heavy black skillet that was 50 years old. **Crackling bread** is corn bread with crispy leftovers from the renderings of pork fat at slaughter time. Traditional **collard greens** are long-simmered and seasoned with ham hocks.

What lobster is to Maine, **catfish** is to the Southern palate. Fried catfish and **hush puppies** (fried cornmeal balls) reign supreme. With a sweet, mild flavor and a firm texture, catfish (now commercially raised in ponds) is one of the most delectable of freshwater fish, despite its

Another stellar example of the Adamesque style is the **Jonathan Lucas House,** built around 1808, at 286 Calhoun St. Several generations of rice barons lived here, establishing rice milling as a big industry in the southeastern United States.

GREEK REVIVAL VERSUS GOTHIC REVIVAL

The **Regency** style came and went quickly in Charleston, filling in a transitional period between Adamesque and the **Greek Revival** style. The most evocative example of Regency is the **Edmondston-Alston House** at 21 E. Battery St., erected by Charles Edmondston in 1825. The purity of the original style was later altered by Charles Alston, a rice planter who added Greek Revival details. From its precincts, General Beauregard watched the attack on Fort Sumter in 1861, and Robert E. Lee once took refuge here when a fire threatened the Mills House Hotel where he was lodged. This historic home is open to the public (see p. 69).

The Greek Revival period flourished roughly from 1820 to 1875. Its defining features are heavy columns and capitals (often Doric), along with a hipped or gabled roof and a wide band of trim. One of the most solid examples of this form of bold architecture is the **Kahal Kadosh Beth Elohim** at 90 Hasell St. (p. 71), the oldest synagogue in continuous use in the United States, first organized in 1749.

ugly appearance. The traditional way to cook it is in grease, but cooks today have created more delicate preparations, serving it with such dainty fixings as lime-and-mustard sauce.

Lowcountry specialties in the Charleston area include such dishes as **shrimp 'n' grits** and **she-crab soup.** Outdoor **oyster roasts** are popular in the late fall, when the bivalves grow big and plump. **Confederate bean soup** is made with onion, celery, bacon, sausage, ham stock, brown sugar, baked beans, and heavy cream.

In a bow to Southern heritage, **wild game** is featured on many a menu. Around October or November, hunters in the South, dressed in blaze orange, set out in the forests to stalk deer. The venison may be eaten right away or frozen for later use in the winter, when a steak might appear on your plate with grits and gravy. In the Carolinas, quail sautéed in butter is a tasty delicacy. More modern cooks season it with wine or sherry. Wild duck—brought down by hunters in blinds on the scenic coastal marshes—may be roasted and stuffed with potato-and-apple dressing.

Eventually, all talk of Southern cooking comes down to **barbecue.** Some cooks slow roast the pork shoulder for 12 hours or so. Traditionalists prefer smoking it with hickory wood, although some use charcoal. No one agrees on the sauce. Will it be a pepper-and-vinegar sauce; a pepper, vinegar, and catsup sauce; or a sweet mustard sauce?

In summer, the fruit pickings are plenty, with local **strawberries, blueberries, cantaloupes,** and **plums** ripening at dusty farm stands. Georgia **peaches** are legendarily sweet and fragrant. The melon of choice is the **watermelon.** The best ones are grown in private gardens (sorry!) or sold at farm stands.

Many Southerners point with pride to the fact that you can get Continental dishes, French-influenced cuisine, and sushi throughout the South today. But visitors to the region deliberately seek out down-home Southern food. Though, unfortunately, it's harder than ever to come by in the increasingly gourmet capitals of Charleston and Savannah—instead, you'll be entertained by some of the most creative young chefs in the U.S.

However, the most spectacular example of the Greek Revival style is at **172 Tradd St.,** built in 1836 by Alexander Hext Chisolm, who made his fortune in rice. The lavish capitals are copies of those designed in Athens in 335 B.C. The architect is thought to be Charles F. Reichardt of New York.

At the turn of the 19th century, Gabriel Manigault, a French Huguenot, was the biggest name in Charleston architecture. His greatest buildings have been torn down, but one that remains is **City Hall,** at the corner of Broad and Meeting streets. Constructed in 1801, this stellar example of Adamesque-Palladian architecture was originally a bank before becoming City Hall in 1818. This historic building is open to the public (see p. 67).

One of the few buildings that can be directly traced to the architectural drawing board of Manigault is the house at **350 Meeting St.** that the architect designed for his brother, Joseph, in 1803. Many critics hail it as one of the most impressive Adamesque homes in America. Manigault's father, also known as Gabriel Manigault, was in his day not only the richest man in Charleston but also one of the wealthiest in the country. The **Joseph Manigault House** is one of the few historic homes in Charleston open to the public (see p. 71).

The best and most helpful practical guide—virtually a street-by-street survey—is *Complete Charleston: A Guide to the Architecture, History and Gardens of Charleston,* by Margaret H. Moore (1997), with photographs by Truman Moore. Sold all over Charleston, the book divides Charleston into 11 neighborhoods and takes you on a tour of each, a voyage of discovery of the city's world-class architecture and lush secret gardens.

Art and Landscape in Charleston and the Lowcountry, by John Beardsley, was published as part of the 21st season of the Spoleto Festival USA The color photographs of Charleston and the Lowcountry alone are reason enough to purchase this guide. You can find both books on Amazon.com.

Another national landmark attributed to Manigault is at **18 Bull St.,** an Adamesque manse constructed at the turn of the 19th century by William Blacklock, a wine merchant. At its lowest point this mansion became a cheap boardinghouse and barely escaped bulldozers in 1958.

Robert Mills, who designed the Washington Monument, filled in when Manigault resettled in Philadelphia. But Mills was never as well received, although he left the monumental **First Baptist Church** (1819–22; see p. 69) on lower Church Street and the five-columned **Fireproof Building** (1822–26) at Chambers and Meeting streets.

When an 1838 fire destroyed a large part of antebellum Charleston, many districts were reconstructed in the Greek Revival style. Doric columns were particularly fashionable, along with rectangular shapes inspired by Greek temples, such as those found in Sicily.

A monumental "pillar" to Greek Revival is the columned **Centenary Methodist Church,** one of the grandest examples of a Greek Doric temple in America, at 60 Wentworth St., an 1842 structure by Edward Brickell White.

Along came Andrew Jackson Downing, the mid-19th-century arbiter of America's taste in architecture, who ridiculed Charleston's obsession with Greek Revival. The way was paved for the emergence of E. B. White, who brought in the **Gothic Revival** design, which prevailed from 1850 to 1885 and was characterized by pointed arches and buttressed stone tracery. The best example of Gothic Revival is the **French Protestant (Huguenot) Church,** at 136 Church St. (see p. 70).

AFTER THE CIVIL WAR

Also dominating the 1850s, the decade before the Civil War, were the architects F. D. Lee and Edward C. Jones. Together and separately they began to change the cityscape of Charleston, creating, for example, the Moorish-style fish market, their most exotic invention—alas, now gone. They pioneered the use of cast iron, which became a dominant feature in city architecture and can still be seen at its most prolific on the western side of Meeting Street, stretching from Hasell to Market streets.

One of the most talented of all Charleston architects, Jones designed the **Trinity Methodist Church,** on Meeting Street, in 1850. This impressive edifice has a pedimented Palladian portico of Corinthian columns. In just 3 years he shifted his style to Italianate, which remained popular until the dawn of the 20th century. The architecture is defined by verandas, low-pitched roofs, and balustrades. An evocative example of the style is the **Colonel John Ashe House,** designed by Jones, at 26 S. Battery St.

In 1853, Jones designed his first commercial building in the Italianate Renaissance Revival style: a bank at **1 Broad St.** At one time this building was owned by George A. Trenholm, a cotton broker and blockade runner, one of several 19th-century power brokers in Charleston who were said to have inspired Margaret Mitchell's character of Rhett Butler in *Gone With the Wind.*

Still one of the city's most magnificent landmarks, the columned building at **200 E. Bay St.** is the most stellar example of the Italian Renaissance Revival style, built over a period of 26 years, from 1853 to 1879. This U.S. Custom House was the creation of Ammin Burnham, a Boston architect who'd created a similar building in his home city. Burnham was largely instrumental in launching the tradition of designing federal buildings, such as post offices, in a classical style. The Roman Corinthian portico of this splendid temple is much photographed.

About 20 years before Charleston got sucked up in the Civil War, all purity in architectural style vanished. Most architects and builders were more interested in a dramatic facade. This period saw the bastardization of a lot of Charleston's landscape. Architects reached out internationally for inspiration—to the Moors, to Persia, to the Norman style of church, or even Gothic Venice, if they were fanciful.

The best example of this bastardized, though architecturally beautiful, style is at **67 Rutledge Ave.,** the home (ca. 1851) that Col. James H. Taylor ordered built "in the style of a Persian villa," with Moorish arches as ornamentation. This was once a famous address, entertaining the likes of such distinguished guests as the 19th-century politician, tastemaker, and orator, Daniel Webster.

And then came the Civil War, when all building ceased except for fortifications. Much great architecture was destroyed during Union bombardments, especially in 1863.

After the war, the **Victorian style** arrived in Charleston and would prevail from 1870 until the coming of World War I. This style did not predominate as much as it did in other American cities because many Charlestonians, wiped out economically from the effects of the Civil War, did not have money to build. Nonetheless, you'll see some fine Victorian manses in Charleston today, notably the **Sottile House,** with its wide verandas opening onto Green Street on the College of Charleston campus.

When Victorian architects did design buildings in Charleston, they often created "fantasies," as exemplified by the startling manse that stands at **40 Montagu St.** Built by food merchant Bernard Wohlers in 1891, the house was restored in 1963. Its unique style combines Charles Eastlake with Queen Anne motifs.

Not all Charlestonians during the latter Victorian Age were building in the Victorian style. Albert W. Todd, for example, an architect and state senator, constructed one of Charleston's most magnificent private residences at **40 Rutledge Ave.** in the Colonial Revival style at the turn of the 20th century. With its verandas and splendid columned portico, this house is worth a detour.

Rainbow Row (79–107 E. Bay St.) is one of the most celebrated blocks in the city. It got its name in the 1930s when the entire block was rejuvenated and then painted in colors used by the colonials. The architecture is mainly of the so-called British style, in that there was a store on the ground floor with the living accommodations on the floors above. Rainbow Row is the longest such Georgian block of buildings in America, and it inspired DuBose Heyward's "Catfish Row" in *Porgy and Bess.*

THE ART OF CHARLESTON

As might be expected, Charleston is far more distinguished by its architecture than by its art. But it's had some peaks and valleys over the years, and today boasts a creative core of artists whose works are displayed at the **Spoleto Festival USA** and in museums in the city—and often showcased in traveling exhibitions around the state.

In the colonial period, the art decorating the antebellum homes of England—most often landscapes or portraits of dogs and horses—was imported from London and brought over by British ships sailing into Charleston Harbor. When families grew rich from rice and indigo, portrait painters, many of them itinerant, did idealized portraits of the founding father of a dynasty and his wife (always made out to be prettier than she was), or else the whole brood gathered for an idealized family portrait.

Out of this lackluster mess, one artist rose to distinguish himself.

CHARLESTON'S RENAISSANCE MAN

Born in South Carolina of Scottish descent, **Charles Fraser** became the best-known artist in Charleston for his miniature portraits, many of which you can see in the **Gibbes Museum of Art** (see p. 70). Although he was also a distinguished landscape painter, he is mainly known today for his miniatures.

When the Marquis de Lafayette came to Charleston in 1825, he sat for a portrait by Fraser. In turn the artist gave the marquis one of his miniatures as a gift. Lafayette later wrote that the portrait was a "very high specimen of the state of arts in America."

Fraser received his artistic training at the age of 13 when he studied with Thomas Coram. He was educated at the Classical Academy, which in time became the College of Charleston. For 11 years he was a lawyer before giving up his practice in 1818 to devote himself to art full time.

As a miniaturist, he captured the essence of many of the city's most distinguished citizens. His color was relatively flat, but his compositions were filled with linear detail, and he was known for his delicate, lyrical art.

Fraser had many other talents as well. He distinguished himself as a civil leader, and he was also a designer, having provided the plans for the steeple on St. John's Lutheran Church at 10 Archdale St. In 1854 he wrote a valuable history of the city, *Reminiscences of Charleston.*

THE CHARLESTON RENAISSANCE

The long, dreary years of the Reconstruction era, when much of Charleston was mired in poverty, did not encourage the growth of great art. In the early 20th century, however, the **"Charleston Renaissance"** was born. This cultural movement spanned the decades between 1915 and 1940 on the eve of the U.S. entry into World War II. Fostered by artists, musicians, architects, and poets, the Renaissance rescued Charleston from the physical devastations of the Civil War and later from the deep mire of the Depression.

Laura Bragg, the director of the Charleston Museum from 1920 to 1931, presided over a salon in her home at 38 Chambers St. In time this parlor became as famous in the South as the salon of Gertrude Stein and her longtime companion, Alice B. Toklas, became in Paris. Much of the Southern literary world, including the novelist and playwright Carson McCullers from Georgia, dropped by.

Elizabeth O'Neill Verner (1883–1979) has emerged as the towering figure of the Charleston Renaissance artists. Charleston-born-and-bred, she studied art in Philadelphia from 1901 to 1903 before returning to Charleston. When she found herself unexpectedly widowed, she turned to art to earn a living to support herself and her two small children.

Verner specialized in beautiful etchings and drawings of Charleston scenes, as exemplified by her *Avenue at the Oaks.* She chose such subjects as churches, beautiful homes, columns, porticos, and wrought-iron gates. But her forte was in depicting scenes of the vendors in the city market, none more evocative than her pastel on silk *Seated Flower Seller Smoking Pipe*. She was instrumental in reviving an interest in art in Charleston during the 1920s and 1930s. As she aged, she switched to pastels and worked almost until the time of her death at the age of 96.

Another major artist of the period was **Alice Ravenel Huger Smith** (1876–1958), a Charleston native who was intrigued by the Lowcountry landscape, with its acres of marshes, cypress swamps, palmettos, rice fields, egrets, herons, and lonely beaches. Her sketches were filled with imagery. After 1924 she worked mainly in watercolor, which she found best for depicting the hazy mist of the Lowcountry. One of her most evocative works is the 1919 *Mossy Tree*.

Another native of South Carolina, **Anna Heyward Taylor** (1879–1956) found her inspiration in Charleston, which she considered a city of "color and charm." Her paintings, in private collections and major galleries today, are steeped in the misty aura of the Lowcountry. Among her finest works is the 1930 *Fenwick Hall* in which she captures the rot, despair, and decay of this laconic plantation before its renovation.

Notable Michigan-born artist **Alfred Hutty** (1877–1954) began a lifelong love affair with Charleston when he was sent here to establish an art school for the Carolina Art Association. His greatest fame came as an etcher, although he was an accomplished painter as well. His works today are displayed in such institutions as the British Museum in London and the Metropolitan Museum in New York. His *White Azaleas-Magnolia Gardens,* done in 1925, captures the luxuriant vegetation of the Lowcountry that was evocative of the Ashley River plantations.

Savannah's Architecture & Art

Savannah's greatest collection of evocative architecture lies in the **Historic District,** where you can admire the old buildings, churches, and squares. Some structures are from the Colonial era; others were perhaps inspired by the Adam brothers or built in the Regency style. There are tons of ironwork and antique buildings in brick or clapboard. Even modest townhouses from the 18th century have been restored to become coveted addresses.

Because many of its residents lacked money in the final decades of the 19th century and the beginning of the 20th, antique structures were allowed to stand, whereas many American cities destroyed their heritage and built modern buildings. When Savannahians started thinking about tearing down their old structures in the 1950s, a forceful preservation movement was launched—and just in time.

THE FIRST CITY

In 1733, at the founding of Savannah, James Oglethorpe faced a daunting challenge. He not only had to secure homes for trustees and colonists, but he also had to construct forts around the new town of Savannah to fend off possible Native American raids, even though the local tribes were friendly.

Since they weren't well built and were later torn down to make way for grander structures, none of the founding fathers' little wooden homes remain today. But the town plan envisioned by Oglethorpe back in London still remains. He wanted an orderly grid composed of 24 squares. In case of rebellion he also wanted "mustering points" where troops could gather to squelch the problem.

Nine years after the colonists arrived in port, they had enough money and building materials to construct their first church, which quickly became the most elaborate structure in town. Called "the Orphan House," the church took its name from the

Bethesda Orphanage founded by evangelist George Whitefield in 1738. Along with Oglethorpe, Whitefield believed that rum drinking caused a yellow fever–like disease but that beer drinking was acceptable. This philosophy was expounded to the congregation of Georgia's first church. Unfortunately, this landmark building no longer stands.

After the Revolutionary War, the port of Savannah began to grow rich on profits it made shipping sago powder, beef, pork, animal skins, tar, turpentine, and other exports. Money generated from this thriving trade with Europe, especially London, was poured into architecture. Grander homes began to sprout on the squares of Savannah. Still, none of these early structures equaled the glory of the rival city of Charleston. While visiting the family of Gen. Nathanael Greene, Eli Whitney invented the cotton gin in 1793, bringing even greater prosperity to the area, which led to grander building.

Little post-Revolutionary architecture survived a disastrous fire that struck in 1796, burning block after block of the city. Built by James Habersham, Jr., in a Georgian style, the remaining structure is a solid brick foundation covered in pink stucco. Today it is a well-recommended restaurant and bar, known as the **Olde Pink House Restaurant** (p. 129), open to the general public at 23 Abercorn St.

In 1820, another devastating fire swept over Savannah, destroying architectural gems that had been erected by builders from both Charleston and the North. The fire erupted just at the time an epidemic of yellow fever broke out. Thousands of slaves died from the fever, temporarily slowing down building efforts because they provided the hard labor on the construction projects. Work on rebuilding Savannah was further slowed by a cholera epidemic in 1834.

But through it all, Savannahians survived and prospered and continued to pour money into elaborate structures, many of which remain today, especially those constructed of brick. The **Federalist** style was very prevalent, as it was along the east coast of America. Some builders, perhaps those with Loyalist hearts, preferred the Georgian style. Locals continued to spend money on churches, notably the **Independent Presbyterian Church** (p. 140), whose architectural beauty competed with that of some of the finest churches of Charleston.

THE REGENCY STYLE SWEEPS SAVANNAH

The cotton planters with their newfound money invited William Jay of London to come to Savannah in 1817. He introduced the **Regency style,** which became all the rage in Savannah.

Some of his structures still stand today. His greatest achievement is the **Owens-Thomas House** (p. 142), the best example of English Regency architecture in the United States. Inspired by classical buildings, the flourishing style was named for King George IV, who ruled as prince regent from 1811 to 1820. The house overlooks Oglethorpe Square and was standing in 1825 to welcome the Marquis de Lafayette when he was the guest of honor in Savannah. The French war hero addressed a crowd of Savannahians from the cast-iron veranda on the south facade of the building. This landmark building was constructed in the main from **tabby,** a concrete mixture of oyster shells, sand, and lime. The Grecian-inspired veranda on the southern facade was the first major use of cast iron in Savannah. As an architectural device, cast iron later swept the city.

Jay also designed the **Telfair Mansion** in a neoclassical Regency style. It was constructed in 1818 for Alexander Telfair, the scion of Edward Telfair, a former Georgia governor and Revolutionary War hero. The mansion was bequeathed to the city for use as a museum, and it was formally opened in 1886 (p. 143). Many notables attended; most of the crowd's interest focused on Jefferson Davis, the former president of the Confederacy.

The Irish-born architect Charles B. Cluskey (1808–71) arrived in Savannah in 1838 and stayed for almost a decade, becoming known for his antebellum architecture influenced by the **Greek Revival** style. The elite of Savannah, prospering from neighboring plantations, hired him to design their townhouses, including the **Champion-McAlpin-Fowlkes house** in 1844. He served as city surveyor of Savannah from 1845 to 1847, when he went to Washington with plans to renovate the White House and Capitol (few of his ideas were carried out, however).

Another antebellum architect, **John Norris** (1804–76), flourished in Savannah between 1846 and 1860. His most famous landmark is the **Savannah Custom House** (p. 139), which was constructed between 1848 and 1852 in the Greek Revival style, with its mammoth portico. He also designed many more notable structures throughout the city in the same general style, including the **Andrew Low House** in 1849 (p. 134).

A competitor of his was John B. Hogg, who hailed from South Carolina. Hogg's most notable structure is the **Trinity United Methodist Church** at 225 W. President St. (see p. 144). The church was built of the famous "Savannah grays," or stucco-covered gray brick. The building became known in Georgia as the "Mother Church of Methodism."

WAR, RECONSTRUCTION & PRESERVATION

Unlike Atlanta, Savannah was not burned to the ground. Even in 1864, after all the wartime deprivation suffered by the long blockade of its port, Savannah was a worthy "gift" when Sherman presented it as a Christmas present to Lincoln.

The Civil War introduced most Savannahians to poverty, and the decades of Reconstruction meant the end of opulence. Oglethorpe's original town plan had stretched from 6 to 24 city squares. Architects of renown avoided building in Savannah, going to richer cities instead.

The famous "Savannah grays" ceased production in the 1880s. Many buildings fell into ruin or decay. Modern structures outside the historic core were haphazardly constructed, although the Victorian era produced some notable architecture to grace the cityscape.

Just when it appeared that Savannah was going to rot away in the hot Georgia sun, the 1950s preservation movement arrived. Historic Savannah was subsequently saved and restored during the latter part of the 20th century.

THE ART OF SAVANNAH

In antebellum days, **portraiture** was the most common form of art. Any moderately well-off family commissioned idealized portraits of its family members, at least the gentleman and lady of the house. Most were either in oil on canvas or in watercolor. In some rare instances, the portraits were done on ivory. The subjects of the portraits are attired in their "Sunday go-to-meeting" garb. Backdrops were romanticized—an elegant drapery, a Grecian column, a distant view of the ocean.

With the coming of the deprivations caused by the Civil War and the lean years of the Reconstruction era, Savannah was more in survivalist mode than in the mood for painting. But as time went on, a number of self-taught artists emerged in Savannah and the Lowcountry. Many of them were black, working in a folk-art medium. Sometimes they painted on unpainted clapboard from some abandoned barn or other structure. The

the arts: BOOKS, MUSIC & FILM

The most famous writer to hail from either city is **(Mary) Flannery O'Connor** (1925–64) of Savannah. Best known for her Southern Gothic style, O'Connor's most respected work is *Wise Blood* (1952), *The Violent Bear It Away* (1960), and *A Good Man Is Hard to Find* (1955).

Midnight in the Garden of Good and Evil (1994) by **John Berendt** is the book that put Savannah on the map (see p. 140). Clint Eastwood's film version came out in 1997. Set in Savannah, *Forrest Gump* (1994) was a huge worldwide commercial success, winning six Oscars, including Best Actor for Tom Hanks. The movie tells the story of a man with an IQ of 75 and his epic journey through life. The famous 'bench scene' that opens the movie was genuinely shot here (p. 28). With Savannah as a setting, *The Legend of Bagger Vance* (2000) was directed by Robert Redford. It stars Will Smith as Bagger Vance and Matt Damon as Rannulph Junuh, the best golfer in the city. Bagger teaches Rannulph the secret of an authentic golf stroke, which turns out to also be the secret to mastering any challenge and finding meaning in life.

Robert Redford's 2010 historical drama *The Conspirator* (the story of Mary Surratt, charged in the Abraham Lincoln assassination, and the first woman to be executed by the U.S government), was also filmed in Savannah (Fort Pulaski served as Surratt's prison).

The Notebook (2004), starring Rachel McAdams and Ryan Gosling, was partly filmed in Charleston. More recently (and much to the horror of most locals), the Bravo reality series *Southern Charm* (2014) follows the lives of a group of wealthy socialites in Charleston.

Arguably Charleston's most famous son of the moment, comedy talk-show host **Stephen Colbert** was chosen to succeed David Letterman as the host of the *Late Show* on CBS in 2014.

When it comes to music, the **Gullah** community has had a huge influence on music in Charleston, especially jazz music (allegedly inspiring "The Charleston," p. 26, and *Porgy and Bess*, p. 27).

Telfair Museum (p. 143) is the showcase for these self-taught artists, displaying Low-country art in various temporary exhibitions.

Among the other artists who have distinguished themselves in modern times is **Leonora Quarterman** (1911–79), who became one of the best-known watercolorists in the South. Her silk-screen prints of Savannah and Georgia coastal scenes are highly prized by collectors today.

Christopher P. H. Murphy (1902–69) was a native of the city who became known for drawings that captured both the cityscape of Savannah and the coastal landscape of the Lowcountry coastline. His originals and reproductions are as sought after as those of Ms. Quarterman.

WHEN TO GO

Although Charleston, Savannah, and St. Augustine can be very hot and steamy in summer (to say the least), temperatures are never extreme the rest of the year (St. Augustine tends to be hotter than its two northern neighbors). Winter temperatures seldom drop below freezing. Spring and fall are the longest seasons, and the wettest months are December to April. Spring is a spectacular time to visit, as the azaleas, dogwoods, and camellias burst into bloom.

Savannah Average Temperatures & Rainfall

	JAN	FEB	MAR	APR	MAY	JUNE	JULY	AUG	SEPT	OCT	NOV	DEC
High (°F)	60	62	70	78	84	89	91	90	85	78	70	62
High (°C)	16	17	21	26	29	32	33	32	29	26	21	17
Low (°F)	38	41	48	55	63	69	72	72	68	57	57	41
Low (°C)	3	5	9	13	17	21	22	22	20	14	14	5
Rain (in.)	3.6	3.2	3.8	3.0	4.1	5.7	6.4	7.5	4.5	2.4	2.2	3.0

Charleston Average Temperatures & Rainfall

	JAN	FEB	MAR	APR	MAY	JUNE	JULY	AUG	SEPT	OCT	NOV	DEC
High (°F)	59	61	68	76	83	87	89	89	85	77	69	61
High (°C)	15	16	20	24	28	31	32	32	29	25	21	16
Low (°F)	40	41	48	56	64	70	74	74	69	49	49	42
Low (°C)	4	5	9	13	18	21	23	23	21	9	9	6
Rain (in.)	3.5	3.3	4.3	2.7	4.0	6.4	6.8	7.2	4.7	2.9	2.5	3.2

St. Augustine Average Temperatures & Rainfall

	JAN	FEB	MAR	APR	MAY	JUNE	JULY	AUG	SEPT	OCT	NOV	DEC
High (°F)	67	70	74	79	85	89	91	90	87	82	75	69
High (°C)	19	21	23	26	29	32	33	32	31	28	24	21
Low (°F)	46	49	53	59	66	71	73	73	72	65	57	49
Low (°C)	8	9	12	15	19	22	23	23	22	18	14	9
Rain (in.)	2.8	3.2	4.1	2.6	3.1	5.8	4.8	6.5	7.3	4.2	2.3	2.4

Charleston, Savannah & St. Augustine Calendar of Events

JANUARY

Lowcountry Oyster Festival, Charleston. Steamed buckets of oysters greet visitors at Boone Hall Plantation (p. 77). Enjoy live music, oyster-shucking contests, kids' events, and other activities at what's reputed to be the world's largest oyster festival. Contact the Greater Charleston Restaurant Association (✆ **843/452-6088;** www.charlestonrestaurantassociation.com) for more information. End of January.

Space Coast Birding and Wildlife Festival, Titusville, FL. An annual festival celebrating, identifying, and analyzing the wilder residents of the area, this one brings in heavy hitters from the worlds of biology and ornithology as well as nature photographers, scientists, writers, and historians. Late January. See www.spacecoastbirdingandwildlifefestival.org.

FEBRUARY

Amelia Island Book Festival, Amelia Island, FL. A gathering of bibliophiles, authors, writers, and those who aspire to be all the aforementioned, this weekend homage to the printed word features some major names, workshops, parties, and more. Late February. Visit www.ameliaislandbookfestival.com.

Southeastern Wildlife Exposition, Charleston. More than 150 of the finest artists and more than 500 exhibitors participate at 13 locations in the downtown area. Enjoy carvings, sculptures, paintings, live-animal exhibits, food, and much more. Call ✆ 843/723-1748 or visit www.sewe.com for details. Mid-February.

Georgia Days Colonial Faire and Muster, Savannah. Georgians turn out to celebrate the founding of their colony in Savannah on February 12, 1733, by James Oglethorpe. Various events are staged, including costumed demonstrators depicting skills used by the early settlers. Admission is free. Call ✆ **912/651-2125** or go to www.georgiahistory.com for more information. Early February.

Savannah Irish Festival, Savannah. This Irish heritage celebration promises fun for the entire family, with music, dancing, and food. There's both a children's stage and a main stage. Contact the Irish Committee of Savannah (☎ **912/604-8298;** www.savannah irish.org) for more information. Mid-February.

MARCH

Festival of Houses and Gardens, Charleston. For nearly 50 years, people have been enjoying some of Charleston's most historic neighborhoods and private gardens on this tour. Contact the Historic Charleston Foundation, 40 E. Bay St. (☎ **843/723-1623;** www.historiccharleston.org), for details. Late-March to mid-April.

Charleston Wine + Food Festival, Charleston. Four days of parties, events, and seminars mark this world-class culinary festival that draws the likes of Bobby Flay. Call ☎ **843/727-9998** or visit www.charleston wineandfood.com for details. Late February to early March.

Charleston Fashion Week, Charleston. This is a 5-night celebration of fashion and the city's burgeoning retail community, featuring up-and-coming designers from the Carolinas and Georgia. Visit www.charlestonfashion week.com for details. Late March.

Savannah Music Festival. Featuring everything from indigenous music from the South to world premieres, this annual music festival attracts fans from all over America. Chamber music and even ballet troupes perform before appreciative audiences. For more information, call ☎ **912/234-3378** or visit www.savannahmusicfestival.org. Late March to early April.

The Savannah Tour of Homes & Gardens, Savannah. Each spring many residents open the doors to their historic homes for 4-day walking tours in which you are allowed to visit six to eight private homes and gardens every day. Luncheons and afternoon teas are also staged. Contact Tour Headquarters at 18 Abercorn St. (☎ **912/234-8054;** www. savannahtourofhomes.org) for more information. Late March.

St. Patrick's Day Celebration on the River, Savannah. The river flows green and so does the beer in one of the largest celebrations held on River Street each year; this is now the second largest Paddy's Day celebration in the U.S. Enjoy live entertainment, lots of food, and tons of fun. Contact the Savannah Waterfront Association (☎ **912/234-0295;** www.riverstreetsavannah.com/stpats or www.savannahsaintpatricksday.com) for more information. St. Patrick's Day weekend (nearest March 17).

APRIL

Cooper River Bridge Run, Charleston. Sponsored by the Medical University of South Carolina, this 10K run and walk starts in Mount Pleasant, goes over the Cooper River Bridge, and ends in the center of Charleston. Call ☎ **843/856-1949** or visit www.bridgerun.com. Early April.

Family Circle Cup, Charleston. Moved from Hilton Head to Family Circle Cup Stadium in Charleston, the Family Circle Cup WTA tournament is one of the oldest on the women's pro tour. For information, call ☎ **843/856-7900** or go to www.familycirclecup.com. Mid-April.

Blessing of the Fleet, Mount Pleasant. This seafood festival, which takes place at Mount Pleasant Memorial Waterfront Park, overlooking Charleston Harbor, celebrates the historic Mount Pleasant shrimping industry and offers a host of other family activities; one highlight is an arts-and-crafts show with some 40 exhibitors. Call ☎ **843/849-2061.** Late April.

Silver Springs International Film Festival, Ocala, FL. New in 2014, this celluloid confab features flicks filmed in central Florida—including *The Creature From the Black Lagoon*—screened at the Marion Theater in downtown Ocala. John Travolta, who lives nearby, is a supporter and showed up to the fest's opening night kickoff with wife Kelly Preston. Visit www.springsfilmfest.com for more information. Early April.

MAY

North Charleston Arts Festival, North Charleston. This is a 9-day, all-encompassing cultural festival, with film presentations, theater, art workshops, street dances, concerts, performances for kids, and an outdoor sculpture competition, among other happenings. Call ☎ **843/554-5700** or go to www.northcharlestonartsfest.com. Early May.

Spoleto Festival USA, Charleston. This is the premier cultural event in the Southeast. This famous international festival—the American counterpart of the equally celebrated one in Spoleto, Italy—showcases world-renowned performers in drama, dance, music, and art in various venues throughout the city. For details and this year's schedule, contact Spoleto Festival USA (© **843/579-3100;** www.spoletousa. org). Late May through early June.

Memorial Day at Old Fort Jackson, Savannah. The day includes a flag-raising ceremony and a memorial service featuring "Taps." Contact the Coastal Heritage Society (© **912/651-6840;** www.chsgeorgia.org) for more information. Late May.

JUNE

Sweet Grass Festival, Charleston. This cultural festival celebrates the region's rich Gullah/Geechee heritage and provides the most extensive showcase of sweet-grass baskets in the Lowcountry. It also features unique handmade arts, crafts, paintings, and live performances. Visitors can enjoy classic barbecue as well as authentic Gullah cuisine. Call © **843/856-9732** or go to www.sweet grassfestival.org. Early June.

Juneteenth, Savannah. This event highlights the contributions of more than 200,000 African Americans who fought for their freedom and that of future generations. This event is a celebration of the Emancipation Proclamation. Although this promise of freedom was announced in January, it was not until the middle of June (actual date unknown) that the news reached Savannah, thus prompting the remembrance of "Juneteenth." For more information, contact the Savannah Convention & Visitors Bureau (© **877/728-2662** or 912/644-6401; http://savannahvisit. com). Mid-June.

SEPTEMBER

Scottish Games and Highland Gathering, Charleston. This gathering of Scottish clans features medieval games, bagpipe performances, Scottish dancing, and other traditional activities. Call the Scottish Society of Charleston (© **843/224-7867;** http:// charlestonscots.org). Third Saturday in September.

MOJA Festival, Charleston. Celebrating the rich African-American heritage in the Charleston area, this festival features lectures, art exhibits, stage performances, historical tours, concerts, and much more. Contact the Charleston Office of Cultural Affairs (© **843/724-7305;** www.mojafestival. com) for more information. Late September to early October.

Savannah Jazz Festival, Savannah. This festival features national and local jazz-and-blues legends. A jazz brunch and music at different venues throughout the city are among the highlights. Call © **912/525-5050** or go to www.savannahjazzfestival.org for more information. Late September.

OCTOBER

A Taste of Charleston, Charleston. Traditionally held at Boone Hall Plantation, this annual event offers an afternoon of food, fun, entertainment, and more. A selection of Charleston-area restaurants offers their specialties in bite-size portions so you can sample them all. For more information, call © **843/452-6088** or visit www.charleston restaurantassociation.com. Early October.

NOVEMBER–DECEMBER

British Night Watch, St. Augustine. Watch the "Grande Illumination Parade" of Redcoats as they circle the historic district before returning to the Plaza de la Constitucion where they fire muskets, followed by Christmas caroling. Visit www.floridashistoriccoast. com for more information. Early December.

Cane Grinding and Harvest Festival, Savannah. More than 75 crafts artists from four states sell and demonstrate their art. Music is provided by the Savannah Folk Music Society. Contact Oatland Island (© **912/395-1212;** www.oatlandisland.org) for more information. Mid-November.

Christmas in Charleston, Charleston. This month-long celebration features home and church tours, Christmas-tree lightings, craft shows, artistry, and a peek at how Old Charleston celebrated the holiday season. For more information on how to participate or to visit, call (C) **800/774-0006** or visit www.christmasincharleston.com. Early November to late December.

Holiday Tour of Homes, Savannah. The doors of Savannah's historic homes are opened to the public during the holiday season. Each home is decorated, and a different group of homes is shown every day. Contact the Downtown Neighborhood Association ((C) **912/236-8362;** www.dna holidaytour.com) for more information. Early to mid-December.

Pirate Gathering, St. Augustine. Wannabe swashbucklers gather for this annual celebration featuring reenactments, pirate battles, sailor's encampment, and Thieves Market. First week in November. Visit www. pirategathering.com for more information.

Nights of Lights St. Augustine (Nov–Jan). Two-month long celebration of the holiday season that sees millions of white lights illuminate colonial St. Augustine, and a roster of special events. For more information call (C) **800/653-2489** or visit www.floridas historiccoast.com/nights).

CHARLESTON

All those romantic notions of the South—stately homes, courtly manners, gracious hospitality, and, above all, sumptuous food—are facts of everyday life in Charleston. This elegant city of ironwork balconies, colorful stucco, lush palmetto palms, and graceful mansions is a magnificent spectacle, truly magical on an early spring evening, when church bells chime, horse carriages trundle through the streets, and folks gather along the harbor. Jasmine and wisteria fragrances fill the air, and the aroma of she-crab soup (a local favorite) wafts from sidewalk cafes. Though it can get very touristy, it is surprisingly easy to lose the crowds. Indeed, the best way to enjoy Charleston is to simply stroll the enchanting streets, soaking up the antebellum architecture and languid atmosphere.

Notwithstanding a history dotted with earthquakes, hurricanes, fires, and Yankee bombardments, Charleston remains one of the best-preserved cities in America's Old South. Founded by English colonists in 1670, today it boasts 73 Colonial buildings, 136 from the late 18th century and more than 600 built before the 1840s.

Does this city have a modern side? Yes, but it's well hidden. Chic shops abound, as do a few supermodern hotels, but Charleston has no skyscrapers. You don't come to Charleston for anything cutting-edge—you come to glimpse an earlier, almost-forgotten era.

You'll gain a sense of this history touring some of its great houses such as **Calhoun Mansion,** one of its historic churches such **St. Michael's Episcopal,** or by visiting the **Charleston Museum** or exploring the **College of Charleston,** set on a truly beautiful campus. But take time to simply wander the back streets, where you will encounter a real, living, breathing city, where many houses have been owned by the same families for generations, and even small cafes and taverns drip with historic charm.

ESSENTIALS

Arriving

BY PLANE   Charleston International Airport (www.chs-airport.com) is in North Charleston on I-26 (5500 International Blvd.), about 12 miles west of the city. The meter rate for a taxi from the airport into the city is $2.52 per mile plus $14 per person in excess of two passengers; typical metered fares to the Historic District range from $29 to $34 ($45 to Middleton Place; $50 to Isle of Palms; $73 to Kiawah Island). The airport **shuttle service** (every 15 min.; © **843/767-1100**) has a $14 fare to hotels in downtown Charleston (a shared ride making several stops). The **local bus,** CARTA Route 11 Dorchester/Airport ($1.75; Mon–Fri 7am–8:40pm hourly; Sat 8pm–8:40pm hourly; Sun 10am–7pm hourly) serves the airport and runs directly into the downtown area (around 50 min.). All major **car-rental facilities,** including Hertz and Avis, are available at the airport. If you're driving, follow the airport-access road to I-26 into the heart of Charleston.

BY CAR   The main north-south coastal route, U.S. 17, passes through Charleston; I-26 runs northwest to southeast, ending in Charleston. Charleston is 120 miles southeast of Columbia via I-26, 98 miles south of Myrtle Beach via U.S. 17, and 106 miles northeast of Savannah via U.S. 17 and I-95 (around 2-hr. drive).

BY TRAIN   Amtrak (© **800/872-7245;** www.amtrak.com) trains arrive at 4565 Gaynor Ave., North Charleston, 11 miles from the Historic District. The station serves the Silver Service/Palmetto route between New York and Washington D.C., and Orlando and Miami. Trains travel twice a day between Savannah and Charleston (1 hr. 45 min.–2 hr.). **Local bus** CARTA runs from the Amtrak station directly into the downtown area ($1.75), but if you arrive at night take a taxi ($20–$30 to the Historic District).

BY BUS   Greyhound (© **800/231-2222;** www.greyhound.com) offers regular service to North Charleston (7 miles from the Historic District) from Columbia and Myrtle Beach, and 1 daily from Savannah (2 hr. 10 min.). **Southeastern Stages** (© **404/591-2750;** www.southeasternstages.com) offers similar routes. The **bus station** is at 3610 Dorchester Rd. (© **843/744-4247**). CARTA Route 11 (see above) also services the Greyhound bus station.

Visitor Information

TOURIST OFFICES   The **Charleston Visitor Center,** 375 Meeting St., at John St. (© **800/774-0006;** www.charlestoncvb.com), just across from the Charleston Museum, provides maps and brochures, and the helpful staff can also assist you in finding accommodations. Numerous **tours** depart hourly from the visitor center, and restroom facilities, as well as parking ($16/day), are available. Be sure to allow time to view the 24-minute multi-image presentation *Forever Charleston* (admission $2) and pick up a copy of the visitor's guide. The center is open daily from 8:30am to 5:30pm (closing at 5pm Nov–Feb; closed Christmas Day, New Year's Day, and Thanksgiving Day). You can download useful maps from the website, showing the streets of the Historic District as well as surrounding areas.

Other area tourist offices include the **North Charleston Visitor Center,** at the Tanger Outlet mall, 4975-B Centre Point Dr. (© **800/774-0006**), open Monday to Saturday 10am to 5pm and Sunday 1 to 5pm; and the **Mount Pleasant Visitor Center,** 99 Harry M. Hallman Jr. Blvd., Memorial Waterfront Park (© **800/774-0006**), open daily 9am to 5pm.

City Layout

Charleston's streets are laid out in an easy-to-follow grid pattern. The main north-south thoroughfares are King, Meeting, and East Bay streets. Tradd, Broad, Queen, and Calhoun streets cross the city from east to west. South of Broad Street, East Bay becomes East Battery.

Neighborhoods in Brief

The Historic District In 1860, according to one Charlestonian, "South Carolina seceded from the Union, Charleston seceded from South Carolina, and south of Broad Street seceded from Charleston." The city preserves its early years at its southernmost point: the conjunction of the Cooper and Ashley rivers. White Point Gardens, right in the elbow of the two rivers, provides a sort of gateway into this area, where virtually every home is of historic or architectural interest. Between Broad Street and Murray Boulevard (which runs along the south waterfront), you'll find such sightseeing highlights as St. Michael's Episcopal Church, the Edmondston-Alston House, the Heyward-Washington House, Catfish Row, and the Nathaniel Russell House.

Downtown Extending north from Broad Street to Marion Square at the intersection of Calhoun and Meeting streets, this area encloses noteworthy points of interest, good shopping, and a gaggle of historic churches. Just a few of its highlights are the Old City Market, the Dock Street Theatre, the Old Powder Magazine, Congregation Beth Elohim, the French Huguenot Church, and St. John's Church. In the guide we've considered Downtown an extension of the Historic District.

North Charleston Charleston International Airport is at the point at which I-26 and I-526 intersect. This makes North Charleston a Lowcountry transportation hub.

Primarily a residential and industrial community, it lacks the charm of the Historic District. It's the home of the North Charleston Coliseum, the largest indoor entertainment venue in the state, and the *Hunley* Confederate Submarine.

West Ashley One of Charleston's six main districts, West Ashley was where colonists first came ashore in the 1670s. Head west across the Ashley River Bridge to pay tribute to Charleston's birth at Charles Towne Landing and visit such highlights as Drayton Hall, Magnolia Gardens, and Middleton Place, all conveniently located along Ashley River Road (SC Hwy. 61). West Ashley is also home to the region's largest indoor shopping mall, Citadel Mall.

Mount Pleasant East of the Cooper River, just minutes from the Historic District, this community is worth a detour. Filled with lodgings, restaurants, and some attractions, it encloses a historic district along the riverfront known as the Old Village, which is on the National Register of Historic Places. Its major attractions are Patriots Point, the world's largest naval and maritime museum (also the home of the aircraft carrier *Yorktown*), and Boone Hall Plantation.

Outlying Areas Within easy reach of the city are the public beaches at Sullivan's Island, historic Fort Moultrie, and ill-fated Fort Sumter, out in Charleston Harbor, where the Civil War began in 1861.

Getting Around

BY BUS Public transport is provided by CARTA (Charleston Area Regional Transportation Authority). The standard bus fare is $1.75 (express $3, transfers 30¢), and service is available from 5:35am to 10pm (until 1am to North Charleston). Between 9am and 3:30pm, after 6pm, and all day Saturday and Sunday, seniors pay 85¢. The fare for persons with disabilities (all day) is 50¢. Exact change is required. A 1-day pass is $6 (3 days is $12), but if you intend to stay primarily in the Historic District these are not necessary (see the DASH service below). Bus 41 connects Downtown with Patriots Point, but for most of the attractions in West Ashley and the outlying areas you will need your own transport. For route and schedule information, call *(* **843/724-7420** or visit www.ridecarta.com.

Ride a Rickshaw

By far the most fun way to get around the Historic District (though not the cheapest) is to hail a tricycle taxi, otherwise known as a rickshaw. In peak season it's easy to find them on Market Street, but you can also call for pick up.

Contact the **Charleston Rickshaw Co.,** daily 9am to 2am (© **843/723-5685;** www.charlestonrickshaw.com). Drivers charge $5.50 per passenger, per 10 minutes.

BY TROLLEY The **Downtown Area Shuttle (DASH)** is the quickest way to get around the main downtown area. The service is **free.** There are currently three routes: **RT210,** which runs along Calhoun Street between the Aquarium and the College of Charleston; **RT211,** which runs between the Historic District and the Visitor Center; and **RT213,** which makes a big loop to the Citadel. All three routes intersect at the Visitor Center and tend to run Monday to Friday 6:30am to 9:30pm and weekends 8am to 9:30pm, every 20 or 30 minutes. To confirm hours and routes, call © **843/724-7420** or visit www.ridecarta.com.

BY TAXI Leading taxi companies are **Yellow Cab** (© **843/577-6565;** www.yellow cabofcharleston.com) and **Safety Cab** (© **843/722-4066**). For pick-ups at the airport, and Amtrak and Greyhound stations, try **Mount Pleasant Shuttle** (© **866/223-7226;** www.mpshuttle.com). Each company has its own fare structure, but city ordinances require all taxi drivers to charge a flat $5 rate for any trip within the Charleston peninsula. Companies are allowed to add a $1 surcharge per passenger beyond the first passenger, plus a gas surcharge ranging from 50¢ (when the gas price reaches $3/gallon) to $3.50 (if gas reaches $6.50/gallon). You must call for a taxi; there are no pick-ups on the street.

BY WATER TAXI **Charleston Water Taxi,** 10 Wharfside St. (© **843/330-2989;** www.charlestonwatertaxi.com) runs an hourly ferry loop service across the Cooper River starting at 9am at the Charleston Harbor Resort & Marina in Mount Pleasant before heading over to Waterfront Park in the Historic District; the ferry then runs up to the Maritime Center (1 block south of the South Carolina Aquarium) before crossing back over to Patriots Point in Mount Pleasant and starting the loop again. Ferries run daily 9am to 8pm late March through late November (June–Aug ferries run Fri–Sat until 11pm). The rest of the year ferries run Saturdays only 10am to 6pm. One-way tickets are $6; 1-day passes are $10. Children 3 and under ride free. Purchase tickets on the boat or online.

BY CAR If you're staying in the city proper, park your car and save it for day trips to outlying areas. You'll find **parking facilities** scattered about the city, with some of the most convenient at Hudson Street and Calhoun Street, both of which are near Marion Square; on King Street between Queen and Broad; and on George Street between King and Meeting. If you can't find space on the street to park, the two most centrally located **garages** are on Wentworth Street (© **843/724-7383**) and at Concord and Cumberland (© **843/724-7387**). The fee is $16 all day.

Leading car-rental companies are **Avis Rent A Car** (© **800/331-1212** or 843/767-7030; www.avis.com), **Budget Car and Truck Rentals** (© **800/527-0700,** 843/767-7051 at the airport, 760-1410 in North Charleston, or 577-5195 downtown; www. budget.com), and **Hertz** (© **800/654-3131** or 843/767-4554; www.hertz.com).

[FastFACTS] CHARLESTON

Dentists Consult **Atlantic Dental Associates,** in 61 West Building, 1483 Tobias Gadson Blvd., Ste. 105 (℃ **843/556-3838;** www. atlanticimplantdentistry. com).

Doctors & Hospitals For a physician referral or 24-hour emergency-room treatment, contact **Roper Hospital,** 316 Calhoun St. (℃ **843/724-2000;** www.ropersaintfrancis.com), or **Doctor's Care** (℃ **843/556-5585;** www. doctorscare.com) for the names of local walk-in clinics. Other local hospitals operating 24-hour

emergency rooms include **East Cooper Medical Center,** 2000 Hospital Dr., Mount Pleasant (℃ **843/881-0100;** www.eastcooper medctr.com), and **Medical University of South Carolina,** 171 Ashley Ave. (℃ **843/792-2300;** www. musc.edu).

Emergencies In an emergency, dial ℃ **911.** If the situation isn't life threatening, call ℃ **843/577-7070** for the fire department and ℃ **843/577-7077** for the police.

Pharmacies Try **CVS Pharmacy,** 59 George St., Downtown (℃ **843/**

720-8523), open Monday to Friday 8am to 10pm, Saturday 9am to 6pm, and Sunday 10am to 6pm (store open 24 hr.). The closest **24-hour** CVS Pharmacy is in North Charleston at 5215 Ashley Phosphate Rd. (℃ **843/767-4500**).

Post Office The main post office is at 83 Broad St. (℃ **843/577-0688**), open Monday to Friday 11:30am to 3:30pm. The East Bay branch, just north of Downtown at 557 E. Bay St. (℃ **800/275-877**), is open Monday to Friday 9am to 5pm, and Saturday 9:30am to 11:30am.

CHARLESTON HOTELS

Charleston has many of the best historic inns in America, surpassing even those of Savannah. **Hotels** and **motels** are priced in direct ratio to their proximity to the **Historic District. Bed-and-breakfast** accommodations range from historic homes to carriage houses to simple cottages, and they're located in virtually every section of the city. For full details and reservations, contact **Historic Charleston Bed and Breakfast,** 57 Broad St. (℃ **800/743-3583;** www.historiccharlestonbedandbreakfast.com; Mon–Fri 9am–5pm).

During the **Spring Festival of Houses** (Mar–Apr) and the **Spoleto Festival USA** (late May–early June; www.spoletousa.org), rates for all types of accommodation go up, and owners charge pretty much what the market will bear. Advance reservations are essential at those times. Note that although the city attracts visitors year-round, March through June tends to be **peak season** in Charleston.

In a city that has rooms of so many shapes and sizes in the same historic building, classifying hotels by price is difficult. Price often depends on the room itself. Some expensive hotels may, in fact, have many moderately priced rooms. Moderately priced hotels, on the other hand, may have special rooms that are quite expensive. When booking a hotel, ask about **package plans**—deals are most often granted to those who are staying 3 days or more.

The downside regarding all these inns of charm and grace is that they are invariably **expensive** when compared to other cities in the South. Staying at an inn or B&B in the Historic District is one of the reasons to go to Charleston and can do more to evoke the elegance of the city than almost anything else. Innkeepers and B&B owners know this all too well and charge accordingly, especially in the summer season.

If you can't afford a stay at one of these historic inns, you can confine your consumption of Charleston to dining in the old city and sightseeing and, at night, retire to one of the many clean, comfortable—and, yes, utterly dull—**chain motels** on the outskirts. The biggest clusters can be found in **North Charleston,** near the international airport (at the junction of I-26 and I-526); at the southern end of I-526 in **West Ashley;** and just across the Cooper River on U.S. 17. Doubles range from $55 to $180. Children 11 and under stay free in their parent's room, and cribs are also free.

Self-Catering Apartments

Anyone looking to really get into the local swing of things in Charleston should consider a short-term rental apartment. For the same price or less than a hotel room, you could have your own one-bedroom apartment with a washing machine, air conditioning, and a fridge to store booze. Properties of all sizes and styles, in every price range, are available for stays of 3 nights to several weeks.

RECOMMENDED AGENCIES

The companies below are especially recommended.

AirBnB (www.airbnb.com) offers over 125 properties in and around Charleston. The San Francisco-based Internet venture connects private property owners with travelers at a variety of price points.

Couchsurfing (www.couchsurfing.org) is another website connecting travelers with folks willing to rent a house, room, or apartment. It offers over 2,000 options in and around Charleston.

Vacation Rentals by Owner (www.vrbo.com) is a hip rental agency that offers over 3,000 rental properties in and around Charleston, everything from 4-bedroom apartments for $310 per night to studios for $165 per night.

The Historic District

VERY EXPENSIVE

Belmond Charleston Place ★★ For a delightful introduction to old-fashioned Southern charm look no further; the Orient-Express Hotels–managed Belmond offers top-notch concierge services, gourmet dining, super-comfy rooms, staff that go above-and-beyond, and the perfect location in the heart of the Historic District. The Thoroughbred Club, located next to the hotel's grand staircase, is a great spot for cocktails, accompanied by live music every night. The 4th-floor pool is a real treat, with an impressive retractable glass roof, a heated saltwater pool, and retro porthole windows overlooking Downtown. Though it all looks like something from the Georgian era, the hotel was actually built in 1986.

205 Meeting St., Charleston, SC 29401. www.charlestonplace.com. © **843/722-4900.** 435 units. $279–$350 double. Parking $32. **Amenities:** 2 restaurants (including Charleston Grill; see review, p. 56); bar; exercise room; indoor/outdoor pool; room service; sauna; spa; free Wi-Fi.

Planters Inn ★★ You'll feel like you have been transported back to the 19th-century at this elegant 1844 inn. Now a Relais & Châteaux property, the structure started life as a large cotton warehouse, just across from the City Market. The spacious, bright rooms feature comfortable four-posters, large flatscreen TVs, upholstered chairs, and beautiful furnishings. Free coffee, tea, and fresh fruit are always available in the lobby, which features a welcoming fireplace in the winter. Note that there is a 3-night minimum during peak periods.

112 N. Market St., Charleston, SC 29401. www.plantersinn.com. © **843/722-2345.** 64 units. $259–$589 double. Parking $20. **Amenities:** Restaurant (see review, p. 58); bar; babysitting; room service; free Wi-Fi.

Where to Stay in Charleston

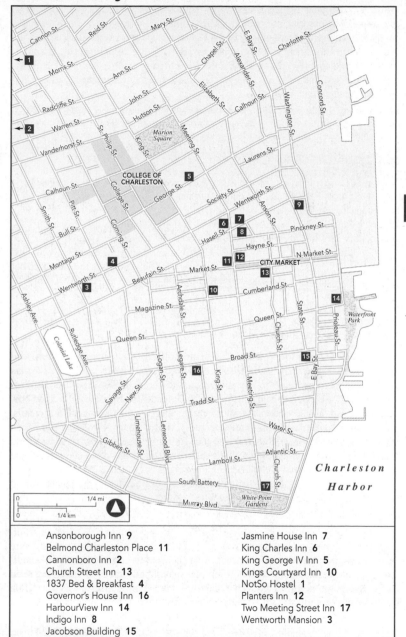

Hotel	#	Hotel	#
Ansonborough Inn	9	Jasmine House Inn	7
Belmond Charleston Place	11	King Charles Inn	6
Cannonboro Inn	2	King George IV Inn	5
Church Street Inn	13	Kings Courtyard Inn	10
1837 Bed & Breakfast	4	NotSo Hostel	1
Governor's House Inn	16	Planters Inn	12
HarbourView Inn	14	Two Meeting Street Inn	17
Indigo Inn	8	Wentworth Mansion	3
Jacobson Building	15		

Wentworth Mansion ★★★ This stunning hotel, framed by magnolia trees and set in a gorgeous 1886 Second Empire mansion, offers some serious pampering. Inside you'll find large, luxurious rooms with modern amenities (including iPod docks and DVD players), as well as a whirlpool tub and a fridge with free drinks. It's not quite as central as the Belmond or the Planters (it's a short walk), but the staff are incredibly friendly (there is 24-hr. concierge service), the complimentary late afternoon wine and aperitifs are superb, and there is a highly rated restaurant, Circa 1886, on the premises. The hotel has no gym, but offers free club membership at Eco Fitness, a 5-minute stroll away.

149 Wentworth St., Charleston, SC 29401. www.wentworthmansion.com. ✆ **888/466-1886.** 21 units. $395–$490 double. Rates include breakfast buffet and afternoon tea and cordials. Free parking. **Amenities:** Circa 1886 Restaurant (see review, p. 56); bar; babysitting; room service; spa; free Wi-Fi.

EXPENSIVE

Ansonborough Inn ★ An old paper warehouse transformed into an atmospheric hotel (built around 1901), the Ansonborough retains its enormous exposed pinewood beams and cavernous three-story lobby. The extra spacious rooms are comfy, with 25-foot ceilings, attractive furniture, modern granite bathrooms, and flatscreen TVs, with quality artwork liberally spread throughout the premises. The rooftop terrace offers fantastic views of the city and makes a romantic spot for afternoon wine and cheese (the delicious pimento cheese is a specialty). The location is fairly central, but note that the hotel lies next to the cruise terminal, so the area can get busy when ships load and unload.

21 Hasell St., Charleston, SC 29401. www.ansonboroughinn.com. ✆ **843/723-1655.** 37 units. $169–$275 double. Rates include continental breakfast. Children 11 and under stay free in parent's room. Parking $15. **Amenities:** Breakfast room; bar; room service; babysitting; free Wi-Fi.

Governor's House Inn ★★★ This luxurious B&B in a two-story wooden mansion is in the heart of the Historic District. The house was built by one James Laurens in 1760 and has a fascinating history, serving as the home of Governor Edward Rutledge, youngest signer of the Declaration of Independence, between 1776 and 1800. Beyond the spiral pinewood staircase there are lovely paneled rooms with canopy beds, fireplaces, lofty ceilings, family antiques, original hardwood floors, and whirlpool baths. Breakfast is good and wholesome (think homemade quiche, sausage and cheese bake), afternoon tea comes with light snacks (chocolate cake, chess bars), and each evening guests are served wine with local cheeses. Note that Wi-Fi can be weak in some rooms, and that allergy sufferers should be aware that Nu, the friendly house cat, gently pads around the hotel.

117 Broad St., Charleston, SC 29401. www.governorshouse.com. ✆ **843/720-2070.** 11 units. $185–$470 double. Rates include full breakfast, afternoon tea, wine and cheese, and sherry after dinner. Free parking. **Amenities:** Breakfast room; free bikes; free Wi-Fi.

HarbourView Inn ★★ Unlike many of its Downtown competitors, this is a modern hotel, though there is an "historic wing" with an original brick wall from the 1830s, and all the rooms are furnished with a nod to the city's past. Flatscreen TVs and iPod docks are paired with wooden four-posters and antique-like furnishings. But the main draw of this hotel is the sensational location overlooking the harbor and Waterfront Park, with an enticing rooftop terrace and lounge chairs to enjoy the complimentary cocktail hour (wine and cookies). Breakfast is delivered to the room. Complimentary "Skyline Tours" are offered on Wednesdays and Saturdays on the rooftop terrace.

2 Venue Range, Charleston, SC 29401. www.harbourviewcharleston.com. ℂ **843/853-8439.** 52 units. Double $159–$499. Rates include continental breakfast. Parking $20. **Amenities:** Babysitting; room service; free Wi-Fi.

Two Meeting Street Inn ★★★   One of the city's most enticing B&Bs, a beautiful Queen Anne mansion given as a wedding present and completed in 1892 (horse-drawn carriage tours actually stop out front). The building features lofty ceilings, Tiffany stained glass windows, an attractive wraparound porch with rocking chairs and soothing views across the water and colorful gardens, and artfully carved oak paneling throughout. Rooms are spacious, comfortable, and loaded with amenities. Bottled water, coffee, and tea are always available, and afternoon tea is a special treat here, with a variety of cheeses, spreads, and cakes. Two-night minimum at weekends.

2 Meeting St., Charleston, SC 29401. www.twomeetingstreet.com. ℂ **843/723-7322.** 9 units. $185–$489 double. Rates include continental breakfast and afternoon tea. No children 11 and under. **Amenities:** Breakfast room; free Wi-Fi.

MODERATE

Cannonboro Inn ★   This handsome wooden mansion was built around 1853 by the wealthy Lucas family, was restored in the 1990s, and is now a friendly B&B oozing Southern hospitality. Breakfasts are excellent (think orange-glazed croissant French toast), and the Charleston tradition of late afternoon wine, cheese, and crackers (at 4pm) is nicely done here. Rooms are furnished with original heart-pine floors, antiques, and four-poster and canopied beds. Three rooms are located in the nearby Guest House, built around 1850 as the carriage house for Wickliffe House (now a wedding venue and Tea Room). Cannonboro is located on the west side of Downtown, between the Medical School and the College of Charleston, but only a brisk walk from the Historic District.

184 Ashley Ave., Charleston, SC 29401. www.charleston-sc-inns.com. ℂ **843/723-8572.** 11 units. $109–$250 double. Rates include full breakfast and afternoon tea and sherry. Free parking. No children 9 and under. **Amenities:** Breakfast room; free bikes; free Wi-Fi.

Church Street Inn ★★   This elegant Festiva Resorts property in the heart of Downtown is well worth considering as an alternative to traditional hotels. This is a time-share residential development, with plush one- and two-bedroom apartments rented to temporary visitors. The apartments are fully self-catering, with kitchens (including dishwashers), living room with sofa bed, DVD players, flatscreen TVs, and dining room. The 24-hour front desk acts as concierge and can help set up tours.

177 Church St. (at Market St.), Charleston, SC 29401. www.festiva-churchstreet.com. ℂ **843/722-3420** or 866/933-7848. 31 units. $159–$209 1-bedroom apartment. Parking $20. **Amenities:** Concierge desk private kitchen; free Wi-Fi.

1837 Bed & Breakfast ★★   This is a quaint B&B owned and operated by two friendly artists, Jane Floyd and Richard Dunn, comprising an early 1800s cotton planter's home and brick carriage house. The third floor rooms are most spacious (no elevator), with a deck and lounge, while the carriage house rooms are more compact, but still pleasant and very clean, with canopied beds, antiques, local artwork, and oriental rugs. Breakfasts are huge and tasty, with specialties like sausage pie, the signature raspberry French toast, and ham frittata with Mornay sauce. Afternoon tea (3–5pm) comes with addictive brownies and chocolate chip cookies. The location is fine, a 5- to 10-minute walk from everything, and your hosts are a font of local knowledge. The free parking can be tight, so get here early if you can (bigger vehicles should make other arrangements; there's a public parking garage less than 2 blocks away for $15). Note that there is a 2-night minimum on weekends and holidays, and that reservations made 14 days or more in advance will require a deposit by check, not credit card.

126 Wentworth St., Charleston, SC 29401. www.1837bb.com. © **843/723-7166.** 9 units. $109–$245 double. Rates include full breakfast and afternoon tea. Free parking. No children 6 and under. **Amenities:** Breakfast room; free Wi-Fi.

Indigo Inn/Jasmine House Inn ★★

These sister properties in the center of town offer similar experiences, though Jasmine House is far more luxurious. Rooms in the Indigo Inn (an indigo warehouse built in 1850) are old but spacious, and simply furnished in period antiques (bathrooms tend to be small, however). The most compelling feature is the lush courtyard and fountain in the center of the complex, the perfect place for the complimentary afternoon wine and cheese (5–6:30pm), and breakfast (generally fruits, donuts, and hard-boiled eggs). Jasmine's apartments are located in an 1843 Greek Revival mansion and are much bigger, and also come with breakfast and afternoon tea. The two properties are one block apart and share the same reception area in the Indigo Inn.

1 Maiden Lane (Jasmine House at 64 Hassel St.), Charleston, SC 29401. www.indigoinn.com. © **843/577-5900.** 40 units Indigo Inn, 11 units Jasmine House. Double $139–$249 Indigo Inn, $149–$316 Jasmine House. Rates include continental breakfast. Parking $10. **Amenities:** Breakfast room; babysitting (at Indigo Inn); Jacuzzi; free Wi-Fi.

Jacobson Building ★★

Constructed by merchant Andrew Kerr in 1794, this ravishing historic property has been converted into a condo-hotel hybrid, with spacious apartments featuring heart-pine floors, soaring 16-foot ceilings, brick fireplaces, modern kitchens, and new tile baths. It's an excellent deal, especially for families and large groups (the two cheaper doubles must be booked with the two larger studios), with a superb location in the heart of the Historic District. The name reflects the building's role as the law offices of I.H. Jacobson in the 1950s (descendants Michael and Jan Jacobson still own and operate the hotel).

19 Broad St., Charleston, SC 29401. www.historiccharlestonaccommodations.com. © **843/727-8262.** 4 units. $100–$400. Parking $12–$20. **Amenities:** Full kitchen (Grand Studio only); free Wi-Fi.

King Charles Inn ★

This distinctive-looking hotel is one of the most affordable options in Downtown Charleston (1 block from the College of Charleston)—in the off season, at least—with small but cozy period rooms. The outdoor pool and free parking add to the appeal. Though it looks older, the inn was actually completed in 1958 on the location of the old Pavilion Hotel, where Edgar Allan Poe spent his weekends 1827 to 1829 (when he was enlisted at Fort Moultrie), and wrote "The Gold Bug." Each room contains a flatscreen LCD TV and an iPod docking station, and the on-site BREW pub and cafe is open for breakfast, complimentary reception (4:30–5:30pm), drinks, and dinner. While there is no gym, adjacent Eco Fitness is open to guests for $5 per day.

237 Meeting St. (btw. Wentworth and Hazel sts.), Charleston, SC 29401. www.kingcharlesinn.com. © **843/723-7451.** 91 units. $149–$289 double. Children 18 and under stay free in parent's room. Free parking. **Amenities:** Restaurant; outdoor pool; fitness center; room service; free Wi-Fi.

Kings Courtyard Inn ★

Just a 3-minute walk from City Market, this historic property started life in 1853 as an inn catering to plantation owners and merchants. Though it's starting to show some wear and tear, the rooms remain charmingly old-fashioned, most with four-posters or canopied beds, fireplaces, and fine views of the two inner courtyards. The four rooms in the Carriage House section are all **pet-friendly.** A decent breakfast and evening wine-and-cheese reception are included. The complimentary wine or sherry upon arrival is a nice touch.

198 King St., Charleston, SC 29401. www.kingscourtyardinn.com. ✆ **800/845-6119.** 41 units. $150–$265 double. Rates include continental breakfast. Children 11 and under stay free in parent's room. Off-season 3-day packages available. Parking $12. **Amenities:** Breakfast room; lounge; Jacuzzi; room service; free Wi-Fi.

INEXPENSIVE

King George IV Inn ★★   A lovely four-story wooden mansion house with heaps of character, comfortable beds, and spotlessly clean rooms. Known also as the "Peter Freneau House," the Federal-style residence dates back to the 1790s and is named after its original owner, the successful merchant, ship-owner, politician, and respected Charleston journalist. All rooms feature fireplaces, 11-foot ceilings, original wide-planked hardwood floors, and plenty of Victorian antiques. Note that the top-floor rooms share a bathroom. You'll be sleeping on anything from antique Gothic rope beds from the 1840s, to Victorian iron or teak masterpieces. The porches—on three levels—offer a soothing retreat and are ideal perches to soak up the street scene. Terry and Debra Flowers are extremely generous hosts (and Harley Davidson enthusiasts). Advance reservations are essential, as this place books up months in advance (great deals are available off-season). Two-night minimum on weekends.

32 George St., Charleston, SC 29401. www.kinggeorgeiv.com. ✆ **843/723-9339.** 10 units, 2 with shared bathrooms. $89–$240 double. Rates include full breakfast. Free parking. **Amenities:** Breakfast room; free Wi-Fi.

NotSo Hostel ★   This is an excellent bargain considering the Historic District is within walking distance (in fact, it's the only hostel in the city). Don't expect a posh hotel—this is a basic but charming 19th-century home, with a wooden porch, bagels and toast for breakfast, clean **dorms** (4 four-person dorms and one eight-person dorm), simple doubles, **camping** (rent camping gear for $10/night), and shared bathrooms. Personal fans are provided when it gets hot. Towels are $1, but linens are included. The **Notso Hostel Annex,** 5 blocks away at 33 Cannon St (same check-in), only contains spacious private rooms, some with private bathrooms, and is much quieter, though the Wi-Fi is often not as good.

156 Spring St., Charleston, SC 29401. www.notsohostel.com. ✆ **843/722-8383.** 5 dorms, 8 units (shared bathrooms); Annex 6 units. $16 camping, $26 dorm, $65–$85 double. Rates include continental breakfast. Free parking. **Amenities:** Breakfast room; communal kitchen; free laundry; free Wi-Fi.

West Ashley

MODERATE

The Inn at Middleton Place ★   Located on the grounds of historic Middleton Place (p. 76), this is the bucolic alternative to Downtown Charleston. The lodge-like rooms are spacious and comfy enough (most with wood-burning fireplaces), though some are in need of renovation—but it's really the surroundings that appeal here. Walking, bike riding, and kayaking on the Ashley River, and horseback riding are some of the activities on offer, and guests are entitled to a free tour of the plantation house (worth $56 for two adults). The daily manager's reception (5–7pm) is a much more relaxed and sociable affair than similar events at hotels such as the Wentworth Mansion or Governor's House Inn. Although the inn serves breakfast, and the plantation restaurant serves lunch and dinner (p. 64), there is nowhere else close to eat at night. Note also that there are no elevators to the upper floors.

4290 Ashley River Rd., Charleston, SC 29414. www.theinnatmiddletonplace.com. ℭ **800/543-4774** or 843/556-0500. 54 units. $149–$235 double. Rates include continental breakfast. Free parking. **Amenities:** Breakfast room; babysitting; bike rentals; outdoor pool; free Wi-Fi.

INEXPENSIVE

Creekside Lands Inn ★   The Creekside is an old but clean and well-maintained budget accommodation, around a 15-minute drive outside Downtown Charleston. The independently owned motel is conveniently located on the Savannah Highway, but once inside, road noise is surprisingly minimal. Most rooms overlook the nearby wetlands of Long Branch Creek (a tidal saltwater creek), and are well equipped with toiletries, towels, microwave, hairdryer, TV, and fridge.

2545 Savannah Hwy. (U.S. 17), Charleston, SC 29414. www.creeksidelandsinn.com. ℭ **843/763-8885.** 55 units. $60–$80 double. Children 17 and under stay free in parent's room. Rates include continental breakfast. Free parking. **Amenities:** Breakfast room; outdoor pool; outdoor barbecue grill; free Wi-Fi.

Oaks Plantation Campground ★★   A large, justly popular campground for motorhomes and tents, with plenty of space and excellent, high-speed Wi-Fi throughout (plus cable TV). The sites are well spaced (including full hook-ups on gravel drive-on pads), and the location is picturesque, with mossy live oaks, lots of shade, and very little road noise. This is a great location, around 10 miles from Downtown Charleston. A huge Publix supermarket and pharmacy lies within walking distance, and there is a gas station next door. There is a pleasant dog run on site.

3540 Savannah Hwy. (U.S. 17), Charleston, SC 29455. www.oakplantationcampground.com. ℭ **843/766-5936.** 200 sites. $32–$45. Free parking. **Amenities:** Outdoor pool; convenience store; laundry; free Wi-Fi.

Mount Pleasant

MODERATE

Old Village Post House ★★★   Located right in the heart of the enticing Old Village section of Mount Pleasant, surrounded by beautiful old homes and just a short walk from the Cooper River, the Post House started life as a 19th-century clapboard general store, and retains its gorgeous white-wood exterior. It's primarily known as a first-class restaurant and tavern these days, but staying in one of its six lovingly restored rooms is a real treat, all tastefully decorated but maintaining worn pinewood floors for added atmosphere. Though the neighborhood is itself a charming place to explore, the inn is only a short drive from all the major attractions in and around the city, but at much cheaper rates than hotels of a similar quality in Charleston; if you have a car, this is a real bargain.

101 Pitt St., Mount Pleasant, SC 29464. www.mavericksouthernkitchens.com/oldvillageposthouse. ℭ **843/388-8935.** 6 units. $145–$163 double. Rates include breakfast. **Amenities:** Restaurant (see review, p. 64); bar; free Wi-Fi.

INEXPENSIVE

Da Noi ★★   The amiable Wenche (pronounced "venka") and Wyatt Fox own and operate this tiny gem of a B&B, through the AirBnB website (p. 48). Their charming wooden house is tucked away between oak trees in a quiet residential neighborhood, a short ride from Downtown Charleston (the owners will drive you in for $10). All guest rooms are upstairs and beautifully decorated, with colorful, period furnishings in a classical French style, antique beds (some four-posters), and cozy armchairs. There are three shared bathrooms and two shared sitting rooms. Note that payment for 2 nights through airbnb.com is a minimum requirement, with cash only accepted on site. The owners offer transport to the airport for $35 one-way.

368 5th Ave., Mount Pleasant, SC 29464. www.airbnb.com/rooms/111689. 𝄞 **843/881-3638.** 4 units. $85–$130 double. Rates include continental breakfast. Free parking. **Amenities:** Breakfast room; free Wi-Fi.

Plantation Oaks Inn ★★   An excellent value 15 miles from Downtown, a hidden gem built on what was once part of the Snee Farm Plantation, owned by Charles Pinckney (p. 77). Today this B&B, with a distinctive timber cabin exterior, is surrounded by 300-year-old live oaks, marshes, and tranquil Horlbeck Creek. The five comfy rooms (three with four posters), are all decorated with antique wood furnishings, Baroque mirrors, and pine paneling, though each one boasts a different color scheme. Fresh cookies are served each day. Two-night minimum on weekends.

1199 Long Point Rd., Mount Pleasant, SC 29464. www.plantationoaksinnbandb.com. 𝄞 **843/971-3683.** 5 units. $99–$155 double. Rates include breakfast. **Amenities:** Free Wi-Fi.

Outlying Areas
INEXPENSIVE
James Island County Park Campground & Cottages ★★★   This county-managed campground is just 5 miles beyond Downtown Charleston, and is incredibly popular all year round. The site lies within 643-acre **James Island County Park,** where a plethora of activities is available, from rock climbing and kayaking, to hiking and mountain biking. The campground offers full hook-ups (water and electricity), primitive campsites, decent free Wi-Fi, and 24-hour staffing, while pet-owners can enjoy the large and well-maintained dog park. Cable TV is not available, but the cottages have satellite TV. The cottages are perfect for families and groups, with three bedrooms and one full bathroom. If you're lucky, you might see alligators wallowing in the nearby ponds. The park is 15 minutes from downtown historic Charleston, and offers a shuttle service for $10 one-way.

871 Riverland Dr., James Island, SC 29412. www.ccprc.com. 𝄞 **843/795-4386.** 10 cottages, 125 campsites. $25 primitive camping, $39–$49 hook-ups, $169 cottages. **Amenities:** Campground store; bike rental ($10/day); pedal boat rental ($6/hr.); kayak rental ($5/hr.); grills and picnic tables; laundry; playground; free Wi-Fi.

WHERE TO DINE

Foodies from all over flock to Charleston for some of the finest dining in the U.S. You get not only the refined cookery of the Lowcountry, but also an array of French and international specialties. The whole concept of "Lowcountry Cuisine" was pioneered here, essentially a blend of traditional Southern, African, French, and Caribbean flavors. Today, hot young chefs continue to experiment and open trendy new restaurants in the Historic District. One trend that unites the city's culinary movers and shakers is farm-to-table: Charleston restaurateurs pride themselves on sourcing meat and produce locally, and seasonally. Though prices tend to be high, on a par with much bigger cities on the east and west coasts, the quality is hard to beat.

Historic District

VERY EXPENSIVE

Charleston Grill ★★★ LOWCOUNTRY/FRENCH   Old-school, formal dining at its very best, with wood-paneled walls and crisp, white tablecloths. Chef Michelle Weaver's menus are work of arts. Dishes are creatively divided into four types: Pure (lighter dishes), Lush (richer meats and seafood), Cosmopolitan (inspired by global cuisines), and Southern (contemporary riffs on regional classics). The food is simply exquisite. Start the meal with a light octopus salad or seared foie gras, before sampling the Southern-fried catfish or venison tenderloin. The lounge section is far more relaxed, with comfy couches and a bar menu of cocktails and snacks, though you can also have dinner here (same menu as the dining room). Every night top-notch musicians—from classical trios to Brazilian jazz combos—serenade diners.

In the Charleston Place Hotel, 224 King St. www.charlestongrill.com. ✆ **843/577-4522.** Main courses $27–$55. Sun–Thurs 5:30–10pm, Fri–Sat 5:30–10:30pm.

Circa 1886 Restaurant ★★★ SOUTHERN/FRENCH   Chef Marc Collins is on top of his game right now, with this restaurant one of the city's leading fine-dining establishments catering to a well-heeled local and tourist clientele. Set in the old carriage house of the Wentworth Mansion (p. 50), the dining room retains much of its historic character, with wood-burning fireplace, stable doors, original heart-of-pine floors, and booths designed to mimic the original carriage openings. Collins uses local suppliers and seasonal produce to riff on Lowcountry and Southern classics (using less butter and cream than is typical). His Carolina flounder is a delicate dish served with smoked scallops, macadamia nuts, and pimento, while the artichokes n' truffles is about as decadent a veggie entree as you are ever likely to taste. Start by nibbling the in-house plantation rice bread rolls or the crab macaroni and cheese and end with the croissant donut or caramel-banana cake. No shorts or T-shirts.

In the Wentworth Mansion, 149 Wentworth St. www.circa1886.com. ✆ **843/853-7828.** Main courses $22–$35. Mon–Sat 5:30–10pm.

Cypress ★★ SOUTHERN/CONTINENTAL   Housed in an 1834 cotton warehouse, this restaurant blends original features—exposed brick walls and beautiful bay windows—with stylish, contemporary furniture and modern chandeliers. The always buzzing dining room attracts plenty of local movers and shakers as well as curious visitors. Chef Craig Deihl's menu relies heavily on Lowcountry ingredients, but the dishes are a creative fusion of Asian, Southern, and Italian flavors, from sweet-and-sour meatballs served with tomato-orange marmalade, to the Japan-inspired crispy wasabi tuna, and the parmesan-baked grits. The **bar menu** is a lot cheaper but just as inventive, with burgers and *báhn mi* sandwiches from $8, and steak fries for $5. The menu also includes selections from Deihl's in-house charcuterie program, the Artisan Meat Share, which produces over 80 types of meats.

167 E. Bay St. www.magnolias-blossom-cypress.com. ✆ **843/727-0111.** Main courses $25–$38. Sun–Thurs 5:30–10pm, Fri–Sat 5:30–11pm.

Fig ★★★ SOUTHERN/INTERNATIONAL   A modern, exceedingly creative bistro helmed by Chef Mike Lata, with a laid-back vibe, friendly and enthusiastic servers, and a simply decorated but welcoming dining room, enhanced with warm colors, and soft lighting. It's another restaurant that follows a farm-to-table philosophy, with ingredients sourced from Lowcountry producers wherever possible. Menus are seasonal, but always include plenty of local seafood; think cornflower-dusted jumbo flounder,

Where to Dine in Charleston

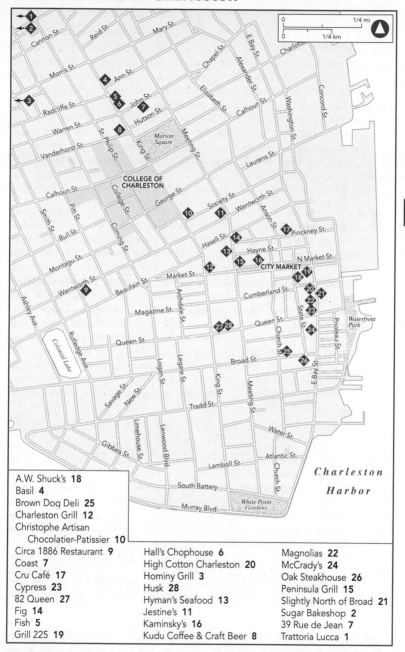

A.W. Shuck's **18**
Basil **4**
Brown Dog Deli **25**
Charleston Grill **12**
Christophe Artisan
   Chocolatier-Patissier **10**
Circa 1886 Restaurant **9**
Coast **7**
Cru Café **17**
Cypress **23**
82 Queen **27**
Fig **14**
Fish **5**
Grill 225 **19**

Hall's Chophouse **6**
High Cotton Charleston **20**
Hominy Grill **3**
Husk **28**
Hyman's Seafood **13**
Jestine's **11**
Kaminsky's **16**
Kudu Coffee & Craft Beer **8**

Magnolias **22**
McCrady's **24**
Oak Steakhouse **26**
Peninsula Grill **15**
Slightly North of Broad **21**
Sugar Bakeshop **2**
39 Rue de Jean **7**
Trattoria Lucca **1**

triggerfish with Carolina gold rice grits, and luscious Caper's Blades oysters. For dessert try the simple but exquisite sticky sorghum cake with calvados ice cream.

232 Meeting St. www.eatatfig.com. © **843/805-5900.** Main courses $28–$32. Mon–Thurs 5:30–10:30pm, Fri–Sat 5:30–11pm.

Grill 225 ★★ STEAK/INTERNATIONAL   This is first and foremost a plush steakhouse, where wet-aged steaks are beautifully served in a wood-paneled dining room resembling an old-fashioned Victorian club (it's located inside the elegant 19th-century style Market Pavilion Hotel.) SDA prime beef sourced from a family-owned supplier in the Midwest, these cuts are for serious connoisseurs. All tenderloin, rib-eye, and veal steaks are aged a minimum of 42 days, while the New York strip is aged for 50 days. You can taste the difference; these steaks have a succulent, rich flavor, as well as an incredible texture that makes them slice like warm butter. Though red meat is the primary focus, the array of Maine lobster dishes and seafood starters are all excellent.

In the Market Pavilion Hotel, 225 E. Bay St. www.marketpavilion.com. © **843/723-0500.** Main courses $16–$23 lunch, $27–$79 dinner. Daily 11am–3pm and 5:30–11pm.

Hall's Chophouse ★★ SEAFOOD/STEAK   With its cherrywood-paneled, clubby interior, this might appear to be just another steakhouse, but as its popularity attests, it supplies one of the most unique dining experiences in the city. Though it's by far the most-visited restaurant, members of the Hall family are often on hand to greet customers (a practice that tends to put off locals but amuse visitors), and the atmosphere is more family-friendly than exclusive. It's Chef Matthew Niessner's 28-day aged steaks, though, that are the main event: supplied by Allen Brothers of Chicago, the USDA prime beef is grilled to perfection, with the wet-aged, buttery rib-eye and porterhouse virtually melting on the tongue. His seafood creations are just as good—try the classic shrimp and grits, or the cedar-plank wild salmon. The lively bar attracts its own cocktails-and-snacks scene at the weekends, and if you attend the Sunday Gospel Brunch (think steak and eggs, biscuits and gravy) you'll be serenaded by local chanteuse Christal Brown-Gibson. *Note to non-meat eaters:* Hall's specially makes vegan and vegetarian dishes on request.

434 King St. www.hallschophouse.com. © **843/727-0090.** Main courses $25–$67. Mon–Sat 4pm–2am, Sun 10am–2pm (Gospel Sunday Brunch).

Peninsula Grill ★★★ SOUTHERN/INTERNATIONAL   The Peninsula rounds out Charleston's most exclusive dining establishments, a beautifully restored circa 1844 building converted into a chic, modern dining room adorned with oil paintings, velvet-lined walls, woven sea grass, and custom-made chandeliers commissioned by respected designer Amelia Handegan. The outdoor seating area in the lush courtyard is illuminated by real copper carriage lanterns. The main theme here is a sophisticated interpretation of Southern cuisine. Tantalizing offerings might include Lowcountry oyster stew with wild mushroom grits to start, followed by grilled bourbon-glazed jumbo shrimp, or local swordfish in red pepper Béarnaise sauce. The wine menu is also one of the city's finest, with over 300 selections. Leave room for the signature "ultimate coconut cake," with its 12 (yes, 12) layers of vanilla-and-coconut deliciousness (you can order a slice or the whole thing to go).

In the Planters Inn, 112 N. Market St. www.peninsulagrill.com. © **843/723-0700.** Main courses $31–$50. Sun–Thurs 5:30–10pm, Fri–Sat 5:30–11pm.

EXPENSIVE

High Cotton Charleston ★★ SOUTHERN/STEAK   High Cotton is a committed member of the Charleston farm-to-table movement, with local suppliers the sources of wonderful small plates to share such as buttermilk-fried oysters, Folly River clams, and Blue Hill Bay mussels. Entrees are especially rich in local vegetables here: pan-roasted tilefish with roasted acorn squash and pistachios, or pan-seared cashew-crusted tofu. Don't skip the sides: the fried Brussels sprouts and roasted fingerling potatoes are attractions in themselves. Meals are served in an elegant dining room, with heart-pine floors and antique brick, and are accompanied by live jazz every evening. The in-house spirits (rum, gin, whiskey, and vodka), have been specially created by Terressentia, a Charleston distiller.

199 E. Bay St. www.mavericksouthernkitchens.com. ✆ **843/724-3815.** Main courses $22–$38. Mon–Thurs 5:30–10pm, Fri 5:30–11pm, Sat 10am–2:30pm and 5:30–11pm, Sun 10am–2pm (brunch with live music) and 5:30–10pm.

Husk ★★ LOWCOUNTRY/SOUTHERN   Helmed by Chef Sean Brock (of *McCrady's* fame), Husk is serious about Southern food. As Brock says on the website, "if it doesn't come from the South, it's not coming through the door." Believe the hype: everything on the menu is a contemporary spin on a Southern classic. Menus are seasonal but may include deviled eggs with pickled okra and trout roe, Caper's Blades oysters, chilled strawberry soup, toasted honey-pecan-glazed confit duck leg, and cornmeal-dusted catfish served with Sea Island red peas and butterbeans. The main dining room, located in a typically gorgeous Charleston house, was constructed in 1893, but converted into a stylish blend of contemporary minimalist design and Victorian fixtures. The bar offers an extensive lineup of historic and modern cocktails, as well as a decent wine list.

76 Queen St. www.huskrestaurant.com. ✆ **843/577-2500.** Main courses $27–$30. Mon–Thurs 11:30am–2:30pm and 5:30–10pm, Fri–Sat 11:30am–2:30pm and 5:30–11pm, Sun 10am–2:30pm and 5:30–10pm.

McCrady's ★★ SOUTHERN/AMERICAN   Local celeb and executive Chef Sean Brock pioneered "new Southern" fine dining at this venerable spot, with produce fresh from local farms and local suppliers. Built by one Edward McCrady in 1788, the building was originally a four-story Georgian tavern. The bar area was once home to horse and buggy stalls, while the second-floor Long Room boasts lofty 15-foot ceilings, stone fireplaces, grand Venetian chandeliers, and handmade Italian chairs. George Washington dined here in 1791, though he would no doubt be amazed by today's fixed-price menu of beautifully presented trout, snapper, flounder, lamb, wagyu beef, and Grassroots Farms chicken. Desserts include the exceptional frozen parfait of grits, with geranium and preserved peach.

2 Unity Alley. www.mccradysrestaurant.com. ✆ **843/577-0025.** Main courses $29–$40; 4-course fixed-price dinner $65; tasting menu $115. Sun–Thurs 5–9:30pm, Fri–Sat 5–10:30pm.

Oak Steakhouse ★ STEAK/SEAFOOD   Set in the elegant former premises of the South Carolina Loan & Trust, dating back to around 1850, this steakhouse also specializes in seafood and shellfish dishes, using regional suppliers such as Clammer Dave's. While the steaks can't quite compete with those at Grill 225 or Hall's, they are a little cheaper and the menu here is more varied, with Italian flavors (house pastas), decent salads, lamb, roast chicken, and an excellent burger served with hand-cut truffle fries. The location is fabulous, with soaring 18-foot ceilings, original heart-of-pine floors, chandeliers, and local contemporary artwork on the walls.

17 Broad St. www.oaksteakhouserestaurant.com. © **843/722-4220.** Main courses $17–$51. Sun–Thurs 5–10pm, Fri–Sat 5–11pm.

Trattoria Lucca ★ ITALIAN   For a well-earned break from all things new Southern and Lowcountry, check out Chef Ken Vedrinksi's family-style Italian restaurant, inspired by the Tuscan city of Lucca. Set in a charming, clapboard Charleston home, the interior sports a fresh, contemporary design, with soft-pillowed banquettes, community-style seating, and a popular bar. The trattoria's fresh, handmade pasta is a real treat ($19–$21), while Italian imported cheese and *salumi* supplement an entree selection that utilizes—in faithful Charleston fashion—local produce. Menus change daily based on what's fresh and in season, but could include local triggerfish with artichokes, scaloppini of Sonoma duck, or the exceptional heritage Duroc pork chop Milanese.

41A Bogard St. www.luccacharleston.com. © **843/973-3323.** Main courses $25–$28. Mon–Thurs 6–10pm, Fri–Sat 6–11pm.

MODERATE

Coast ★ SEAFOOD   One of the best seafood specialists in the city, with a beach bar theme enhanced by cavernous 40-foot ceilings and rustic tin roofs. The restaurant is justly proud of its hickory-and-oak wood-burning grill, which adds an extra layer of flavor to its fresh fish. Otherwise, it's tough to choose a favorite here because everything is fresh, inventive, and tasty: simple peel-and-eat shrimp, fish tacos, creole-fried oysters, and the more-complex seafood linguini, crab-encrusted tilapia, and sensational cashew-encrusted grouper. The ceviche is always tongue-tingling and super fresh, and the wine list features organic and biodynamic producers.

39D John St. www.holycityhospitality.com/coast-bar-and-grill. © **843/722-8838.** Main courses $15–$28. Sun–Thurs 5:30–10pm, Fri–Sat 5:30–11pm.

Cru Café ★★★ AMERICAN/INTERNATIONAL   Located in a small 18th-century house, this two-room cafe is a local favorite, with a simple but bright white-walled and wood-floored interior that feels a bit like eating in someone's dining room. John Zucker's hidden gem is no longer so hidden, but his gourmet twists on classic comfort food are still worth the effort. Small plates include the simple but zesty fried green tomatoes and sesame tuna, while entrees might feature ginger-seared salmon and lemon risotto; the wonderful local swordfish served with wild mushroom grits, taso gravy, truffle arugula, and tobacco onion; or the heavenly pecan-smoked duck breast. End with the simple but glorious bread pudding. Note that if you are on a budget, lunch is a relative bargain.

18 Pinckney St. www.crucafe.com. © **843/534-2434.** Main courses $11–$14 lunch, $22–$29 dinner. Tues–Thurs 11am–3pm and 5–10pm, Fri–Sat 11am–3pm and 5–11pm.

82 Queen ★ LOWCOUNTRY   Fine dining from one of the pioneers of Lowcountry cuisine, with 11 simple but elegantly decorated dining rooms dating back to the early 1700s, replete with original wood floors and period furnishings. Adding to the ambience, at the heart of the restaurant stands a huge magnolia tree, surrounded by a Beaux Arts courtyard. Established in 1982, the restaurant remains true to its roots, with a menu that showcases the fusion of African, French, and American flavors that goes into local food. Start with the Carolina crab cake or crispy oysters before sampling classics such as barbecue shrimp and grits, Southern chicken with toasted rice, country ham gravy, and haricot verts, or the simple but irresistible lobster and fries.

82 Queen St. www.82queen.com. © **843/723-7591.** Main courses $11–$16 lunch, $13–$17 Sun brunch, $24–$39 dinner. Mon–Thurs 11:30am–3pm and 5–10pm, Fri 11:30am–3pm and 5–10:30pm, Sat 11am–3pm and 5–10:30pm, Sun 11am–3pm.

Fish ★ SEAFOOD Unsurprisingly, this is a fish restaurant, with locally sourced fresh-off-the-boat seafood used by Chef Nico Romo in a blend of French- and Asian-inspired dishes. He's devised an intriguing menu, divided into large, medium, and petite plates, showcasing fresh flounder, scallops, and triggerfish, but also an amazing bouillabaisse and crawfish *croque madame*. There's also a curious dim sum section ($12), with smaller bites such as lobster rolls and frog leg Rangoon. The property, a beautifully restored 1837 Charleston townhouse, features contemporary artwork, a purple heart-wood bar, and a sleek main dining room with distressed mirrors and cork walls. A leafy courtyard provides outdoor seating when weather allows.

442 King St. www.fishrestaurantcharleston.com. © **843/722-3474.** Petite plates $7–$10, medium plates $16–$19, large plates $18–$29. Daily 5:30–10pm.

Magnolias ★★ SOUTHERN Purveyors of upscale Southern cuisine since 1990, blending traditional ingredients and techniques with contemporary flair. The dining room reflects the food, with a fusion of exposed timber beams and wood floors with a crisp, modern design and simple, contemporary chairs and tables. Signature dishes include the "Down South Egg Roll," which is stuffed with collard greens, chicken, and Tasso ham, or the shellfish over grits (shrimp, sea scallops, and lobster). Everything is good here, but my favorite starters are the cornmeal-fried oysters (you can really taste the briny, juicy oysters under the batter) and boiled peanut hummus, while for entrees the fresh fish always delivers—think blackened catfish over Carolina dirty rice and fried green tomatoes, or the cedar-plank rainbow trout.

185 E. Bay St. www.magnolias-blossom-cypress.com. © **843/577-7771.** Main courses $10–$19 lunch, $19–$32 dinner, $10–$19 Sun brunch. Mon–Thurs 11:30am–10pm, Fri–Sat 11:30am–11pm, Sun 10am–10pm.

Slightly North of Broad ★★ SOUTHERN/INTERNATIONAL Another restaurant firmly committed to its local suppliers, with a simple but enticing Southern menu that offers "medium plates" in addition to standard entrees. Highlights include the pan-seared duck breast, the roasted lamb rack with roasted cauliflower, and the perennial favorite Maverick shrimp and grits with sausage, country ham, fresh tomatoes, and green onions. Vegetarians are well catered to—the butternut squash bisque is truly sublime—while the small but tempting dessert menu includes a warm sour cream apple pie that's hard to resist.

192 E. Bay St. www.mavericksouthernkitchens.com. © **843/723-3424.** Main courses $10–$16 lunch, $18–$34 dinner. Mon–Fri 11:30am–3pm and 5:30–11pm, Sat–Sun 5–11pm.

39 Rue de Jean ★ FRENCH/SUSHI This intriguing restaurant offers an unusual combo of French bistro food and Japanese sushi that just about works. The selection of *moules* (mussels) in various sauces is exceptional, and the French side of the menu includes rainbow trout, pork chop Brittany, braised rabbit, baked Atlantic cod, and even roasted bone marrow. The sushi, sashimi, and maki rolls won't impress connoisseurs, but are always fresh and make for a nice change. The property itself boasts an equally mixed-up history, starting life as a brick warehouse in 1880, redesigned in 1943 in the Art Moderne style, and now sporting a 19th-century Parisian brasserie

The City Market—a Good Food Guide

Charleston's **City Market** (p. 67) at 188 Meeting St. is a great place to load up on (relatively cheap) local snacks and dishes. Eat here or take out to enjoy at Waterfront Park. Student favorite **Caviar & Bananas** ★★ (✆ 843/577-7757; www.caviarandbananas.com; daily 9am–6pm) is best known for its mouth-watering sandwiches (especially the duck confit and the po-boy), but the salads are also excellent, and there are plenty of gluten-free options. **Food for the Southern Soul**'s 'Cue-Osk (✆ 843/577-5230; www.foodforthesouthernsoul.com; daily 9:30am–6pm) knocks out decent pulled pork ($6), beef brisket ($7), and mac and cheese ($2). Those with a sweet tooth have plenty of options. **Southern Sisters** (✆ 843/801-2665; www.southernsisters bakers.com) knocks out the famous Benne Wafer's, Charleston lemon coolers, and pecan tea cookies, while nearby **Kaminsky's**, 78 N. Market St. (✆ 843/853-8270; www.kaminskys.com) serves up ciders, coffees, hot toddies, and sumptuous desserts.

theme: red-leather banquettes, metal-top bar, exposed brick, rattan chairs, and outdoor tables under umbrellas.

39 John St. www.holycityhospitality.com/39-rue-de-jean. ✆ **843/722-8881.** Main courses $8–$20 lunch, $16–$27 dinner, $8–$19 Sun brunch. Mon–Sat 11:30am–11pm, Sun 10am–11pm.

INEXPENSIVE

A. W. Shuck's ★ SEAFOOD   Knocking out affordable seafood since 1978, Shuck's is still an oyster bar at heart, with a huge range of bivalves ranging from Chesapeake Bay Selects to Carolina Cups. Having said that, the range of seafood here is phenomenal. The blue crab dip is worth the trip alone, and Ivan's Steampot is a sumptuous combo of mussels, beer-can clams, oysters, shrimp, and steamed snow crab legs, with smoked sausage, new potatoes, and corn on the cob. For a quicker snack opt for the burgers, shrimp, or oyster po-boys, or the grilled mahi mahi tacos. We'd quite happily stop by just for the peach-bourbon bread pudding. The whole, sprawling establishment is housed in an early 20th-century warehouse built by biscuit giant Nabisco.

70 State St. www.a-w-shucks.com. ✆ **843/723-1151.** Main courses $9–$20. Sun–Thurs 11am–10pm, Fri–Sat 11am–11pm.

Basil ★★ THAI   This always-buzzing Thai restaurant offers another rare excursion from Lowcountry cuisine in the center of the city. All your usual favorites are here and are great value and pretty authentic. Choose stir-fried meats (beef, chicken, pork, shrimp) and the method of cooking (with basil, ginger garlic, and so on) or opt for a classic green or red curry, pad thai, or shrimp-fried rice.

460 King St. www.eatatbasil.com. ✆ **843/724-3490.** Main courses $10–$12 lunch, $14–$17 dinner. Mon–Thurs 11am–2:30pm and 5–10:30pm, Fri–Sat 11am–2:30pm and 5–11pm, Sun 5–10pm.

Brown Dog Deli ★★ DELI   A popular local cafe serving tasty sandwiches (including the famed duck club as well as gluten-free options), seafood chowder, and hot dogs fixed all sorts of ways (try the pimento cheese, celery salt, and Deep River chips). I always opt for a salad here ($10)—Hailey's sweet summer salad, or the spinach and goat, though the Hawaiian salmon burger ($8) with its blackened filet of Alaskan salmon and pineapple-mango salsa is hard to resist. The deli occupies a cozy, hip space adorned with album covers and old comics, but if weather allows enjoy your lunch in the pleasant outdoor eating area, washed down with old-fashioned ginger ale. The Brown Dog tends to get very busy at lunch but ask to sit at the community table and you won't have to wait long.

40 Broad St. www.browndogdeli.com. ℂ **843/853-8081.** Main items $7–$14. Mon–Thurs 11am–6pm, Fri–Sat 11am–8pm, Sun 11am–4pm.

Christophe Artisan Chocolatier-Pâtissier ★★ BAKERY/CAFE

Mouth-watering handmade chocolates from Christophe Paume, a third-generation French chocolatier from Toulouse, are offered here. Locals line up for his boxes of multi-colored truffles (the caramel sea salt flavor is mind-blowing), but you can also stop in to sample his delectable almond croissants, macaroons, and cookies, best enjoyed with a cup of French-press coffee. On the savory side there's fresh croissants (the flaky, French kind), and wholesome baguette sandwiches (which often sell out early).

90 Society St. www.christophechocolatier.com. ℂ **843/297-8674.** 9-piece chocolate assortment $21. Mon–Thurs 8am–7pm, Fri–Sat 8am–9pm, Sun 10am–6pm.

Hominy Grill ★★ LOWCOUNTRY

Owned and operated by chef Robert Steh-ling, the Hominy looks a bit like a Southern country cafe, with a an old-fashioned, rustic interior in a clapboard building daubed with a giant "Hominy Grits" mural. The menu offers fresh and creative Lowcountry fare, but at much more affordable prices than more lauded kitchens. The appetizers and smaller plates are some of the best in the city—sample the jalapeño hushpuppies with sorghum butter, okra and shrimp beignets with salsa and cilantro-lime sour cream, or pimento cheese with crispy fried onions on a pretzel roll. If you're still hungry, the best entrees are local classics such as sautéed chicken livers with country ham gravy, or the absolutely wicked Charleston "Nasty Biscuit" with fried chicken breast, cheddar cheese, and sausage gravy.

207 Rutledge Ave. www.hominygrill.com. ℂ **843/937-0930.** Main courses $6–$19. Mon–Fri 7:30am–9pm, Sat 9am–9pm, Sun 9am–3pm.

Hyman's Seafood ★★ SEAFOOD

This old-fashioned seafood place offers exceptional value, a family-style joint you might expect to find in a small fishing village, with family photos, old plates, and wood planks lining the walls. Plenty of folks come here to order the crispy flounder served with chutney on the side, which is some-thing of a local institution, but the menu also features meaty crab cakes, salmon cro-quettes, and a vast choice of soups, salads, po-boys, and traditional Southern entrees. Highlights include shrimp and grits, Charleston-style fish and chips (haddock), and the fresh fish of the day—prepared as you like it, or stuffed with crab. Hyman's was estab-lished back in 1890 as a dry goods business (the wrought-iron staircase is original), but became a restaurant in 1986. It's still owned by the Hyman family.

215 Meeting St. www.hymanseafood.com. ℂ **843/723-6000.** Main courses $10–$25. Sun–Thurs 11am–10pm, Fri–Sat 11am–11pm.

Jestine's ★ SOUTHERN/SOUL FOOD

This is a spot for typical Southern home-cooking, from cornbread and steamed shrimp while you wait, to fried green tomatoes, baskets of fried chicken, and brown-sugar glazed ham. The sides are all worth adding: okra gumbo, mashed potatoes, and collard greens. The restaurant is named for Jestine Matthews, born in the Lowcountry in 1885, a daughter of a freed slave and a Native American woman. Jestine once cooked for the grandparents of the current owner, and the restaurant is inspired by her enticing style of home cooking.

251 Meeting St. www.jestineskitchen.com. ℂ **843/722-7224.** Main courses $6–$16. Tues–Thurs 11am–9:30pm, Fri–Sat 11am–10pm, Sun 11am–9pm. Closed Christmas Day and Jewish holidays.

Kudu Coffee & Craft Beer ★★ CAFE/BAR   This local hangout could just as easily fall in the bar category, though coffee connoisseurs should make a pilgrimage here during the day. Sip freshly ground roasts from Counter Culture Coffee in the tranquil courtyard, accompanied by hefty croissants, sandwiches, quiche, and pastries. It's a cozy place that morphs into a beer-aficionado paradise in the evenings, with a menu of 22 quality craft brews on tap (from $5) and several bottled ciders (the alcoholic kind). The only downer: no Wi-Fi.

4 Vanderhorst St. www.kuducoffeeandcraftbeer.com. ℂ **843/853-7186.** Coffee $2–$5, beers from $5, main courses $5–$10. Mon–Wed 6:45am–9pm, Thurs–Sat 7am–9pm, Sun 8am–8pm.

Sugar Bakeshop ★★ BAKERY   Get your cake and cupcake fix at this local bakery, founded by two New York City transplants. Their flavor combinations are inventive, and the frostings delectably rich, made with homemade butter cream that melts in your mouth. The chocolate chip cookie ($1) is the best seller, but my faves are the lemon curd cakes and the fresh strawberry cakes—actually any of the luscious fresh fruit-filled versions. Mini-cupcakes are also available ($2).

59½ Cannon St. www.sugarbake.com. ℂ **843/579-2891.** Cupcakes $3/each, $33/dozen; whole cakes $22–$42. Mon–Fri 10am–6pm, Sat 11am–5pm.

West Ashley

MODERATE

Middleton Place Restaurant ★★ LOWCOUNTRY/SOUTHERN   This plantation restaurant (see p. 76) offers lunch and dinner in a replica of an original rice mill. Lunch set menus are a great deal, with specialties including hoppin' John (a peas-and-rice dish) and ham biscuits, pulled pork with mustard barbecue, and corn pudding. Dinner (a la carte) is likely to include chicken-and-dumplings, catfish stew, and a concoction of shrimp, sausage, and grits. Leave room for the seasonal cobbler (served with house-made vanilla ice cream) or the South Carolina pecan pie.

4300 Ashley River Rd. www.middletonplace.org/restaurant.html. ℂ **843/556-6020.** Set lunch menu $18, main courses dinner $14–$27. Mon noon–3pm, Tues–Sun noon–3pm (Mar–Oct from 11am) and 6–9pm.

Mount Pleasant

MODERATE

Old Village Post House ★★ LOWCOUNTRY/CONTINENTAL   This is the best place to eat across the Cooper River, in the heart of Mount Pleasant's Old Village. Menus change, but might include Charleston crab soup to start, beef Bolognese or cast-iron South Carolina quail for a main, and Boone Hall Farms strawberry pie to finish. Vegetarian options are often just as creative: try the cauliflower pudding with truffle glaze, or the strawberry spinach salad. The Tavern Room is a relaxed alternative to the main dining area, with views across the outdoor patio.

101 Pitt St. www.mavericksouthernkitchens.com/oldvillageposthouse. ℂ **843/388-8935.** Main courses $13–$26. Mon–Thurs 5:30–10pm, Fri–Sat 5:30–11pm, Sun 10am–3pm and 5:30–10pm.

EXPLORING CHARLESTON

I always head for the **Battery** (officially, the White Point Gardens) to get into the feel of this city. It's right on the end of the peninsula, facing the Cooper River and the harbor. It has a landscaped park, shaded by palmettos and live oaks, with

Charleston Attractions

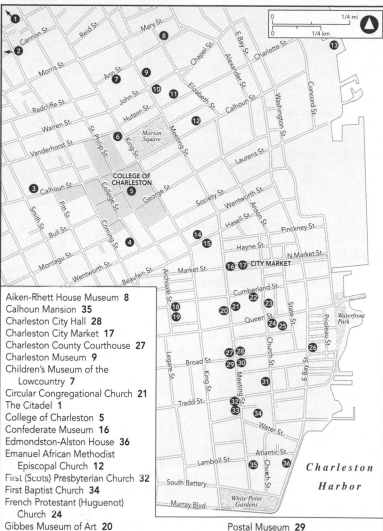

Aiken-Rhett House Museum **8**
Calhoun Mansion **35**
Charleston City Hall **28**
Charleston City Market **17**
Charleston County Courthouse **27**
Charleston Museum **9**
Children's Museum of the
  Lowcountry **7**
Circular Congregational Church **21**
The Citadel **1**
College of Charleston **5**
Confederate Museum **16**
Edmondston-Alston House **36**
Emanuel African Methodist
  Episcopal Church **12**
First (Scots) Presbyterian Church **32**
First Baptist Church **34**
French Protestant (Huguenot)
  Church **24**
Gibbes Museum of Art **20**
Heyward-Washington House **31**
Joseph Manigault House **10**
Kahal Kadosh Beth Elohim **14**
Karpeles Manuscript Library **2**
Mount Zion African Methodist Episcopal Church **4**
Nathaniel Russell House Museum **33**
Old Bethel United Methodist Church **3**
Old Exchange and Provost Dungeon **26**
Old Slave Mart Museum **25**

Postal Museum **29**
The Powder Magazine **22**
Second Presbyterian Church **11**
South Carolina Aquarium **13**
St. John's Lutheran Church **18**
St. Mary's Roman Catholic Church **15**
St. Matthew's Lutheran Church **6**
St. Michael's Episcopal Church **30**
St. Philip's Episcopal Church **23**
Unitarian Church in Charleston **19**

You can visit nine of the city's most visible historic attractions by buying a 2-day **Heritage Passport ticket** for $53 (there is no discounted ticket for children or seniors). Assuming you intend to visit all nine sights, the passport is excellent value, saving well over 40% on normal admission (though if you have children, it's less of a deal, since most sights offer discounted admission for kids). The ticket provides entry to the Charleston Museum, the Heyward-Washington House, the Joseph Manigault House, Middleton Place, Drayton Hall, the Nathaniel Russell House, Gibbes Museum, the Aiken-Rhett House, and the Edmondston-Alston House. The ticket allows one-time admission to each of those attractions, during the course of two consecutive days. Three-day passports are $63, while 7-day passports are $73. Tickets are available only from **Charleston Visitor Center,** 375 Meeting St., North Charleston Visitor Center, and Mt. Pleasant Visitor Center (see p. 44).

walkways lined with old monuments and other war relics. The view toward the harbor goes out to Fort Sumter. It wasn't always like this. During the early 18th century, the park was the site of the town gallows, where numerous ne'er-do-wells were hanged. From here you can stroll along the seawall on East Battery to **Waterfront Park,** where you can sit on the porch swings and watch dolphins frolicking in the river.

The Historic District

Aiken-Rhett House Museum ★★ HOUSE MUSEUM   Constructed around 1820 by Charleston merchant John Robinson, the Aiken-Rhett House is perhaps one of the city's most atmospheric piles, an elegantly decayed mansion purchased by Irish immigrant-made-good William Aiken, Sr. in 1827. Taking over the property in 1833, his son (who served as state governor from 1844–46), **William Aiken, Jr.,** and wife Harriet Lowndes, transformed it into one of the grandest residences in Charleston with crystal and bronze chandeliers, classical sculpture, paintings, and antiques. Harriet died in 1892, after which the house was inherited by her daughter Henrietta, and her son-in-law, Major A.B. Rhett. The Aiken's personal art gallery was beautifully restored in 2014, furnished with many of the original works the couple purchased on their tour of Europe in 1858. Original outbuildings include the kitchens, laundry, slave quarters (the Aiken's had up to 14 slaves working at the house), carriage house and stables, privies, and cattle sheds.

48 Elizabeth St. www.historiccharleston.org. © **843/723-1159.** Admission $10 ($16 with Nathaniel Russell House Museum). Mon–Sat 10am–5pm, Sun 2–5pm.

Calhoun Mansion ★★★ HISTORIC HOUSE   The largest, most ostentatious, fascinating, and plain over-the-top mansion in Charleston was built in 1876 for successful entrepreneur **George Walton Williams.** Designed in the Italianate style, the property comprises 35 rooms, a grand ballroom, Japanese water gardens with koi ponds, a private elevator, three levels of piazzas, ornate chandeliers, a 90-foot cupola, and decorative painting and lighting designed and installed by Louis Comfort Tiffany. When Williams died in 1903, the house was inherited by his son-in-law, railroad financier **Patrick Calhoun** (thus the name). Restored by local attorney Gedney M. Howe in the 1980s and 1990s, the house was sold again in 2004 and remains privately owned, albeit open for tours throughout the year.

16 Meeting St. www.calhounmansion.net. ℂ **843/722-8205.** Admission $15. Guided tours daily 11am–5pm, on the hour and half-hour.

Charleston City Hall ★ HISTORIC SITE   This handsome building was constructed between 1800 and 1804 in what is known as the Adamesque style, serving as a branch of **The First Bank of the United States** (the original brick walls were covered with Italian marble stucco in 1882). The property became **City Hall** in 1818, and, remarkably, the council chamber on the second floor remains the center of city government. On the lower level, view the short audiovisual presentation on the history of the building before proceeding through security and heading up to the council chamber itself. Assuming a meeting is not in session, docents will point out rare artifacts and paintings in the gallery here, including one of **George Washington** by John Trumbull (1791) and a portrait of President **James Monroe** by Samuel F. B. Morse.

80 Broad St. ℂ **843/577-6970.** Free admission. Mon–Fri 8:30am–1pm and 2–5pm.

Charleston City Market ★★★ HISTORIC MARKET   Charleston's City Market dates back to 1788 and remains a fun if touristy place to explore, crammed with arts-and-crafts stalls, restaurants, and the city's famed Gullah "basket ladies" working on sweet-grass baskets. The complex comprises the Greek Revival-style **Market Hall,** completed in 1841 (and containing the **Confederate Museum** upstairs, p. 69), and 4 blocks of open-air buildings and sheds, most of which were built between 1804 and the 1830s.

Market St., btw. Meeting and East Bay sts. www.thecharlestoncitymarket.com. ℂ **843/937-0920.** Free admission. Daily 9:30am–6pm (art market Fri–Sat 6:30–10:30pm).

Charleston County Courthouse ★ HISTORIC SITE   Next door to City Hall, the old courthouse rounds out Charleston's historic civic heart. The structure dates back to 1753, when the Carolina statehouse was built on this site, but was reconstructed in 1792 in a grand Neoclassical style for use as the Charleston district courts. It was conceived by Irish architect **James Hoban,** best known for designing **The White House** in Washington D.C. a few years later. Today the courthouse is still in use, but is definitely worth a peek inside—it's open to the public during normal business hours. A small display on the first floor charts the history of the building, with the walls lined with portraits of South Carolina's great and good.

84 Broad St. ℂ **843/577-6970.** Free admission. Mon–Fri 9am–5pm.

Charleston Museum ★★ MUSEUM   Get to grips with the long and intriguing history of the Charleston region at this illuminating museum opposite the Visitor Center. Permanent galleries include the **Lowcountry History Hall,** beginning with ancient artifacts from Native Americans who first inhabited the area, and charting the struggles of the first African American slaves and European settlers. Exhibits include rare slave badges, which allowed slaves to be hired out as laborers. The museum's **Armory** contains historic weaponry dating from 1750 to the twentieth century, while **Becoming Americans** explores Charleston's role in the American Revolution, with personal items of **Francis Marion**—aka the "Swamp Fox"—on display.

360 Meeting St. www.charlestonmuseum.org. ℂ **843/722-2996.** Admission $10 adults, $5 children 3–12. Adult combination ticket for the Charleston Museum, the Joseph Manigault House, and Heyward-Washington House $22. Mon–Sat 9am–5pm, Sun 1–5pm.

Children's Museum of the Lowcountry ★ MUSEUM Little ones will enjoy a couple of hours in this fun, hands-on museum, with nine themed areas including Charleston Market, a supermarket designed for kids, and the Medieval Creativity Castle, where they can dress as a prince or princess, explore secret passageways, and check-out a puppet show.

25 Ann St. www.explorecml.org. ℂ **843/853-8962.** Admission $10 per person, free for kids under 12 months. Tues and Fri 9am–7pm, Wed–Thurs and Sat 9am–5pm, Sun 1–5pm.

Circular Congregational Church ★ CHURCH Founded by Dissenters in 1681, this is one of the oldest churches in the South, its burial grounds dating back to 1695. In 1861, a fire destroyed the third incarnation of the building, and bricks from "Old Circular" were used to build the fourth and present church, completed in 1892. The name was maintained though this church is only partly circular (more like a cloverleaf), featuring instead a neo-Romanesque style inspired by Henry Hobart Richardson. The congregation is now related to the United Church of Christ and the Presbyterian Church (U.S.A.). The graveyard is worth a stroll, with the oldest inscribed gravestone dating from 1729, while the Greek Revival **Parish House ★★** at the back is a rare architectural work by **Robert Mills,** dating from 1806 and the only remnant of the original Circular Church.

150 Meeting St. www.circularchurch.org. ℂ **843/577-6400.** Mon–Fri 8:30am–noon. Free guided tours (call ahead to confirm times).

The Citadel ★ HISTORIC SITE The home of the **Military College of South Carolina** and the South Carolina Corps of Cadets was originally conceived as an arsenal for the state militia, with the first buildings completed in 1829 around what is now Marion Square. The arsenal was converted to a military academy in 1842, and in 1922 it began the move to its present Ashley River Campus. The 24 attractive buildings of the college feature Romanesque and Moorish design, with crenelated battlements and sentry towers, but the real highlight of any visit occurs on Friday (when college is in session), when the public is invited to a **precision-drill parade** on the quadrangle at **3:45pm.** For a history of the college, visit the **Citadel Museum** (ℂ **843/953-6846;** free admission) inside the Daniel Library on campus, which displays historic photographs, uniforms, and archival documents.

171 Moultrie St., at Elmwood Ave. www.citadel.edu. ℂ **843/225-3294.** Free admission. Visitors may enter the campus for self-guided tours daily 8am–7pm (after 7pm, entry is only for on-campus events); all academic buildings, Mark Clark Hall, Summerall Chapel, and McAlister Field House are open, but barracks are strictly off-limits. Museum Sun–Fri 2–5pm, Sat noon–5pm. Closed religious, national, and school holidays.

College of Charleston ★★★ UNIVERSITY This infrequently visited gem boasts a gorgeous campus studded with romantic Victorian buildings, statuary, moss-draped live oak trees, and well-manicured gardens. Visit at the weekends, when it's extra sleepy, and the whole thing feels like a movie set portraying the Old South.

Founded in 1770, C of C is the oldest college in South Carolina (today it's a public university). Highlights include **Randolph Hall,** the main building, designed by Philadelphia architect William Strickland and constructed 1828–29. What you see today is mostly the result of the 1850 renovation, which added six Ionic columns. The **Porters Lodge** (bearing the Greek inscription for "Know Thyself"), was completed in 1852 in a similar Roman Revival style, while the **Towell Library** was completed in 1856. The oldest building on campus is the **President's House** at 6 Glebe St., which was constructed in 1770 as the parsonage of St. Philip's Church. Download a campus map from the website, or pick one up from Admissions in Craig Hall at 65 George St.

66 George St. www.cofc.edu. (*) **843/805-5507.** Campus daily 24 hr.

Confederate Museum ★ MUSEUM Since 1898, the United Daughters of the Confederacy (descendants of Confederate soldiers who commemorate the Civil War, especially the part played by Southern women), has operated this small museum on the second floor of Market Hall. The museum is a little disorganized but the simple displays of old flags, uniforms, swords, rare Confederate postage stamps, and other Confederate memorabilia are fascinating nonetheless. Try and pick out the actual white handkerchief used to surrender Fort Sumter in 1861, and a lock of General Lee's hair.

188 Meeting St. (*) **843/723-1541.** Admission $5. Jan–Feb Thurs–Sat 11am–3:30pm, Mar–Dec Tues–Sat 11am–3:30pm.

Edmondston-Alston House ★★ HISTORIC HOUSE On High Battery, an elegant section of Charleston, this house (built in 1825 by Charles Edmondston, a Charleston merchant and wharf owner) was one of the earliest constructed in the city in the late Federal style. In 1837 Edmondston sold it to Charles Alston, a Lowcountry rice planter, who modified it in Greek Revival style. The house has remained in the Alston family, who open the first two floors to visitors (on guided tours only). Inside are heirloom furnishings, silver, and paintings. It was here in 1861 that General Beauregard joined the Alston family to watch the bombardment of Fort Sumter. Later that year Robert E. Lee found refuge here when his hotel uptown caught fire.

21 E. Battery. www.edmondstonalston.com. (*) **843/722-7171.** Admission $12 adults, $8 students and children 6–13, free for children 5 and under. Guided tours Tues–Sat 10am–4:30pm, Sun–Mon 1–4:30pm. Last tour 4:15pm.

Emanuel African Methodist Episcopal Church ★ CHURCH Founded in 1791 by free blacks and slaves, this is the oldest AME church in the South. With a sanctuary holding 2,500, it still has one of the largest black congregations south of Baltimore. The original gas lanterns hanging inside date from its founding. In 1822, one of the church's founders, ex-slave Denmark Vesey, urged the congregation into an insurrection, but authorities learned of the rebellion and the church was burned (Vesey was hanged). The church was reorganized in 1865, and eventually rebuilt in 1891 into the present structure you can visit today.

110 Calhoun St. www.emanuelamechurch.org. (*) **843/722-2561.** Free admission. Mon–Thurs 9am–1pm and 2–4pm, Fri 9am–3pm.

First Baptist Church ★ CHURCH Established in 1682, this was the first Baptist church in the South (the church was actually organized in Maine and moved to Charleston in 1696). In 1751, the pastor, Oliver Hart, founded the Charleston Baptist Association, the earliest organization for the education of Baptist ministers in the South. He fled from the British in 1780, never to return. The present Greek Revival–style sanctuary was designed in 1822 by **Robert Mills,** the first American-born architect. The sanctuary has been the victim of many natural disasters, including a tornado in 1885, an earthquake in 1886, and Hurricane Hugo in 1989, but was faithfully restored after each event.

61 Church St. www.fbcharleston.org. (*) **843/722-3896.** Free guided tours Tues–Thurs 10:30am–noon and Fri 1–3pm (call ahead to confirm).

First (Scots) Presbyterian Church ★ CHURCH   This is the fifth-oldest church in Charleston, founded in 1731 by Scottish immigrants who broke away from the Circular Congregational Church (First Scots is now part of the Presbyterian Church U.S.A.). The seal of Scotland in the windows over the main entrance can still be seen. The church was constructed in 1814; its design was inspired by St. Mary's Cathedral in Baltimore, whose architect, Benjamin Latrobe, also designed the U.S. Capitol. The walls of this massive brick church are 3-feet thick and covered with stucco, and twin towers rise above a pillared portico. The church bell that was donated to the Confederacy during the Civil War, to be melted down for use as cannonballs, was eventually replaced by an English bell made in 1814, the same time of the church's construction.

53 Meeting St. www.first-scots.org. ℂ **843/722-8882.** Free admission. Mon–Fri 8:30am–5pm (call ahead to confirm).

French Protestant (Huguenot) Church ★ CHURCH   This pretty white confection is the only remaining French Calvinist church in the U.S., offering weekly church services in English as well as an annual service in French each spring. It was founded in 1681 by Huguenot refugees from Protestant persecutions in France. The first church built on this site in 1687 was destroyed in 1796 in an attempt to stop a fire. It was replaced in 1800, only to be dismantled in 1844 to make way for the present Gothic Revival building designed by Edward B. White. The church suffered heavy damage by shellfire during the Civil War and was nearly demolished in the earthquake of 1886. The original Tucker organ—one of the rarest in the country—is from 1845.

136 Church St. (at Queen St.). www.huguenot-church.org. ℂ **843/722-4385.** Free admission. Tours Spring and Fall Mon–Thurs 10am–4pm and Fri 10am–1pm (call ahead to confirm times; office hours Mon–Fri 9:30am–1:30pm).

Gibbes Museum of Art ★★ ART MUSEUM   Charleston's premier art gallery hosts seven temporary exhibitions each year (ranging from photography and prints to contemporary art and painting), in addition to the on-going **"Charleston Story,"** drawn from the museum's permanent collection of some 10,000 objects. Items rotate every January and July (about 150 works can be displayed at one time), but are always chosen to highlight how the city has developed over the last 400 years; think colonial portraits by the likes of **Benjamin West,** art from the **Charleston Renaissance** of 1915 to 1940, and Southern Modern and contemporary art, including work by Georgia-born **Jasper Johns.**

135 Meeting St. www.gibbesmuseum.org. ℂ **843/722-2706.** Admission $9 adults; $7 seniors, students, and military; $5 children 6–18; free for children 5 and under. Tues–Sat 10am–5pm, Sun 1–5pm. Closed holidays.

Heyward-Washington House ★ HISTORIC HOUSE   In a district of Charleston called Cabbage Row, this red-brick Georgian-style house was built in 1772 by Daniel Heyward, aka "the rice king," and later acquired by his son Thomas Heyward, Jr., a signer of the Declaration of Independence. President **George Washington** bedded down here during his weeklong stay in 1791. Many of the fine period pieces in the house are the work of **Thomas Elfe,** one of America's most famous cabinetmakers. The restored 1740s kitchen is the only one of its kind in the city that is open to the public. It stands behind the main house, along with the servants' quarters and the garden.

87 Church St. (btw. Tradd and Broad sts.). www.charlestonmuseum.org. ℂ **843/722-0354.** Admission $10. Combination ticket for Heyward-Washington House, the Joseph Manigault House, and

the Charleston Museum $22. Mon–Sat 10am–5pm, Sun 1–5pm. Tours begin every half-hour until 4:30pm.

Joseph Manigault House ★ HISTORIC HOUSE   This elegant red-brick mansion was built in 1803 for wealthy rice planter Joseph Manigault (a descendant of French Huguenots). The house features a curving central staircase and an outstanding collection of Charlestonian, American, English, and French period furnishings. Manigault inherited several rice plantations and over 200 slaves from his grandfather in 1788, cementing his fortune by marrying into the Middleton family (of Middleton Place, p. 76), and later the Drayton family (of Drayton Hall, p. 75).

350 Meeting St. (at John St.). www.charlestonmuseum.org. (C) **843/722-2996.** Admission $10 adults. Combination ticket for the Joseph Manigault House, the Heyward-Washington House, and the Charleston Museum $22. Mon–Sat 10am–5pm, Sun 1–5pm. Last tour 4:30pm.

Kahal Kadosh Beth Elohim ★★ SYNAGOGUE   This is the second-oldest synagogue building in the U.S. and the oldest in continuous use. The congregation was formed in 1749, and the synagogue was erected in 1794, although it was destroyed by fire in 1838. The present building was constructed in 1840 as one of the country's finest examples of Greek Revival architecture. This was also the birthplace of **Reform Judaism** in the U.S., with the roots of the movement going back to 1824 and the synagogue one of the founding members in 1873 of what became the Union for Reform Judaism. **Francis Salvador,** a member of the congregation, was delegate to the South Carolina Provincial Congresses of 1775 and 1776 and the first known Jew to die in the Revolutionary War. The small synagogue **museum** tells the story of the congregation with rare artifacts, including prayer books dating from 1766.

90 Hasell St. www.kkbe.org. (C) **843/723-1090.** Free admission. Museum Mon–Fri 10am–4pm. Free 30-min. guided tours Mon–Thurs 10am–noon and 1:30–3:30pm, Fri 10am–noon and 1–3pm, Sun 1–4pm.

Karpeles Manuscript Library ★★ MUSEUM   The small but remarkable Karpeles Manuscript Library occupies the grand Greek Revival **St. James Methodist Chapel,** completed in 1856. Thanks to the Karpeles Library (based in Santa Barbara), the elegant interior displays a mind-blowing array of original documents, letters, and manuscripts, from the concluding page of Darwin's "Origin of Species" and a page of Karl Marx's "Das Kapital," to the founding documents of baseball. Exhibits are usually thematic and change every 4 months.

68 Spring St. www.rain.org/~karpeles. (C) **843/853-4651.** Free admission. Tues–Fri 11am–4pm.

Mount Zion African Methodist Episcopal Church ★ CHURCH   This distinctive Neoclassical church was the first brick building owned by African-Americans in Charleston. Originally completed in 1848 as the Glebe Street Presbyterian Church, it was purchased in 1882 by members of the Emanuel A.M.E. Church when that sanctuary had become too crowded. The 54th and 55th Massachusetts Regiment worshiped here while stationed in Charleston. The church is known for offering the best choral music in Charleston, with six different choirs. Music ranges from classical hymns to original and unarranged black spirituals, many from the 18th century.

5 Glebe St. www.mtzioncharleston.com. (C) **843/722-8118.** Free admission. Mon–Wed and Fri 11:30am–1:30pm.

Nathaniel Russell House Museum ★★★ HOUSE MUSEUM   One of America's finest examples of Neoclassical architecture, this red-brick mansion was built in 1808 for Nathaniel Russell, one of Charleston's richest merchants. The interior contains an astounding elliptical staircase, spiraling unsupported for three floors, and opulent period furnishings, especially the music room with its golden harp and Neo-classical-style sofa. The excellent guided tours provide context not only about the Russell family, but also the enslaved African Americans responsible for maintaining their luxury lifestyle. The original kitchen house contains artifacts such as pottery shards, beads, and part of a slave tag, dug up from around the house.

51 Meeting St. www.historiccharleston.org. ℂ **843/724-8481.** Admission $10. Guided tours Mon–Sat 10am–5pm, Sun and holidays 2–5pm. Last tour 4:30pm.

Old Bethel United Methodist Church ★ CHURCH   This elegant clapboard gem is the third-oldest surviving church building in Charleston. Founded and paid for by both white and black citizens, it was built in 1797, with the finishing touches applied in 1807. By 1840, its African-American members had left to form their own congregation, and 12 years later the church was moved to the western part of its lot for them to use. A new church, **Bethel Methodist,** was completed in 1854 on the original space at 57 Pitt Street for the white worshipers in a grand Greek Revival style. In 1880, Old Bethel moved again, across the street to its present location, where it still serves a predominantly African-American congregation.

222 Calhoun St. ℂ **843/722-3470.** Free admission. Open to the public, but no set hours. Bethel Methodist Church open Mon–Thurs 9am–4:30pm and Fri 9am–2pm.

Old Exchange and Provost Dungeon ★ MUSEUM   Built as the Customs House in 1771, this grand Palladian edifice served as a British barracks and prison in the Revolutionary War; local martyr **Isaac Hayne** spent his last night here before being hanged in 1781. The building housed the **Charleston Post Office** from 1815 to 1896 (with brief interruptions due to earthquake and war), and in 1913 it was sold to the Daughters of the American Revolution. Today the main floor contains exhibits on the history of the town and the building, while the top floor is home to the **Great Hall** and Isaac Hayne Room, and the lower-level **dungeon** displays mannequins and dioramas of pirates and patriots.

122 E. Bay St. www.oldexchange.com. ℂ **843/727-2165.** Admission $9; $14 with Old Slave Mart. Daily 9am–5pm. Closed Thanksgiving Day and Dec 23–25.

Old Slave Mart Museum ★★ MUSEUM   Completed in 1859, on the eve of the Civil War, slave auctions were held in this shed, once part of a complex of buildings known as **Ryan's Mart.** Slaves stood chained on auction tables here, 3-feet high and 10-feet long, placed lengthwise so potential buyers could examine them during the sale. Slave auctions ended in 1863. Now a poignant museum dedicated to African-American history and the slave trade, rare recordings of ex-slaves are preserved inside, along with a permanent exhibit, "Triumph over Slavery."

6 Chalmers St. ℂ **843/958-6467.** Admission $7. Mon–Sat 9am–5pm.

Postal Museum ★ MUSEUM   This tiny specialist museum charts Charleston's postal history, housed in a room inside the elegant **Post Office Building** built in 1896. The building still serves as the post office today (Mon–Fri 11:30am–3:30pm).

Meeting St., at Broad St. ℂ **843/868-8118.** Free admission. Mon–Fri 9am–5pm.

The Powder Magazine ★ MUSEUM   Completed in 1713, this is the oldest public building in South Carolina. The "magazine" was used as an arsenal up to 1743 for the defense of the British settlement of Charles Towne against Native Americans, pirates, and Spanish and French warships. During the Revolutionary War it was re-used by the Continental Army, later serving as stables, print shop, blacksmith shop, wine cellar, and horse carriage house before being purchased by the National Society of Colonial Dames in 1902. The building now serves as a small museum of early Charleston history, displaying armor, costumes, antiques, and interactive exhibits popular with kids (who enjoy getting locked in the stocks outside).

79 Cumberland St. www.powdermag.org. © 843/722-9350. Admission $5. Mon–Sat 10am–4pm, Sun 1–4pm.

St. John's Lutheran Church ★ CHURCH   Dubbed the "Mother Church of Lutherans in South Carolina," this graceful Federal-style building dates from 1818, though the congregation was founded by German immigrants in 1742. The Italianate steeple with bell-shaped roof was added in 1859. Its church bell was melted down and given to the Confederacy for use as cannonballs in the Civil War, and it wasn't until 1992 that the bell was replaced.

5 Clifford St. www.stjohnscharleston.org. © 843/723-2426. Free admission. Tours Mon–Fri 9am–4pm (by appointment only).

St. Mary's Roman Catholic Church ★ CHURCH   Formally known as **St. Mary of the Annunciation,** this is the oldest Roman Catholic church in the state, with a congregation that dates back to 1789. The original brick church of 1801 was destroyed by fire in 1838, but was rebuilt 1 year in the plain Classical Revival style visible today, replete with Tuscan portico and parapet. Many of the tombstones in the churchyard are in French, indicating the early French influence that prevailed at the church (many of the early congregants were exiles from Haiti).

89 Hasell St. www.catholic-doc.org/saintmarys. © 843/724-8495. Free admission. Mon–Fri 9:30am–3:30pm.

St. Matthew's Lutheran Church ★ CHURCH   Founded by German-speaking settlers in 1840, this was the second Lutheran congregation formed in the city. The current Gothic Revival building, erected in 1872 and rebuilt after a fire in 1965, is best known for its slim, 255-foot steeple, which remains the tallest in the state. The beautiful stained-glass windows in the chancel are part of the original structure.

405 King St. www.smlccharleston.org. © 843/723-1611. Free admission. Mon–Fri 8:30am–4:30pm.

St. Michael's Episcopal Church ★ CHURCH   A National Historic Landmark, this is one of the most impressive of America's Colonial churches, and it remains the oldest in Charleston. The church was constructed between 1752 and 1761 in a typical Colonial style, and has changed little since then. Seen for miles around, its 186-foot steeple is a Charleston landmark, its clock bell towers imported from England in 1764. The steeple tower was used as a compass-positioning point for artillery targets during the Revolutionary and Civil wars. Both George Washington and Robert E. Lee attended services here.

71 Broad St. www.stmichaelschurch.net. © 843/723-0603. Free admission. Mon–Fri 9am–4pm, Sat 8:30am–noon.

St. Philip's Episcopal Church ★ CHURCH   This impressive church is nicknamed the "Lighthouse Church" because a light was once put in its distinctive steeple to guide ships into the harbor. The present building dates from 1838 (the steeple was added in 1850), and houses the oldest congregation in South Carolina (with roots back to 1680). During the Civil War, the church bells were donated to the Confederacy to be melted down and recast into cannonballs. Buried in the churchyard are such notables as John C. Calhoun (former Vice President of the United States), signers of the Declaration of Independence Edward Rutledge and Charles Pinckney, and DuBose Heyward (author and playwright).

142 Church St. www.stphilipschurchsc.org. © **843/722-7734.** Free admission. Mon–Fri 10am–noon and 2–4pm (call ahead to verify times).

Second Presbyterian Church ★ CHURCH   Dedicated in 1811, this is the oldest Presbyterian church in Charleston, and it's been designated by the Presbyterian Church of the United States as Historical Site Number One. When it was first constructed, it was so large and cavernous that the minister's voice couldn't be heard. Two pastors in a row died of pneumonia because of the winter chill. Remodeling in the late 1800s added a boiler beneath the church floor, thereby solving the heating problem, and architectural changes in 1833 that raised the floor by 3 feet and lowered the ceiling by 16 feet eventually solved the acoustical issues.

342 Meeting St. (at Charlotte St.). www.secondpresbyterianchurch.org. © **843/723-9237.** Free admission. Call ahead if you plan to visit the church.

South Carolina Aquarium ★★ AQUARIUM   Take a break from colonial history at Charleston's state-of-the-art aquarium, filled with thousands of enchanting creatures and plants native to the Carolinas. Jutting into the Charleston Harbor for 2,000 feet, the focal point is the two-story **Great Ocean Tank,** containing more than 800 animals, including deadly sharks but also stingrays and a 220-pound loggerhead sea turtle. One of the most popular exhibits is the **Saltmarsh Aviary,** where you can buy $3 shrimp cups to feed the stingrays gliding around a 6,000-gallon tank. Newer attractions include the **Madagascar Journey,** home to ring-tailed lemurs, a Nile crocodile, and white-spotted bamboo sharks; and the **4-D Theater,** where 3-D movies are enhanced by moving floors and gusts of wind.

100 Aquarium Wharf. www.scaquarium.org. © **843/720-1990.** Admission $25 adults ($30 with 4-D Theater), $15 children 2–11 ($20 with 4-D Theater), free for children 1 and under. Mar–Aug daily 9am–5pm, Sep–Feb daily 9am–4pm.

Unitarian Church in Charleston ★ CHURCH   The oldest Unitarian church in the South, this is also the second-oldest church in Charleston and one of the country's most stellar examples of the Perpendicular Gothic Revival style. Its construction began in 1774 but was halted when the Revolutionary War broke out, and was only completed in 1787. The church was remodeled and enlarged in 1852 by local architect Francis Lee, who designed the fan-vaulted ceiling, nave, and chancel, using the Chapel of Henry VII in Westminster Abbey in London for his inspiration.

4 Archdale St. www.charlestonuu.org. © **843/723-4617.** Free admission. Fri–Sat 10am–1pm (call ahead to reserve a tour).

North Charleston

H. L. Hunley Confederate Submarine ★★★ MUSEUM   The 40-foot Confederate submarine *H. L. Hunley,* a hand-cranked vessel fashioned of locomotive boilers, sank the Union blockade vessel USS *Housatonic* in February 1864. The sinking of the Union ship launched the age of submarine warfare, but the submarine and its eight-member crew mysteriously vanished off Sullivan's Island shortly after completing its historic mission. The vessel was finally located in 1995 by a team led by author Clive Cussler, sparking headlines across the world. The submarine was raised 5 years later and brought to the old Charleston navy base for preservation. The bones of its crew members were buried in a historic ceremony on April 17, 2004, at **Magnolia Cemetery,** 70 Cunnington Ave. (www.magnoliacemetery.net). The sub, which rests in a tank in the Lasch laboratory, is still being studied and remains the property of the U.S. Navy. On weekends you can peek down at the vessel itself on 20-minute tours, peruse exhibits, and see facial reconstructions of the crew members.

Warren Lasch Conservation Center, 1250 Supply St., Bldg. 255, N. Charleston. www.hunley.org. *f* **877/448-6539.** Admission $12, free for children 5 and under. Sat 10am–5pm, Sun noon–5pm.

West Ashley

Charles Towne Landing State Historic Site ★★ HISTORIC SITE   This
663-acre park on the Ashley River, 3 miles northwest of Downtown, is located on the site where English settlers first landed in 1670, thereby establishing the birthplace of the Carolina colony and the plantation system that eventually spread throughout the American South. Little remains from that period, but the visitor center and museum contains lots of interactive exhibits describing the history of the settlement, while a trail, with the option of listening to a prerecorded audio tour ($5), runs through the site. In the summer interpretive park rangers in 17th-century dress tend heirloom crops such as rice, indigo, and cotton; fire cannons and muskets; and deliver information about the daily life of the era's indentured servants. You can explore *The Adventure II,* a life-size reproduction of a trading ship or ketch of the 17th century, reconstructed earthwork fortifications, and the **Animal Forest,** a 22-acre zoo of species that were native to the area at the time of the original settlement (pumas, bison, alligators, black bears, otters, bobcats, and wolves).

500 Old Towne Rd. (S.C. 171, btw. U.S. 17 and I-26). www.friendsofcharlestownelanding.org. *f* **843/852-4200.** Admission $10 adults, $6 children 6–15. Daily 9am–5pm. Closed Dec 24–25.

Drayton Hall ★★ HISTORIC HOUSE   This is one of the oldest surviving planta-
tions, built between 1738 and 1742 for wealthy rice producer John Drayton and owned by the Drayton family until 1974. Framed by majestic live oaks, the Georgian-Palladian house and its hand-carved woodwork and plasterwork represent New World craftsmanship at its finest. Because such modern elements as electricity, plumbing, and central heating have never put in an appearance, the house is much as it was in its early years; in fact, it is displayed unfurnished. You can also visit an African-American cemetery and take self-guided walks along the river.

3380 Old Ashley River Rd. (S.C. 61). www.draytonhall.org. *f* **843/769-2600.** Admission $20 adults, $10 children 12–18, $6 children 6–11, free for children 5 and under. Mon–Sat 9am–3:30pm, Sun 11am–3:30pm (exit closes at 5pm). Tours on the half-hour. Closed Thanksgiving Day and Christmas Day. Take U.S. 17 S. to S.C. 61; it's 9 miles northwest of Downtown Charleston.

Magnolia Plantation & Gardens ★★★ HISTORIC HOUSE   The original
seat of the Drayton family dates back to 1676, when Thomas and Ann Drayton built the first hall on this site. Their rice plantation, which was worked by slaves, soon made the Draytons rich, though the first mansion burned just after the Revolution, and the second was set afire by General Sherman. What you see today is attractive but not altogether genuine: the house was reconstructed in stages after the Civil War, though the oldest section was actually built before the Revolutionary War and transported here from Summerville. The house is filled with museum-quality Early American furniture, porcelain, quilts, and other Drayton family heirlooms, with guides providing

illuminating background throughout the tour. Learn about the current owners in the **History Room** at the end of the tour.

The flowery **gardens** of camellias and azaleas—among the most beautiful in America—reach their peak bloom in March and April but are colorful year-round. Basic admission includes entry to the gardens (including an herb garden, horticultural maze, topiary garden, and biblical garden), a petting zoo, and a waterfowl refuge.

Other sites include five 19th-century cabins that have been restored and furnished to reflect the homes of slaves and workers in different periods, a **Nature Boat** ride along the Ashley River ($8), and a **Nature Train** ($8) that carries guests on a 45-minute ride around the plantation's perimeter. The **Audubon Swamp Garden,** also on the grounds, is an independently operated 60-acre cypress swamp that offers a close look at local wildlife such as egrets, alligators, wood ducks, otters, turtles, and herons.

3550 Old Ashley River Rd. (S.C. 61.) www.magnoliaplantation.com. 📞 **800/367-3517.** Admission to garden and grounds $15 adults, $10 children 6–12, free for children 5 and under. Plantation house tour $8 extra ages 6 and up; children 5 and under not allowed to tour the house. Admission to Audubon Swamp Garden $8 ages 6 and up, free for children 5 and under. Magnolia Plantation and Audubon Swamp Gardens Mar–Oct daily 8am–5:30pm, Nov–Feb daily 9am–4:30pm.

Middleton Place ★★ HISTORIC HOUSE   The Middleton family has been one of Charleston's most influential dynasties since the 17th century, though this once massive rice plantation was established in the 1730s by planter John Williams. **Henry Middleton,** president of the First Continental Congress, whose son, Arthur, was a signer of the Declaration of Independence, inherited the estate in the 1740s, but most of the property was destroyed in the Civil War and the earthquake of 1886. What remains is still incredibly beautiful: the remaining properties have been restored over many years, and the 65 acres of fabulous **gardens** are laced with ornamental lakes, terraces, and plantings of camellias, azaleas, magnolias, and crape myrtle.

Built in 1755 by Henry Middleton as a gentlemen's guest quarters, what remains of the Dutch-gabled main house contains collections of fine silver, furniture by Thomas Elfe, rare first editions by Mark Catesby and John James Audubon, and portraits by Benjamin West and Thomas Sully. In the stable yards, craftspeople demonstrate life on a plantation of yesteryear. A plantation lunch is served at the **Middleton Place Restaurant** (p. 64).

4300 Ashley River Rd. (S.C. 61). www.middletonplace.org. 📞 **800/782-3608** or 843/556-6020. Admission to gardens and stable yard $28 adults, $10 children 6–13, free for children 5 and under. House tour $15 adults, $15 children 6–13. Daily 9am–5pm. Take U.S. 17 W. to S.C. 61 (Ashley River Rd.) 15 miles northwest of Downtown Charleston.

Old St. Andrew's Parish Church CHURCH   Founded and built in 1706, this simple Anglican structure is the oldest surviving church in Charleston. Part of the church was constructed from bricks used as ballast on ships arriving in the port, and a number of historic tombs are found in the courtyard. In late March or early April—depending on flowers in bloom and the Easter holiday—the church sponsors its annual **Tea Room and Gift Shop** fundraiser, with waitresses dressed in period costumes serving such delicacies as magnolia pie. During the fundraiser, an on-site gift shop is open Monday to Saturday 11am to 1:30pm, selling cookbooks, jams, jellies, and crafts made by parish members.

2604 Ashley River Rd. (S.C. 61). www.oldstandrews.org. 📞 **843/766-1541.** Free admission. Mon–Fri 8am–2pm.

Just 12 miles north of Mount Pleasant via U.S. 17 (15 miles from the center of Charleston), the Avian Conservation Center and its **Center for Birds of Prey** (① **843/971-7474;** www.thecenter forbirdsofprey.org), 4872 Seewee Rd., Awendaw, is set on a leafy 152-acre site. Founded in 1991, the center's medical clinic treats more than 500 injured birds of prey each year. The collection includes around 40 species of eagles, falcons, hawks, owls, vultures, and other birds of prey from all parts of the world. The center is open Thursday to Saturday 10am to 5pm. Guided walking tours run Thursday to Saturday at 10:30am and 2pm, and free-flight demonstrations are staged Thursday to Saturday 11:30am and 3pm. Admission is $15 for adults, $10 for ages 6 to 16, and free for ages 5 and under.

Mount Pleasant

Boone Hall Plantation & Gardens ★★ HISTORIC HOUSE   This unique plantation is approached by a famous three-quarter mile **Avenue of Oaks** ★★★, huge old moss-draped trees planted in 1743 by Captain Thomas Boone. The original wooden house was constructed in 1790, but what remains is just a replica Colonial Revival mansion completed in 1935; die-hard history purists may be disappointed, but the grounds are stunning and very much worth visiting The first floor of the plantation house is elegantly furnished and open to the public. Outbuildings include the circular smokehouse of 1750 and original slave cabins constructed of bricks made on the plantation between 1790 and 1810. **Boone Hall Farms** opened in 2006, selling produce grown on the plantation and offering seasonal pick-your-own crops (strawberries run Apr–June).

1235 Long Point Rd. (U.S. 17/701). www.boonehallplantation.com. ① **843/884-4371.** Admission $20 adults, $18 seniors 65 and over, $10 children 6–12, free for children 5 and under. Mid-Mar to Labor Day Mon–Sat 8:30am–6:30pm, Sun noon–5pm; after Labor Day to Mid-Mar Mon–Sat 9am–5pm, Sun noon–5pm. Take U.S. 17/701 9 miles north of Charleston.

Charles Pinckney National Historic Site ★ HISTORIC SITE   Principal author and a signer of the U.S. Constitution, **Charles Pinckney** once lived on this coastal plantation, though little remains of his old home. Nevertheless, the memory of the "forgotten founder" is preserved at the small **visitor center,** located in a Lowcountry farmhouse dated to around 1828 (a 20-minute orientation video is shown on request). Outside, only 28 acres of Pinckey's once massive Snee Farm plantation remain undeveloped, accessible by a half-mile interpretive walking trail. Pinckney inherited the plantation in 1782, but was forced to sell it in 1817 to pay off debts.

1254 Long Point Rd. www.nps.gov/chpi. ① **843/881-5516.** Free admission. Daily 9am–5pm. Take U.S. 17/701 6 miles north of Charleston.

Patriots Point Naval & Maritime Museum ★★★ MUSEUM   The real showstopper at this family-friendly complex, just across the Cooper River from Downtown Charleston, is the **USS** *Yorktown,* one of America's most famous navy ships. This aircraft carrier was commissioned in 1943 and named after the ship sunk at the Battle of Midway 1 year earlier. It served in World War II and off Vietnam between 1965 to 1968, finally being decommissioned in 1970. Though *Yorktown* is the main attraction, you can also peruse the **Shipyard Museum,** explore the USS *Clamagore,* a 1945 submarine, and the USS *Laffey,* a destroyer commissioned in 1944, serving in World War II and Korea.

40 Patriots Point Rd. www.patriotspoint.org. ℂ **843/884-2727.** Admission $20 adults, $17 seniors 62 and over, $12 children 6–11, free for children 5 and under. Daily 9am–6:30pm. Closed Christmas Day.

Outlying Attractions

Fort Moultrie ★ Only a palmetto-log fortification at the time of the American Revolution, the half-completed fort was attacked by a British fleet in 1776. Col. William Moultrie's troops repelled the invasion in one of the first decisive American victories of the Revolution. The fort was subsequently enlarged into a five-sided structure with earth-and-timber walls 17 feet high. The British couldn't take it, but an 1804 hurricane ripped it apart. By the War of 1812, it was back and ready for action. **Osceola,** the fabled leader of the Seminoles in Florida, was incarcerated at the fort and eventually died here. During the 1830s, **Edgar Allen Poe** served as a soldier at the fort. He set his famous short story "The Gold Bug" on Sullivan's Island. The fort also played roles in the Civil War, the Mexican War, the Spanish-American War, and even in the two world wars, but by 1947, it had retired from action.

1214 Middle St., Sullivan's Island. www.nps.gov/fosu/historyculture/fort_moultrie.htm. ℂ **843/883-3123.** Admission $3 adults, $1 seniors 62 and over, free for children 15 and under. Federal Recreation Passports honored. Daily 9am–5pm. Closed Christmas Day and New Year's Day. Take S.C. 703 from Mt. Pleasant to Sullivan's Island.

Fort Sumter National Monument ★★★ It was here on April 12, 1861, that Confederate forces launched a 34-hour bombardment that started the **Civil War,** aka the "War Between the States." Union forces eventually surrendered, and the rebels occupied federal ground that became a symbol of Southern resistance. Amazingly, Confederate troops held Sumter for nearly 4 years, although it was almost continually bombarded by the Yankees. When evacuation finally came, the fort was nothing but a heap of rubble.

Park rangers are on hand to answer questions, and you can explore gun emplacements and visit a small **museum** filled with artifacts related to the siege. A complete tour of the fort takes about 2 hours. **Fort Sumter Visitor Education Center** at Liberty Square (back in Downtown Charleston), displays information on the events leading up to the first shots at Fort Sumter.

Most people take the tour of the fort offered by **Fort Sumter Tours,** 360 Concord St. (ℂ **800/789-3678** or 843/881-7337; www.fortsumtertours.com). You can board at either of two locations: **Liberty Square,** or Mount Pleasant's **Patriots Point.** Sailing times change every month or so, but from March to Labor Day, there generally are three sailings per day from each location, beginning at 9:30 or 10:45am. Winter sailings are less frequent. Call for details. Each departure point offers ample parking, and the boats are clean, safe, and equipped with modern conveniences.

In Charleston Harbor. ℂ **843/881-7337.** Free admission to fort; boat trip $18 adults, $16 seniors, $11 children 6–11, free for children 5 and under. Fort open Mar–Aug daily 10am–5:30pm; check website for other dates. Fort Sumter Visitor Education Center at Liberty Square open daily 8:30am–5pm.

Organized Tours

BY HORSE & CARRIAGE   **Old South Carriage,** 14 Anson St. (ℂ **843/723-9712;** www.oldsouthcarriagetours.com), offers narrated horse-drawn-carriage tours through

Charleston Outside the Historic District

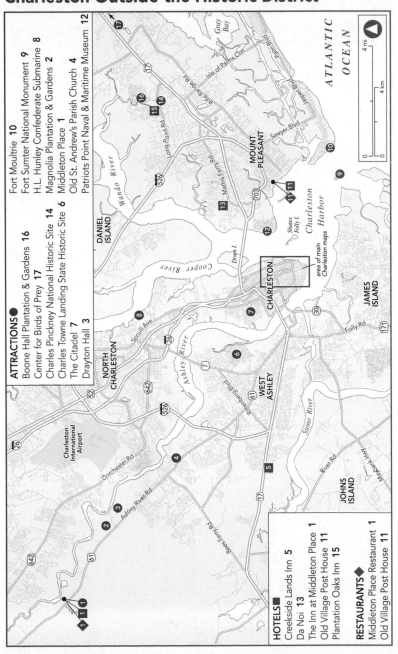

ATTRACTIONS ●

Boone Hall Plantation & Gardens **16**
Center for Birds of Prey **17**
Charles Pinckney National Historic Site **14**
Charles Towne Landing State Historic Site **6**
The Citadel **7**
Drayton Hall **3**
Fort Moultrie **10**
Fort Sumter National Monument **9**
H.L. Hunley Confederate Submarine **8**
Magnolia Plantation & Gardens **2**
Middleton Place **1**
Old St. Andrew's Parish Church **4**
Patriots Point Naval & Maritime Museum **12**

HOTELS ■

Creekside Lands Inn **5**
Da Noi **13**
The Inn at Middleton Place **1**
Old Village Post House **11**
Plantation Oaks Inn **15**

RESTAURANTS ◆

Middleton Place Restaurant **1**
Old Village Post House **11**

the Historic District daily from 9am to 5pm (Jan–Feb 10am–4pm). A 1-hour carriage tour spans a distance of 2½ miles, covering 30 blocks of the Historic District. The cost is $23 for adults and $15 for children 4 to 11.

BY MULE TEAM   **Palmetto Carriage Works,** 8 Guignard St. (© 843/723-8145; www.carriagetour.com), uses mule teams instead of the usual horse and carriage for its guided tours of Old Charleston. Tours originate at the Big Red Barn behind the Rainbow Market. The cost is $23 for adults and seniors and $15 for children 4 to 11. It operates daily from 9am to 5pm.

BY BOAT   **Spiritline Cruises,** 360 Concord St., Ste. 201 (© 800/789-3678 or 843/722-2628; www.spiritlinecruises.com), offers Harbor and Dinner Cruises. **Dinner Cruises** run 7 to 9:30pm, boarding at 6:30pm at Patriots Point, with rates $54 per person (Sun–Thurs), or $60 per person (Fri–Sat). Meals are usually pretty good—local farm-to-table produce with live entertainment from local musicians. **Harbor Tours** are $20, with daily departures March through November from Aquarium Wharf at 360 Concord St. (11am, 1pm) and Patriots Point (3pm). The 90-minute cruise passes the Battery, Charleston Port, Castle Pinckney, Drum Island, Fort Sumter, and the aircraft carrier *Yorktown.*

WALKING TOURS   Charlestonians are proud to talk about the historical quirks of their city, and as such, several tour operators compete for your walking tour business. A well-recommended staple is **Charleston Strolls** (© 843/766-2080; www.charles tonstrolls.com), which conducts a 2-hour walking tour every day beginning at 10am and 2pm (from the Mills House Hotel, 115 Meeting St.), which touches on the salient points of the city's sometimes bloody history. Tours are $20 per person, or else $10 for ages 7 to 12 (6 and under free).

Another wildly popular guided stroll through old Charleston is the candlelight tour by **Ghosts of The South** (© 843/343-9255; www.charlestonghostsofthesouth.com). It lasts around 80 minutes and costs $20. Departing year-round every night at 8 and 10pm, tours originate at Sheila's Shamrock Gift Shop, 84c North Market St. As the name suggests, the tour delves into Charleston's haunted history (hotels, houses, and graveyards), and isn't really suitable for young children.

Outdoor Activities

BEACHES   Three great beaches are within a 25-minute drive of the center of Charleston.

In the West Islands, **Folly Beach,** which had degenerated into a funky Coney Island–type amusement park, has made a comeback following a multimillion-dollar cleanup, but it remains the least pristine beach in the area. The best bathroom amenities are located here, however. At the western end of the island is the **Folly Beach County Park,** 1100 West Ashley Ave. (Nov–Feb daily 10am–5pm; Mar–Apr and Sep–Oct daily 10am–6pm; May–Labor Day daily 9am–7pm; free admission; parking $7–$10), with bathrooms, parking, and shelter from the rain. To get here, take U.S. 17 East to S.C. 171 South to Folly Beach.

In the East Cooper area, both the **Isle of Palms** and **Sullivan's Island** offer miles of public beaches, mostly bordered by beachfront homes. Windsurfing and jet-skiing are popular here. Take U.S. 17 East to S.C. 703 (Ben Sawyer Blvd.). S.C. 703 continues through Sullivan's Island to the Isle of Palms.

Kiawah Island has the area's most pristine beach—far preferable to Folly Beach, to my taste—and draws a more upmarket crowd. The best beachfront is at

Beachwalker County Park (Nov–Feb daily 10am–5pm, Mar–Apr and Sept–Oct daily 10am–6pm, May–Labor Day daily 9am–7pm; free admission, parking $7–$10), on the southern end of the island at 8 Beachwalker Drive. Get there before noon on weekends; the limited parking is usually taken by then. Canoe rentals are available for use on the Kiawah River, and the park offers not only a boardwalk, but also bathrooms, showers, and a changing area. Take U.S. 17 East to S.C. 171 South (Folly Beach Rd.), and turn right onto S.C. 700 Southwest (Maybank Hwy.) to Bohicket Road, which turns into Betsy Kerrison Parkway. Where Betsy Kerrison Parkway dead-ends, turn left on Kiawah Parkway, which takes you to the island. For details on the major resorts on Kiawah Island and the Isle of Palms, see p. 88.

BIKING   Charleston is basically flat and not traffic-clogged except on its main arteries at rush hour. Biking is a popular local pastime, and most of the city parks have biking trails. The most popular run is across the 2.5-mile, eight-lane **Arthur Ravenel Jr. Bridge,** which links downtown Charleston to Mount Pleasant. For the best bike rentals, contact the **Bicycle Shoppe** at 280 Meeting St. (© **843/722-8168;** www.the bicycleshoppecharleston.com). Rentals begin at $7 for 1 hour or $28 per day. ID and credit card required.

BOATING   A true Charlestonian is as much at home on the sea as on land. Sailing local waters is a popular family pastime. One of the best places for boat rentals is **Isle of Palms Marina,** 1207 Palm Blvd., Isle of Palms (© **843/886-0209;** www.iop.net), where 18-foot boats, big enough for seven people, rent for around $240 for half a day, plus fuel. A larger boat, big enough for 10, goes for about $375 to $450 for a half day, plus fuel.

FISHING   Freshwater fishing charters are available year-round along the Lowcountry's numerous creeks and inlets. The waterways are filled with flounder, trout, spottail, and channel bass. Some of the best striped-bass fishing available in America can be found at nearby Lake Moultrie.

Offshore-fishing charters for reef fishing (where you'll find fish such as cobia, black sea bass, and king mackerel) and for the Gulf Stream (where you fish for sailfish, marlin, wahoo, dolphin, and tuna) are also available. Both types of charters can be arranged at the previously recommended **Isle of Palms Marina** (© **843/886-0209**). A fishing craft holding up to 10 people rents for $900 for 6 hours, including everything but food and drink. Reservations must be made 24 hours in advance.

Folly Beach Fishing Pier (© **843/588-3474;** www.ccprc.com), 101 East Arctic Ave., Folly Beach, is a 25 feet wide wood pier that extends 1,000 feet into the Atlantic Ocean. Facilities include restrooms, a tackle shop, and a restaurant. It's accessible to people with disabilities, and open daily May to September 6am–11pm (Dec–Feb 8am–sunset; Mar and Nov 7am–sunset; Apr and Oct 6am–10pm; free admission, parking $5–$10).

GOLF   Charleston is said to be the home of golf in America. Charlestonians have been playing the game since the 1700s, when the first golf clubs arrived from Scotland. With 26 public and private courses in the area, there's a golf game waiting for every buff.

Wild Dunes Resort, Isle of Palms (© **843/886-2164;** www.wilddunes.com), offers two championship golf courses designed by Tom Fazio. The **Links Course ★★★** is a 6,387-yard, par-70 layout that takes the player through marshlands, over or into huge sand dunes, through a wooded alley, and into a pair of oceanfront finishing holes once called "the greatest east of Pebble Beach, California." The **Harbor Course** offers

6,402 yards of Lowcountry marsh and Intracoastal Waterway views. This par-70 layout is considered to be target golf, challenging players with 2 holes that play from one island to another across Morgan Creek. Greens fees at these courses can range from $95 to $175, depending on the season. Both courses are open daily 7am to 6pm.

   Charleston Golf, Inc. (*©* **800/774-4444;** www.charlestongolfguide.com; Mon–Fri 8:30am–5pm) represents 20 golf courses, offering packages that range from $112 to $269 per person March to August. Prices include greens fees on one course, the use of a golf cart, a hotel room based on double occupancy, and taxes. Travel pros here will customize your vacation with golf-course selections and tee times; they can also arrange rental cars and airfares. Reservations must be made 1 week in advance.

HIKING   The most beguiling hiking trails begin around Buck Hall in **Francis Marion National Forest** (*©* **843/887-3257;** www.fs.usda.gov/scnfs), located some 40 miles north of the center of Charleston via U.S. 17-N. The site consists of 250,000 acres of swamps, with towering oaks and pines. Within the national forest, **Buck Hall Recreation Area** (*©* **877/444-6777;** www.recreation.gov), reached by U.S. 17/701 north from Charleston, has camping sites ($15–$25 per night), plus a boat ramp and fishing. Other hiking trails are at **Edisto Beach State Park,** 8377 State Cabin Rd., on Edisto Island (*©* **843/869-2156;** admission $5; daily 8am–6pm).

Especially for Kids

For more than 300 years, Charleston has been the home of pirates, patriots, and presidents. Your child can see firsthand the **Great Hall** at the **Old Exchange** (p. 72), where President Washington danced; view the **Provost Dungeons** (p. 72), where South Carolina patriots spent their last days; and touch the last remaining structural evidence of the **Charleston Seawall.** Children will take special delight in **Charles Towne Landing** (p. 75) and **Middleton Place** (p. 76). At **Fort Sumter** (p. 78), they can see where the Civil War began. Children will also enjoy **Magnolia Plantation** (p. 75), with its Audubon Swamp Garden.

   Kids and navy vets will love the aircraft carrier **USS *Yorktown,*** at **Patriots Point** (p. 77). Its World War II, Korean, and Vietnam exploits are documented in exhibits, and general naval history is illustrated through models of ships, planes, and weapons.

SHOPPING

The densest and most appealing collection of upscale shops in the Carolinas is on **King Street.** The **Shops at Belmond Charleston Place,** located on the ground floor of Charleston Place Hotel, along King and Market streets (www.charlestonplace.com), comprises a mix of designer brands (Gucci, L'Occitane, Calypso St. Barth, Louis Vuitton, Kate Spade, and so on). A short stretch of trendy, youth-conscious boutiques known as **Upper King Street Design District** (www.littleworksofheart.typepad.com/upperkingcharleston) is where about a dozen forward-thinking artisans ply their penchant for jewelry, millinery, and crafts.

Antiques

George C. Birlant and Co. ★★   This tantalizing store has been selling quality antiques since 1922. It specializes in carefully selected 18th- and 19th-century English antique furniture, silver, china, crystal, and brass. The store is also known for the bespoke "Charleston Battery Bench," a wood-and-iron bench made from 1880s molds and South Carolina cypress. The Birlant building itself is a real gem, constructed around 1850. Hours are Monday to Saturday 9am to 5:30pm. 191 King St. www.birlant. com. ℰ **843/722-3842.**

Livingston Antiques ★   Established in 1969 out in West Ashley, this is one of the largest antique dealers in the South. The specialization here is 18th- and 19th-century English furniture, but you'll also find high-quality pottery and porcelain: majolica, Staffordshire, Jasperware, and Delft. Hours are Tuesday to Saturday 10am to 5pm. 2137 Savannah Hwy. www.livingstonantiques.com. ℰ **843/556-3502.**

Art

Chuma Gullah Gallery ★★   This enlightening gallery in City Market specializes in the art of the Gullah people (descendants of enslaved Africans) of coastal South Carolina. The work of lauded Gullah artist Jonathan Green is especially prominent, as is John Jones (best known for his *Color of Money* series). The gallery is open daily 9:30am to 6pm. 188 Meeting St (inside City Market). www.gallerychuma.com. ℰ **843/722-1702.**

Lowcountry Artists Gallery ★★   Founded in 1982, this gallery is an exciting showcase for local artists. It's a very eclectic ensemble; all mediums and styles of painting are represented, as well as blown glass, pottery, and sculpture. Hours are Monday to Saturday 10:30am to 6pm and Sunday 1 to 5pm. 148 E. Bay St. www.lowcountry artists.com. ℰ **843/577-9295.**

Studio 151 Fine Arts ★   This fine-art gallery was established by a group of prominent local artists including Colleen Wiessmann, Shelby Parbel, Rosie Phillips, Bob Graham, and Amelia Whaley. Many of the artists are often in the store and are happy to chat with customers. Hours are Monday to Thursday 10am to 5pm, Friday and Saturday 10am to 8pm, and Sunday 11am to 5pm. 175 Church St., at Market St. www. studio151finearts.com. ℰ **843/579-9725.**

Wells Gallery ★   Art lovers will want to make the trip out to the Sanctuary Resort on Kiawah Island to visit this elegant gallery, a showcase for contemporary local artists such as Curt Butler, Russell Gordon, E.B. Lewis, and Karen Larson Turner. Hours are Monday to Saturday 10am to 5pm. 1 Sanctuary Beach Dr. www.wellsgallery.com. ℰ **843/576-1290.**

Books

Blue Bicycle Books ★★★   Charleston's premier secondhand book seller (it also buys books), owned by local writer Jonathan Sanchez. With over 50,000 volumes in the store, it boasts the largest collection of used, rare, and new titles in Charleston and the Lowcountry. Hours are Monday to Saturday 10am to 7:30pm, and Sunday 1 to 6pm. 420 King St. www.bluebicyclebooks.com. ℰ **843/722-2666.**

College of Charleston Bookstore ★★   This college bookstore is actually run by Barnes & Noble. Inside you'll find a fabulous choice of books, textbooks, school spirit clothing, school supplies, and gifts. Hours are Monday to Friday 7:45am to 5:30pm, Saturday 9am to 5:30pm, and Sunday noon to 5:30pm. 160 Calhoun St (Lightsey Center, College of Charleston Campus). ℰ **843/953-5518.**

Preservation Society of Charleston Bookstore ★★   Founded in 1920, the Preservation Society of Charleston runs this great local bookstore. It boasts a decent choice of titles on Charleston and South Carolina history, Gullah and African American history, and the Civil War, as well as old maps, prints, etchings, and DVDs. Hours

are Monday to Saturday 10am to 5pm, Sunday 10am to 4pm. 147 King St. www.preserva
tionsociety.org. ℰ **843/722-4630.**

Cookware

Charleston Cooks! ★★   This local kitchen supply mini-chain also offers Southern cooking lessons. It's a rustic, bright space selling everything from cookware and
cookbooks to baking and bar essentials (including some really cool bottle openers).
Open Monday to Saturday 10am to 9pm, and Sunday noon to 6pm. 194 E. Bay St. www.
charlestoncooks.com. ℰ **843/722-1212.**

Crafts & Gifts

Charleston Crafts ★★★   Owned by a cooperative of local artists since 1989
(exhibiting artisans are required to be residents of South Carolina), this store is a real
treat. Inside you'll see the artistic sweet-grass baskets of Alethia Manigault, the unique
jewelry designs of Caroline Sandlin, the lathe-turned bowls of Charles Black, and the
stained-glass panels of Don Carberry, among many others. It's open daily 10am to
6pm. 161 Church St. www.charlestoncrafts.org. ℰ **843/723-2938.**

Jewelry

Croghan's Jewel Box ★★   This venerable jewelry store was established in the
18th century by one William Joseph Croghan, and the current shop still occupies the
same spot. The stock here is unusual and unique, with a blend of vintage-inspired and
contemporary pieces. The store is also justly famous for the quality of its personalized
engraving service. Hours are Monday to Friday 9:30am to 5:30pm and Saturday 10am
to 5pm. 308 King St. www.croghansjewelbox.com. ℰ **843/723-3594.**

Dazzles ★   Stylish, contemporary jewelry from a host of very hot designers. Think
Natalie K, Mindy Lam, and Lalique. Hours are Monday to Saturday 10am to 6pm;
there is another branch at 86 Queen St. 202 King St. www.dazzlesjewelry.com.
ℰ **843/722-5997.**

Paulo Geiss Jewelers ★   Another Charleston institution, though this family
business was actually founded in Brazil back in 1919. The family moved to South
Carolina in 1964, but the first Charleston store opened 20 years later. Today Paulo
Geiss keeps his family legacy alive working with top contemporary manufacturers and
designers. Hours are Monday to Friday 10am to 5:30pm, and Saturday 10am to 5pm.
116 E. Bay St. www.geissjewelers.com. ℰ **843/577-4497.**

Joggling Boards

Old Charleston Joggling Board Co. ★★★   Heard of the joggling board?
These bizarre local devices date back to the early 1830s, designed by Mrs. Benjamin
Kinloch Huger as a mild form of exercise for her rheumatism (the board allows you to
bounce, gently, on the spot). It's essentially a long plank of wood supported by two
struts, which bends (but doesn't break) when you sit on it. Kids love them. This company revived the old art in 1970. Hours are Monday to Friday 8am to 5pm. 650 King St.
www.oldcharlestonjogglingboard.com. ℰ **843/723-4331.**

Pharmacy

Pitt Street Pharmacy ★★   This old-time drugstore opened in 1938, across the
bridge from downtown Charleston in Mount Pleasant. Though it almost qualifies as an

historic sight, it still operates as a regular pharmacy, with all the usual products and off-the-shelf remedies for sale, and prescriptions filled. Hours are Monday to Saturday 9am to 6pm. 111 Pitt St., Mount Pleasant. www.pittstreetpharmacy.com. ✆ **843/884-4051.**

Textiles

Lulan Artisans ★★★ Founded by Eve Blossom, this fashionable store brings together contemporary American textile designers and talented Asian artisans. All the natural hand-woven fabrics, silks, organic cotton and linens on sale are created by 650 weavers, spinners, dyers, and finishers in Cambodia, Laos, Thailand, Vietnam, and India. Hours are Monday to Friday 11am to 5pm. 469 King St. www.lulan.com. ✆ **843/722-0118.**

ENTERTAINMENT & NIGHTLIFE

The Performing Arts

Charleston's major cultural venue is the **Dock Street Theatre,** 135 Church St. (✆ **843/577-7183;** www.charlestonstage.com), a 463-seat theater. The original was built in 1736 but burned down in the early 19th century, and the Planters Hotel (not related to the Planters Inn) was constructed around its ruins. In 1936, the theater was rebuilt in a new location. It's the home of the **Charleston Stage Company,** a local not-for-profit theater group whose season runs from mid-September to May. Dock Street hosts performances ranging from Shakespeare to *My Fair Lady*. It's most active during the **Spoleto Festival USA** (p. 47) in May and June. The box office (✆ **843/577-7183**) is open Monday to Friday 10am to 5pm, Saturday 10am to 5pm and a half-hour before curtain, and Sunday from 10am to 3pm.

The **Charleston Symphony Orchestra,** 14 George St. (✆ **843/723-7528;** www.charlestonsymphony.com), performs throughout the state, but its main venues are the Gaillard Auditorium and Charleston Southern University. The season runs from September to May.

Bars, Clubs & Live Music

Big John's Tavern ★★ Open since 1955, this is one of Charleston's oldest bars, and a popular hangout for cadets from the Citadel. The space reopened in 2014 after a renovation and revamp of the menu, bringing it back to its no-frills, dive bar roots. Believe the hype—the roast beef sandwiches ($9) here really are the best in town. Inside there's the old long bar, cozy booths, and a separate pool room. The bar is open daily 4pm to 2am. 251 E. Bay St. ✆ **843/723-3483.**

Blind Tiger Pub ★★ This old tavern is best known for its live bands and its atmospheric courtyard, a great place to unwind after a hard day of sightseeing. The pub building was erected in 1803 by George Keith as a commercial property (the ornate facade on Broad Street was put up in 1877), and though the small, cramped interior features the old wooden bar, exposed beams, and a cluster of oak tables, it's the outdoor area that really pulls in the locals. Crumbling, ivy-covered brick arches and walls create a series of atmospheric nooks and patios. Live music from local artists is featured most nights of the week. Beers are just $3 during the Monday-to-Friday happy hour (5–8pm). The bar is open Monday to Saturday 11:30am to 2am, and Sunday 11am to 2am. 36–38 Broad St. www.blindtigercharleston.com. ✆ **843/577-0088.**

The Black Fedora

This **"comedy mystery theatre"** at 164 Church St. is lots of fun for families, with two or three comic mysteries running most evenings (in play form). The Pirate Mystery Treasure Show is especially thrilling for little ones, while the hilarious Sherlock Holmes parody is more suitable for pre-teens and above.

Tickets are $24 for adults, $22 for students, and $15 for children 12 and under. Visit www.charlestonmysteries.com or call ✆ **843/937-6453** for the latest schedule. The book and gift shop on site is open Tuesday to Sunday noon to show time.

Charleston Beer Works ★   No-nonsense sports bar in the trendy Upper King area. It's a casual, friendly space, with 40 beers on tap (including regional microbrews, $5–$6), a tasty food menu, and plenty of TVs to watch that big game. Local bands usually perform Thursday to Saturday nights. Open daily from 11:30am to 2am (happy hour Mon–Fri 4–7pm). 468 King St. www.charlestonbeerworks.com. ✆ **843/577-5885.**

First Shot Lounge ★   This plush hotel lounge bar is a classy place to start your evening, with a decent cocktail menu and a wide selection of wines and beer. The bar is decked out like a Victorian gentleman's club, and overlooks the fountain courtyard. There's also a selection of tasty appetizers and sandwiches. Open daily from 4 to 10:30pm. In the Mills House Wyndham Grand Hotel, 115 Meeting St. ✆ **843/577-2400.**

Gin Joint ★★★   This compact bar is one of the city's finest, with mixologists that really know what they're doing and quality cocktails. The usual offering contains 5 to 8 separate ingredients and pours: the exceptionally smooth "South of the Border" comprises tequila, Agwa Coca Liqueur, lime, Meyer lemon, mint, and Angostura bitters, for example. The bar snacks are equally creative—think soft pretzels with Sriracha cheese sauce, and Pad Thai popcorn ($6). It's open Sunday to Wednesday 5pm to midnight, Thursday to Friday 5pm to 2am, and Saturday 3pm to 2am. 182 E. Bay St. www.theginjoint.com. ✆ **843/577-6111.**

Mad River ★   This sports bar boasts one of the most unique venues in Charleston, the Old Seaman's Chapel on Market Street. Inside, the original high vaulted ceilings and stained-glass windows from the church have been retained, but you can also enjoy a drink on the patio outside. The big screen makes this a popular spot to watch the game, while late-nights DJs create more of a club atmosphere, with plenty of dancing. Happy hour (Fri 5–8pm) beers are $3. It's open daily from 11am to 2am. 32 N. Market St. www.madrivercharleston.com. ✆ **843/723-0032.**

Mynt ★   This is the newest bar/nightclub combo to open in downtown Charleston—things change fast, however, so check its current status before making plans. A fashionable cocktail bar for young professionals on weekdays, with an abstract, multicolored ceiling and mosaic bar, Mynt morphs into dance club–mode Friday and Saturday nights (though it remains the preserve of the upwardly mobile). There's a dress code here: no sneakers, hats, baggy trousers, or jerseys. Mynt is open daily 5pm to 2am. 135 Calhoun St. www.myntsouthcarolina.com. ✆ **843/718-1598.**

The Sounds of Charleston

The best night out in the city is this must-see performance of gospel, Gershwin, music of the Civil War, light classics, and jazz—all the elements of Charleston's rich musical stew. The **Sounds of Charleston** (📞 800/838-3006; www.soundofcharleston.com) concert lasts around 90 minutes, with shows starting at 7pm. The schedule changes seasonally, but there is usually one show per week (less June to August). Tickets cost $28 for adults, $26 for seniors, $16 for students, and are free for children 12 and under. Get tickets online or at the any of the local Visitor Centers.

Prohibition ★★ A stylish bar and restaurant inspired by the Jazz Age, with reclaimed wood walls, a long, elegant bar, and pressed-tin ceiling. The fun menu is a spin on Southern and American classics (see the "Capone Burger" or "Bootlegger Wings"), while draught beers include suds from local microbrewery Holy City Brewing. The inventive cocktail menu continues the speakeasy theme—try the bacon-maple old-fashioned ($11). Live jazz, swing, and big band music sets the mood most night, while DJs take over on weekends. The bar is open Tuesday to Saturday 5pm to 2am, and Sunday 11am to midnight. 547 King St. www.prohibitioncharleston.com. 📞 843/793-2964.

Rooftop at the Vendue ★★ Relax on the comfy banquettes at the main bar in the Venue hotel, or walk up to the two-level rooftop patio bar (make sure you walk right to the top level for the best views of the city). On a clear evening this is the best place to start your night. Hours are Monday to Friday 4pm to midnight, and Saturday and Sunday 11am to midnight. 19 Vendue Range. www.thevendue.com/rooftop-bar. 📞 800/845-7900.

Southend Brewery & Smokehouse ★★ Though this is as much a restaurant as a bar (serving high-quality Southern and American classics), it's the craft beers brewed on site that brings in the crowd. Order a sample tray for $10, or a pitcher of Rip Tide Red, Pict's Stout, or Love Me Two Times Blonde for $16. The bar occupies the 19th-century Wagener Building, a place that is supposedly Charleston's most haunted spot. Live music every Friday 10pm to 1:30am (mostly alternative rock, soul, and country). The bar is open daily 11:30am to 2am. 161 E. Bay St. www.southendbrewery.com. 📞 843/853-4677.

SIDE TRIPS FROM CHARLESTON

If you only have a couple of days or so, you will probably want to spend them in the center of Charleston. However, if you are here for a week—or on your second visit to the city—make time for the surrounding Lowcountry to see some of the old plantations and islands that lie within this historic region. The most popular of the latter are the **Isle of Palms, Sullivan's Island** (p. 80), and **Kiawah Island.** In July and August, these breeze-swept barrier islands are the place to be. Some of the islands now contain upscale resorts, and all have long, sandy beaches. White-tailed deer and bobcats live in the maritime forests in the area, and the endangered small tern and loggerhead turtles still nest and lay their eggs on some of these islands. There are no tourist information offices on these islands except at Kiawah. For information, see the Charleston Visitor Center (p. 44).

To the north lies the section of coast known as the **Grand Strand** and, eventually, **Myrtle Beach.** The Grand Strand annually hosts as many as 14 million visitors, who also come for shopping, excellent golfing, sightseeing, and live theater. Myrtle Beach has grown into a year-round family destination, with theme parks and beaches galore. I've also covered historic **Georgetown, Pawley's Island,** and **Murrells Inlet.** For **Beaufort** and **Hilton Head Island,** see p. 159.

KIAWAH ISLAND

27 miles SW of Downtown Charleston

This eco-sensitive residential and resort island covers just over 11 square miles, with stunning beaches and world-famous golf courses the main attraction. Legendary quarterback Dan Marino and Miami Heat's Ray Allen have holiday homes here. Named for the Kiawah people who inhabited the islands in the 17th century, today the island is primarily a gated beach and golf resort, the **Kiawah Island Golf Resort** (www.kiawahresort. com), though day-visitors are welcome. **Kiawah Beachwalker Park** is also open to the public. The resort fronts a lovely 10-mile stretch of Atlantic beach; magnolias, live oaks, pine forests, and acres of marsh characterize the interior of the island.

Kiawah Resort runs many challenging **golf courses,** including one designed by Jack Nicklaus at **Turtle Point.** Kiawah is also one of the

KIAWAH golf & tennis

GOLF Designed by Jack Nicklaus, **Turtle Point Golf Course** (© 843/768-2121; www.kiawahresort.com) is an 18-hole, par-72, 7,054-yard course at **Kiawah Island Golf Resort.** Greens fees range $175 to $225 (Kiawah Island Golf Resort guests pay less than day-visitors). The **Ocean Course** (© 843/768-2121), designed by Pete Dye, was home of the 1991 Ryder Cup, 1997 World Cup, 2003 World Cup, and 2012 PGA Championships. It's an 18-hole, par-72, 7,296-yard course, the finest in South Carolina. It was even featured in the 2000 movie

The Legend of Bagger Vance. Call for rates.

TENNIS One of the greatest **tennis resorts** in the South is also found at the **Kiawah Island Golf Resort** (© 843/768-2121), with 28 hard-surface or Har-Tru clay courts in two tennis complexes. The per-hour cost is $34 per hour for resort guests and $44 for non-guests. Racquet rental is $8 per hour. Open daily, from 8am to 8pm in summer, 8am to 7pm in spring and fall, and 9am to 5pm in winter.

nation's top **tennis** resorts, with its 28 hard-surface and Har-Tru clay courts. Anglers are also attracted to the island, especially in spring and fall.

The Kiawah people ceded the island to the English colonists from Charlestown in 1675, and it remained privately owned for years; the influential Vanderhorst family bought it in 1775. Cotton production began here in 1802, but in 1864 Union troops demolished the Vanderhorst plantation house. Daily passenger and freight services by boat between Kiawah and Charleston didn't get going until 1911, and it wasn't until 1950 that the Vanderhorst finally sold the island (to a logging and timber company). Resort development began in the 1970s, and today the island maintains a full-time resident population of approximately 1,400.

Essentials

GETTING THERE

From Charleston, take U.S. 17 E. to S.C. 171 S. (Folly Beach Rd.); turn right onto S.C. 700 (Maybank Hwy.) southwest to Bohicket Road, which turns into Betsy Kerrison Parkway. Where Betsy Kerrison Parkway reaches a traffic circle, turn left on Kiawah Parkway, which takes you to the island. There is no public transport to the island.

VISITOR INFORMATION

The **Kiawah Island Visitor Center,** 21 Beachwalker Dr. (© 843/768-9166; www. kiawahisland.org), is open Monday through Friday 9am to 3pm.

Exploring Kiawah Island

Kiawah has the area's most pristine **beach**—far preferable to nearby **Folly Beach**—and draws a more upmarket crowd. The best beachfront is at **Kiawah Beachwalker Park,** 8 Beachwalker Dr. (© 843/768-2395), on the western end of the island. Get here before noon on weekends; the limited parking is usually gone by then. Canoe rentals are available for use on the Kiawah River, and the park offers not only a boardwalk, but also bathrooms, showers, and a changing area. The park is open daily November to February 10am to 5pm, March to April and September to October 10am to 6pm, and May to Labor Day 9am to 7pm. Admission is $7 per vehicle March to October ($10 on Sat–Sun, May–Labor Day), and free November to February. You can rent a beach chair and beach umbrella for $10 per day.

Where to Dine

Ocean Room at the Sanctuary ★★★ AMERICAN/STEAK   This is the top place to dine on Kiawah Island, and definitely worth a splurge if you stay for dinner. Excellent staff, fabulous steaks, and also top quality "Southern-style" sushi in the **Sushi Lounge** section. The seasonal menus feature local produce and can include anything from the famed ribeye steak and Kansas City strip, to ricotta gnocchi and the catch of the day. Leave room for the whipped sweet potato cheesecake. The views of the beach and resort grounds are breathtaking. No flip flops or denim.

Kiawah Island Golf Resort, 1 Sanctuary Beach Dr. www.kiawahresort.com/dining/the-ocean-room. *C* **843/768-6253.** Main courses $25–$65; set menu (5:30–6:30pm only) $49; sushi small plates $5–$21. Tues–Sat 5:30–10pm.

EDISTO ISLAND ★

45 miles SW of Downtown Charleston

Isolated, and offering a kind of melancholy beauty, **Edisto Island** is named after the Edisto tribe of Native Americans, now long gone. Paul Grimball was the first English settler, arriving here in 1683 (the tabby ruins of the Grimball House are still visible). By the late 18th century, Sea Island cotton had made the slave-holding plantation owners wealthy, and some houses from that era still stand. Today the island primarily attracts families from Charleston and the Lowcountry to its **white sandy beaches.** Popular activities include shrimping, surf-casting, deep-sea fishing, and sailing.

Essentials

GETTING THERE

Take U.S. 17 W. for 21 miles, then head south along Hwy. 174 the rest of the way. There is no public transport to the island.

Exploring Edisto Island

Edisto Beach State Park (www.southcarolinaparks.com/edistobeach), 8377 State Cabin Rd., sprawls across 1,255 acres, opening onto 2 miles of beach. There are also signposted nature trails through forests of live oak, hanging Spanish moss, and palmetto trees, and an ancient shell midden (**Spanish Mount Point**), created by the Edisto Indians around 2,000 B.C., made up mostly of oyster shells. Enjoy a picnic lunch under one of the shelters or visit the **Interpretive Center** (Tues–Sat 9am–4pm; *C* **843/869-4430**) featuring interactive displays on the ACE Basin estuarine reserve, the largest such natural reserve on the East Coast.

Admission to the park is $5 for adults, $3 for ages 6 to 15, and free for ages 5 and under. The park is open daily 8am to 6pm.

The park also has 111 campsites with full hookups and 5 primitive campsites for tents. Campsites cost $21 to $38 per night (the price is the same for RV hookups). Primitive tent sites are $15 to $20 per night. Call *C* **843/869-2756** for reservations.

Where to Dine

Old Post Office ★★ SOUTHERN   Rustic purveyor of Lowcountry cuisine from chef Cherry Smalls. Start with the house-made pimiento cheese or fried oyster

Swamp Boat Adventures ★★

The 163-acre swamps of **Cypress Gardens,** 3030 Cypress Gardens Rd. (U.S. 52), Moncks Corner (℃ **843/553-0515;** www.cypressgardens.info), some 24 miles north of Charleston, were once used as a freshwater reserve for Dean Hall, a huge Cooper River rice plantation, and were given to the city in 1963. Today the giant cypress trees draped with Spanish moss provide an unforgettable setting for flat-bottom swamp boats that glide among their knobby roots. Footpaths in the garden wind through a profusion of azaleas, camel-lias, daffodils, and other colorful blooms. Visitors share the swamp with alligators, pileated woodpeckers, wood ducks, otters, barred owls, and other abundant species. The gardens are worth a visit at any time of year, but they're at their most colorful in March and April. Also on-site are a reptile center, aquarium, and aviary, plus a butterfly house. Admission is $10 adults, $9 seniors 65 and over, $5 children 6 to 12, free for children 5 and under. Boat rides are an additional $5. The gardens are open daily 9am to 5pm.

cocktail. The main courses include, of course, a fabulous wild-caught shrimp and grits, topped with mousseline sauce, but also good alue ribeye steaks, cayenne-and-honey–sizzled catfish, blueberry chicken, and delicate crab cakes. All main courses are served with house salad, fresh baked bread, stone-ground grits, and vegetable of the day. The late 18th-century clapboard building was once a post office and general store.

1442 Hwy. 174, at Store Creek. www.theoldpostofficerestaurant.com. ℃ **843/869-2339.** Main courses $22–$29. Mar–Oct Tues–Sat 5:30–10pm, Nov–Feb Wed–Sat 5:30–10pm. Closed Jan.

Po-Pigs BO-B-Q ★★ BARBECUE   Superb barbecue from Pam and "BoBo" Lee, with all the Southern fixin's, in a gut-busting all-you-can-eat buffet (the chicken and pulled pork are especially good). They also offer BBQ plates or sandwiches, and delicious fried chicken. The buffer includes a huge variety of Southern vegetables, including turnip greens, okra, field peas, and squash casserole. Note that Po-Pigs was planning to move into new premises closer to the beach at the time of research.

2410 Hwy. 174. ℃ **843/869-9003.** Buffet $10. Thurs–Sat 11:30am–9pm.

THE ISLE OF PALMS

13 miles E of Downtown Charleston

A residential community facing the Atlantic Ocean, this barrier island, with its salt marshes and wildlife, has been transformed into a vacation retreat, but one that is more downscale than Kiawah Island. The attractions of Charleston are close at hand, but the Isle of Palms is also self-contained, with dining, an array of accommodations, and two championship **golf courses.** Seven miles of wide, **white sandy beach** is the island's main attraction, and beach volleyball, sailing, and windsurfing are popular. The more adventurous will go crabbing and shrimping in the creeks.

The island's original inhabitants were the Seewee people, now long gone. Charlestonians have been flocking to the Isle of Palms for holidays since 1898. The first hotel opened here in 1906.

ISLE OF PALMS: fishing & golfing

FISHING   Offshore-fishing charters for both reef fishing (where you'll find fish such as cobia, black sea bass, and king mackerel) and Gulf Stream fishing (where you fish for sailfish, marlin, wahoo, dolphin, and tuna) can be arranged at **Isle of Palms Marina** (✆ **843/886-0209**). A fishing craft holding up to three people rents for $375 to $525 inshore, including everything but food and drink. Offshore 12-hour rentals are also available for $950 to $1,995. Reserve 1 week in advance.

GOLF   **Wild Dunes Resort** (✆ **843/ 886-6000;** www.wilddunes.com) offers two championship courses designed by Tom Fazio. The **Links Course** ★★★ is a 6,387-yard, par-70 layout that takes the player through marshlands, over or into huge sand dunes, through a wooded alley, and into a pair of oceanfront finishing holes once called "the greatest east of Pebble Beach." The **Harbor Course** ★★ offers 6,402 yards of Lowcountry marsh and Intracoastal Waterway views. This par-70 layout is considered target golf, challenging players with 2 holes that play one island to another across Morgan Creek. Greens fees at these courses range from $100 to $190. Both courses are open year-round daily 7am to 6pm.

Essentials

GETTING THERE

From Charleston, take U.S. 17 N. to S.C. 517, then S.C. 703 to Isle of Palms. I-26 intersects with I-526 heading directly to the island via the Isle of Palms Connector (S.C. 517). There is no public transport to the island.

Exploring the Isle of Palms

The **beachfront** is the center of activity on the Isle of Palms. Popular **Front Beach** is located on Ocean Boulevard, between 10th and 14th avenues. You can rent a bodyboard from a nearby stand, play a friendly game of volleyball, or comb the beach for shells like sand dollars, whelks, and angel wings. The central **Isle of Palms County Park** section of the beach at No. 1, 14th Ave. (where the Isle of Palms Connector enters the island), has the most facilities and is open daily (Nov–Feb 10am–5pm; Mar–Apr and Sept–Oct 10am–6pm; and May–Labor Day 9am–7pm). Admission is $7 per vehicle March to October ($10 Sat–Sun May–Labor Day), and free November to February. You can rent a beach chair and beach umbrella for $10 per day.

A true Charlestonian is as much at home on the sea as on land. Sailing local waters is a popular family pastime. One of the best places for rentals is **Isle of Palms Marina** (✆ **843/886-0209;** www.iop.net), where 18-foot boats, big enough for seven people, rent for around $240 for 4 hours, plus fuel. A larger pontoon boat, big enough for 10, goes for $395 to $475 for 4 hours, plus fuel.

Where to Dine

Acme Lowcountry Kitchen ★★★ LOWCOUNTRY   Universally acknowledged as the best restaurant on the island, by locals and visitors alike. The laid-back beach vibe reflects the amazing downhome food. All the classics are perfect here: fried green tomatoes, creamy shrimp and grits, lobster tails, Carolina succotash, lump crab cake, and peanut butter pie. But for a real treat order the crab-stuffed flounder with chipotle cream sauce. If you can't make lunch or dinner try visiting for breakfast, which features burritos, benedicts, and fresh biscuits.

31 J. C. Long Blvd. www.acmelowcountrykitchen.com. © **843/886-0024.** Main courses dinner $15–$29, breakfast $8–$12; sandwiches $9–$10. Daily 8am–2pm and 5–10pm.

The Boathouse at Breach Inlet ★ SEAFOOD   This rustic seafood restaurant overlooks the marina and remains a popular local staple. The menu combines fresh seafood with Lowcountry cooking; there's plenty of crab, lobster, and shrimp, but also sweet jalapeño hushpuppies, steaks, spicy shrimp and grits, and stewed okra. Arrive early for an aperitif on the rooftop bar, which boasts spectacular ocean views. The boathouse itself is an artfully designed replica of a typical early 20th-century coastal South Carolina building. The rowboats hanging from the ceiling are the real thing, however—some over 100 years old.

101 Palm Blvd. www.boathouserestaurants.com. © **843/886-8000.** Main courses $19–$32. Mon– Thurs 5–10pm, Fri–Sat 5–11pm, Sun 11am–2pm and 5–10pm.

HAMPTON PLANTATION STATE HISTORIC SITE ★★

47 miles NE of Charleston

This elegant Georgian plantation house makes for a fascinating half-day trip, just under 50 miles northeast of downtown Charleston on U.S. 17. The **Hampton Plantation,** 1950 Rutledge Rd., McClellanville, was owned by five generations of the Horry/ Rutledge family from the mid 1700s until 1971. It boomed thanks to rice and indigo, and at its peak in 1790, the plantation owned 340 slaves. Today the grand facade remains but the rooms are bare and unrestored, left as a slightly eerie memorial to antebellum Carolina. Regular 40-minute **guided tours** (adults $8, children ages 6–15 $4, free ages 5 and under), the only way to get inside, provide background and explain some of the architectural details on display. Tours usually take place Saturday and Sunday at 10am, noon, and 2pm; and on Monday, Tuesday, and Friday at noon and 2pm. The grounds also contain nature trails where you might spot the endangered red-cockaded woodpecker or swallow-tail kite. Admission to the park is free. The grounds are open daily April to October 9am to 6pm, and November to March 9am to 5pm.

Visit **www.southcarolinaparks.com/hampton** or call © **843/546-9361** for more information.

GEORGETOWN ★★

61 miles NE of Charleston

A short drive north of Hampton Plantation, the Colonial era comes alive at **Georgetown.** Named after King George II, this enclave of only 9,000 people boasts more than 50 historic homes and buildings dating back as far as 1737. When Elisha Screven laid out the town in 1729, he couldn't have known that it would become a lively shopping enclave. Masted ships sailed from this riverfront, bound for England with their cargoes of indigo, rice, timber, and "king cotton." You can take a leisurely stroll along the **Harbor Walk,** tour the antebellum homes, or dine at some of my favorite spots. Georgetown is rarely crowded with visitors. Located 12 miles from the Atlantic, this community is South Carolina's third-oldest city.

Essentials
GETTING THERE
From Charleston, it's an easy drive straight up U.S. 17/701 to Georgetown. Greyhound/Southeastern Stages run one bus per day from Charleston to Georgetown (9:15am; 1 hr. 20 min.; $20). The bus returns at 1:05pm. Coast RTA bus #16 runs between Georgetown and Myrtle Beach via Pawleys Island and Murrells Inlet ($1.50 one-way) at least 5 times daily. Visit **www.coastrta.com** or call $\textcircled{c}$ **843/488-0865.**

VISITOR INFORMATION
Providing information about sights, accommodations, and tours, the **Georgetown Chamber of Commerce,** 531 Front St. ($\textcircled{c}$ **800/777-7705** or 843/546-8436; www. georgetownchamber.com), is most helpful. The staff will also provide you with maps and brochures. It's open Monday to Friday 9am to 5pm.

Exploring Georgetown
Georgetown's **Rice Museum ★**, 633 Front St. ($\textcircled{c}$ **843/546-7423;** www.ricemuseum. org), is known locally as the "Town Clock" after the oversized timepiece that dominates the **Old Market Building.** This fascinating museum chronicles the history of the local rice trade from 1750 through dioramas, maps, artifacts, and other exhibits. Next door in old Kaminski Hardware Building, the Maritime Museum Gallery contains the 50-foot-long **Browns Ferry Vessel,** built in the early 1700s and sunk around 1730—it is the oldest vessel on exhibit in the United States (it was discovered in 1976).

The museum is open Monday to Saturday 10am to 4:30pm, and Sunday 11:30am to 3:30pm. Admission is $7 for adults, $5 seniors 60 and over, $3 students and children 6 to 21, and free for children 5 and under.

A short walk away, the **Kaminski House Museum ★**, 1003 Front St. ($\textcircled{c}$ **843/546-7706;** www.kaminskimuseum.org), is a beautiful clapboard Colonial home built around 1769 for wealthy merchant Paul Trapier. Today the elegant interior is notable for its outstanding collection of American and English antiques from the 18th and 19th centuries. Harold and Julia Kaminski purchased the house in 1931, and willed it to the city in 1972. There's also a museum shop with local arts and crafts, and books on the history of Georgetown. Admission is $7 adults, $5 seniors, $3 children 6 to 12, and free for children 5 and under. The museum is open Monday to Saturday 9am to 5pm.

At the junction of Broad and Highmarket streets, **Prince George Winyah Episcopal Church** ($\textcircled{c}$ **843/546-4358;** www.pgwinyah.com), 300 Broad St., was built between 1740 and 1755 with brick from English ships' ballast (the steeple was added in 1824). The church was occupied by British troops during the Revolutionary War and by Union troops during the Civil War. The latter occupation resulted in a great deal of damage. The English stained glass behind the rebuilt altar was once part of a slaves' chapel on the nearby Hagley Plantation. In the churchyard is one of the state's oldest cemeteries, with the earliest marker dating back to 1767. Sanctuary tours run March to October, Monday to Friday 11am to 4pm. Admission is free, but donations are welcome.

Where to Stay
Mansfield Plantation ★★★   Step back in time at this old rice plantation, established way back in 1718 on the banks of the Black River. The house lies at the end of "Oak Alley," a long avenue with large live-oak trees draped in moss. Beyond lies an original encampment of slave cabins, church, and slave school house. Rooms

GEORGETOWN'S great OUTDOORS

CANOEING & KAYAKING Black **River Outdoors Center** at Kensington Gardens, U.S. 701, 3 miles north of Georgetown (tickets at ℂ **800/979-3370;** or www.blackriveroutdoors.com), offers two- ($35), 4- ($55), and 6-hour ($75) Guided Kayak EcoTours of the Salt Marsh, Cypress Swamp, or Sandy Island. Full-day canoe rentals cost $50, with kayaks going for $35/day.

GOLF One of the popular Georgetown championship courses, **Wedgefield Plantation ★**, just north of Georgetown (ℂ **843/546-8587**), is on the site of a former Black River rice plantation and has wildlife in abundance. It was designed by Porter Gibson in 1972. Greens fees are $19 to $32, including

cart. The signature hole is the par-4 14th, with both tee and approach shots over water.

RIVER CRUISES Rover Tours (ℂ **843/546-8822;** www.roverboattours. com) operate from Georgetown Harbor. The *Carolina Rover*, a 40-foot pontoon boat, offers a 3-hour trip including a docked stop on North Island, home to Winyah Bay Lighthouse. The 45-minute excursion to this rather remote island includes a nature walk and beach shelling. Trips usually leave three times a day, Monday to Saturday, but the schedule depends on the tides (call ahead). It costs $33 for adults and $22 for children 11 and under.

at Mansfield are tastefully decorated in period style, but the breakfasts are the real highlight, served in a fabulous dining room crammed with antiques. Everything is good, but the stuffed French toast is sublime. The indefatigable Kathryn Green is a wonderful host and will bend over backwards to make your stay a happy one. The house is around a 10-minutes' drive from central Georgetown. The plantation served as the backdrop for scenes from movie *The Patriot* (2000).

1776 Mansfield Rd., Georgetown, SC 29440. www.mansfieldplantation.com. ℂ **843/546-6961.** 9 units. $150–$200 double. **Amenities:** Breakfast room; BBQ grill; library; free bikes; free Wi-Fi.

Shaw House Bed and Breakfast ★ Experience true southern hospitality in this enticing early Colonial American home. Congenial innkeepers Mary and Joe Shaw are knowledgeable hosts, and their rooms are exquisitely decked out in period furnishings, four posters, and drapes. The house overflows with antiques and can seem cluttered, but the overall effect is charming—the view over the old rice fields adds to the ambience.

613 Cypress Court, Georgetown, SC 29440. www.bbonline.com/sc/shawhouse. ℂ **843/546-9663.** 3 units. $100 double. Additional person $15. Rates include full breakfast. **Amenities:** Breakfast room; library; free bikes; free Wi-Fi.

Where to Dine

Alfresco Bistro ★ ITALIAN Locals love this tiny Italian gem, offering an appetizing break from Lowcountry cuisine. Great location right on the water, with a large outdoor dining area and patio, and warm, mustard-colored walls (the former bank building dates back to around 1919). Local ingredients are used throughout—think wild mushroom lobster bisque, goat-cheese truffles, mac and cheese with lobster, and poached Atlantic salmon over Mediterranean orzo.

812 Front St. ℂ **843/344-3869.** Main courses $10–$15. Mon–Sat 11am–10pm.

River Room ★★ SEAFOOD   Expect generous portions of fresh seafood at this popular joint; with its blend of local and international dishes, the River Room offers the best of casual Southern coastal dining. The signature shrimp and grits with smoked sausage is always good, but the shrimp and scallop pasta is also stuffed with seafood. The Carolina grouper is the best of the fresh fish, served blackened with basil cream sauce. The structure itself was completed in 1888 as the J.B. Steele Building, a commercial property for dry goods and groceries; the restaurant opened here 100 years later. The historic ambience is maintained with the original walls, hardwood floors, and a selection of nautical and early 20th-century antiques, while the dining room actually extends 50 feet over the Sampit River, affording spectacular views of the harbor. Don't miss the restaurants' giant reef aquarium, crammed with marine life.

801 Front St. www.riverroomgeorgetown.com. © **843/527-4110.** Main courses $10–$25. Mon–Sat 11am–2:30pm and 5–10pm.

Thomas Cafe ★ LOWCOUNTRY   There's been a restaurant here since 1929, and this 1950s-style diner, replete with cozy wooden booths, black-and-white checkered floor, and a long counter with stools, is a popular local spot for breakfast and light lunches. Stick with classics such as the fried green tomatoes, Southern-fried flounder, fried chicken, and rice and gravy. It also knocks out great sandwiches—try the Philly cheese steak. Most dishes are less than $10 and an excellent deal.

703 Front St. © **843/546-7776.** Breakfast $6–$9, lunch specials $8, sandwiches $6–$9. Mon–Fri 7am–2pm, Sat 7am–noon.

PAWLEYS ISLAND

73 miles NE of Downtown Charleston

Just 13 miles north of Georgetown and one of the oldest resorts in the South, **Pawleys Island** has been a popular hideaway for vacationers for more than 3 centuries. Over the years, everyone from George Washington to Franklin Roosevelt to Winston Churchill has visited. During the 18th century, rice planters made the island their summer home so that they could escape the heat and humidity of the Lowcountry and enjoy ocean breezes. Storms have battered the island, but many of the weather-beaten old properties remain, earning the island the appellation "arrogantly shabby."

Today the barrier island is less than 4 miles long and mostly just one-house wide, separated from the mainland by a salt marsh and accessible by two short causeways. The **beaches** here are among the best maintained, least polluted, and widest along coastal South Carolina; however, access to public beach areas is severely limited.

Essentials

GETTING THERE

Driving to Pawleys Island from Charleston, just take U.S. 17 N. towards Myrtle Beach. There is no direct bus service, but Coast RTA bus #16 runs to Pawleys Island from Georgetown and Myrtle Beach via Murrells Inlet ($1.50 one-way) at least 5 times daily. Visit **www.coastrta.com** or call © **843/488-0865.**

Exploring Pawleys Island

Many visitors come to Pawleys Island just to shop for handicrafts, such as the famous Pawleys Island **rope hammock.** The best place to purchase one is the **Original Hammock Shop** (© **800/332-3490** or 843/237-9122), 10880 Ocean

golf ON PAWLEYS ISLAND

Caledonia Golf & Fish Club, 369 Caledonia Dr., Pawleys Island (✆ **800/483-6800** or 843/237-3675; www.fishclub.com), opened in 1993. Tees are marked by replicas of native waterfowl that inhabit the old rice fields. The centerpiece of the course is a clubhouse, a replica of a 1700s colonial plantation house. Architect Mike Strantz, a former assistant to Tom Fazio, took care to highlight the natural beauty of the area: huge, centuries-old live oaks, pristine natural lakes, scenic views of the old rice fields, and glimpses of native wildlife. Greens fees are $94 to $160.

Hwy., in operation since 1938. It's open year-round Monday to Saturday from 9:30am to 6pm and on Sunday from noon to 5pm. At various plantation stores in the area (known as the hammock shops), you'll also find pewter, miniature doll furniture, clothing, candles, Christmas items, brass, and china. The only other real sight on the island is the **Litchfield Plantation,** a stately manor house (ca. 1740) at the end of a quarter-mile avenue of live oaks (24 Ave. of the Oak), making it oft-photographed (the house itself is closed to the public; the hotel closed in 2012). In the island's **Historic District** you can view a number of signs with historic information about the antebellum homes here, though none are open to visitors (most are available for summer rental, though).

Where to Stay

Litchfield Beach & Golf Resort ★★ This 600-acre family-friendly resort offers a plethora of activities, from kayaking and biking along the Waccamaw Neck Bikeway, to relaxing at the pool with lazy river, and simply lounging on the beach. You can choose from suites, condominiums, villas, and houses with a variety of sizes and layouts, but all feature period-style decor (flowery bedspreads and drapes, Victorian lampshades, carved wood beds, and old prints on the walls), microwave, fridge, and coffee facilities. If the on-site health club featuring indoor pool, steam room, gym, table tennis, and racquetball isn't enough, guests can enjoy discounts at 4 nearby golf courses.

14276 Ocean Hwy. www.litchfieldbeach.com. ✆ **888/766-4633.** 950 units. $79–$357 suite. 3-night minimum stay July–Aug. Free parking. **Amenities:** Restaurant; bar; babysitting; health club; Jacuzzi; three 18-hole golf courses; sauna; 17 tennis courts (lit); free Wi-Fi.

Pelican Inn ★★★ Wonderful cypress wood property built just off the beach in the 1840s, best appreciated by veteran B&B lovers who enjoy family-style communal meals. Breakfast and lunch are served on the porch, featuring high-quality Lowcountry cuisine and plenty of socializing. There are hammocks scattered all over the property, a boardwalk to the beach, and beach chairs and boogie boards provided. Rooms are cozy (and air-conditioned), though some share a bathroom—make sure you book an en-suite room if this is important. Perhaps unsurprisingly in this part of the world, a ghost tale is associated with the inn, notably the tale of the "Gray Man"—ask the owners. The inn is open only from Memorial Day weekend through Labor Day weekend.

506 Myrtle Ave., Pawleys Island, SC 29585. www.pawleyspelican.com. ✆ **843/325-7522.** 8 units. $250 double room. Rates include full breakfast and lunch. **Amenities:** Dining room; BBQ grill; bike rentals; free Wi-Fi.

Sea View Inn ★ This old-fashioned beach house oozes local charm, though it's not for everyone: the property is a little frayed around the edges, there are no TVs or phones in the rooms, and no air-conditioning (not a great option in summer). Yet the rooms are spotless, the staff always helpful, and the private beach is spectacular—lounge in a rocking chair on the veranda to enjoy the view. It's a bit like staying in your Southern grandma's house, circa 1950 (it's actually been here since 1937). All three meals are served as part of the standard plan (food charge is just $20/day), and the food is pretty good—no-nonsense Lowcountry cuisine cooked by the no-nonsense kitchen staff. Note that showers are shared in the main inn, and Wi-Fi is only available in one corner of the back lounge.

414 Myrtle Ave., Pawleys Island, SC 29585. www.seaviewinn.com. ℭ **843/237-4253.** 20 units. $130–$275 double. **Amenities:** Dining room; free Wi-Fi (in lounge only).

Where to Dine

Frank's Restaurant ★ LOWCOUNTRY/INTERNATIONAL Local institution Frank's Restaurant opened in 1988 in the old Marlow's Supermarket building (here since the 1940s). The elegant interior is enhanced by an original antique mahogany bar, handcrafted in the late 19th century. Start with the classic she-crap soup before sampling the pan-fried cornmeal-encrusted grouper, or the grilled-shrimp skewers with coconut rice fritters. In 1992, Frank's Outback opened behind the main restaurant in Frank Marlow's mother's old house; the best feature is the huge covered outdoor seating area, set in a garden under a canopy of trees. The menu is similar but a little more creative (think house-made jalapeño-pimento cheese with fried wonton chips), and there's also section of wood-fired pizzas.

10434 Ocean Hwy. www.franksandoutback.com. ℭ **843/237-3030.** Main courses $23–$39; Frank's Outback main courses $27–$37; pizza $15. Mon–Sat 5–9:30pm (Frank's Outback closed Mon).

MURRELLS INLET

81 miles NE of Downtown Charleston

Murrells Inlet, "the seafood capital of South Carolina," is often invaded by Myrtle Beach hordes in quest of a seafood dinner. To join them, just take U.S. 17 north from Georgetown and prepare to dig in. This centuries-old fishing village has witnessed a parade of humanity, from Confederate blockade runners to federal gunboats, from bootleggers to today's pleasure craft. The island was also visited by Edward Teach, better known as Blackbeard. During the 1600s, Blackbeard's ship allegedly left a sailor on Drunken Jack Island, just off Murrells Inlet, by accident; when the ship returned 2 years later, the crew discovered the abandoned sailor's bones bleaching in the sun, along with 32 empty casks of rum.

In addition to its seafood restaurants (a few are recommended in this chapter), Murrells Inlet is home to **Brookgreen Gardens,** one of the most-visited attractions along the Grand Strand.

Essentials

GETTING THERE

Driving from Charleston, just take U.S. 17 N. towards Myrtle Beach. There is no direct bus service, but Coast RTA bus #16 runs from Murrells Inlet to Myrtle Beach, and to Georgetown via Pawleys Island (all $1.50 one-way) at least 5 times daily. See www.coastrta.com or call ℭ **843/488-0865.**

Exploring Murrells Inlet

Some 3 miles south along U.S. 17 from Murrells Inlet, towards Pawleys Island, **Brookgreen Gardens ★★**, 1931 Brookgreen Dr. (© 843/237-4218; www.brook green.org), is a world-class sculpture garden and wildlife park that's a source of enormous civic pride to virtually everyone in South Carolina. It occupies the low-lying flatlands of what functioned 200 years ago as a rice plantation. After the destruction of the original plantation house, the gardens were laid out in 1931 to accommodate the world's largest collection of American garden sculptures, all crafted between 1850 and the present. Archer Milton Huntington and his wife, the sculptor Anna Hyatt Huntington, planned the garden walks in the shape of a butterfly with outspread wings. All walks lead back to the central space, a contemporary building that occupies the site of the original plantation house. On opposite sides of this space are the Small Sculpture Gallery and the original plantation kitchen, now the site of one of the snack bars. An outstanding feature within the wildlife park is the **Cypress Bird Sanctuary,** a 90-foot-tall aviary housing species of wading birds within half an acre of cypress swamp. The curators of this garden recommend spending at least 2 hours wandering along its byways. Terrain is flat and makes for easy walking. The price of admission grants access to the park and garden for 7 consecutive days.

Admission is $14 for adults, $12 for seniors 65 and older, $7 for children 4 to 12, and free for ages 3 and under. Hours are daily 9:30am to 5pm. In April, the gardens remain open until 8pm. The gardens are closed December 25.

Huntington Beach State Park ★, just across U.S. 17 from Brookgreen Gardens (© 843/237-4440; www.southcarolinaparks.com), offers one of the best **beaches** along the Grand Strand. Entrance is $5 for adults, $3 for seniors, $3 for children 6 to 15, and free for children 5 and under. The 2,500-acre park has a wide, firm beach, which is slightly orange. Anna Hyatt Huntington and her husband, Archer, the creators of Brookgreen Gardens, once owned this coastal wilderness. The park is the site of their winter home and Iberian-style castle, **Atalaya** (daily 9am–5pm), built between 1931 and 1933. Admission to the house is an additional $2 (for ages 6 and up). Guided tours (45 min.) of Atalaya are offered March to October, while audio tours ($4) are available year round.

In the park are 137 campsites, along with picnic shelters, a boardwalk, terrific birding, bike rentals, and toilets. Swimming in specially marked sections is excellent, as is fishing from the jetty at the north side of the beach, or crabbing along the boardwalk. Campsites are rented on a first-come, first-served basis, at a cost of $21 to $41 per day (price depends on whether the particular site has electricity or water). The park is open daily April to October 6am to 10pm, December to February 6am to 6pm, and March and November 6am to 8pm.

Where to Dine

Capt. Dave's Dockside ★ SEAFOOD/SOUTHERN
One of the many seafood stalwarts along the waterfront and "Marsh Walk," with the best seating overlooking the water. The food is good (it's the only spot with a charcoal-burning grill), though like all the restaurants here, a little pricey—you are primarily paying for location. Signature dishes worth sampling include fish and grits (filet of mahi-mahi with Andouille sausage gravy), Carolina crab cakes, and grouper dishes, though these are the most expensive. Save room for the New Orleans bread pudding and Key lime pie.

On the Waterfront (4037 Hwy. 17 Business). www.davesdockside.com. © 843/651-5850. Main courses $16–$33. Mon–Sat 4pm–midnight, Sun 10am–2pm.

Dead Dog Saloon ★ AMERICAN/SEAFOOD Enjoy the spectacular views from this waterfront bar and restaurant, the place to be if you want to eat good food and have a good time. You'll be regaled by comedians and singers most nights, with the packed bar becoming pleasantly rowdy as the evening wears on, especially weekends. Great seafood (including tasty fish and chips) and hush puppies, of course, but also juicy burgers, steaks, barbecue, friendly servers, and live bands (mostly alternative rock and country). Half-priced drinks during happy hour 4–6pm Monday to Friday.

On the Waterfront (4079 Hwy. 17 Business). www.deaddogsaloon.com. ℂ **843/651-0664.** Main courses $20–$27. Daily 7am–1am.

MYRTLE BEACH

Named for its abundance of crape myrtle trees, **Myrtle Beach** is the largest, liveliest, and most developed beach resort along the Grand Strand, with the greatest number of attractions, entertainment facilities, and restaurants. In stark contrast to Charleston, the tone here is that of a family resort, with many hotels providing programs and diversions for children. The range of activities on offer is simply overwhelming. In addition to boating and a wealth of watersports, fishing is first-rate, whether you cast your line from the surf (permitted all along the beach), a public pier, or a "head boat"—charter boats that are available at marinas up and down the Strand. Golfers can swing a club at any of 120 courses (high season for golf is from February to November), while tennis enthusiasts can whack balls at more than 200 public and private tennis courts along the Grand Strand. While environmentalists are concerned that all this development puts the region's natural beauty at risk—and longtime promoters fear that Myrtle Beach's family-friendly atmosphere may be threatened—corporate entrepreneurs continue pouring money into the area, and the region's metropolitan population of around 330,000 continues to grow.

Essentials

GETTING THERE **Myrtle Beach International Airport,** on Harrelson Boulevard, 3 miles southwest of downtown (ℂ 843/448-1589; www.flymyrtlebeach.com), is a major hub for **Spirit Airlines** (ℂ 800/772-7117; www.spiritair.com), with direct flights from Boston, New York, Fort Lauderdale, and numerous seasonal destinations. There is also scheduled air service via **Delta/Delta Connection** (ℂ 800/221-1212; www.delta.com), **American Eagle** (ℂ 800/433-7300; www.aa.com), **Allegiant Air** (ℂ 702/505-8888; www.allegiantair.com), **United Express** (ℂ 800/864-8331; www.united.com), and seasonally from Toronto via **WestJet** (ℂ 888/937-8538; www.westjet.com) and **Porter Airlines** (ℂ 888/619-8622; www.flyporter.com). For cities farther west than Chicago you'll need to change planes at least once.

Many hotels operate free shuttles to and from the airport, but taxis are always available (fares by meter). **Coast RTA** (ℂ **843/438-3747**) runs bus #747N and #747S between the airport, Ocean Blvd. and the Sheraton Myrtle Beach Convention Center and Hotel. The fare is $7 one-way or $10 round-trip.

All the major car rental companies have desks at the airport. The U.S. 17 Bypass runs north and south, about 2 miles inland from the Grand Strand's coastline. U.S. 17 Business (also known as the North or South King's Hwy.) runs about a half-mile inland from the coastline, through the most congested neighborhoods of Myrtle Beach. Direct access to most of the highway networks of inland South Carolina is via U.S. Highway 501, which runs eastward to Myrtle Beach from I-95. The city is around 95 miles and 2 hours by car from Charleston.

MYRTLE beaches

The main attraction here, and the reason people started visiting in the first place, is the **beach.** Myrtle Beach sand is mostly hard packed and the color of brown sugar, to which it's often compared. During the resort's rapid growth during the 1980s and 1990s, city planners deliberately interspersed residential zones with commercial zones, thereby relieving clusters of honky-tonk with carefully landscaped communities of private homes and condos.

The beach has lifeguards and plenty of fast-food joints. Amazingly, there are no public toilets. South Carolina law, however, obligates hotels to allow beach buffs to use their facilities. (Many male beachgoers don't bother to go inside the hotels but use walls instead—a habit that has provoked endless local-newspaper comment.)

At the southern tier of the beach, **Myrtle Beach State Park,** 4401 South King's Hwy.,

Myrtle Beach (© **843/238-5325;** www. myrtlebeachstatepark.net), offers 312 acres of pine woods and access to a sandy beach. Admission to the park is $5 for adults, $3 for children 6 to 15, and free for children 5 and under. Seniors age 65 and over who are residents of South Carolina pay an entrance fee of $3. The park contains toilets and picnic tables, and it's possible to fish from Myrtle Beach pier for $5 for ages 16 and older, $3 for South Carolina seniors, and $3 for children ages 6 to 15. The park is full of nature trails and offers 302 campsites, priced from $31 to $52 per night for full-service campsites, $21 to $42 per night for electrical and water (but not sewage) connections. Simple campsites with none of the above-mentioned hookups rent for $18 to $31 per night. Free Wi-Fi is available for overnight guests. The park is open March to November daily 6am to 10pm, and December to February daily 6am to 8pm.

Buses from **Greyhound** (© **800/231-2222;** www.greyhound.com) and **Southeastern Stages** (© **404/591-2780;** www.southeasternstages.com) arrive and depart from **J & D Travel,** 511 7th Ave. N (© **843/448-2472**), just 4 blocks from the seafront. Buses from Charleston run just once a day, departing at 9:15am, travelling via Georgetown, and arriving in Myrtle Beach at 11:35am. The bus makes the return journey at 12:05pm.

Warning: Although their borders blend almost imperceptibly, the communities of Myrtle Beach and North Myrtle Beach maintain distinctly different systems of numerating their roads and streets. Hundred-dollar cab fares have been racked up by passengers who weren't clear about which of the two communities they were going to.

VISITOR INFORMATION The **Myrtle Beach Area Chamber of Commerce Visitor Center** is at 1200 N. Oak St. (© **800/356-3016** or 843/626-7444; www.visit myrtlebeach.com), open Monday to Friday 8:30am to 5pm, Saturday 9am to 5pm, and Sunday 10am to 2pm (from Labor Day to Apr, the center closes at 2pm on Saturday and all day Sunday). The **Airport Welcome Center** (same contacts) is open daily 8am to 7pm. The online "Official Myrtle Beach Area Vacation Guide" is jam-packed with specific area information (visit the website).

Exploring Myrtle Beach

The Art Museum of Myrtle Beach ★★
Formally the Franklin G. Burroughs-Simeon B. Chapin Art Museum, this little gem offers a dose of culture—art with a beach view—for those rainy afternoons. Inside this grand old beach villa dating back

to 1924 are 2 floors and 10 galleries with exhibitions that change throughout the year, anything from local paintings to Australian Aboriginal art. In the small educational center you can learn about local history and watch a video on the development of Myrtle Beach. Stop by the gift shop to buy handicrafts and prints by southern artists such as Jonathan Green.

3100 South Ocean Blvd. www.myrtlebeachartmuseum.org. (☎ **843/238-2510.** Free admission (suggested donation $5). Tues–Sat 10am–4pm, Sun 1–4pm.

Broadway at the Beach ★★★ This is one of the biggest, most fun, and most-visited shopping, dining, and entertainment venues in South Carolina. It sprawls across a vast area around 23-acre Lake Broadway in the heart of town. Some of its most notable features include the pyramid-shaped Hard Rock Cafe, as well as Margaritaville, MagiQuest, WonderWorks, and Ripley's Aquarium (see reviews below). There are more than 150 shops, 24 restaurants and food outlets, 3 hotels, a 16-screen movie theater, a gaggle of theme-oriented bars (many with big-screen TVs for sports-watching), and a gaggle of late-night bars and dance clubs that includes everything from country-western line dancing to salsa.

1325 Celebrity Circle (by Route 17 Bypass, btw. 22nd and 29th blvds). www.broadwayatthebeach. com. (☎ **843/444-3200.** Jan–Feb daily 10am–6pm; March–May and Sept daily 10am–9pm; June–Aug daily 10am–11pm; Oct–Dec Mon–Sat 10am–9pm, Sun 10am–6pm.

Family Kingdom Amusement Park ★★ This is one of the declining numbers of old-fashioned sea-front amusement parks, replete with roller coasters, carousels, cotton candy, and the **Giant Wheel**—at over 100 feet, the second-largest Ferris wheel in South Carolina. A few of the park's attractions were salvaged from the Pavilion, a now-defunct venue that evokes nostalgia in the hearts of many local residents. The majority of the park's 37 rides, however, are high-tech enough to generate excitement, and traditional enough to still evoke memories of Clarence the Clown and spun-sugar candy. The 2,400 foot, figure-eight **Swamp Fox** wooden roller coaster is a classic.

Open since 1966, the site now covers some 16 acres and includes the **Splashes Oceanfront Water Park,** just across Ocean Boulevard from the main amusement park. This includes two speed slides, eight child-friendly water slides, lots of splashing fountains, water flumes, and an interconnected series of lazy river–style swimming pools.

300 S. Ocean Blvd. www.family-kingdom.com. (☎ **843/626-3447.** Free admission to water park and amusement park with amusement park rides $2–$6 per person; amusement park all-day ride pass $27 for all ages; water park all-day pass $22 for persons 48 in. and taller, $9 for persons shorter than 48 in.; 1-day combo pass for both amusement park and water park $37 per person. Water park late May–Aug daily 10am–6pm; amusement park Apr–Sept daily usually 4pm–midnight.

Horry County Museum ★ Myrtle Beach is in Horry County (pronounced "O-ree"), with the small city of Conway on the Waccamaw River (15 miles northwest of the beach) acting as the county seat. Other than strolling the pleasant Riverwalk here, lined with good restaurants, it's worth popping into the county museum, housed in the old Burroughs School built in 1905. The museum is small but contains a fascinating array of exhibits on the area, including the surprising revelation that alligators and even black bears lurk in the nearby woods and creeks. Displays also focus on the southeastern woodland cultures that dominated the coastal plain of South Carolina long before Europeans arrived, and shed light on county namesake Peter Horry (1743–1815), the son of French Huguenot parents and a local hero of the American Revolutionary War.

805 Main St., at 9th Ave., Conway. www.horrycountymuseum.org. ℂ **843/365-3596.** Free admission. Tues–Sat 9am–5pm.

L.W. Paul Living History Farm ★★

Managed by the Horry County Museum (see above), this 17-acre working farm recreates life in rural South Carolina circa 1900 to 1955. Though none of the buildings are original (local businessman Larry Paul funded its construction in 2006), the wooden outhouses and period interiors are faithful replicas, and the activities on offer are lots of fun. Kids will especially enjoy picking peanuts, shelling corn, grinding grits, milking cows, pumping water, spinning cotton, and making butter. Costumed guides plow with mules, make lye soap, work at the blacksmith shop, cure meat, pick and string tobacco, and cook cane syrup in huge, bubbling vats.

2279 Harris Shortcut Rd., at Hwy. 701 N., Conway. www.horrycountymuseum.org. ℂ **843/365-3596.** Free admission. Tues–Sat 9am–4pm. Closed on government holidays.

MagiQuest ★★

Here's how it works: You (and presumably the children who accompany you) will select a magic wand (which you get to keep forever), after which the adventures begin as you learn how to harness its power. Within a 20,000-square-foot space, you can befriend a pixie, learn from an ancient wizard, battle a goblin, outwit a dragon, and even take part in a "duel," producing the kinds of effects of which Harry Potter—at any stage of his development as a wizard—would be proud. The theme is medieval, Celtic, and mystical, with plenty of problems on-site for the solving, and lots of opportunities for the power of youth and truth to triumph over the forces of darkness and evil. Suspend disbelief, bring a sense of make-believe, and marvel at the way someone has found to harness the ongoing attraction for myths, lore, legend, the supernatural, and superheroes.

At Broadway at the Beach, 1185 Celebrity Circle. www.magiquest.com. ℂ **843/916-1800.** Admission for all ages $26 (75 min.), $35 (90 min.), $40 (100 min.); guests without wands can enter for $5; discounts available for returning guests; grandparents accompanying their grandchildren and children 4 and under free admission. Mon–Fri noon–8pm, Sat–Sun 10am–8pm.

Myrtle Waves Water Park ★

Myrtle Beach is *hot* in summer, so it's little wonder that June to August this park is crammed with families escaping the heat. The state's largest water park has 1.2 million gallons and some 20 acres of curves, waves, and swerves. Some 200,000 visitors come annually for more than 30 rides and various attractions, including an Ocean in Motion Wave pool; the LayZee River, a slow, 3-mph ride around the park; and Bubble Bay, a 7,000-foot leisure pool for toddlers with a trio of cascading water umbrellas. Other amusements include a Saturation Station with splashes, slides, and waterfalls, and Turbo Twisters, the world's tallest tubular slides (10 stories high).

3000 10th Ave. N. (U.S. 17 Bypass at Mr. Joe White Ave.). www.myrtlewaves.com. ℂ **843/913-9250.** Admission $24 for those 42 in. and over, $19 for 41 in. and under; discounts after 3pm. Parking $2, lockers $6. June to mid-Aug daily 10am–7pm, late May and mid-Aug to early Sept Sat–Sun and some weekdays 10am–5pm (call ahead for specific days).

Ripley's Aquarium ★★

This is the most-visited attraction in South Carolina, and deservedly so. Visitors are surrounded on all sides by menacing 10-foot sharks as they travel through Dangerous Reef, a 750,000-gallon tank. The question always asked is why don't these monsters gobble up the other fish in the tank. The answer: They're so well fed they don't bother. Most of the habitats in the various holding tanks are saltwater. The only freshwater exhibit is the Rio Amazon, displaying fearsome piranhas, aruanas, and pacu. You can spend at least 4 hours here, enjoying such pleasures as Rainbow Rock, with its view of thousands of brilliantly colored fish from the Pacific. Children are drawn to the Sea-for-Yourself Discovery Center, an interactive, multimedia playground, and "Pirates: Fact and Folklore," an exhibit about the privateers who once sheltered themselves in South Carolina's coves and inlets. Dive shows and marine education sessions are presented hourly.

At Broadway on the Beach, 1110 Celebrity Circle. www.ripleysaquarium.com. ✆ **800/734-8888** or 843/916-0888. Admission $21 ages 12 and over, $12 ages 6–11, $5 ages 2–5, free ages 1 and under. June–Aug daily 9am–10pm, Sept–May daily 9am–9pm.

SkyWheel Myrtle Beach ★★   For a bird's-eye view of the beach, take a ride on this revolving behemoth. The 187-foot-tall Ferris wheel opened on the new 1.2 mile-long Oceanfront Boardwalk in 2011, offering sensational views along the Grand Strand. One ride comprises three smooth loops (8–10 min.) inside one of 42 glass-enclosed, air-conditioned gondolas (2–6 people per gondola). For a really romantic date, rent the "VIP" gondola for a mere $50, where you'll enjoy glass floors, leather seats, and a double ride (six loops).

1110 N Ocean Blvd. www.myrtlebeachskywheel.com. ✆ **843/839-9200.** Admission $13 adults, $9 children 3–11, free children 2 and under. Sun–Thurs 11am–7pm, Fri–Sat 11am–9pm (hours change seasonally, so call ahead to confirm).

WonderWorks ★★   Kids love this hands-on learning experience, beginning with the crazy-looking building itself—it's upside down. Inside are over 100 high-tech games, interactive exhibits, and simulations that will keep kids enthralled for half a day. The activities are designed as a fun way to introduce scientific principles—the Hurricane Shack recreates 71-mph winds to mimic hurricanes, a gallery of paintings that contain optical illusions, and a tank of freezing-cold water you can test with your hand to experience what the Atlantic was like the day the Titanic sank. The displays end with an indoor ropes course (included in general admission), and the Lazer Tag Game, which is extra.

Broadway at the Beach, 1313 Celebrity Circle. www.wonderworksonline.com/myrtle-beach. ✆ **843/626-9962.** Admission $24 adults, $15 seniors 55 and over and kids 4–12. Sun–Thurs 10am–9pm, Fri–Sat 10am–10pm (hours vary by season, so call ahead to confirm).

Golf

Golf is one of the major attractions of Myrtle Beach—indeed, this is arguably America's greatest golf vacation destination. Golfers can tee off at more than 100 **championship golf courses ★★★ (www.mbn.com),** making it possible to play a different course every day for 3 months straight. Many local courses host major professional and amateur tournaments. Some of the most visible tournaments attract huge interest locally; examples include the PGA Tour Superstore World Amateur Handicap Championship, in late August; the Palmetto High Golf Championship, held in March and again in September, wherein golf teams from high schools throughout the country compete against each other; and the Veterans Golf Classic, a May event that's open only to active military personnel and qualified veterans.

Variety is a contributing factor to the success and popularity of Myrtle Beach and Grand Strand golf courses, which come in many shapes, sizes, and degrees of difficulty. Courses have been designed by some of the best-known names in golf: Jack Nicklaus, Arnold Palmer, Rees Jones, Tom Fazio, Gary Player, Don Ross, Dan Maple, Tom Jackson, and Pete Dye.

Ligers, Tigers & Bubbles

For a break from all that craziness along the beach, animal lovers should check out the two unusual attractions offered by **Myrtle Beach Safari** (✆ **843/361-4552;** www.myrtlebeachsafari.com). The main event is the **Wild Encounters Tour,** a guided walk through a 50-acre preserve of 60 big cats and other exotic creatures. You can meet and play with great apes, watch tigers swim and run at full speed, hold a tiger cub, and meet "Bubbles" the African elephant. This is also the only place in the world where you get up close and personal with a Liger (a mix of tiger and lion). It's not cheap: tours are $239 per person (the minimum age for the tour is 6), though purchasing a photo at the Preservation Station in Barefoot Landing (see below) gives a $40 discount on the tour fee. Tours run 3 to 5 days a week from mid-March to mid-October, beginning at 10am and lasting approximately 3 hours. The preserve is 17 miles south of Barefoot Landing, but for the privacy of the animals, exact directions are only given to those who have tour reservations.

Alternatively, you can visit the **T.I.G.E.R.S. Preservation Station** (✆ **843/361-4552**) at Barefoot Landing, 4898 South Highway 17, North Myrtle Beach. Here you can also meet some of the animals up close, typically tiger cubs or young chimps and orangutans. Entrance is free, but photo sessions are $79 for any group of up to five. All proceeds from photo sessions and portrait sales go directly to support international wildlife conservation projects through the Rare Species Fund (www.rarespecies fund.org). The station is also open mid-March to mid-October, though times vary.

Golf-course architects have taken care to protect the habitats of indigenous wildlife. Players find themselves in the midst of towering Carolina pines or giant live oaks draped in Spanish moss. Some courses overlook huge bluffs with the Atlantic Ocean or Intracoastal Waterway in the background. Some of the courses feature such unusual attractions as a private airstrip adjoining a clubhouse, a cable car that crosses the Intracoastal Waterway, and alligators lurking in water hazards. Some courses are built on the grounds of historic rice plantations, which offer Old South atmosphere.

Although golf is played year-round, spring and autumn are the busiest (and most expensive) seasons. Many golf packages include room, board, and greens fees. For information, call **Myrtle Beach Golf Holiday** (✆ **800/845-4653;** www.golfholiday. com).

Aberdeen Country Club, 701 Bucks Trail, Longs, S.C. 9, North Myrtle Beach (✆ **843/399-2660** or 843/235-6061; www.playaberdeen.com), is a 27-hole course designed by Tom Jackson, charging greens fees of $31 to $67. Along the banks of the Waccamaw River, this course has Bermuda greens, along with a pro shop and a practice area with a driving range.

Arcadian Shores Golf Club, 701 Hilton Rd. (✆ **866/326-5275** or 843/449-5217; www.arcadianshores.com), an 18-hole, par-72 course opened in 1974, was created by noted golf architect Rees Jones. Just 5 miles north of Myrtle Beach off U.S. 17, the course has bent-grass greens winding through a stately live-oak grove. Electric carts are required, and greens fees are $31 to $67.

Azalea Sands Golf Club, 2100 U.S. 17 S., North Myrtle Beach (✆ **800/253-2312** or 843/272-6191; www.azaleasandsgc.com), opened in 1972. The 18-hole course

Myrtle Beach

sporting MYRTLE BEACH

FISHING Because of the warming temperature of the Gulf Stream, fishing is good off Myrtle Beach from early spring until around Christmas. You can pursue king mackerel, spadefish, amberjack, barracuda, sea bass, and Spanish mackerel, along with grouper and red snapper. Great fishing is available from **Crazy Sister Marina,** 4123 Business Highway 17, at Murrells Inlet (© **866/557-3474** or 843/651-3676; www.crazysister.com). Private sport fishing charters are available, while regular trips on the "Head Boat" run from a 4-hour afternoon shark-fishing excursion ($40) to an all-day deep-sea fishing expedition ($84). The rates include rod and reel, bait, tackle, and license. Once a month, between March and November, Crazy Sister hosts the Overnight Gulf Stream fishing expedition for the true fishing enthusiast. The cost of the 25-hour trip, which departs Saturday at 1:30pm and returns Sunday at 2:30pm, is $220. The

rate includes rod and reel, bait, tackle, and license; an electric reel is an additional $20. On this trip, the price of the electric reel may well be worth it.

SAILING & KAYAKING Crazy Sister Marina also offers cruises that afford stunning views of the Grand Strand. The **Saltwater Marsh Adventure** is a 2-hour ecology trip that allows you to see marine life in its true element. Rates are $21 for adults and $15 for children 12 and under. The **Sunset Evening Cruise** along the coast of Myrtle Beach lasts 75 minutes. Rates are $12 for adults and $6 for children under 12 (both outings are free for children 2 and under).

You can rent kayaks and Hobie Cat sailboats at **Sail and Ski,** 515 Hwy. 501, Myrtle Beach (© **843/626-7245**), from April to September. Usually rented only to experienced sailors, the boats cost $35 to $50 per hour. Escorted 2-hour kayak tours through local mangrove swamps are around $60 each.

features white-sand traps and blue lakes. Designed by architect Gene Hamm, it's a popular course for golfers of all handicaps. Greens fees range from $40 to $55.

Beachwood Golf Club, 1520 U.S. 17 S., Crescent Section, North Myrtle Beach (© **800/526-4889** or 843/272-6168; www.beachwoodgolf.com), is another course designed by Gene Hamm. Opened in 1968, it has 18 holes, charging greens fees ranging from $55 to $70. It's a par-72 course with blue tees of 6,844 yards.

Caledonia Golf and Fish Club, 369 Caledonia Dr., Pawleys Island (© **800/483-6800** or 843/237-3675; www.fishclub.com), is set atop what used to be a series of marshy rice paddies, and some of its links are graced with century-old oak trees. This golf course has an intelligent layout favored by pros, and a clubhouse whose architecture was inspired by an antique Lowcountry plantation house. Its only drawback is a location that's about a 30-minute drive south of Myrtle Beach. A flotilla of charter boats and deep-sea fishing pros are associated with this place as well. Greens fees range from $102 to $190.

Grande Dunes ★★, 8700 Golf Village Lane (© **843/315-0333**; www.grandedunes.com/golf), features two of the newer and better courses. The Resort Club is an 18-hole course set on a bluff overlooking the Intracoastal Waterway with panoramic views. Consistently rated as one of the best courses in the nation, it is a par-72 course with numerous elevation changes and wide Bermuda-grass fairways, including 34 acres of lakes. Greens fees are $50 to $141. The adjacent Members Club course was designed by Nick Price, but is off-limits to non-members.

Paddleboard lessons are $120 for 90 minutes, while an introduction to kiteboarding is $99 for 1 hour.

PADDLEBOARDING   To enjoy the up-and-coming pastime of paddleboarding (standup paddling on modified surfboards), contact **Carolina Paddle Co.** (✆ 843/222-3132; www.carolinapaddlecompany.com), 3937 Mega Dr., Unit 78, Myrtle Beach. Private lessons are $85 for 2 hours, or as low as $50 for a group of four people or more. Rentals run from $40 for 4 hours to $60 for 8 hours, and $75 for 24 hours.

TENNIS   The **Myrtle Beach Tennis Center,** 3302 Robert M. Grissom Parkway (✆ 843/918-2440) features a pro shop and 10 courts, eight of which are lighted for night play. Courts are $2 per person, per hour. The center is open Monday to Friday 8am to 9pm, and Saturday 8am to 6:30pm most of the year (reduced hours Dec–Feb). **Grand Dunes**

Tennis Club, U.S. 17 Bypass, across from Dixie Stampede, at Myrtle Beach (✆ 843/449-4486), has 10 composition courts, eight of which are lighted for night play. Courts cost $30 for two people and $50 for four people. There's also an on-site pro shop and fitness room. It's open Monday to Saturday 8:30am to 6pm, and Sunday noon to 5pm.

WATERSPORTS   To rent jet skis and other watersports vehicles, contact **Myrtle Beach Watersports** (✆ 843/497-8848; www.myrtlebeachwatersports.com). It operates out of four locations along the Grand Strand; 4495 Mineola Ave., Little River (North Myrtle Beach; ✆ 843/280-7777); 2100 Little River Neck Rd., North Myrtle Beach (✆ 843/280-8400); Marina at Grande Dunes, 8201 Marina Parkway, in Myrtle Beach (✆ 843/839-2999); and Clarion Inn, 101 Fantasy Harbour Blvd., Myrtle Beach (✆ 843/903-3456).

Legends ★★★, 1500 Legends Dr. (U.S. 501), Myrtle Beach (✆ **800/299-6187** or 843/236-9318, www.legendsgolf.com), features three choices for championship golf designed by Pete Dye and Tom Doak, with a gorgeous clubhouse modeled after the home of the Royal & Ancient Golf Club in Scotland. The complex comprises Legends Heathland, Legends Parkland, and Legends Moorland; the latter boasts many of the most feared holes in Myrtle Beach, in addition to the shortest par four guarded by "Hell's Half-Acre." Greens fees range $49 to $104 at all three courses.

The 36-hole, par-72 **Myrtlewood Golf Club,** 1500 48th Ave. (U.S. 17 Business), North Myrtle Beach (✆ **800/283-3633** or 843/913-4516; www.myrtlewoodgolf.com), was designed by architect Arthur Hills. Bordering the Intracoastal Waterway, the Pine-Hills course is the fourth oldest at Myrtle Beach, measuring 6,640 yards. Also at Myrtlewood, the Palmetto Course is one of the best in the area, with bent-grass putting greens. It stretches for 6,953 yards. Greens fees range $31 to $69.

Where to Stay

The Grand Strand is lined with hotels, motels, condominiums, and cottages, and you'll rarely have trouble finding a room. The highest rates are charged June 15 to Labor Day. Myrtle Beach is becoming more of a year-round destination, however, and you can find great off-season discounts in the winter. Golfers, in particular, take advantage of these low-cost rooms in the off season. The hotels and inns below are recommendations from a very long list.

MODERATE

Hampton Inn Myrtle Beach-Broadway @ The Beach ★★ This popular chain operates several properties in the Myrtle Beach area, but this is my overall favorite. It is not on the beach (the sand is 1 mile away), but it is close to the heart of the action in the sprawling Broadway at the Beach complex. It's also a better choice for couples and singles, especially if you intend to sample the nightlife, which is right on the doorstep (some rooms actually overlook Margaritaville). Rooms are modern, comfy, and fairly standard chain fare, with fast Wi-Fi, 40-inch flatscreen TVs, and plush, queen- or king-size beds.

Broadway at the Beach, 1140 Celebrity Circle, Myrtle Beach, SC 29577. www.hamptoninn.com. ℂ **800/426-7866** or 843/916-0600. 141 units. $119–$239 double. Children 17 and under stay free in parent's room. Rates include deluxe continental breakfast. Free parking. **Amenities:** Breakfast room; bar; exercise room; Jacuzzi; 2 pools (1 indoor); sauna; free Wi-Fi.

Island Vista ★★★ This beachfront property is the pick of the family-friendly resorts, beautifully located in a relatively tranquil residential section of town. All the rooms are clean and comfy, but this place really is all about the views. Standard rooms are dubbed "ocean view," but make sure you ask for a high floor (above six). For a real treat, splurge on an exquisite oceanfront room or suite (not the same as an "ocean view" room), with a balcony; the views day or night are spectacular. Kids will love the indoor and outdoor pools, hot tub, and the lazy river—you can even order pizza from the in-house restaurant and grab free DVD movies from the resort's extensive library. Adults will enjoy the fun Tiki Bar, open in the warmer months. Needless to say, this is not the best option for couples or singles looking for a quiet time, especially during school holidays.

6000 N. Ocean Blvd., Myrtle Beach, SC 29577. www.islandvista.com. ℂ **855/732-6250.** 149 units. $80–$220 double. **Amenities:** Restaurant (see review, p. 109); bar; children's activities; 3 pools (all 3 indoor and outdoor); free Wi-Fi.

Ocean Reef Resort ★★ This is another family resort option, set on a busier stretch of beach than Island Vista, but still apart from the really boisterous section and with slightly cheaper rooms. It has all the water slides, lazy rivers, and colorful toddler pools (indoor and outdoor) to entice the kids, and like Vista it also provides DVD movies for free (however all games in the games room are $1). The oceanfront rooms also offer gorgeous sea views, and most rooms in the hotel were renovated in 2014. Best for families with young kids.

7100 N. Ocean Blvd. (at 71st Ave. N.), Myrtle Beach, SC 29572. www.oceanreefmyrtlebeach.com. ℂ **855/571-0904** or 843/449-4441. 333 units. $69–$230 double. Children 17 and under stay free in parent's room. Discounts (up to 25%) available on the website. Free parking. **Amenities:** Restaurant; bar; children's activities and water playground; exercise room; Jacuzzi; 3 pools (1 indoor); room service; sauna; free Wi-Fi.

INEXPENSIVE

Coral Beach Resort & Suites ★★ This is the affordable family resort, right on the beach but a long walk from the center of town. It's old, but generally clean: try and look at your room before accepting it, if you can; the hotel is gradually renovating but some rooms are still stuck in the 1980s. As with the other beachfront hotels, paying extra for an oceanfront room, as high up as possible, is well worth it. Kids, as always, will love the amenities, from the hot tubs, lazy river, and pools (the outdoor area is most fun), to the pool tables, grill area, and especially the bowling alley.

1105 S. Ocean Blvd., Myrtle Beach, SC 29577. www.coralbeachmyrtlebeachresort.com. (℃ **800/314-8060** or 843/448-8421. 310 units. $44–$155 double. Free parking. **Amenities:** Restaurant; bar; children's activities; exercise room; 4 Jacuzzis (3 indoor); 8 pools (2 indoor) and kiddie water park; spa; free Wi-Fi.

Serendipity Inn ★★★ This is a rare find in Myrtle Beach—a family-run B&B. Phil and Kay Mullins are wonderful hosts and a font of local knowledge, running this small, no-frills place in a quiet, residential area of town just 5 minutes walk from the beach. Standard rooms are small but homey, with comfy beds, fridge, microwave, and TV, while the more spacious apartments are equipped with kitchenettes. Extras include the free use of two bikes, a great hot tub, pool, and DVDs. The breakfast is pretty good, with fruits, a hot dish, pastries, yogurt, and bagels It's popular with "snowbirds" from up north in winter, so book ahead (monthly rates for mini-suites start at just $750).

407 71st Ave. N., Myrtle Beach, SC 29572. www.serendipityinn.com. (℃ **800/762-3229** or 843/449-5268. 15 units. $55–$149 double. Rates include continental breakfast. Take King's Hwy. (U.S. 17 N.) to 71st Ave. N., then turn east toward the ocean. **Amenities:** Breakfast room; babysitting; outdoor pool; hot tub; free bikes; free Wi-Fi.

CAMPING

You'll find plenty of campsites along the Grand Strand, many on the oceanfront (see **Myrtle Beach State Park,** p. 101), and rates drop considerably after Labor Day. Most welcome families, and many don't allow any single person younger than 25. Set directly on the ocean, about halfway between Myrtle Beach and North Myrtle Beach, 430 sites are available at **Apache Family Campground,** 9700 Kings Rd. (℃ **800/553-1749** or 843/449-7323; www.apachefamilycampground.com). Amenities include a swimming pool and recreation pavilion, water, electricity, shade shelters, modern bathhouses with hot water, sewer hookups, laundry, trading post, playground, public telephones, and ice. Reserve here year-round, except for the week of July 4th. Rates are $32 to $64, depending on the season.

Where to Dine

Eating out is a real pleasure in Myrtle Beach, with a plethora of choices from mouthwatering Lowcountry classics, fresh seafood and steaks, to tempting pastries and desserts. Prices are no measure of quality here; dining costs are unexpectedly moderate at even the better restaurants.

EXPENSIVE

Collectors Cafe ★ MEDITERRANEAN Artsy cafe, replete with jazz music, ambient light, and the work of local painters displayed throughout (and for sale). Eat in one of six themed areas, from the elegant main room or Old Victorian Gallery, to the cozy Lion's Den with comfy lounge chairs, or snug Hideaway with its giant hanging sculpture. The food is Mediterranean-inspired but rich in local ingredients: scallop cakes, filet mignon, and rack of lamb, served with garlic-roasted cauliflower, ginger-scented basmati rice, cashews, and fenugreek-cream curry sauce. Having said that, Collectors is getting a reputation as a spot for tasty desserts and coffee these days, rather than a full meal. It's all incredibly addictive: the tiramisu, the peanut butter mousse pie, or the Key lime pie are top choices.

7740 N. King's Hwy. www.collectorscafeandgallery.com. (℃ **843/449-9370.** Main courses $25–$35. Mon–Fri 11:30am–2:30pm, Mon–Sat 5:30pm–midnight.

Cypress Room ★★★ LOWCOUNTRY/INTERNATIONAL The best place for a splurge on the strip, with the Southern breakfast especially popular: the sweet-potato

best of THE BEACH CHAINS

Plenty of folks come to Myrtle Beach in search of those classic party chains such as Margaritaville (Jimmy Buffet owns several joints in town), where decent food is just the beginning of a big night out involving plenty of booze and live music. Here are some of the better venues.

Hard Rock Cafe 1322 Celebrity Circle, Broadway at the Beach (℃ **843/946-0007;** www.hardrock.com/cafes/myrtle-beach). The giant 70-foot pyramid makes this outpost of the rock n' roll franchise hard to miss, though the food is otherwise standard Hard Rock fare (burgers, nachos, and American comfort food). Check out guitars owned by Carlos Santana, Eric Clapton, BB King, and Brian Wilson, and black leather boots worn by Johnny Cash. It's open Sunday to Thursday 11am to 11pm, and Friday and Saturday 11am to midnight.

Jimmy Buffett's Margaritaville 1114 Celebrity Circle, Broadway at the Beach (℃ **843/448-5455;** www.margaritaville myrtlebeach.com). Love it or loathe it, this classic slice of Americana is a big hit in Myrtle Beach, so expect a wait to be seated. The food is so-so but pricey, and you really need to be into the booze, the music, and the whole "parrot head"

scene to make the most of this. It's open Sunday to Thursday 11am to 10:30pm, and Friday and Saturday 11am to 11pm.

Johnny Rockets 1216 Celebrity Circle, Broadway at the Beach (℃ **843/448-8575;** www.johnnyrockets.com). The 1950s–style diner chain serves up decent burgers, fries, and shakes, for reasonable prices in this part of town. It's open daily 11am to 9pm.

LandShark Bar & Grill 1110 N. Ocean Blvd (℃ **843/788-0001;** http://myrtle beach.landsharkbarandgrill.com). Part of the Jimmy Buffet empire, this hip seafront venue serves up great comfort food (chicken wings, burgers, tater tots, club sandwiches, and so on), and plenty of LandShark beer. It's open Sunday to Thursday 11am to 10pm, and Friday and Saturday 11am to 11pm.

Planet Hollywood 2915 Hollywood Dr., opposite Broadway at the Beach (℃ **843/448-7827;** www.planetholly woodintl.com). This franchise seems a little dated these days, but the Myrtle Beach outpost is still a lot of fun, with friendly staff, a decent gift shop, amazing fries, and the bizarre Thursday morning (8:30–11am) "breakfast bingo." It's otherwise open daily 11am to 10pm.

pancakes with maple-pecan butter are crazy good. Dinners are more expensive and elegant affairs but still feature wholesome Lowcountry cuisine, including baked goat-cheese tart, crispy fried oysters, crab cakes, beef short ribs, and sensational she-crab soup. The decor really is all cypress wood, and the ocean views through the floor-to-ceiling windows are magnificent.

In the Island Vista Resort, 6000 N. Ocean Blvd. www.islandvista.com/dining. ℃ **843/449-6406.** Reservations recommended. Main courses $5–$10 breakfast, $15–$29 dinner. Daily 7:30–10am and 5:30–9pm.

Greg Norman's Australian Grille ★ INTERNATIONAL/AUSTRALIAN This Australian-themed restaurant is especially good for big, juicy steaks, all wood-grilled and premium black angus. The seafood isn't bad either, with the buffalo shrimp dip and local grouper the standouts. Lunch is a much better deal, with a classic Foster's beer-battered shrimp and chips and the Greg Norman signature blackened sirloin burger with apple-wood smoked bacon hard to resist. The outdoor area right on the water is an enticing spot for drinks, and you can snag cheap snacks (from $5) and booze (beer $3) at the daily happy hour (4–7pm).

At Barefoot Landing, 4930 Hwy. 17 S., N. Myrtle Beach. www.gregnormansaustraliangrille.com. ℂ **843/361-0000.** Reservations recommended. Main courses $10–$17 lunch, $26–$41 dinner. Daily 11am–3pm and 4:30–10:30pm. Pub 4pm–midnight (happy hour 4–7pm).

The Parson's Table ★★★ STEAKHOUSE/INTERNATIONAL   Though located out of town in the village of Little River, this gem is well worth the drive. The main dining room was actually the original Little River Methodist Church built in 1885, serving as a church until 1952. The original hand-hewn heart-of-pine floors, and original clapboard pine siding are still here, while the stained glass was added more recently from churches all over the state (some from the old Baptist Church of Mullins). The ravishing beveled glass over the doorway came from the White Mansion in Lumberton, North Carolina. The food more than lives up to the decor. Steaks are the main event, but the menu features a wide range of dishes, from spinach and wild mushroom curry, to fresh local flounder, and jumbo crab cakes. Each dish comes with a suggested wine pairing: who knew a crisp (white) Crios de Susana Balbo Torrontes would make the perfect compliment for shrimp and grits?

4305 McCorsley Ave., Little River (11 miles east of central Myrtle Beach on U.S. 17). www.parson stable.com. ℂ **842/249-3702.** Main courses $16–$30. Mon–Sat 4:30–9pm.

MODERATE

Joe's Bar & Grill ★ AMERICAN   Joe's is a classic crab shack, with a cozy all-wood interior lined with fishing paraphernalia, real fireplace, and the Raccoon Cove Deck Bar out back, overlooking a saltwater marsh. Though it does seafood, this is another spot that excels at steaks, with the signature 6-ounce filet mignon melt-in-your-mouth good. It also knocks out scrumptious lamb chops, an unusually large range of veal dishes, and plenty of local specials, including the Southern-tradition trout, stuffed with crabmeat and coated in cornmeal, shrimp and grits, and Lowcountry-style crab cakes, served with a spicy black bean cake and hollandaise sauce. Check out the early-bird special Sunday to Thursday between 5 and 6pm for substantial savings.

810 Conway St., N. Myrtle Beach. www.joesbarandgrillonline.com. ℂ **843/272-4666.** Main courses $19–$32. Daily 5–9:30pm. Closed for 3 weeks in Jan. Drive 15 miles north on U.S. 17; it's across from Barefoot Landing in N. Myrtle Beach.

Sea Captain's House ★ AMERICAN   This oceanfront diner is loaded with character, built back in 1930 as a family beach cottage and serving as a restaurant since the 1960s. The views of the sea and beach remain a major draw, while the menu, unsurprisingly, is loaded with fresh seafood. Crab-cake benedict is the pick for breakfast, while shrimp and grits, she-crab soup, and sea-island shrimp (Carolina shrimp served in a marinade of olive oil, apple cider vinegar, capers, and onion), feature at dinner. The Sunday brunch buffet is extra popular; for just $10, this is a real bargain, and even includes those shrimp and grits. Reservations recommended.

3002 N. Ocean Blvd. www.seacaptains.com. ℂ **843/448-8082.** Breakfast $7–$11; lunch platters, salads, and sandwiches $11–$15; lunch and dinner main courses $18–$25. Daily 7–10:30am, 11:30am–2:30pm, and 4:30–10pm.

INEXPENSIVE

The Ultimate California Pizza ITALIAN   This South Carolina chain serves up the best pizza on the Strand, with six locations in and around Myrtle Beach. This branch is a popular local hangout, with a huge menu of toppings, from the spicy

nights out IN MYRTLE BEACH

As you'd expect of a major resort, there's plenty to see and do at night in Myrtle Beach, but it's not just pubs and clubs. Much of the entertainment is geared towards families.

The **Alabama Theatre** (℗ **843/272-1111;** www.alabama-theatre.com), Barefoot Landing, 4750 Hwy. 17 S., N. Myrtle Beach, features country-music supergroup Alabama and similar acts in musical productions such as "ONE The Show," with performances daily at 7:30pm. Tickets usually range $35–$48 for adults, $18 for children 3 to 16, and free for children 2 and under (in adult's lap).

Calvin Gilmore's **The Carolina Opry,** 8901 N. King's Hwy. at U.S. 17. (℗ **800/843-6779;** www.thecarolinaopry.com) presents family-friendly 2-hour country shows blending high-energy music, comedy, and dance most nights at 7pm. Tickets range $35 to $50 for adults, $23 for students, $17 for children 3 to 16, and are free for children 2 and under.

Legends in Concert, 2925 Hollywood Drive (℗ **800/960-7469;** www.legendsinconcert.com), is an entertaining tribute show, featuring surprisingly good impersonators of Michael Jackson, Elton John, the Blues Brothers, and of course, Elvis. Tickets range $38 to $49 adults, $14 to $46 for children 3 to 16, and are free for children 2 and under.

The **Medieval Times & Dinner Show,** 2904 Fantasy Way (℗ **888/935-6878** or 843/236-4655; www.medievaltimes.com) is a kitschy but fun night out for kids and adults, with costumed serving "wenches" and jousting knights, and medieval-themed music and food. Tickets are $52 for adults, and $26 for children 12 and under.

The **Palace Theater** at Broadway at the Beach, 1420 Celebrity Circle (℗ **800/905-4228** or 843/448-0588; www.palacetheatremyrtlebeach.com), is the place for live entertainment shows, Broadway-style theatre productions, and musicals from around the world. Monday to Saturday showtime is 8pm, with additional shows Wednesday 10am and Thursday 2pm (tickets vary according to performance, but are usually around $30).

Young ones will love the over-the-top **Pirates Voyage,** 8901 N. Kings Hwy. (℗ **843/497-9700;** www.piratesvoyage.com) dinner-show experience. Roast pork and chicken are served whilst the Crimson and Sapphire pirates do battle in full-size pirate ships on a 15-foot indoor lagoon. Shows start most days at 6pm, and cost $49 to $54 for adults, and $24 to $29 for children 4 to 11.

Mexican (salsa, green peppers, ground beef, roasted red peppers, onion, crumbled tortilla chips, and jalapeño peppers), to Thai chicken (sweet-chili Thai sauce, mozzarella, roasted red peppers, green onions, roasted chicken, and chopped peanuts). It also knocks out great wings, subs, and pastas.

In the Market Common, 4003 Deville St. www.ultimatecaliforniapizza.com. ℗ **843/839-9880.** Pastas, sandwiches, and subs $6–$8; pizzas $8–$19. Daily 11am–11pm.

SAVANNAH

S ome 17 miles up river from the Atlantic, Savannah has always been one of the most ravishing cities in the American South, long before John Berendt and his *Midnight in the Garden of Good and Evil* added some mystery and chic to the place in the 1990s. Few cities in America can match Savannah for sheer romantic beauty: live oaks dripping with Spanish moss, stately antebellum mansions, mint juleps sipped on the veranda, magnolia trees, peaceful marshes, horse-drawn carriages, and ships sailing up the river. Savannah's famed squares add an extra touch of elegance, spacious, lush spaces that break up the Historic District with statues, memorials and plenty of greenery.

Savannah is similar to Charleston, but definitely not the same. The free spirit, the passion, and even the decadence of Savannah resemble that of Key West or New Orleans more than they do the Bible Belt, downhome interior of Georgia. It's a lot wilder—and a little edgier—than Charleston, with high levels poverty beyond the handsome streets of the old center.

Founded in 1733 by British colonists led by Gen. James Oglethorpe, Savannah's precious stock of historic homes had fallen into deep decay by the 1950s, and it's largely thanks to volunteers and local organizations such as the Historic Savannah Foundation that anything survives. Tourism really took off after the publication of *Midnight in the Garden of Good and Evil,* of course, and even today, "The Book" remains a source of curiosity for many visitors, and a livelihood for many locals. In fact Savannah's boasts several respected literary scions, including Flannery O'Connor (p. 138) and Conrad Aiken, the American poet, critic, writer, and Pulitzer Prize winner.

Today the economy and much of the city's day-to-day life still revolve around port activity. For the visitor, however, it's the Historic District, a beautifully restored and maintained area, that's the big draw. More than 800 of Old Savannah's 1,100 historic buildings have been restored, using original paint colors—pinks and reds and blues and greens. This "living museum" is now the largest urban National Historic Landmark District in the country—some 2½ square miles, including 20 one-acre squares that still survive from James Oglethorpe's dream of a gracious city.

ESSENTIALS

Arriving

BY PLANE **Savannah Hilton Head International Airport** (© 912/964-0514; www.savannahairport.com) is about 8 miles west of downtown (15 min. drive), just off I-16 at 400 Airways Ave. See p. 231 for details of airlines and flights. The airport **visitor center** is open daily 9am to 10pm

(✆ **912/966-3743**). **Taxis** into the city center charge a flat fare: the Historic District is $28, Hutchinson Island is $34, hotels near the airport are $10–$15, Hilton Head Island is $85, and Tybee Island is $53. These rates apply to one person—there's an extra $5 charge for each additional person in the taxi, and a $1 airport surcharge.

CAT (p. 116) runs the 100X Airport Express **bus service** between the airport and Joe Murray Rivers, Jr. Intermodal Transit Center, 610 W. Oglethorpe Ave., on the western edge of the Historic District (a 10 min. walk from Telfair Square, and 6 min. from the Visitor Center). The bus operates Monday to Saturday every hour from around 6am to 7pm, and Sundays 9:30am to 4:30pm. Fares are just $1.50 one-way.

The **K-Shuttle** (✆ **877/243-2050**; www.kshuttle.com) is a minivan service that runs between the airport and the resorts of **Hilton Head Island,** daily from 10am to 11:45pm every 1 to 2 hours. Rates are $45 one-way or $80 round-trip.

BY CAR   From the north or south, I-95 passes 10 miles west of Savannah, with several exits to the city, while U.S. 17 runs through the center. From the west, I-16 ends in downtown Savannah, and U.S. 80 also runs through the city from east to west. The city lies 106 miles southwest of Charleston via I-95 and U.S. 17 (around 2 hr. drive), 250 miles southeast of Atlanta via I-16 and I-75 (3 hr. 30 min.), and 140 miles north of Jacksonville, Florida, via I-95 (around 2 hr.)

BY TRAIN   The **train station** is at 2611 Seaboard Coastline Dr. (✆ **912/234-2611**), some 4 miles southwest of downtown; take a cab into the center (around $10). The station serves the **Amtrak** Silver Service/Palmetto route between New York, Washington D.C., Orlando, and Miami. Trains travel twice a day between Savannah and Charleston (2 hr.). For schedules and fare information, contact ✆ **800/872-7245** or visit www.amtrak.com.

BY BUS   Greyhound (✆ **800/231-2222**; www.greyhound.com) and **Southeastern Stages** (✆ **404/591-2750**; www.southeasternstages.com) offer regular service to Savannah from Charleston (1 daily; 2 hr.), Atlanta (5 daily; 4 hr. 30 min.), and Jacksonville (7 daily; from 2 hr. 15min.). The **bus station** is at 610 W. Oglethorpe Ave. (✆ **912/232-8186**), at the CAT local bus terminal on the edge of the Historic District (6-min. walk from the Visitor Center).

Visitor Information

TOURIST OFFICES   The friendly and efficient **MLK Visitor Information Center,** 301 Martin Luther King Jr. Blvd., on the west side of the Historic District (✆ **912/944-0455**; www.visitsavannah.com), is open Monday to Friday 8:30am to 5pm and Saturday and Sunday 9am to 5pm. The center offers an audiovisual presentation ($5 adults, $2 children), organized tours, and self-guided walking, driving, or bike tours with excellent maps and brochures.

Alternatively, the **Visit Savannah Visitor Information Center** is at 101 E. Bay St., just up from the riverfront (✆ **877/728-2662** or 912/644-6400), open Monday to Friday 8:30am to 5pm.

There are smaller visitor kiosks at the **River Street Visitor Information Center,** 1 W. River St. (on the riverfront; ✆ **912/651-6662**), open daily 9am to 8pm (Jan–Feb until 6pm), **Forsyth Park** at 621 Drayton St. (✆ **912/233-7848**), open daily 8am to 7pm, and **Ellis Square** at 26 Barnard St. (✆ **912/525-3100**), open daily March to July 10am to 10pm (Feb and Nov until 8pm; Dec–Jan until 6pm; Aug–Oct until 9pm).

City Layout

In Savannah, every other street—north, south, west, and east—is punctuated by greenery. The grid of **21 scenic squares** was laid out in 1733 by Gen. James Oglethorpe, the founder of Georgia. The design—still in use—has been called "one of the world's most revered city plans." It's said that if Savannah didn't have its history and architecture, it would be worth a visit just to see the city layout.

Bull Street is the dividing line between east and west. On the south side are odd-numbered buildings, on the north side even numbered.

Neighborhoods in Brief

The Historic District The primary reason to visit Savannah, the Historic District encompasses both the Riverfront and the City Market, described below. It's officially bordered by the Savannah River and Forsyth Park at Gaston Street, and Montgomery and Price streets. Within its borders are more than 2,350 architecturally and historically significant buildings in a 2½-square-mile area.

Riverfront River Street is where the Historic District meets the Savannah River, though in terms of architecture and atmosphere it is a little different (and lower down) than the more stately streets to the south. Once lined with warehouses holding King Cotton, it has been the subject of massive urban renewal, turning this strip into a row of restaurants, art galleries, shops, and rowdy bars. The original source of the area's growth was the river, which offered a prime shipping avenue for New World goods bound for European ports. In 1818, about half of Savannah fell under quarantine during a yellow-fever epidemic. River Street never fully recovered and fell into disrepair until its rediscovery in the mid-1970s.

City Market Two blocks from River Street and bordering the Savannah River, the City Market district was the former social and business mecca of Savannah (the actual market building was demolished in the 1950s). The city of Savannah decided to save what remained of the district in the 1980s. Today the district comprises a 4-block area of restored warehouses and shop fronts adjacent to Ellis Square, offering everything from antiques to collectibles, including many Savannah-made products. And everything from seafood and pizza to French and Italian cuisine is served here. Live music often fills the nighttime air. Some of the best jazz in the city is presented here in various clubs.

Victorian District The Victorian District, south of the Historic District, holds some of the finest examples of post–Civil War architecture in the Deep South. The district is bounded by Martin Luther King Jr. Boulevard and by East Broad, Gwinnett, and Anderson streets. Houses in the district are characterized by gingerbread trim, stained-glass windows, and imaginative architectural details. In all, the district encompasses an area of nearly 50 blocks, spread across some 165 acres. The entire district was added to the National Register of Historic Places in 1974. Most of the two-story homes are wood frame and were constructed in the late 1800s on brick foundations. The district, overflowing from the historic inner core, became the first suburb of Savannah.

Getting Around

The grid-shaped Historic District is best seen on foot—the real point of your visit is to take leisurely strolls with frequent stops in the many squares. **Parking garages** and **lots** in the city center are plentiful but do fill up at peak times. The most central are the

River Street Lots (Mon–Fri 8am–5pm, $1/hr.), the **Bryan St. Garage** ($1/hr.; $2 overnight; Sat–Sun $5) with entrances on Drayton and Abercorn streets, and the **Whitaker St. Garage** ($2/hr., max. daily rate $16) at 7 Whitaker St. Visit www.savan nahga.gov for the latest rates.

BY CAR   Outside the Historic District your own wheels will be much more convenient, and they're absolutely essential for sightseeing outside the city proper.

All major car-rental firms have branches in Savannah and at the airport, including **Hertz** (ⓒ **800/654-3131** or 912/964-9595 at the airport; www.hertz.com); **Avis** (ⓒ **800/331-1212;** www.avis.com), with locations at 422 Airways Ave. (ⓒ **912/964-1781**) and at the airport (ⓒ 912/964-0234); and **Budget** (ⓒ **800/527-0700;** www. budget.com), with offices at 7070 Abercorn St. (ⓒ 912/966-1771) and the airport (ⓒ 912/354-4718).

BY BUS   **Chatham Area Transit (CAT)** runs the city bus network. You'll need exact change for the $1.50 fare; transfers are free. The **central bus station** is the Joe Murray Rivers, Jr. Intermodal Transit Center, 610 W. Oglethorpe Ave., where you can buy passes Monday to Friday from 7am to 8pm. Day passes are $3, 7-day passes are $16, and a 10-ride pass is $15. Bus #4 runs out to the Oglethorpe Mall, while bus #20 runs to Skidway Island State Park, though if you intend to stay in the Historic District you won't need to use regular buses much. More useful are the CAT-operated **free shuttles**. Park your car in the **Liberty St. Parking Garage** (Mon–Fri only; $1/hr.), and take the free **Liberty St. Parking Shuttle** to Bryan Street (Mon–Fri 6:20–9:10am and 3:40–6:20pm). Otherwise the extremely useful **"dot" Express Shuttle** (Mon–Sat 7am–9pm, Sun 11am–9pm; free) runs all over downtown every 20 minutes or less, passing the Visitor Center, Forsyth Park, and a number of parking garages. The **River St. Streetcar** (Fri–Sun noon–9pm; free), an authentic 1930s trolley, runs along the Savannah River waterfront, from Morrell Park to the western end of the strip, though it is sometimes suspended for maintenance. For route and schedule information, call CAT at ⓒ **912/233-5767** or visit www.catchacat.org.

BY FERRY   The **Savannah Belles Ferry** runs from River Street at City Hall (Hyatt Hotel), across to Hutchinson Island, the Savannah International Trade and Convention Center, and the Westin Savannah Harbor Resort & Spa. The service is **free,** and runs daily 7am to midnight, every 20 to 30 minutes (no service Thanksgiving, Christmas, and New Year's Day).

BY TAXI   The base rate for taxis is $2, plus 32¢ per 1/6 mile thereafter, not to exceed $3.60 for the first mile and $1.92 per mile thereafter. For 24-hour taxi service, call **Yellow Cab** at ⓒ **912/604-9845** (www.yellowcabofsavannah.com).

[FastFACTS] SAVANNAH

Dentist   Call **Abercorn South Side Dental,** 11139 Abercorn St. (ⓒ **912/925-9190;** www.dentistsavan nahfriday.com), for complete dental care and emergencies Monday to Friday 8:30am to 3pm.

Doctors & Hospitals   There are 24-hour emergency-room services at **Candler General Hospital,** 5353 Reynolds St. (ⓒ **912/819-6000;** www. sjchs.org), and at **Memorial University Medical Center,** 4700 Waters Ave.

(ⓒ **912/350-8000;** www. memorialhealth.com).

Emergencies   In an emergency, dial ⓒ **911.** If the situation isn't life threatening, call ⓒ **912/651-6756** for the fire department and

912/651-6675 for the police.

Pharmacies Drugstores are scattered throughout Savannah. The most central **CVS Pharmacy** is at 119 Bull St., at State St. (**912/232-1129**), open Monday to Saturday 8am to 8pm, and

Sunday 10am to 6pm. The nearest **24-hour** CVS is at 4725 Waters Ave. (**912/355-7111**), near Memorial Hospital, 5 miles south of the riverfront.

Post Office Post offices and sub–post offices are centrally located and

generally open Monday to Friday 8am to 4:30pm. The most central office is at **Telfair Square,** 118 Barnard St., open Monday to Friday 9am to 5pm.

SAVANNAH HOTELS

The undisputed stars in Savannah are the charming small inns in the Historic District, most in restored old homes that have been renovated with modern conveniences. Price ranges can vary greatly, though like Charleston, rates are generally expensive compared to other parts of the country. Advance reservations are necessary in most cases, since many of the best properties are quite small. **High season** is from March through June (Mar–Apr is often the busiest time), and again from late September through November. You will find that the cheapest rates will usually be on weekdays during **low season,** which is January, February, and late July to early September. The price ranges listed below include both low and high seasons. Very expensive hotels often have some smaller, more moderately priced units. It never hurts to ask.

If you can't afford a stay at one of Savannah's historic inns, you can opt for one of the numerous **chain motels** on the outskirts. The biggest cluster can be found near the **airport** around exit 104 of I-95, 13 miles west of Downtown; further south around exit 94 (16 miles from Downtown), known as **Savannah South;** and along Hwy-204 (Abercorn St. extension), 5 to 6 miles south of the city center, in what's known as the **Midtown** area. With so many choices, rooms in these properties are usually exceptionally good deals, with most motels offering doubles for well under $100 outside peak periods and holidays.

Self-Catering Apartments

Anyone looking to get into the local swing of things in Savannah should consider a **short-term rental apartment.** For the same price or less than a hotel room, you could have your own one-bedroom apartment with a washing machine, A/C, and a fridge to keep your booze in. Properties of all sizes and styles, in every price range, are available for stays of 3 nights to several weeks.

RECOMMENDED AGENCIES

The companies below are especially recommended.

Airbnb (www.airbnb.com) offers over 280 properties in and around Savannah. The San Francisco-based Internet venture connects private property owners with travelers at a variety of price points.

Couchsurfing (www.couchsurfing.org) is another website connecting travelers with folks willing to rent a house, room, or apartment. It offers over 1,450 options in and around Savannah.

Vacation Rentals by Owner (www.vrbo.com) is a hip rental agency that offers over 360 rental properties in and around Savannah, everything from one-bedroom historic condos for $130 per night to six-bedroom mansions for $585 per night.

Along the Riverfront

EXPENSIVE

Bohemian Hotel ★★ Hip Marriott-owned hotel purpose-built in 2009 right on the water, with a buzzy rooftop bar and restaurant popular with the Savannah in-crowd (see Rocks on the Roof, p. 153). The hotel is decorated throughout with an exceptional art collection. The rooms feature a blend of whimsical 18th-century decor (lots of driftwood, brass, and leather), and contemporary style (iPod docking stations, huge LCD TVs), with velvet drapes separating the bathroom from the bedroom. Pricey but cool—best for young (or young-at-heart) couples that want to splurge.

102 W Bay St., Savannah, GA 31401. www.bohemianhotelsavannah.com. © **912/721-3800.** 75 units. $242–$369 double. One child under 18 stays free when using existing beds (extra beds $20); breakfast $15. Parking (valet) $25. **Amenities:** Restaurant; bar; spa; fitness center; room service; free Wi-Fi.

Savannah Marriott Riverfront ★ This fairly standard business hotel just about beats the Hyatt behemoth further down the strip, with a wonderful waterside location at the quiet eastern end of the riverfront. Like most of Savannah's big central hotels it primarily caters to business travelers and conference-attendees, but the staff are extra helpful, and the facilities are all top notch, including the gym (a rarity in Savannah). If you do stay, opt for a river-view room so you can admire all those huge ships floating by, day and night.

100 General McIntosh Blvd., Savannah, GA 31401. www.marriott.com. © **912/233-7722.** 387 units. $209–$279 double. Children 12 and under stay free in parent's room. Breakfast $15. Parking $19. **Amenities:** 4 restaurants; 2 bars; fitness center; Jacuzzi; 2 pools (1 indoor); room service; spa; Wi-Fi ($13/day or $16 for high-speed; free in lobby and public areas).

Westin Savannah Harbor Golf Resort & Spa ★ Savannah's largest hotel lies in splendid isolation on the other side of the river from the Historic District. Getting across is easy however, thanks to the free ferry (p. 116). As you'd expect, the amenities and rooms—which face either the golf course or the river—are the usual Westin standard (the staff is great), but thanks to the daily resort fee, this is really only worthwhile if you intend to use the resort facilities or play golf at least once during your stay (tee fees from $68). The hotel also offers shuttles ($40) and free access to the beaches of Daufuskie Island, and lounging on the pool deck overlooking the city is certainly an added bonus. The Westin is another hotel popular with tour groups and conferences.

1 Resort Dr., Savannah, GA 31401. www.westinsavannah.com. © **912/201-2000.** 403 units. $215–$292 double. From I-95 and Savannah International Airport, take exit 17A to I-16 toward Savannah; follow sign for Rte. 17–Talmadge Bridge; take the Hutchinson Island exit onto Resort Dr. Resort fee of $23/day covers Internet, putting greens/driving range, and self-parking ($22 valet). **Amenities:** 4 restaurants; 3 bars; babysitting; 18-hole golf course; exercise room; Wi-Fi (included in resort fee; see above); Jacuzzi; outdoor pool; spa; room service; sauna.

MODERATE

River Street Inn ★ Housed in a 19th-century cotton warehouse on the river, this B&B offers excellent value considering the location, though some of its rooms are starting to show their age. The air-conditioning can also be a little temperamental—ask to move if it's too hot. In general rooms are nicely decorated in a period style, with four-poster and canopy beds, hardwood floors, and oriental rugs. Note that the river views are stunning, but balconies are usually tiny. The complimentary wine and hors d'oeuvres reception isn't always held every day—check in advance if this is important

Where to Stay in Savannah

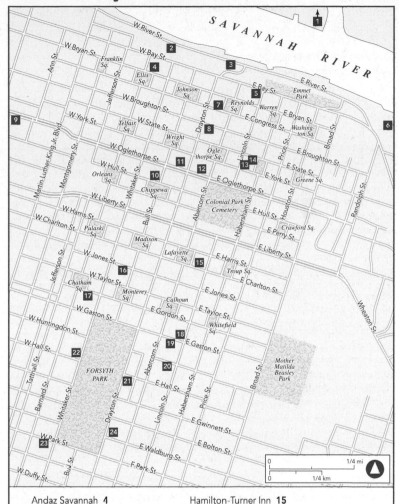

Andaz Savannah **4**
Azalea Inn & Gardens **20**
Ballastone Inn **11**
Bohemian Hotel **2**
Catherine Ward House Inn **24**
Dresser Palmer House **19**
East Bay Inn **5**
The 1895 Inn **12**
Eliza Thompson House **16**
Foley House Inn **10**
Forsyth Park Inn **22**
Gastonian **18**

Hamilton-Turner Inn **15**
Kehoe House **14**
Mansion on Forsyth Park **21**
Marshall House **8**
Park Avenue Manor **23**
Planters Inn **7**
River Street Inn **3**
Savannah Bed & Breakfast Inn **17**
Savannah Marriott Riverfront **6**
17 Hundred 90 Inn **13**
Thunderbird Inn **9**
Westin Savannah Harbor Golf Resort & Spa **1**

to you. The property dates back to 1819, and was expanded in 1853. Excellent rates are available online.

124 E. Bay St., Savannah, GA 31401. www.riverstreetinn.com. ℂ **912/234-6400.** 86 units. $131–$179 double. Children 13 and under stay free in parent's room. Parking $6–$10 in public garage. **Amenities:** 2 restaurants; exercise room; free Wi-Fi.

Historic District
VERY EXPENSIVE

Ballastone Inn ★★   This luxurious and highly romantic hotel lies next door to the Juliette Gordon Low Birthplace (p. 141). The building dates back to 1838 but was enlarged in the 1880s and is today littered with period antiques and authentic reproductions. High Tea (afternoon tea) at 4pm is a special treat here, with delicious finger food (smoked salmon sandwiches, freshly baked scones with Devonshire cream, or Meyer lemon scones with orange butter), and teas served on an antique tea silver service (wine is charged). When it comes to the rooms, all of them are decorated in a period style, but quality differs a lot depending on price point. I've categorized the hotel as "very expensive" because the best, most atmospheric rooms—like Mulberry Tulips and Scarlett's Retreat—tend to be pricey. "Low Country" is much cheaper but nowhere near as comfortable.

14 E. Oglethorpe Ave., Savannah, GA 31401. www.ballastone.com. ℂ **912/236-1484.** 16 units. $179–$335 double. Rates include full breakfast, afternoon tea, and evening hors d'oeuvres. Free parking. No children 15 and under. **Amenities:** Breakfast room; bar; spa; free Wi-Fi.

Hamilton-Turner Inn ★★★   As one of the city's most famous homes, this hotel is almost a tourist attraction in its own right (though you can only see inside if you are a guest). The lavish rooms here run from suites to basic doubles, but all feature contemporary interpretations of period styles, with antique-style beds, bold color schemes, and sparkling new bathrooms. The mansion was built for successful businessman Samuel Pugh Hamilton in 1873, right on Lafayette Square, and was the first home in Savannah to have electricity (in 1883). It was purchased by Dr. Francis Turner in 1915. Joe Odom, who featured in *Midnight in the Garden of Good and Evil,* held wild parties in the house, and it's a regular staple of ghost tours in the area (ask the staff about the various "sightings").

330 Abercorn St., Savannah GA 31401. www.hamilton-turnerinn.com. ℂ **912/233-1833.** 17 units. $199–$384 double. Rates include breakfast and evening wine reception. Children 9 and younger not allowed. Free parking. **Amenities:** Breakfast room; business center; concierge desk; free Wi-Fi.

EXPENSIVE

Andaz Savannah ★★★   The Hyatt-owned Andaz occupies prime territory on historic Ellis Square, but this is not another old mansion: the hotel was purpose-built in 2009, with nary an antique bed in sight. Anyone looking for a contemporary, stylish boutique hotel—again, this is not an historic inn—should consider the slick, comfy rooms here. Extras include complimentary soft drinks and snacks in the minibar (alcoholic drinks are charged), a decent 24-hour gym and enticing pool area with rooftop terrace. Rates including the substantial buffet breakfast tend to be $20 more.

14 Barnard St., Savannah, GA 31401. www.savannah.andaz.hyatt.com. ℂ **912/233-2116.** 151 units. $189–$244 double. Parking $16 ($20 valet). **Amenities:** Bar; restaurant; concierge; room service; exercise room; outdoor pool; spa; free Wi-Fi.

Azalea Inn & Gardens ★★★   Located near Forsyth Park, this is another romantic inn a little out of the way, but with the added bonus of a tranquil outdoor pool and incredibly welcoming hosts Teresa and Micheal Jacobson. Food and drink is a major part of any stay here, beginning with the gourmet breakfasts, and including the fresh-ground local coffee, tea, soda, and fresh-baked desserts (think apple crumble bars) available at any time. While every room is cozy and has heaps of charm, my faves are the Magnolia Room, with hardwood floors and private balcony overlooking the pool, and the luxury suites at the poolside Cottage Garden House.

217 E. Huntingdon St., Savannah, GA 31401. www.azaleainn.com. ✆ **912/236-6080.** 10 units. $179–$375 double (Cottage Garden House $299–$409). Rates include full breakfast. Parking $5. **Amenities:** Outdoor pool; free Wi-Fi.

Catherine Ward House Inn ★★   This Victorian clapboard gem is another B&B close to Forsyth Park. Built for Irish immigrant Captain James Ward and his wife Catherine in 1886, the house is a spectacular example of High Victorian Italianate architecture. Fully renovated most recently in 2005, rooms are charming and spotlessly clean, though bathrooms tend to be very small. Sipping your coffee in the shady court-yard is a real pleasure, the staff are amazingly helpful, and the breakfasts really exceptional.

118 E. Waldburg St., Savannah, GA 31401. www.catherinewardhouseinn.com. ✆ **912/234-8564.** 9 units. $179–$259 double. Rates include full breakfast. No children 13 or under. Free parking. **Amenities:** Breakfast room; free Wi-Fi.

Dresser Palmer House ★★   This spectacular Italianate townhouse was built in 1876 for cotton merchant Henry Dresser and Samuel Palmer, who ran the largest hardware store in Savannah. It is now one of the most appealing B&Bs in the city. Its beautiful ironwork porch, where you can sip coffee in the morning, is matched by a soothing garden, patio, and koi pond at the back. Rooms are spacious and decked out in an elegant 19th-centuty style (the charming "waltz out" windows allow you to exit the room straight to the patio), but this is another place especially recommended for foodies. Breakfasts are gourmet events prepared by skilled chefs, accompanied by fresh pastries made on the premises, and the afternoon wine and cheese features qual-ity styles and brands. The house is 1 block from Forsyth Park, in a quiet residential neighborhood.

211 E. Gaston St., Savannah GA 31401. www.dresserpalmerhouse.com. ✆ **912/238-3294.** 16 units. $179–$329 double. Rates include full breakfast and afternoon wine and hors d'oeuvres 5–6pm. Free parking. **Amenities:** Breakfast room; concierge desk; free Wi-Fi.

The 1895 Inn ★★   Incredibly popular B&B housed in an artfully refurbished Queen Anne-style mansion loaded with antiques and Victorian art. With just four rooms on offer you will need to reserve this option many months in advance. The rooms are elegantly furnished (the Renaissance Room includes an original Toulousc-Lautrec engraving), and beautifully maintained, but it's really the hosts, Bob Ray and Ed Bryant, that make the whole experience so smooth and personal. Staying here really brings the concept of "Southern hospitality" to life.

126 E. Oglethorpe Ave., Savannah, GA 31401. www.the1895inn.net. ✆ **912/231-8822.** 4 units. $175–$195 double; 2-night minimum stay on weekends and holidays. Adults 21 and over only. Rates include full breakfast, afternoon wine and cheese 5–6pm, and late-evening dessert. Free parking. **Amenities:** Breakfast room; DVD library (DVD players in room); free Wi-Fi.

Foley House Inn ★★   This luxurious B&B on Chippewa Square really stands out for its food. The delicious Southern breakfasts are followed by decadent afternoon sweets and tea (3–5pm) with treats such as white-chocolate-raspberry cheesecake and chocolate chip cheese balls, and evening wine and hors d'oeuvres (6–7pm), the perfect start to a night out. Rooms are a blend of old-world charm and modern amenities, with everyone (even the cheaper ones) attractively adorned with original fixtures and exposed brick. The inn is pet-friendly, so don't be surprised to see guests with dogs.

14 W. Hull St., Savannah, GA 31401. www.foleyinn.com. © **912/232-6622.** 19 units. $199–$349 double. Rates include full breakfast, afternoon hors d'oeuvres, wine, and cordials. Pets allowed. No children 11 and under. **Amenities:** Breakfast room; free Wi-Fi.

Forsyth Park Inn ★ This handsome 1890s Queen-Anne clapboard mansion occupies a prime spot overlooking the park. The spacious rooms are decked out in modern furnishings inspired by 19th-century styles, with 14-foot ceilings, tiled fireplaces, original hardwood parquet floors, and views of Forsyth Park or the pretty walled courtyard garden and fountain. I especially enjoyed the rocking chairs on the veranda.

102 W. Hall St., Savannah, GA 31401. www.forsythparkinn.com. © **912/233-6800.** 11 units, 1 cottage with kitchenette. $185–$295 double; $250 cottage. Rates include full breakfast, evening hors d'oeuvres, late-night desserts, and coffee. **Amenities:** Breakfast room; free Internet.

Gastonian ★★ Luxury B&B comprising two ravishing Regency-Italianate style mansions dating back to 1868. Today the inn is part of the Relais & Chateaux group, and offers the high standards of service and comfort you'd expect. Those Savannah extras—early evening wine with hors d'oeuvres, and late night desserts—are exceptional here (chocolate sherry bars anyone?). As with other Savannah properties of this type, room quality does vary considerably with price, but here at least the cheaper Classic Queen rooms are just as full of character, if smaller, than the others. Furnishings are simple but classic, with wood beds, stained-glass windows, and fireplaces.

220 E. Gaston St., Savannah, GA 31401. www.gastonian.com. © **912/232-2869.** 17 units. $169–$279 double. Rates include full breakfast, afternoon wine reception with hors d'oeuvres (4:30–6pm), and desserts and cordials (8–10pm). Free parking. **Amenities:** Breakfast room; concierge service; free Wi-Fi.

Kehoe House ★★ Kehoe boasts a great location on a central but peaceful square. All the rooms feature wood floors and period furnishings, but it is definitely worth paying extra to get a room with access to the veranda, especially when you can take breakfast out there. Breakfasts here are delicious, with usually a choice of two wicked options (think blueberry bread pudding, pecan French toast, or lemon ricotta pancakes). Successful Irish immigrant William Kehoe built the house in 1892 after creating a fortune in the iron business.

123 Habersham St., Savannah, GA 31401. www.kehoehouse.com. © **912/232-1020.** 13 units. $179–$269 double. Rates include full breakfast, evening tea, and hors d'oeuvres. Parking $12. Adults 21 and over only. **Amenities:** Breakfast room; concierge desk; free Wi-Fi.

Mansion on Forsyth Park ★★ The sister property of the Bohemian (p. 118) is similarly crammed with Richard Kessler's exceptional art collection (displayed in its own "Grand Bohemian Art Gallery"), but that's where the comparisons end. This is actually a genuine Romanesque beauty, just across from the park, its art and period furnishings enhanced with onyx and Verona marble, Lalique chandeliers, and Versace furniture. Leading local architect E.S. Eichberg built the mansion in 1888, but it was completely renovated in 2005. All the rooms blend lavish contemporary and historic furnishings and styles, and all feature spacious marble-clad bathrooms with whirlpool tubs or Swiss showers. I recommend the Concierge Floor, though, which is on the top floor and comes with complimentary breakfast and wine reception 5 to 8pm. Avoid rooms on the park side of the property if you are a light sleeper. Handy free shuttles run to the Bohemian on the riverfront every half-hour until 10pm. On site you have the lauded 700 Drayton Restaurant, as well as two plush lounges, the Bösendorfer or Casimir's Lounge featuring live entertainment, and a rooftop terrace overlooking the park.

700 Drayton St., Savannah, GA 31401. www.mansiononforsythpark.com. © **912/238-5158.** 125 units. $170–$349 double. Parking $20. **Amenities:** Restaurant (700 Drayton, see review, p. 128); 2 bars; exercise room; outdoor pool; room service; spa; Wi-Fi ($10/day).

MODERATE

East Bay Inn ★★   Enticing and good-value B&B close to River Street in an excellent, central location ideal for exploring the city on foot. The property dates back to 1852, when it was completed for trader Edward Padefford as a simple commercial building (the last cotton merchant closed in 1910). Today the comfortable rooms inside feature old-fashioned wooden beds, exposed brick walls, and beautiful furniture. Rooms at the front have the best views, but note that the street is busy and can be noisy. Dog-owners love this place because it boasts six pet-friendly rooms.

225 E. Bay St., Savannah, GA 31401. www.eastbayinn.com. © **912/238-1225.** 28 units. $107–$219 double. Rates include continental breakfast and evening reception with beverages, cheese, and hors d'oeuvres (5:30–7pm). Parking $12. Pets welcome. **Amenities:** Breakfast room; free Wi-Fi.

Eliza Thompson House ★★   One of Savannah's most attractive mansions, Eliza Thompson House is another spot perfect for a romantic getaway. The garden courtyard, with its Koi pond (and iron sculpture by late Georgia-based artist Ivan Bailey), makes for a tranquil hideaway, while the house itself dates from 1847. It was built for Eliza and Joseph Thompson (a cotton merchant), with an enticing fireplace in the lobby. It has no elevators of course. The carriage house in the courtyard is a replica, constructed in the 1980s in the style of New Orleans' French Quarter. A number of ghostly sightings have been recorded in the house over the years, but in typical Savannah fashion this is considered more a quaint and interesting part of the local tradition rather than anything scary.

5 W. Jones St., Savannah, GA 31401. www.elizathompsonhouse.com. © **912/236-3620.** 25 units. $120–$209 double. Rates include continental breakfast, evening wine, and cheese reception (5:30–7pm), and desserts and coffee (8:30–10pm). Children 17 and under not allowed. Parking $12. **Amenities:** Breakfast room; free Wi-Fi.

Marshall House ★   This aging gem was opened in 1851 by enterprising innkeeper Mary Marshall, making it the city's oldest hotel. In the Civil War it served as a hospital, while Joel Chandler Harris, author of the famous "Uncle Remus" stories (of Br'er Rabbit and company), lived here in the late 1860s. The budget Petite Queen Rooms are small as you'd expect, old and a little worn, but the location in the heart of the historic district cannot be beat and the wine reception is usually a sociable event. If you can afford it, the Broughton Balcony Rooms are the best in the hotel and a real treat, opening out onto the spacious, wrought-iron veranda.

123 E. Broughton St., Savannah, GA 31401. www.marshallhouse.com. © **800/589-6304** or 912/644-7896. 68 units. $116–$244 double. Rates include continental breakfast. Parking $15. **Amenities:** Restaurant; bar; free Wi-Fi.

Park Avenue Manor ★★★   This gorgeous and justly popular B&B was converted from a beautiful 1889 Victorian home, showcasing the very best of Southern hospitality. Located at the southwest corner of Forsyth Park, it's a little apart from the main section of the Historic District, but that hardly matters. This is a bit like living in a Savannah mansion of your own; all the rooms are upstairs and are furnished with four-posters, antique chairs, and period Savannah engravings. The patio at the back is perfect for a quiet couple of hours of reading. Coffee, tea, and hot chocolate are available all day, the breakfasts are works of art, and Maurice Norman is a gracious and knowledgeable host. With just five rooms and relatively low prices, you must make reservations here several months in advance.

107–109 West Park Ave., Savannah GA 31401. www.parkavenuemanor.com. ✆ **912/233-0352.** 5 units. $109–$199 double. Rates include full breakfast. No children under 16. Free parking. **Amenities:** Breakfast room; free Wi-Fi.

Planters Inn ★★   This hotel has perhaps the best location in the city, right on historic Reynolds Square with room service from the Olde Pink House (p. 129) next door. Built in 1912, the inn lies on the historic site of John Wesley's first parish in the 1730s. Rooms are simply but tastefully decorated with four-poster rice beds and fireplaces, though note that many overlook the parking garage and can be a little noisy—check before you settle in. Use of the nearby Lava 24 Fitness Center is complimentary for guests.

29 Abercorn St., Savannah GA 31401. www.plantersinnsavannah.com. ✆ **912/232-5678.** 60 units. $109–$229 double. Rates include continental breakfast and evening wine and cheese reception Mon–Sat. Parking $16. **Amenities:** Bar; breakfast room; limited room service; free Wi-Fi.

Savannah Bed & Breakfast Inn ★★   This B&B occupies a fabulous location on Chatham Square, just 1 block from Forsyth Park. The stone-fronted townhouse, completed around 1853, is also a very good deal, with comfy rooms and superb home-cooked food—the freshly baked chocolate cookies are irresistible. The Value Rooms are cozy and romantic, with exposed brick walls, period oil paintings, and views of Chatham Square (Chatham Room is the best). For a splurge, the Live Oak Suite is definitely worth the extra bills, with much more space, living room, four-poster rice bed with canopy crown, and a kitchenette.

117 W. Gordon St. (at Chatham Sq.), Savannah, GA 31401. www.savannahbnb.com. ✆ **912/238-0518.** 18 units. $119–$229 double. Rates include full breakfast, afternoon tea (4–6pm), and bedtime milk and cookies after 8pm. Free parking. **Amenities:** Breakfast room; Wi-Fi (in some, free).

17 Hundred 90 Inn ★★   As the name suggests, this intriguing B&B has foundations that date all the way back to 1790, with major additions in the 1820s and 1888, with the separate Guest House building a beautiful Georgian built in 1875 just across the road. Everything was completely renovated in 2011. Rooms are furnished in the usual blend of antique furniture and modern amenities, while the continental breakfast is standard fare. In grand Savannah tradition, the main building is reputed to have its own ghost. There's even a section on the website dedicated to "hauntings". Note that parking is limited and first-come first served.

307 E. President St., Savannah, GA 31401. www.17hundred90.com. ✆ **912/236-7122.** 17 units. $119–$179 double. Rates include continental breakfast. Limited free parking. **Amenities:** Bar; breakfast room; free Wi-Fi.

INEXPENSIVE

Thunderbird Inn ★   This kitschy, retro motel, circa 1964, is really the only budget option in the Historic District worth considering. Lowest rates are available in July, August, and January. It's friendly and clean, though some rooms are getting rather worn and Wi-Fi can be spotty. The "KrispyKreme" breakfast (free donuts) is a nice dose of Americana, as are the free MoonPies and popcorn on arrival (though they sometimes run out). The inn only has two free bikes for guest use, so you'll have to be early to nab them. Late check-out is $3.

611 W. Oglethorpe Ave., Savannah, GA 31401. www.thethunderbirdinn.com. ⓒ **912/232-2661.** 42 units. $66–$145 double. Children 18 and younger stay free when using existing beds. Rates include continental breakfast. Parking $5. **Amenities:** Breakfast room; free Wi-Fi.

Outlying Areas
INEXPENSIVE

Savannah Oaks RV Resort ★ To get really good budget deals you'll need to stay in an outlying motel, or camp out, and commute into the Historic District. Savannah Oaks RV Resort is just 12 miles from the center, on the banks of the Ogeechee River, and offers sites for tent camping as well as RVs. Kids will love the clean (and warm) pool, clean showers, and playground. The whole 24-acre site is picturesquely located amongst Spanish moss-laced live oak trees, and there's a store, gas station, and laundry facilities. The Gray Line Hop on/Hop off tour (p. 147) offers pick-up at the site.

805 Fort Argyle Rd., Savannah, GA 31419. (2½ miles west of I-95, 4½ miles west of U.S. 17). www. savannahoaks.net. ⓒ **912/748-4000.** 42 units. $39–$45 full hook-ups. **Amenities:** Store; laundry; outdoor pool; playground; boat ramp; hot showers; free Wi-Fi.

Skidaway Island State Park ★★★ Open year-round, this state park is the best choice in the area for camping. The sites are spacious and wooded, with plenty of full hookups for RVs as well as 3 comfy cabins (with kitchens) for those without gear. The tranquil park itself features 1- and 3-mile nature trails to a fun observation tower, grills, picnic tables, an outdoor pool, and a laundry, while the bathrooms are some of the cleanest you'll find. I recommend renting the bikes ($10 for 2 hr.). On arrival, you purchase a $5 state parking pass valid for the entire stay.

52 Diamond Causeway, Savannah, GA 31411. www.gastateparks.org/info/skidaway. ⓒ **912/598-2300.** 87 sites. Full hook-ups and tent camping $35–$40, cabins $125. Parking $5 one-time fee. **Amenities:** Outdoor pool; grills; laundry: hiking trails; free Wi-Fi.

WHERE TO DINE

Savannah is known for the excellence of its seafood and Southern restaurants. Assuming you are not stuffed by the constant round of breakfast, afternoon tea, wine and cheese, and evening desserts laid on by Savannah's historic inns, food lovers will have a real ball here. The city's restaurants are among the best in Georgia, rivaled only by those in Atlanta. The best dining is in the Historic District, and along River Street, bordering the water. Some of Savannah's restaurants, like Elizabeth on 37th, are ranked among the finest in the entire South. Others, like Mrs. Wilkes' Dining Room, are places to go for real Southern fare. And then there's TV celebrity chef **Paula Deen,** long-time native of the city and purveyor of much-loved Southern-style cooking. Some visitors still make the trip to Savannah solely to visit her feted restaurant, The Lady & Sons, despite Deen being dumped by the Food Network in 2013 after a controversy involving racial slurs.

Along the Riverfront
EXPENSIVE

Chart House ★ STEAK/SEAFOOD This attractive waterside spot is part of a nationwide chain, best known for entrees such as macadamia-crusted fish, fresh

Unlike the old City Market, **Forsyth Farmers' Market** (www.forsythfarmers market.com) is a genuine fresh-food market with a huge variety of local organic produce and poultry for sale. The market operates on Saturdays between 9am and 1pm, at the southern end of Forsyth Park. Think delicious nuts from Alake's Pecans, sweet treats from the Chocolate Lab, local honey, and Cup to Cup Coffee Roasters.

scallops, and the blue-cheese filet mignon, but especially the hot chocolate lava cake ($11). This addictive dessert is a rich chocolate cake with a molten center of Godiva liqueur, served warm, and smothered with chocolate sauce, Heath bar crunch, and vanilla ice cream. The sleek modern interior of the restaurant lies inside a sugar-and-cotton warehouse dating from the 18th-century.

202 W. Bay St. www.chart-house.com. © **912/234-6686.** Main courses $19–$42. Mon–Thurs 5–10pm, Fri 5–10:30pm, Sat 11am–10:30pm, Sun 11am–10pm.

MODERATE

Barracuda Bob's Bar and Grill ★★ AMERICAN SEAFOOD/SOUTHERN
One of the newer kids on the block is also one of the most fun, serving fresh seafood and classic bar snacks (think Guinness wings and pepperjack fries) in a buzzing tavern by the river. Standouts include the gator gumbo, tilapia, shrimp, scallops, and crab cake, but Bob's also does a great line in fresh salads for lunch. Live music from 7pm on most Wednesdays (mostly acoustic and alternative rock).

19 E. River St. © **912/777-4381.** Main courses $11–$30. Mon–Fri 11am–10:30pm, Sat–Sun 11am–11:30pm.

Olympia Cafe ★★ GREEK This riverside restaurant, with a bright, modern interior and a casual vibe popular with tourists, specializes in authentic Greek and Mediterranean cuisine, utilizing plenty of local seafood (flounder, snapper, shrimp, grouper, and the like). All the other classics are here: moussaka, spanakopita (spinach cheese pie), and stuffed grape leaves, and others. Smaller snacks such as gyros, sandwiches, and burgers are served in the express area, and the cafe lives up to its name by also crafting great cups of coffee and cappuccino—plenty of visitors stop by just for the hot drinks and homemade baklava.

5 E. River St. www.olympiacafe.net. © **912/233-3131.** Main courses $15–$25. Daily 11am–10pm.

Vic's on the River ★★ SEAFOOD/LOWCOUNTRY Fine dining on the riverfront, with an exquisite dinner menu featuring plenty of local seafood. Items change, but specialties such as the pecan-crusted local flounder, and jumbo lump crab cakes, are usually available. Lunch is a cheaper affair, with a range of sandwiches ($8–$14) and light meals (fish tacos for $13). The building dates back to 1859, and was designed by renowned architect John Norris as a cotton warehouse for merchant John Stoddard. The spacious dining rooms are simply decorated but retain some of the historical features: high ceilings, wide windows, chandeliers, and hardwood floors. The name of the restaurant refers to one of the owners, Dr. Irving Victor, aka "Dr. Vic." A live singer with pianist performs daily.

26 E. Bay St. (entrance also at 15 E. River St.). www.vicsontheriver.com. © **912/721-1000.** Main courses $15–$31. Sun–Thurs 11am–10pm, Fri–Sat 11am–11pm.

Where to Dine in Savannah

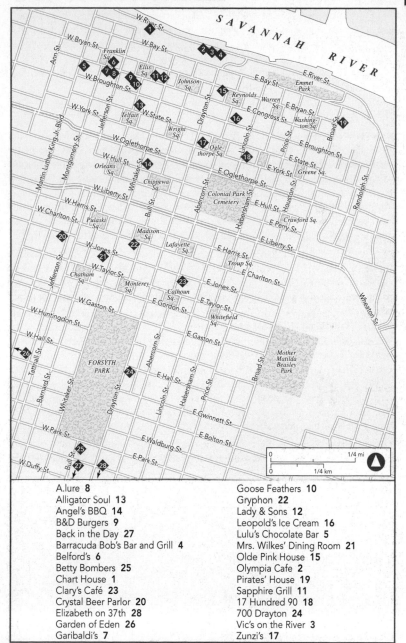

A.lure **8**
Alligator Soul **13**
Angel's BBQ **14**
B&D Burgers **9**
Back in the Day **27**
Barracuda Bob's Bar and Grill **4**
Belford's **6**
Betty Bombers **25**
Chart House **1**
Clary's Café **23**
Crystal Beer Parlor **20**
Elizabeth on 37th **28**
Garden of Eden **26**
Garibaldi's **7**

Goose Feathers **10**
Gryphon **22**
Lady & Sons **12**
Leopold's Ice Cream **16**
Lulu's Chocolate Bar **5**
Mrs. Wilkes' Dining Room **21**
Olde Pink House **15**
Olympia Cafe **2**
Pirates' House **19**
Sapphire Grill **11**
17 Hundred 90 **18**
700 Drayton **24**
Vic's on the River **3**
Zunzi's **17**

The Historic District

VERY EXPENSIVE

Alligator Soul ★★ NEW SOUTHERN   This upscale Southern cuisine from Chef Stephen McLain represents one of Savannah's most enjoyable eating experiences. The farm-to-table menus are seasonally inspired and might include anything from a twist on fried green tomatoes and shrimp-and-grits, to stuffed lamb loin, rabbit, and buffalo. The setting is magnificent—underground cellars built as a grain warehouse around 1885.

114 Barnard St., Telfair Square. www.alligatorsoul.com. (C) **912/232-7899.** Main courses $22–$36. Daily 5:30–10pm.

Sapphire Grill ★★ AMERICAN/LOWCOUNTRY   Chef Chris Nason opened his feted restaurant back in 1998, and it still sets the benchmark for local market-to-table cuisine. His restaurant is relatively small, with soft lighting and a rustic contemporary style that incorporates exposed brick, reclaimed wood, and bold modern art. His interpretation of Savannah's antebellum culinary heritage includes sesame-spiked calamari with ginger-coriander pesto, pineapple-sage shortbread, and benne-encrusted local black grouper with jasmine rice. You can also simply pick your meat (steak, duck, lamb) or seafood (salmon, scallops, tuna) and then select the sauce (the white truffle butter is hard to beat).

110 W. Congress St. www.sapphiregrill.com. (C) **912/443-9962.** Main courses $22–$42. Sun–Thurs 6–10:30pm; Fri–Sat 5:30–11:30pm.

700 Drayton ★★★ INTERNATIONAL/LOWCOUNTRY   Arguably Savannah's best restaurant, this shrine to fine dining occupies the oldest and most evocative part of the Mansion on Forsyth Park (see p. 122), a lavish space enhanced with high ceilings, striking contemporary art installations, and Victorian antiques. Start with rope-cultured mussels (served with chorizo and grilled baguette) or the fried green tomatoes, dressed up with banana pepper chow chow (a spicy relish), and caraway goat cheese. The entrée selection always comprises local seafood—think wreckfish with boursin-cheese grits, or scallops in yellow coconut curry—but the meats are especially well done. Options might include New Zealand venison loin served with seasonal succotash and sweet potato steak fries, or a broiled pork chop with hazelnut cream.

In the Mansion on Forsyth Park, 700 Drayton St. www.mansiononforsythpark.com. (C) **912/721-5002.** Main dinner courses $26–$34. Daily 7–11am, 11:30am–2pm, and 5–10pm.

EXPENSIVE

A.lure ★★ LOWCOUNTRY   This stylish contemporary take on Lowcountry food is one of the up-and-coming stars of the local scene. Helmed by Chef Charles Zeran, the restaurant sources all its meat, fish, and produce locally. Combining Lowcountry gourmet, fresh seafood, and farm-to-fork into a unified concept, the menu is playful and highly creative. It's tempting to make a meal from the appetizers: perhaps a gruyère-and-onion tart, lamb carpaccio, and cornmeal-dusted chicken livers. The main dishes are just as enticing, laced with Italian and Asian influences: think Thai duck curry, nori-dusted catch of the day, and seafood pastas. Still, my favorite is the shrimp and grits, a creamy, leek-inflected delight.

309 W. Congress St. www.aluresavannah.com. (C) **912/233-2111.** Main courses $14–$35. Daily 5–10:30pm (bar 4pm–midnight).

Belford's ★ LOWCOUNTRY   Fine steaks and seafood in the City Market district. Highlights include the house-made crab cakes (and she-crab stew), the fresh shrimp, greens and grits, the smoked salmon, and the lip-smacking Angus beef steaks. Save room for Marlowe's white-chocolate cheesecake. Sunday brunch comes with a complimentary glass of sparkling wine. The beautiful red-brick premises were built in 1902 for Savannah's Hebrew Congregation. W.T. Belford, a successful food wholesaler, purchased the building in 1913.

315 W. St. Julian St. www.belfordssavannah.com. ✆ **912/233-2626.** Lunch $10–$22, dinner $15–$42, Sun brunch $8–$21. Mon–Sat 11am–4pm and 5–10pm, Sun 11am–10pm. Closed Thanksgiving, Christmas Eve (night), and Christmas Day.

Garibaldi's ★ SEAFOOD/ITALIAN   This fine Italian restaurant features an elegant Neoclassical dining room with high ceilings, chandeliers, and Roman columns— all very romantic. The refined Italian-inspired menu makes a welcome break from all things Southern, though local seafood still features prominently. The crab cakes, oysters, and clams are all good, but I would opt for the seafood fettuccini or delicious clams and linguine in a garlic-white-cream sauce. The building was constructed around 1871 to serve as the Germania Fire House (operated by German-born volunteers).

315 W. Congress St. www.garibaldisavannah.com. ✆912/232-7118. Main courses $11–$34. Mon–Thurs and Sun 5–10:30pm, Fri–Sat 5pm–midnight.

Lady & Sons ★★ SOUTHERN   Paula Deen established her now wildly popular restaurant in 1989 with the help of her sons, Jamie and Bobby. In 2003 the restaurant moved into this much larger former White Hardware building dating from around 1810. Most folks come here for Deen's Southern buffet, which is a great deal and loaded with all the usual crowd-pleasers. You can also order a la carte: shrimp and grits, Savannah crab cakes, strip steaks, grouper, and even chicken pot pie often appear on the menu, though items do change. It's all super touristy, of course, but the quality is good and plenty of locals still come here. Despite losing her show on the Food Network in 2013, Deen's cookbooks have continued to sell like hotcakes, and you should expect long lines outside her flagship restaurant at peak times. Reservations recommended.

102 W. Congress St. www.ladyandsons.com. ✆ **912/233-2600.** Main courses $19–$33; all-you-can-eat buffet $18. Mon–Sat 11am–10pm, Sun 11am–5pm (buffet only).

Olde Pink House ★★★ SEAFOOD/SOUTHERN   One of Savannah's great culinary experiences, adjacent to the Planters Inn (p. 124), this local institution remains extremely popular. It knocks out all the Lowcountry favorites, albeit with a touch of gourmet flair. Local grouper is stuffed with crab, then smothered in white-wine lemon sauce, mashed potatoes, and mixed beans, while the mouth-watering bourbon-molasses grilled pork tenderloin is served with sweet potato, pecan vanilla butter, and collards. For appetizers it's hard to top the lump crab hush puppies with spicy peach remoulade. The property itself dates way back to 1771, and is indeed covered in a layer of pink stucco.

23 Abercorn St., Reynolds Sq. ✆ **912/232-4286.** Main courses $9–$35. Sun–Mon 5–10:30pm, Tues–Sat 11am–10:30pm.

17 Hundred 90 ★★ AMERICAN/SOUTHERN   The elegant restaurant at this hotel (p. 124) is a cozy, historic space with stone slab floors, exposed brick walls, and a timbered roof. The traditional menu comprises delights such as homemade

Savannah is probably the last place you'd expect to find a Jewish food festival, but the annual event—referred to locally as **"Shalom, Y'all"**—is a genuine celebration of all things matzoh ball, latke, and challah. The festival usually takes place at the end of October in Forsyth Park, when around 10,000 people trawl the various stalls selling snacks and small plates. Admission is free, and most snacks are $1.

honey-dripped biscuits, jambalaya, and shrimp and grits with Tasso gravy, but also a decent range of burgers, sandwiches, and vegan and vegetarian options. The lounge area serves as a popular cocktail bar, with Ladies Night every Wednesday (8–10pm) and happy hour Monday to Friday 4 to 7pm.

307 E. President St. www.17hundred90.com. ✆ **912/236-7122.** Main courses $19–$34. Daily 11am–3pm and 5–9pm (lounge until midnight).

MODERATE

Crystal Beer Parlor ★★ AMERICAN   Though it still serves good draft beers, this is primarily a restaurant rather than a pub, established in 1933 just to the west of the Historic District. The menu offers solid American comfort food, from all-beef brown-ale burgers with hand-cut fries to crab stew and rack of lamb. The salad menu is also very extensive, and there is plenty of fresh seafood. You can wash it all down with good old Pabst, Miller, and Dixie lager beers. The atmospheric red-brick building dates from the early 1900s, serving as a speakeasy in the early 1930s, with an interior that looks like a 1950s bar and diner.

301 W. Jones St., at Jefferson St. ✆ **912/232-9754.** Main courses $9–$19. Sun–Thurs 11am–10pm, Fri–Sat 11am–11pm.

Gryphon ★★ CAFE   This elegant cafe is operated by the Savannah College of Art and Design (some SCAD students do work here), housed in the grand 1926 Scottish Rite building on Madison Square. The handsome interior, replete with carved-mahogany bookcases and original stained-glass panels, really sets this place apart. The menu features primarily local, organic produce, with a selection of gourmet sandwiches (try the ratatouille with smoked gouda), and light meals such as spinach pie with feta and dill, or wild Georgia shrimp.

337 Bull St., at Charlton St., Madison Sq. http://web.scad.edu/experience/gryphon. ✆ **912/525-5880.** Main courses $11–$15. Mon–Sat 11am–6pm, Sun 11am–3pm.

Mrs. Wilkes' Dining Room ★★★ SOUTHERN   The best fried chicken in the South (seriously!) and a wonderful Southern eating experience all around. Menus change, but the large tables-for-ten are usually topped with platters of fried chicken, sweet-potato soufflé, black-eyed peas, okra gumbo, corn muffins, and biscuits, shared family-style. There might be meatloaf, mac and cheese, rice and gravy, candied yams, and beef stew. The inspiration for this festival of Southern deliciousness was Sema Wilkes, who took over the boardinghouse here in 1943 and kept feeding hungry patrons right up to her death in 2002, at the age of 95. The property itself dates back to 1870, though the dining room looks like it's frozen in the 1950s.

107 W. Jones St. (west of Bull St.). www.mrswilkes.com. ✆ **912/232-5997.** Lunch $18. No credit cards. Mon–Fri 11am–2pm.

Pirates' House ★ AMERICAN/SOUTHERN   This is more of a kitschy tourist attraction than a straight restaurant, but it's still a fun place to eat for families (the owners play up an alleged connection with *Treasure Island* and the fictional Captain Flint). The attractively weathered clapboard property dates back to 1753, with a decent claim to be the oldest building in the city (even though it's been modified many times since then). Although it started life as a rough-and-ready sailors' tavern, it doesn't have much to do with pirates anymore, and instead specializes in home-style food like chicken gumbo, crab-melt sandwich, and fried catfish. The popular Southern-style buffet runs daily 11am to 3pm.

20 E. Broad St. www.thepirateshouse.com. © **912/233-5757.** Main courses $18–$26 dinner; lunch buffet $14. Sun–Thurs 11am–9:30pm, Fri–Sat 11am–10pm.

INEXPENSIVE

Angel's BBQ ★★★ BARBECUE   This hole-in-the-wall joint has become a minor Savannah legend, thanks to its sumptuous meats, creative sauces, and delicious sides. Opt for the classic pulled pork or BBQ beef brisket sandwiches, accompanied by "angel fries" (fries topped with BBQ–baked beans and cheese), and collard greens with peanuts. Your choice of barbecued meat by the pound ($12) comes with house sauce. Other homemade sauces include "golden idol," a mustard-based South Carolina sauce, and the "Memphis sweet," a Memphis-style sauce sweetened with molasses.

21 W. Oglethorpe Lane. www.angels-bbq.com. © **912/495-0902.** Main courses $7–$12. Tues 11:30am–3pm, Wed–Sat 11:30am–6pm.

B&D Burgers ★★ BURGERS   Savannah's premier burger joint knocks out some of the juiciest sandwiches in the South. With three branches, on the surface B&D might seem like a typical fast-food franchise, but this is a local mini-chain, established in Savannah in 2001, and the atmosphere is more like a diner inside. The concept revolves around build-your-own burgers. You choose your patty (beef, bison, turkey, or veggie), temperature (rare to well done, beef and bison only), then the type of bun, and a huge range of toppings (50¢ each) from sauces and cheeses to veggies and onion rings, pineapple, and other wondrous ingredients.

209 W. Congress St., Ellis Sq. www.bdburgers.net. © **912/238-8315.** Burgers $9–$15. Mon–Wed 11am–midnight, Thurs–Sun 11am–2am.

Back in the Day ★★ BAKERY   This popular local pit-stop offers delicious, handcrafted cakes, brownies, artisan breads, pies, cookies, cupcakes, and espresso from Cup to Cup Coffee Roasters. It's also worth considering a visit for a light lunch (11am–3pm), with fresh sandwiches (like grilled cheese, and bacon with onion jam), and a couple of veggie options (including a salad). The bourbon-bread pudding is impossible to resist.

2403 Bull St. www.backinthedaybakery.com. © **912/495-9292.** Sandwiches $8–$10. Tues–Sat 8am–5pm.

Clary's Café ★ AMERICAN   Established in 1903 as a drugstore, venerable Clary's was really made famous by *Midnight in the Garden of Good and Evil*. Though it's essentially a fairly average diner, it's the literary connection—author John Berendt is said to pop in on occasion, as is Lady Chablis—that keeps pulling the tourists in. Breakfast is a good time to visit, with the eggs benedict and country-fried steak the standouts on a very large, traditional menu. At other meals try the baked French onion soup ($6), the grilled Reuben sandwich, burgers, or pecan pie, washed down with a real malted milkshake ($4).

404 Abercorn St. (at Jones St.). www.claryscafe.com. ℭ **912/233-0402.** Breakfast $6–$14, main courses $6–$13. Mon–Fri 7am–4pm, Sat–Sun 8am–4pm.

Garden of Eden ★★ SOUL FOOD A little out of the way on the west side of the district, but well worth the effort. This is central Savannah's go-to Soul Food joint, established by locals Pastor Joseph Williams and Connie Williams. Folks line up here for the lip-smacking breakfasts, while daily lunch specials (meat and two sides) are just $5. Think genuine Southern-fried chicken and catfish, and the best macaroni and cheese anywhere. It's not all deep-fried and cheese however; the Garden adds a healthy spin by offering baked and grilled meats, and fresh vegetables seasoned with smoked turkey. Leave room for the pound cake. Children 4 and under eat for free.

714 Martin Luther King Jr. Blvd. ℭ **912/349-1420.** Main courses $5–10. Mon–Fri 6am–6pm, Sat 11am–6pm.

Goose Feathers ★★ CAFE/BAKERY Cozy cafe serving wholesome light meals as well as wickedly decadent desserts. Though it's not a Southern tradition, the real must-try item here is the "whoopie pie" (various sweet-cream fillings surrounded by two moist cakes), from $3. Seasonal flavors to watch out for include raspberry, piña colada, pumpkin, and cinnamon. Otherwise breakfast comprises a variety of bagels, butter croissants, homemade oatmeal with fresh fruit, eggs benedict, and the signature "Breakfast Panini," while a huge range of salads and sandwiches are available for lunch.

39 Barnard St. ℭ **912/233-4683.** Main courses $5–$8. Mon–Fri 7am–3pm, Sat–Sun 8am–3pm.

Leopold's Ice Cream ★★★ ICE CREAM Don't leave Savannah without paying homage to this local institution. Serving frozen treats since 1919, Leopold's still makes all its flavors on the premises, according to original recipes devised by the Leopold brothers (who emigrated here from Greece). Though the original store closed in 1969, the family reopened the business in this new location in 2004 (original fixtures salvaged from the old store include the black-marble soda fountain and wooden interior phone booth). Purists will enjoy the tutti-frutti or pistachio flavors, but the lavender, sugar plum fairy, and rum bisque are some of the more adventurous options on offer.

212 E. Broughton St. www.leopoldsicecream.com. ℭ **912/234-4442.** Scoops $3–$5. Mon–Thurs 11am–10pm, Fri–Sat 11am–11pm, Sun 11am–10pm.

Lulu's Chocolate Bar ★★ CAFE/BAR Savannah is fast getting a reputation for quality bakeries, coffee houses, and dessert specialists, and this is one of the best. Stylish Lulu's serves cakes and coffee during the day, while later in the evening it reverts to a cool bar, with a range of specialty cocktails and martinis. The main event here is the mind-blowing "Rapture Sundae," a concoction of vanilla ice cream, frozen chocolate mousse, fresh berries, and pitchers of caramel, and dark and white chocolate sauces ($14–$18, serves 2–3 people).

42 Martin Luther King Jr. Blvd. www.luluschocolatebar.net. ℭ **912/480-4564.** Desserts $3–$14. Sun–Thurs noon–midnight, Fri–Sat 2pm–2am.

Zunzi's ★★ INTERNATIONAL/SOUTH AFRICAN This great little sandwich take-out got a huge boost after appearing on the Food Network. The signature Conquistador chicken sandwich is the most popular order. The food here is really internationally inspired, though there's a definite South African influence (burger Jo-burg–style, homemade South African sausage, and South African iced tea, for example). The food quality is good, and the sandwiches are huge—try the "Godfather," which is big enough for two people. Vegetarians are especially taken care of, with numerous options (wraps, sandwiches, curries, and pastas). Expect long lines at lunchtime.

108 E. York St. www.zunzis.com. *(€)* **912/443-9555.** Main courses $7–$11. Mon–Sat 11am–5pm.

The Victorian District

VERY EXPENSIVE

Elizabeth on 37th ★★★ MODERN SOUTHERN Fabulous haute cuisine served in a gorgeous early 1900s mansion, with dining rooms that drip with Southern plantation elegance: period paintings and antiques, soft lighting, high ceilings, and marble fireplaces. Talented chef Kelly Yambor utilizes fresh coastal seafood, local produce, and the restaurant's own house-grown herbs and edible flowers to re-imagine Southern classics. Items change, but could include creations such as baked creamy sage grits and roasted vegetable hash, delicate parmesan-dusted local flounder served with Grass Roots Farms' spiced quail hash, or roast chicken with wild mushrooms. Mouth-watering local oysters, blue crabs, and Virginia sea scallops always feature.

105 E. 37th St. www.elizabethon37th.net. *(€)* **912/236-5547.** Main courses $30–$40; 7-course fixed-price menu $90. Daily 6–9pm.

INEXPENSIVE

Betty Bombers ★★★ AMERICAN This local gem lies just south of Forsyth Park inside American Legion Post 135 (p. 152), a friendly diner rarely frequented by tourists. Everything on the menu is tasty and good—the chili, tacos, burgers, and sandwiches—but it's the chicken wings (10 for $10) that really bring in the regulars, served with a choice of mouth-watering dipping sauces. The other main draw? The opening hours, with food served right up to the 2am close on weekends.

1108 Bull St. *(€)* **912/272-9326.** Main courses $7–$13. Tues–Wed 11am–midnight, Thurs–Sat 11am–2am.

Outlying Areas

MODERATE

Johnny Harris Restaurant ★★ AMERICAN This Savannah institution has been in business since 1924 (the present location dates from 1936), though today it seems more like an upscale, 1950s diner. After all these years the two specialties of the house remain the famed "bar-B-que" meats, and the "batterless" fried chicken (the Johnny Harris Famous Bar-B-Que Sauce Company was a spin-off), but everything is good. I really like the half hickory-smoked chicken and the baby-back ribs, brushed with their totally addictive spicy honey BBQ sauce.

1651 E. Victory Dr. (Hwy. 80). www.johnnyharris.com. *(€)* **912/354-7810.** Main courses $7–$26. Sun–Thurs 11:30am–9:30pm, Fri–Sat 11:30am–10:30pm.

EXPLORING SAVANNAH

Savannah is easy to explore on foot, though the free buses are handy when the heat picks up. A good place to start is **River Street** overlooking the Savannah River, lined with bars and restaurants, and a great place to stroll or take a boat ride. A short walk east will take you to **Morrell Park** and the **Waving Girl** statue, a tribute to Florence

On a bluff above the Savannah River, **Factors Walk** and **Factors Row** are arrays of redbrick structures named for the men who graded cotton in these buildings in the heyday of the 19th-century King Cotton economy. They were called "Factors." The structures themselves were built by skilled architects, who had to contend with a bluff rising sharply from the river. On this bluff, they designed a series of multi-tiered buildings that were made from ballast stone and brick, hauled across the Atlantic.

Rice and cotton were the main crops held in the warehouses along Factors Walk, both flourishing industries at the time. During Savannah's peak as a seaport, ships from all over the world docked adjacent to the row of warehouses so their exports could be directly loaded into their holds.

The rows of warehouses were made accessible by a network of iron bridgeways over cobblestone ramps. Today this section, lying between Bull and East Broad streets, is filled with shops and restaurants. Ramps lead from the Bay Street level down the bluff to restaurant-lined **River Street,** which you can explore after checking out Factors Row and Factors Walk.

Margaret Martus, who once waved to all the vessels going in and out of the harbor. Also here is the small **Olympic Flame Cauldron,** which was lit during the 1996 Atlanta Olympics (Savannah was the sailing venue). South of the river lies Savannah's **Historic District.** Though the area is peppered with intriguing sights—many of them old mansions—the soul of the city is its great network of **squares** (see p. 136), really subtropical parks shaded by canopies of live oaks, dogwoods, and blooming magnolias. **Johnson Square** is the oldest and largest, though **Reynolds Square** makes an equally attractive starting point of any tour, marked by the statue of **John Wesley.**

The Historic District

Andrew Low House ★★ HISTORIC HOUSE   Once the wealthiest man in Savannah, Scottish immigrant **Andrew Low** had this fine Neoclassical residence built in 1848 overlooking Lafayette Square. Made of stucco over brick, with elaborate ironwork, shuttered piazzas, carved woodwork, and crystal chandeliers, it is now one of the city's most beguiling house museums. Each of its opulent rooms is beautifully furnished in period furniture. Low was a fascinating and tragic character, imprisoned by the North in the Civil War, entertaining an aging **Robert E. Lee** in 1870, hosting English author **William Makepeace Thackeray** in 1853 and 1856 (during his lecture tours), and married twice, with both wives dying young. Low died in England in 1886, but was buried back in Savannah beside the graves of his two wives. Andrew's son **William Low** subsequently inherited the house, though his place in history has been overshadowed by his wife **Juliette Gordon Low** (see Juliette Gordon Low Birthplace, p. 141). Juliette moved into the house after her marriage in 1886, and was living here when she founded the **Girl Scouts of the USA** in 1912. She died in the southeast bedroom in 1927, and left the **carriage house** to the Girl Scout Council of Savannah (p. 139).

329 Abercorn St. www.andrewlowhouse.com. ℭ **912/233-6854.** Admission $10. Tours (on the hour and half-hour) Mon–Sat 10am–4pm, Sun noon–4pm. Closed major holidays and first 2 weeks in Jan.

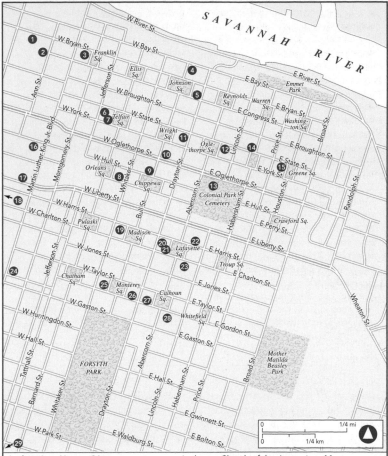

Andrew Low House **21**
Cathedral of St. John the Baptist **22**
Christ Church Episcopal **5**
Colonial Park Cemetery **13**
Davenport House Museum **14**
First African Baptist Church **3**
First Bryan Baptist Church **1**
Flannery O'Connor Childhood Home **23**
Georgia State Railroad Museum **18**
Girl Scout First Headquarters **20**
Green-Meldrim Home **19**
Harper Fowlkes House **8**
Independent Presbyterian Church **9**
Juliette Gordon Low Birthplace **10**
Laurel Grove South Cemetery **29**

Lutheran Church of the Ascension **11**
Massie Heritage Center **28**
Mercer Williams House Museum **25**
Owens-Thomas House **12**
Ralph Mark Gilbert Civil Rights Museum **24**
Savannah Children's Museum **18**
Savannah History Museum **17**
SCAD Museum of Art **16**
Second African Baptist Church **15**
Ships of the Sea Maritime Museum **2**
Telfair Academy **6**
Temple Mickve Israel **26**
Trinity United Methodist Church **7**
U.S. Custom House **4**
Wesley Monumental United Methodist Church **27**

Savannah has 24 historic **squares,** and it is these that really make the city such a special place—there's nothing quite like them anywhere else in the U.S. **Johnson Square** was the first to be laid out by James Oglethorpe in 1733 (it's still the largest of the city's 24 squares). The main attraction here is the monument to Revolutionary War hero **General Nathanael Greene,** who was reinterred under the obelisk in 1901. To the south lies leafy **Wright Square,** the burial site of **Tomochichi,** a leader of the Creek nation and ally of Oglethorpe. He is commemorated by a monument in the southeast corner of the square erected in 1899 (his original resting place was controversially covered by a memorial to war hero William Washington Gordon in the 1880s). **Ellis Square** is one of the city's oldest and busiest centers, but what you see today was re-created and re-opened in 2010: the original square was destroyed in the 1950s to make way for a parking garage (now demolished). Today a statue of local singer

Johnny Mercer looks over the space. South of Ellis lies **Telfair Square,** one of the original four laid out by Oglethorpe, while **Reynolds Square** to the east contains a bronze statue honoring **John Wesley,** founder of Methodism (Wesley preached in Savannah 1735–38). Other highlights include grand **Chippewa Square,** laid out in 1815 and containing an equestrian statue of Savannah founder **General James Oglethorpe,** created by famed sculptor Daniel Chester French in 1910. The "park bench" scene in which Tom Hanks opens *Forrest Gump* (1994) was actually filmed on the north side of the square, though the bench itself was just a prop. If you're more interested in scenery than history, aim for **Pulaski Square** on Barnard Street, between Harris and Charlton streets, home to the most picturesque live oaks in the city. The most beautiful square in the city, however, is **Monterey Square,** located on Bull Street, between Taylor and Gordon streets.

Cathedral of St. John the Baptist ★★ CATHEDRAL

This is the oldest Catholic Church in Georgia, dating back to 1799, though the current Victorian Gothic incarnation, with its distinctive twin spires, was rebuilt in 1900 after a devastating fire (work went on for another 13 years). The whole cathedral was completely renovated between 1998 and 2000, with each of the 24 Renaissance-style murals by local artist Christopher Murphy (completed 1912), painstakingly restored, a new altar and baptismal font fashioned out of Carrara marble, and a new pulpit featuring engravings of the four evangelists (this was rebuilt in 2004 after an arson attack). Inside, you'll also see marble railings, 1904 stained-glass windows from Austria, large carved wooden Stations of the Cross (created in Munich, Germany, and installed in 1900), and a 2,081-pipe Noack tracker organ (1987).

222 E. Harris St. www.savannahcathedral.org. ✆ **912/233-4709.** Free admission. Mon–Fri 9–11:30am and 12:30–5pm; open for Mass Sat noon and 5:30pm; Sun 8am, 10am, 11:30am, and 1pm.

Christ Church Episcopal ★ CHURCH

Savannah was founded as a Church of England settlement, and its center of religious life was this church—the first one established in the colony in 1733. As a result, it is known as the "Mother Church of Georgia." The third and present building on this site was designed by James H.

Button Gwinnett, one of the signers of the Declaration of Independence, is buried in Savannah's Colonial Park Cemetery. He died of wounds suffered in a duel with General Lachlan McIntosh, another Georgian Revolutionary hero, and buried in the same place.

The feud between the two men stemmed from insults McIntosh leveled against Gwinnett after the disastrous Georgia invasion of British Florida in 1777 (Gwinnett was already angry that McIntosh had been promoted to brigadier general in the Continental Army instead of himself). McIntosh called Gwinnett a "scoundrel and lying rascal," in front of the Georgia Assembly. Infuriated, Gwinnett challenged McIntosh to a duel on what is now the cemetery grounds. Both men were shot in the leg, at which point their seconds stopped the duel. McIntosh, though injured, had only sustained a flesh wound. Gwinnett's thigh injury was far more serious, and he died 3 days after being taken to a hospital. McIntosh was tried for murder but acquitted. Mrs. Gwinnett refused to condemn McIntosh for the death of her husband.

Nonetheless, Gwinnett's friends in the Savannah colony turned on McIntosh, and for his own protection he was ordered to leave the city and join George Washington at Valley Forge. In time, he redeemed himself by leading troops successfully at the Siege of Savannah in 1779, and spending 2 years as a British prisoner of war. He became an esteemed, though poor, citizen of Savannah in his later years, and died in 1806. Ironically, the two old enemies, Gwinnett and McIntosh, are buried very near each other.

Cooper in Greek Revival style and was consecrated in 1840. The church was nearly destroyed by fire in 1898, but was rebuilt within its original walls. Famous clergy in the history of this church include John Wesley (1736) and George Whitehead (1738). The first Sunday school conducted in Georgia was held here, and the first hymnal in English was published here. The current assistant rector, the Rev. Julia Sierra Wilkinson, became the first woman and the first African-American priest in the history of the parish in 2012. The 1819 **Revere Bell** is one of the rarest in the country. The bell bears this ominous engraving: "THE LIVING TO THE CHURCH I CALL, AND TO THE GRAVE I SUMMON ALL."

28 Bull St. www.christchurchsavannah.org. (C) **912/238-0434.** Most Fri–Sat 10:30am–3pm.

Colonial Park Cemetery ★★ HISTORIC CEMETERY The oldest burial ground (ca. 1750) in Savannah is filled with magnolia trees and is such a beautiful setting that the city turned it into a park in 1896. Many distinguished Georgians are buried here, including Archibald Bulloch, first President of Georgia, and James Habersham, acting royal Governor of the Province (1771–73), but none are more famous than the two duelers who fought one of the most notorious battles of insults in the state (see box below). More than 700 victims of the 1820 yellow fever epidemic are also buried here, along with numerous other men killed in duels. The cemetery was closed to new burials in 1853. Unsurprisingly, it is now a popular destination for **ghost tours** (see p. 147).

201 E. Oglethorpe Ave., at Abercorn St. www.savannahga.gov. (C) **912/944-0455.** Free admission. Daily Nov–Mar 8am–5pm, Apr–Oct 8am–8pm.

Davenport House Museum ★ MUSEUM   Completed around 1820 for master builder Isaiah Davenport, this Federal-style home was one of the first in Savannah to be restored by the Historic Savannah Foundation in the 1950s, opening as a museum in 1963. The period wallpaper, furniture, ceramics, and textiles inside are either from the period or are period reproductions. Davenport lived here until his death in 1827, and the contents of the house have been selected to reflect the inventory taken at that time.

324 E. State St. www.davenporthousemuseum.org. ☏ **912/236-8097.** Admission $9 adults, $7 students 18–21, $5 children 6–17, free for children 5 and under. Mon–Sat 10am–4pm, Sun 1–4pm. Closed major holidays.

First African Baptist Church ★ CHURCH   This was the first African Baptist church founded in America. It was established in 1773 by **George Leile,** a slave whose master allowed him to preach to other slaves when they made visits to plantations along the Savannah River. Leile was granted his freedom some time before the Revolutionary War began, and in 1782 he sailed to Jamaica with the British. **Andrew Bryan,** another former slave who purchased his freedom, took over the congregation and built the first, simple wooden church in 1794 (see below). In 1832 the congregation purchased the newly vacated First Baptist Church on Franklin Square, rebuilding the current, relatively plain church over it brick by brick, completing it in 1859. It became the first brick building in Georgia to be owned by African Americans. The pews located in the balcony are original and were made by slaves. Before the Civil War, a hidden basement served as part of the Underground Railroad for escaped slaves.

23 Montgomery St., Franklin Sq. www.firstafricanbc.com. ☏ **912/233-6597.** Tours $7 adults, $6 students and seniors over 60, free for children 5 and under. Tours Tues–Sat 11am and 2pm, Sun 1pm. Sun worship 9am and 10am.

First Bryan Baptist Church ★ CHURCH   In 1832 the congregation of First African Baptist Church (see above), split over a doctrinal dispute. One group moved to Franklin Square but retained the original name, while another remained on the site of Andrew Bryan's original wooden chapel, eventually becoming known as **First Bryan Baptist Church.** Though the current Greek Revival structure was built between 1873 and 1888, the site is extremely significant in African-American history, being the oldest parcel of real estate in America to be owned by blacks. Bryan himself was able to purchase his freedom for 50 pounds sterling, and lived until 1812.

559 W. Bryan St. www.fbbcsav.org. ☏ **912/232-5526.** Free tours by appointment only.

Flannery O'Connor Childhood Home ★★ HISTORIC HOUSE   This house museum is dedicated to Savannah's most respected literary scion. **Flannery O'Connor** (1925–64), author of *Wise Blood* (1952) and *The Violent Bear It Away* (1960), lived in this house from her birth in 1925 to 1938. The interior has been restored to reflect the Depression era, with enthusiastic tour guides relating fascinating stories about the O'Connor family and Mary Flannery's early life. Though she died tragically young (of complications from lupus), O'Connor is also highly regarded for her short stories, including the collection *A Good Man Is Hard to Find* (1955). She won the O. Henry Award three times.

207 E. Charlton St. www.flanneryoconnorhome.org. ☏ **912/233-6014.** Admission $6 adults, $5 students, free for 15 and under. Fri–Wed 1–4pm.

Georgia State Railroad Museum ★★ MUSEUM   Train aficionados will love this tribute to America's once mighty railroads. Located at the old Savannah Shops

Ignored by most tourists, the **U.S. Custom House** ★★ is a stately Greek Revival gem, designed by New York architect John Norris and completed in 1852. The oldest federal building in Georgia, it's an austere granite temple with a "Tower-of-the-Winds" portico. It also lies on historic ground: **James Edward Oglethorpe**'s one-story frame house originally stood on the site in 1733, and **John Wesley** delivered his first sermon in Savannah here in 1736.

The U.S. Custom House stands at 1 E. Bay St. (✆ **912/652-4264**), and remarkably, still serves its original purpose. As a public building you are free to look around during office hours (Mon–Fri 8am–5pm), check out the stunning main staircase, and view temporary exhibits on display in the main lobby.

Complex of the **Central of Georgia Railway,** some of the museum buildings date back to the 1850s, including the massive Roundhouse (rebuilt in the 1920s with a still-operating turntable), Machine Shop, Tender Frame Shop, and Blacksmith Shop. The yards were closed in 1963, and now contain several vintage steam and diesel engines, office cars, and cabooses. You can actually take a ride on the No. 30 steam locomotive built in 1913, and the No. 119 diesel built in 1947—check the website for the current schedule.

The railway yards' Carpentry Shop houses the **Savannah Children's Museum** ★ (✆ **912/651-4292;** www.savannahchildrensmuseum.org), a fun diversion for little ones that comprises several hands-on play stations and exhibits, all outside. The museum is open Tuesday to Saturday 10am to 4pm, and Sunday 11am to 4pm (also open on Mondays during school holidays). Admission is $8 for 1-year-olds and over.

655 Louisville Rd. www.chsgeorgia.org/Railroad-Museum.html. ✆ **912/651-6823.** Admission $10 adults, $6 children 2–12. Daily 9am–5pm.

Girl Scout First Headquarters ★ HISTORIC HOUSE   Girl Scouts current and former tend to be the most enthusiastic visitors to this small but historic property, though anyone with an interest in American social history should take a look. Built as the carriage house attached to the Andrew Low House (see p. 134), Girl Scout founder Juliette Low willed the property to the movement in 1927. It is now a Girl Scout muscum and program center owned and operated by the Girl Scouts of Historic Georgia. The short film, exhibits, and rare artifacts inside chronicle the history of Girl Scouting in the USA, an eye-opening reminder of what Girls Scouts have achieved over the years.

330 Drayton St. www.gshg.org. ✆ **912/233-6014.** Admission $3. Mon–Tues and Thurs–Sat 10am–4pm. Closed major holidays.

Green-Meldrim Home ★★ HISTORIC HOUSE   This impressive house was built on Madison Square between 1853 and 1861 for wealthy, English-born cotton merchant Charles Green, but its moment in history arrived when it became the Savannah headquarters of **Gen. William Tecumseh Sherman** at the end of his devastating rampage across Georgia in 1864, euphemistically known as the "March to the Sea." It was from here that the general sent his now infamous (at least, in Savannah) Christmas telegram to President Lincoln, offering him the city as a Christmas gift. Ex-city mayor and judge Peter Meldrim purchased the house in 1892, explaining the current name. Since 1943 it's served as the Parish House for St. John's Episcopal Church next door,

6 | A visit TO THE MIDNIGHT MURDER HOUSE

A landmark Italianate building, paid for by Civil War Gen. Hugh W. Mercer, great-grandfather of Johnny Mercer, the **Mercer Williams House** was completed around 1869. It became known as "the envy of Savannah." Decades later, it was rumored that Jacqueline Onassis wanted to purchase it for use as a private home.

Mostly its fame was promulgated by the John Berendt book *Midnight in the Garden of Good and Evil* (1994). It was here, in May 1981, as related in the book, that the wealthy homosexual antiques dealer Jim Williams (who bought the house in 1969), fatally shot his lover, that blond "walking streak of sex," Danny Hansford, age 21. The house was also the setting where Williams gave his legendary

Christmas parties each year. In January 1991, Williams died of a heart attack at the age of 59 in the same room where he'd been accused—and acquitted—of shooting Hansford.

For years, heirs to Williams's estate have been downplaying its prurience and emphasizing, with much justification, Williams's role as a bon vivant and the savior of at least 60 historic houses in and around Savannah. The Williams family, which still owns the house, has agreed, for a fee, to open it for tours.

Buy your ticket in the carriage house behind the house, inside a gift shop loaded with objects of which Jim, a decorator, might have approved, and a few that he might have found sappy and sentimental. You'll be ushered into one

but open to the public as one of the best examples of Gothic Revival architecture in the South. Though little remains of its original furnishings, rooms have been restored in a period style, and some fixtures have survived: the American black walnut wood floors, stucco crown moldings, Carrara marble mantles, and large mirrors in gold leaf frames purchased from Austria.

14 W. Macon St. www.stjohnssav.org. ✆ **912/233-3845.** Admission $10 adults, $5 students, free for pre-school children. Tues and Thurs–Fri 10am–4pm (last tour 3:30pm), Sat 10am–1pm (last tour 12:30pm).

Harper Fowlkes House ★★ HISTORIC HOUSE This ravishing Greek Revival mansion dates back to 1842, though most of what you see today are Second Empire-style renovations completed in the 1890s. The name reflects the last owner, **Alida Harper Fowlkes,** who purchased the property in 1939, and willed it to the Society of the Cincinnati in 1985 (the society is an organization of men who are direct descendants of George Washington's officers during the Revolution). All of the current furnishings were Alida's, including the silver, china, and crystal. The chandeliers are originals, created around 1847, as is the Federal-style mahogany clock in the hallway, and the 1930 Persian rug and 1740 Queen Anne-style chair in the Front Double Parlor.

230 Barnard St, Orleans Sq. www.harperfowlkeshouse.com. ✆ **912/234-2180.** Admission $10. Wed–Fri 10am–3pm, Sat 10am–1pm.

Independent Presbyterian Church ★★ CHURCH This grand and elegant Regency-style church was built by the first Presbyterian congregation in Georgia, founded in 1755. Their original church burned down in 1796, while the first incarnation on the current site was modeled after St. Martin in the Fields in London and was completed in 1819. This version also burned down, in the great fire of 1889, but the current faithful reproduction was completed in 1891, replete with a magnificent spire of an ongoing series of tours, each lasting about 30 minutes. Tours depart from the carriage house and gift shop, at the compound's back entrance (430 Whitaker St.).

Don't think for a second that questions about Williams's sexuality, his promiscuity, or the murder will be engaged. Guides firmly advise before tours even begin that these are AAA Tours (including only questions about art, architecture, and antiques). Photos are rigidly forbidden, and a strong-willed guide will emphatically urge you "not to touch, drool on, dribble on, or engage the furniture or art objects in any way."

The house has been used as the setting for movies, including Clint Eastwood's film *Midnight in the Garden of* *Good and Evil* in 1997 (check out the photos of Kevin Spacey and co.), *Swamp Thing* (1982), and *Return of Swamp Thing* (1989). The Mercer Williams House is gorgeously furnished in a style that befits a sophisticated millionaire. It is not an authentic re-creation of a Federalist or mid-Victorian home, thanks to the presence of comfortable 20th-century sofas, personalized photos, art objects, and the "eclectic" vision of its style setter.

The **Mercer Williams House Museum** is at 429 Bull St., Monterey Square (✆ **912/236-6352**; www.mercerhouse. com). Admission is $13 for adults and $8 for students with ID (both college and grad school). Tours run every 40 minutes Monday to Satuday 10:30am to 4:10pm and Sunday noon to 4pm.

and one of the most beautiful interiors in the city. Future president Woodrow Wilson was married here in 1885.

207 Bull St., at Oglethorpe Ave. www.ipcsav.org. ✆ **912/236-3346.** Free admission. Mon–Fri 9am–4pm. Services on Sun 11am and 5:15pm, Wed noon.

Juliette Gordon Low Birthplace ★ HISTORIC HOUSE   Juliette Gordon Low—the founder of the Girl Scouts—lived in this Regency-style house from her birth in 1860 until she married William Low in 1886 (p. 134). It's now maintained both as a memorial to her and as a Girl Scout national center. The Victorian additions to the 1818–21 house were made in 1886, just before Juliette's wedding. Today the house, which is relatively modest by Savannah standards, contains a large number of artworks that originally belonged to the Gordon family and Juliette, including memorabilia associated with the founding of Girl Scouts in 1912.

10 E. Oglethorpe Ave. www.juliettegordonlowbirthplace.org. ✆ **912/233-4501.** Admission $9 adults, $8 students 5–21 and Girl Scouts, free for children 4 and under. Mon–Sat 10am–4pm, Sun 11am–4pm (Nov–Feb closed Wed). Closed major holidays and first 2 weeks in Jan.

Lutheran Church of the Ascension ★ CHURCH   Few churches in Georgia have had the bizarre history of this landmark. Its origins are in 1734, when Austrians emigrating from Salzburg founded the church. Although most of the Salzburgers settled in a community called Ebenezer outside Savannah, not all of them did. The Reverend Johann Bolzius, who had created the Ebenezer New Jerusalem Lutheran Church, came back to Savannah in 1741 to found this church for the Salzburgers who had settled in the historic core. A wooden structure originally stood on this site, until a Greek Revival church replaced it in 1844. Thirty-five years later, architect George B. Clarke added the second floor and the medieval-style turrets. Today it's a fine example of the Grecian-Doric style that swept eastern America.

When General Sherman invaded Savannah in 1864, the church pew cushions were used as beds by his soldiers, and the pews themselves were used as firewood. The church was turned into a hospital for the sick and wounded. Although the building was damaged, it was not destroyed. Today it's known for its spectacular "Ascension Window" inside the sanctuary behind the pulpit, and for its rose window featuring Martin Luther and his coat of arms in front of the building.

120 Bull St. on Wright Sq. www.ascensionsavannah.org. (C) **912/232-4151.** Mon–Fri 9am–1pm.

Massie Heritage Center ★ MUSEUM   Here's a stop in the Historic District for the kids. Geared to school-age children, the center features various exhibits about Savannah, including such subjects as the city's Greek, Roman, and Gothic architecture; the Victorian era; and a history of public education. Other exhibits include a period costume room and a 19th-century classroom, where children can experience a classroom environment from days gone by.

207 E. Gordon St., Calhoun Sq. (C) **912/201-5070.** Admission $7 adults, $6 seniors, $5 children 5–17, $2 children 1–4. Mon–Sat 10am–4pm, Sun noon–4pm.

Owens-Thomas House ★★ MUSEUM   This ornate house, designed by William Jay and completed in 1819, is considered one of the finest examples of English Regency architecture in the U.S. The house contains decorative art ranging from the late 18th to the early 19th century, as well as a rare example of intact urban slave quarters. The home was built for cotton merchant and banker Richard Richardson and his wife Francis Bolton, whose brother was married to Ann Jay, the architect's sister. Revolutionary hero **Marquis de Lafayette** was a guest here in 1825, and in 1831 the mayor of Savannah, George Welshman Owens, purchased the property. It remained in his family until 1951, when Margaret Thomas, George Owens' granddaughter, bequeathed it to the Telfair Museum of Art (p. 143).

124 Abercorn St. www.telfair.org/visit/owens-thomas. (C) **912/233-9743.** Admission $15 adults, $5 students, free for children 4 and under. Tours every 15 min. Sun 1–5pm, Mon noon–5pm, Tues–Sat 10am–5pm. Last tours at 4:30pm.

Ralph Mark Gilbert Civil Rights Museum ★★ MUSEUM   This museum is fraying at the edges and might appear to be closed from the outside, but it chronicles an important but under-represented aspect of Savannah history and deserves your support. Start with the 17-minute film shown in the old chapel (2nd floor), and then move on to the poignant exhibits commemorating the fight for African-American equality and civil rights in the region. The building was constructed in 1914 for the African American-owned Wage Earners Bank, and **Dr. Ralph M. Gilbert** (1899–1956) was pastor of the First African Baptist Church between 1939 and 1956, leading the Civil Rights movement in the area.

460 Martin Luther King Jr. Blvd. (C) **912/231-8900.** Admission $8 adults, $6 seniors 65 and over, students $4. Tues–Sat 10am–4pm.

Savannah History Museum ★★ MUSEUM   This enlightening museum is located within the historic Central of Georgia Railway train shed, charting Savannah's past from 1733 to the American Revolution and Civil War, to the Industrial Revolution, and the present day. Just across the street from the museum, **Battlefield Memorial Park** commemorates the Battle of Savannah in 1779, the second bloodiest battle of the American Revolution.

303 Martin Luther King Jr. Blvd. www.chsgeorgia.org. (C) **912/651-6825.** Admission $7 adults, $4 children 2–12. Mon–Fri 8:30am–5pm, Sat–Sun 9am–5pm.

SCAD Museum Of Art ★★ MUSEUM   Savannah's foremost art gallery mounts over 20 different exhibits every year, mostly from highly renowned contemporary artists. The museum's permanent collection of 45,000 artworks includes books, antique maps, paintings by Hogarth, Van Dyck, Gainsborough, and Reynolds; modern and contemporary works by Salvador Dalí, Annie Leibovitz, Robert Mapplethorpe, Robert Rauschenberg, and Andy Warhol; and haute couture from Yves Saint Laurent, Oscar de la Renta, and Givenchy, among others. The building itself is an artful 2011 renovation of an 1853 structure, maintaining the original walls of handmade Savannah gray bricks.

601 Turner Blvd. www.scadmoa.org. ✆ **912/525-7191.** Admission $10 adults, $8 seniors, $5 students, free for children 13 and under. Tues–Wed and Fri 10am–5pm, Thurs 10am–8pm, Sat–Sun noon–5pm. Closed major holidays.

Second African Baptist Church ★ CHURCH   This early African-American congregation (ca. 1802) was known for training more ministers—black or white—than any other church in the country. The current structure dates from 1925, replacing the earlier wooden church. Two historic events took place here. First, General William Tecumseh Sherman read the **Emancipation Proclamation** to Savannah citizens at this church in 1864, promising the newly freed slaves 40 acres and a mule. Second, Dr. Martin Luther King, Jr., proclaimed his "I have a dream" sermon here before the famous march on Washington in 1963.

123 Houston St. www.secondafrican.org. ✆ **912/233-6163.** Free admission. Mon–Fri 10am–2pm.

Ships of the Sea Maritime Museum ★★ MUSEUM   This enjoyable museum showcases Savannah's long role as a port city with nine galleries of ship models, paintings, and maritime antiques. The collection is housed in Scarbrough House, an elegant Greek Revival mansion completed in 1819 for William Scarbrough, president of the Savannah Steamship Company. Exhibits include a model of Scarbrough's steamship *Savannah,* launched in New York in 1818 and the first steamship to cross the Atlantic.

41 Martin Luther King Jr. Blvd. www.shipsofthesea.org. ✆ **912/232-1511.** Admission $9 adults, $7 seniors and students 6–12, free for children 5 and under. Tues–Sun 10am–5pm. Closed major holidays.

Telfair Academy ★★ MUSEUM   Savannah's top 19th-century art museum is housed in an appropriately elegant Regency-style mansion completed in 1819 for Alexander Telfair, son of Revolutionary War hero and Georgia governor Edward Telfair. Today its period rooms contain a selection of 19th- and 20th-century American and European art, including an especially good collection of American Impressionism and Ashcan School Realism. Works by Childe Hassam, Frederick Frieseke, George Bellows, and George Luks are usually on display. One of the most popular paintings, however, is the monumental (and highly romanticized) *Black Prince at Crecy* by English-born portrait painter Julian Russell Story. The Telfair also owns the largest public collection of visual art by Lebanese writer Kahlil Gibran (best known as author of *The Prophet*), as well as Sylvia Shaw Judson's sculpture *Bird Girl,* which appeared on the original cover of *Midnight in the Garden of Good and Evil* (it was relocated here from Bonaventure Cemetery, p. 146).

In 2006, the adjoining **Jepson Center for the Arts** opened at 207 W. York St. (✆ **912/790-8800**). This stylish modern building, designed by Moshe Safdie, showcases major traveling exhibitions of contemporary art as well as installations of works from the Telfair's permanent collection. Exhibits change, but you are likely to see work by Jasper Johns, Chuck Close, Roy Lichtenstein, Jeff Koons, Robert Rauschenberg, and Frank Stella.

121 Bernard St. www.telfair.org. © **912/232-1177.** Single admission to Telfair or Jepson Center $12 adults, $5 students, free for children 4 and under; ticket including Telfair, Jepson Center, and Owens-Thomas House $20 adults, $18 seniors, $10 students. Mon noon–5pm, Tues–Sat 10am–5pm (Jepson Center open until 8pm Thurs), Sun 1–5pm (Jepson Center open at noon). Closed major holidays.

Temple Mickve Israel ★ SYNAGOGUE   At Monterey Square, this temple is home to Georgia's oldest Jewish congregation, the third-oldest congregation in the U.S. Designed by architect Henry G. Harrison, who had previously designed only Christian churches, this is the nation's only Gothic synagogue (ca. 1878). Its founding members were Spanish, Portuguese, and German Jews who came to Savannah in 1733 to escape persecution in their homelands. With them, the group carried a precious relic, the **Sepah Torah,** the oldest Torah in America. The temple today houses a museum with more than 1,800 historical artifacts on view, including portraits, religious objects, documents, and letters to the congregation from presidents George Washington, Thomas Jefferson, and James Madison.

20 E. Gordon St., on Monterey Sq. www.mickveisrael.org. © **912/233-1547.** $6 donation suggested. Tours and museum Mon–Fri 10am–12:30pm and 2–3:30pm. Closed major Jewish holidays.

Trinity United Methodist Church ★ CHURCH   This church, built between 1848 and 1850, is known as the "Mother Church of Savannah Methodism." It is hardly the most opulent church in Savannah, but it holds a fascination for students of architecture. It is known for its hand-hewn pine on its interior. It was constructed of stucco over Savannah gray brick, and its interior design is evocative of the Wesley Chapel in London. The formula for the Savannah gray brick is no longer in existence, having died with its inventor.

225 W. President St. www.trinity1848.org. © **912/233-4766.** Free admission. Mon–Fri 9am–3pm; Sun service 11am.

Wesley Monumental United Methodist Church ★ CHURCH   Built between 1876 and 1890, this Gothic Revival church is a memorial to John and Charles Wesley, the founders of Methodism (and who came to Savannah in the 1730s). It is based on designs for Queen's Kirk in Amsterdam and holds 1,000 parishioners surrounded by stained-glass windows dedicated to the historic figures of Methodism. (Queen's Kirk is the popular name for Nieuwe Kerk, the most-visited church in Amsterdam, standing next to the Royal Palace on Dam Square.) Wesley Monumental took a long time to erect because of financial problems in the Reconstruction era and a catastrophic outbreak of yellow fever in Savannah.

429 Abercorn St. www.wesleymonumental.org. © **912/232-0191.** Free admission. Fri 10am–noon, Sun 9:30am–noon; Sun service 8:45am and 11am.

The Victorian District

Laurel Grove South Cemetery ★ HISTORIC CEMETERY   Many of the city's most prominent African Americans are buried in this cemetery, developed in 1850 and one of the oldest black cemeteries in America. Both antebellum plantation slaves and free blacks during the Reconstruction era were buried here, including **Andrew Bryan** (1716–1812), a pioneer Baptist preacher in the area.

2101 Kollock St. www.savannahga.gov. © **912/651-6772.** Free admission. Daily 8am–5pm.

About 10 miles south of downtown Savannah is the charming community of **Isle of Hope ★**. First settled in the 1840s as a summer resort for the wealthy, it's now a showcase of rural antebellum life. To reach Parkersburg (as it was called in those days), citizens traveled by steamer down the Wilmington River or by a network of suburban trains. Today you can reach Isle of Hope by driving east from Savannah along Victory Drive to Skidaway Road. At Skidaway, go right and follow it to LaRoche Avenue. Take a left and follow LaRoche until it dead-ends on Bluff Drive.

This is the perfect place for a lazy afternoon stroll. The short path is home to authentically restored cottages and beautiful homes, most enshrouded with Spanish moss cascading from the majestic oaks lining the bluff. A favorite of many local landscape artists and Hollywood directors, Bluff Drive affords the best views of the Wilmington River.

As you head back toward Savannah, drive down Skidaway Road. On your left is **Wormsloe Historic Site ★★**, 7601 Skidaway Rd. (*©* **912/353-3023;** www.gastateparks.org/wormsloe). The former colonial estate of Noble Jones (1702–75), Wormsloe is mostly in ruins now, but it's worth a look. After you enter the gates, you proceed down an unpaved oak-lined drive, and the ruins lie less than half a mile off the road. Dr. Jones was one of Georgia's leading colonial citizens and a representative to the continental Congress. Today costumed interpreters add context during programs and events. The on-site **museum** displays artifacts unearthed at the plantation, and screens a short film about the site and the founding of Georgia in 1733. Wormsloe is open Tuesday to Sunday 9am to 5pm. Admission is $10 for adults, $9 for seniors, $5 for children 6 to 17, and $2 for children 5 and under.

Outlying Attractions

Fort McAllister State Park ★★ HISTORIC SITE Lying 10 miles southwest of downtown Savannah on U.S. 17, on the banks of the Ogeechee River, Fort McAllister is a restored Confederate earthwork fortification. Constructed in 1861–62, it withstood nearly 2 years of Union naval bombardments before it finally fell on December 13, 1864, in a bayonet charge that ended General Sherman's infamous March to the Sea. There's a visitor center with an excellent **Civil War Museum** and 13-minute audiovisual presentation, and also walking trails and campsites.

3894 Fort Mcallister Rd., Richmond Hill. www.gastateparks.org/FortMcAllister. *©* **912/727-2339.** Admission $8 adults, $7 seniors, $5 children 6–17, $2 for 5 and under. Parking $5. Park daily 7am–10pm; museum daily 8am–5pm.

Old Fort Jackson ★★ HISTORIC SITE About 2½ miles east of the center of Savannah via the Islands Expressway is Georgia's oldest standing fort, with a 9-foot-deep tidal moat around its brick walls. In 1778, a mud battery was built here to try and stop the British from occupying Savannah during the Revolutionary War, but it was soon abandoned (and the British duly seized the city). The original brick fort was begun in 1808 and named for **James Jackson,** Revolutionary War veteran, and state governor. The fort was manned during the War of 1812, though it saw no action. It was enlarged and strengthened between 1845 and 1860 and saw its greatest use as headquarters for the Confederate river defenses during the Civil War—it was finally

MARTINIS IN THE cemetery

All fans of *Midnight in the Garden of Good and Evil* must pay a visit to the now world-famous **Bonaventure Cemetery,** 330 Bonaventure Rd. (📞 **912/651-6843;** www.bonaventurehistorical.org), a Southern Gothic gem on the low-lying eastern edge of the city. Filled with obelisks and columns and dense shrubbery and moss-draped trees, it's open daily 8am to 5pm. The helpful **Visitors Center** is only open Saturday and Sunday 10am to 4pm. Free **guided tours** provided by the Bonaventure Historical Society run on the second Sunday of each month at 2, 2:30, and 3pm, and the preceding Saturday at 2pm. Admission and the tours are free. You get here by taking Wheaton Street east out of downtown to Skidaway to Bonaventure Road. (You don't want to approach it by boat like Minerva the "voodoo priestess" and John Berendt did—and certainly not anywhere near midnight.)

This cemetery lies on the grounds of what was once a great oak-shaded plantation, built by Col. John Mulryne. In the late 1700s, the mansion caught fire during a formal dinner party; reportedly, the host quite calmly led his guests from the dining room and into the garden, where they settled in to finish eating while the house burned to the ground in front of them. At the end, the host and the guests threw their crystal glasses against the trunk of an old oak tree. It's said that on still nights you can hear the laughter and the crashing of the crystal. In The Book, Mary Harty calls the ruins the "scene of the Eternal Party. What better place, in Savannah, to rest in peace for all time—where the party goes on and on."

It was at the cemetery that John Berendt had martinis in silver goblets with Miss Harty, while they sat on the bench gravestone of poet **Conrad Aiken.** She pointed out to the writer the double gravestone bearing the names of Dr. William F. Aiken and his wife, Anna, parents of Conrad. They both died on February 27, 1901, when Dr. Aiken killed his wife and then himself. The Aikens are buried in Lot 78H. Songwriter **Johnny Mercer** is also buried here, in Lot 49H.

But not **Danny Hansford,** the blond hustler of the book. You can find his grave at Lot 6, Block: G-8 in the **Greenwich Cemetery,** next to Bonaventure. **Jim Williams** is buried in Gordon, Georgia, a 3½-hour drive northwest of Savannah.

occupied by Sherman's troops in December 1864. Its arched rooms, designed to support the weight of heavy cannons mounted above, now contain 13 exhibit areas.

1 Fort Jackson Rd. www.chsgeorgia.org/old-fort-jackson.html. 📞 **912/232-3945.** Admission $7 adults, $4 children 2–12. Daily 9am–5pm.

Pin Point Heritage Museum ★★ MUSEUM   About 12 miles south of downtown Savannah, overlooking the marshes along the Moon River, this fascinating museum commemorates the history of the local **Gullah/Geechee** community. The site is located in the old A.S. Varn & Son oyster and crab factory, which closed in 1985. Pin Point is a tiny Gullah fishing community founded in 1896 by former slaves and their descendants, from Ossabaw and the surrounding islands. The Sweetfield of Eden Baptist Church (still here) was founded 1 year later. Current Supreme Court Justice **Clarence Thomas** was born in Pin Point in 1948; his family spoke Gullah as a first language (Gullah is the historic creole language of the Low Country, based heavily on West African languages). Note the limited opening hours.

9924 Pin Point Ave. (off Hwy. 204). www.pinpointheritagemuseum.com. 📞 **912/667-9176.** Admission $7. Thurs and Sat 9am–5pm.

Organized Tours

If it's a *Midnight in the Garden of Good and Evil* tour you seek, then you've obviously come to the right place. Virtually every tour group in town offers tours of the *Midnight* sites, many of which are included on their regular agenda. *Note:* Some tour outfits will accommodate only groups, so if you're traveling alone or as a pair, be sure to make that known when you make your tour reservations.

BY HORSE & CARRIAGE A delightful way to see Savannah is by **horse-drawn carriage.** An authentic antique carriage carries you over cobblestone streets as the coachman spins tales of the town's history. The 1-hour tour ($20 adults, $10 children 5–11) covers 15 of the 20 squares (daily 9am–3pm, every 30 min.). Reservations are required. Contact **Carriage Tours of Savannah** (© **912/236-6756;** www.carriagetour sofsavannah.com).

BY BUS **Old Town Trolley Tours** (© **912/233-0083** or 888/910-8687; www.trol leytours.com) operates tours of the Historic District ($31 for adults, $11 for children 4–12), with pickups at most downtown inns and hotels, as well as a 1-hour **Ghosts & Gravestones Tour** ($29 adults), detailing Savannah's ghostly past (and present), and even a **Paula Deen Tour** ($50 for adults, $26 for children 4–12). Call ahead to make reservations for all tours.

Oglethorpe Gray Line Tours (© **866/374-8687;** www.grayline.com) offers narrated hop-on, hop-off trolley bus tours of the main museums, squares, parks, and homes. Tours cost $20 per person and one loop lasts 90 minutes (daily 9am–4pm, every 25 min.).

WALKING TOURS **Savannah Walks,** from a headquarters at Abercorn Street just south of Reynolds Square (© **912/238-9255;** www.savannahwalks.com), offers three well-orchestrated guided walking tours. The most mainstream is the **Savannah Stroll,** a well-articulated ramble through the city's most central parks and thoroughfares, offering an anecdotal introduction to the city's history, lore, and legend. They also have a tour focusing on Savannah's triumphs, torments, and despair during the War Between the States (**Civil War Savannah**). Both tours last 90 minutes and are offered twice daily, at 10am and 1pm. After dark, the venue gets spookier, with a **Savannah Ghosts** tour, a 90-minute exposure of the city's flair for the macabre, with departures at 7:30 and 9:30pm. Each of the tours requires an advance reservation, and costs $18 for adults and $9 for children 6 to 14. Your guide might be a part-time student at Savannah College of Art and Design (SCAD) or an older, long-term resident of the city, but the likelihood is high that he or she will have some dramatic flair and a gift for oratory as well.

Ghost Talk Ghost Walk takes you through colonial Savannah on a journey filled with stories and legends based on Margaret Debolt's book *Savannah Spectres and Other Strange Tales.* If you're not a believer at the beginning of the guided tour, you may be at the end. The tour starts at John Wesley's monument in Reynolds Square. For information, call © **912/233-3896** or visit www.ghosttalkghostwalk.com. Hours for tour departures can vary. The cost is $10 for adults and $5 for children 12 and under.

BY BOAT **Riverboat cruises** are offered aboard the *Savannah River Queen,* operated by the **River Street Riverboat Company,** 9 E. River St. (© **800/786-6404** or 912/232-6404; www.savannahriverboat.com). You get a glimpse of Savannah as Oglethorpe saw it back in 1733. You'll see the historic cotton warehouses lining River Street and the statue of Florence Martus, known as Savannah's Waving Girl, as the huge modern freighters see it when they arrive daily at Savannah. **Harbor Sightseeing Cruises** are $22 for adults and $13 for children 4 to 12.

Dolphin Eco Tours, a narrated nature cruise, leaves from the Bull River Marina, 8005 Old Tybee Rd. (U.S. 80 E.). Call ℰ **912/898-9222** or visit www.bullrivermarina. com for information. Passengers are taken on the 1993 40-foot pontoon boat *Natures Way,* for an encounter with the friendly bottle-nosed dolphin. Scenery and wildlife unfold during the 90-minute cruise down the Bull River. Trips are daily noon, 2pm, and sunset spring through fall, weather permitting. Fares are $20 for adults, $18 for seniors, and $10 for children 3 to 12. There's a 30-passenger limit.

Outdoor Activities

BIKING Savannah doesn't usually have a lot of heavy traffic except during rush hours, so you can bicycle up and down the streets of the Historic District, visiting as many of the green squares as you wish. There's no greater city bicycle ride in all the state of Georgia. The best place for **rentals** is **Perry Rubber Bike Shop** (ℰ **912/236-9929;** www.perryrubberbikeshop.com), 240 Bull St., open Monday to Saturday 10am to 6pm and Sunday noon to 5pm. Full-day rentals are $35 (half-day is $20). Many inns and hotels also provide bikes for their guests. Note that riding on the sidewalks, and through (rather than around), the squares is illegal. **Savannah Bike Tours** (ℰ **912/704-4043;** www.savannahbiketours.com), 41 Habersham St, runs relaxed, daily 2-hour guided tours on bikes (bikes provided). Tours are $25 for ages 12 and above, and $10 for children 11 and under.

FISHING **Amick's Deep Sea Fishing,** 6902 Sand Nettles Dr. (ℰ **912/897-6759;** www.amicksdeepseafishing.com), offers daily charters featuring a 41-foot 1993 custom-built boat. The rate is $120 per person and includes rod, reel, bait, and tackle. Bring your own lunch. Beer and soda are sold on board. Reservations are recommended, but if you show up 30 minutes before the scheduled departure, there may be space available—Amick's accepts individuals, not just groups. The boat departs at 7am and returns at either 3 or 5pm.

GOLF **Bacon Park Golf Course,** Shorty Cooper Drive (ℰ **912/354-2625;** www. baconparkgolf.com), offers three nine-hole courses (two designed by Donald Ross in 1926), with greens fees around $35 for an 18-hole round, including cart. Golf facilities include a lighted driving range, putting greens, and a pro shop. It's open daily dawn to dusk.

Henderson Golf Club, 1 Henderson Dr. (ℰ **912/920-4653;** www.hendersongolf club.com), includes an 18-hole championship course, a lighted driving range, a PGA professional staff, and golf instruction and schools. The greens fees are $33 Monday to Friday and $39 Saturday and Sunday. It's open daily 7am to 7pm.

Or try the 9-hole **Mary Calder Golf Club,** 1201 West Lathrop Ave. (ℰ **912/238-7100**), where the greens fees, including cart, are $20 per day Monday to Friday and $25 per day Saturday and Sunday. It's open daily 7am to 8pm (or 5:30pm in winter).

JOGGING "The most beautiful city to jog in"—that's how the president of the **Savannah Striders Club** (www.savystrider.com) characterizes Savannah. The historic avenues indeed provide an exceptional setting for your run. Visit the website for details of where to run and of organized group runs.

RECREATIONAL PARKS **Bacon Park** (see "Golf," above, and "Tennis," below) includes 1,021 acres, with archery, golf, tennis, and baseball fields. **Daffin Park,** 1001 E. Victory Dr. (ℰ **912/351-3851**), features playgrounds, tennis, basketball, baseball, a swimming pool, a lake pavilion, and picnic grounds. Both parks are open daily 8am to 11pm (Oct–Apr until 10pm).

Located at Montgomery Cross Road and Sallie Mood Drive, **Lake Mayer Community Park** (☎ 912/652-6780) consists of 75 acres featuring a multitude of activities, such as public fishing and boating, lighted jogging and bicycle trails, a playground, and pedal-boat rentals.

TENNIS **Bacon Park Tennis Center,** 6262 Skidaway Rd. (☎ 912/351-3850), offers 16 hard, lighted courts open Monday to Thursday 9am to 9pm, and Friday to Sunday 9am to 5pm. The **Daffin Park Tennis Complex,** 1001 E. Victory Drive (☎ 912/351-3851), offers six supervised clay courts and three lighted hard courts, open daily 8:30am to 7pm. Court fees at both places are $6 per player. **Forsyth Park,** at Drayton and Gaston streets (☎ 912/351-3850), has four courts open daily 7am to 9pm that are free. Use of the eight lighted courts at **Lake Mayer Park,** Montgomery Cross Road, is also free. They are open daily 8am to 11pm.

Especially for Kids

Savannah is an extremely family-oriented city, with many of its major attractions offering programs and tours targeted specifically at kids. The **Massie Heritage Center** (p. 142) and **Savannah Children's Museum** (p. 139) are two sights specifically geared to little ones, but the **Georgia State Railroad Museum** (p. 138) is also lots of fun—especially on days when the steam train is running. Consider also the **ArtZeum** at the **Jepson Center for the Arts** (p. 143), a hands-on gallery that encourages children to explore art using large installations they can walk into, architectural building blocks, a magnetic sculpture wall, and other interactive displays.

Weekends at **Fort Pulaski** (p. 156) and **Old Fort Jackson** (p. 145) are especially entertaining, with musket and soldier demonstrations, cannon firing, encampments of costumed troops, special programs, and demonstrations.

Any member of the Girl Scouts will of course be excited to visit the **Juliette Gordon Low Birthplace** (p. 141), home and memorial to the founder of the movement, in addition to **Girl Scout First Headquarters** (p. 139). The **Andrew Low House** (p. 134) is also associated with Juliette.

Most kids love the **Pirates' House** restaurant (p. 131) with its creaky floors loaded with historic kitsch, *Treasure Island* memorabilia, and ghost stories. Talking of haunted houses, older children will enjoy Savannah's many **ghost tours** (p. 147).

Just outside the city, the **Oatland Island Wildlife Center,** 711 Sandtown Rd. (☎ 912/395-1212; www.oatlandisland.org), open daily 10am to 5pm is a great place to let off steam and see gray wolves, armadillos, cougars, snakes, bobcats, and various birds of prey in a natural setting. Admission is $5 for adults, $3 for children 4 to 17, and free for kids 3 and under. For **day-trips** further afield, including **Tybee Island,** see Chapter 7 (p. 157).

SHOPPING

River Street is a souvenir shopper's delight, with some 9 blocks (including Riverfront Plaza) of interesting shops, offering everything from crafts to clothing. The **City Market** district (www.savannahcitymarket.com), a 4-block area of restored warehouses between Ellis and Franklin squares, boasts art galleries, boutiques, and sidewalk cafes along with a horse-and-carriage ride. Bookstores, boutiques, and antiques shops are located between Wright Square and Forsyth Park.

Further outside the center, **Oglethorpe Mall** (www.oglethorpemall.com; Mon–Sat 10am–9pm, Sun noon–6pm), at 7804 Abercorn St., has more than 100 specialty shops and four major department stores, as well as restaurants and fast-food outlets. The massive **Savannah Mall** (www.savannahmall.com; Mon–Sat 10am–9pm, Sun noon–6pm), 14045 Abercorn St., offers two floors of shopping, plus a food court with its own carousel.

Antiques

Alex Raskin Antiques ★★★ Fascinating store in a gorgeous Italianate house, crammed with antiques, historic curios, rugs, works of art, and vintage furniture. It's open Monday to Saturday 10am to 5pm. 441 Bull St. (in the Noble Hardee Mansion), Monterey Sq. www.alexraskinantiques.com. ℰ **912/232-8205.**

Habersham Antiques Market ★★★ It's worth venturing out of the city center to this prime antiques market, an ensemble of 70 dealers inside the old Smith Brothers building. On offer is everything from vintage clothing and jewelry and antique toys, to French copper kitchenware and old crystal. Open Monday to Friday 9:30am to 5:30pm and Saturdays 10am to 5pm. 2502 Habersham St., at 41st St., 1 block north of Victory Dr. www.habershamantiquesmarket.com. ℰ **912/238-5908.**

J.D. Weed & Co. ★★ Antique store just outside the center for serious collectors but also for the simply curious, with an especially rare collection of old Southern furniture. Usually open Monday to Friday 8:30am to 5pm and Saturday 8:30am to noon. 102 W. Victory Dr. www.jdweedco.com. ℰ **912/234-8540.**

Jere's Antiques ★ Specialist in fine antiques but especially English and Continental furniture from the 18th, 19th, and 20th centuries. It also designs and builds bespoke furniture. Open Monday to Saturday 9am to 5pm. 9 N. Jefferson St. www.jeres antiques.com. ℰ **912/236-2815.**

Arts & Crafts

Fresh Exhibitions ★ Formerly the Desotorow Gallery, this space is now operated by Art Rise Savannah (www.artrisesavannah.org), and only open limited hours, but the changing exhibits inside are usually of a very high quality. Open Saturdays 1 to 4pm, or by appointment. 2427 De Soto Ave. www.freshexhibitions.org. ℰ **912/376-9953.**

Gallery 209 ★ Two floors of original paintings, sculpture, woodwork, gold and silver jewelry, enamel work, batik prints, pottery, photography, and stained glass, primarily by local artists. The gallery occupies an appropriately aged-looking 1820s cotton warehouse on the riverside. It's open daily 10:30am to 9pm. 209 E. River St. www.gallery209savannah.com. ℰ **912/236-4583.**

Village Craftsmen ★★ This is the store of a co-op of local artisans from Savannah and the Lowcountry region. Quality is good and there's a huge range of products for sale: quilts, handmade soap, jewelry, paintings, sweet-grass baskets, Gullah art, glass art, and photographs of old Savannah. Open daily 10am to 6pm. 223 W. River St. www.villagecraftsmensavannah.com. ℰ **912/236-7280.**

Books

Barnes & Noble ★ If you're looking for the nearest branch of this national chain you'll need to drive or take the bus to Oglethorpe Mall. It's a big one, with the usual extras like free Wi-Fi and in-store cafe. The store is open daily 9am to 10pm (Fri–Sat until 11pm). 7804 Abercorn, Ext. 72. www.barnesandnoble.com.com. ℰ **912/353-7757.**

The Book Lady Bookstore ★★★ Cozy, independently owned store selling used, rare, out-of-print, and new books since 1978. Its stock of over 50,000 books includes an extensive collection on Georgia and Southern history. It's open Monday to Saturday 10am to 5:30pm. 6 E. Liberty St. www.thebookladybookstore.com. © **912/233-3628.**

E. Shaver, Bookseller ★★ Located right on Madison Square in a Greek Revival mansion, this is one of the city's oldest and most appealing bookstores, offering a huge range of hard and softback books, antique maps, and prints. It's open Monday to Saturday 9:30am to 5:30pm. 326 Bull St., Madison Sq. www.eshaverbooks.com. © **912/234-7257.**

Candy & Other Foods

Lowcountry Gourmet Foods ★ Load up with posh condiments at this friendly local store, selling aged balsamic vinegars, extra-virgin olive oils, barbecue sauces, and gourmet seasonings. It's open Monday to Thursday and Saturday 10am to 6pm, Friday 10am to 7pm, and Sunday 11am–5pm. 10 W. Broughton St. www.lowcountrygourmetfoods. com. © **912/233-7500.**

River Street Sweets ★★ Beloved family-owned candy store established in 1973, best known for the Savannah Pralines you'll see all over town, but also chocolate bear claws, glazed pecans, homemade pecan pies and praline pound cakes. Check out the vintage machine still making 50 different flavors of taffy. It's open daily 9am to 10pm. 13 E. River St. www.riverstreetsweets.com. © **912/447-0200.**

The Salt Table ★★ Popular concept store with free tasting samples of hundreds of different salts, seasonings, sugars, teas, Amish popcorn, and local honey. It's open Monday to Thursday 10am to 6pm, Friday and Saturday 10am to 8pm, and Sunday 11am to 6pm. 51 Barnard St. www.salttable.com. © **912/234-4602.**

Savannah Bee Company ★★ The flagship store of this burgeoning local chain (founded in 2002), does sell a vast range of honey and raw honeycomb, from wildflower to Tupelo styles, but has also become known for its associated beauty products (body lotions, soaps, and so on). It's open Monday to Saturday 10am to 7pm, and Sunday 11am to 5pm. There's also a branch at 1 W. River St. 104 W. Broughton St. www. savannahbee.com. © **912/233-7873.**

Savannah's Candy Kitchen ★★ This riverside sweet store was founded by Stan "The Candy Man" Strickland, over 30 years ago. It's turned into another successful chain, thanks to its traditional Southern treats such as Savannah cakes, pecan pies, pecan log rolls, glazed pecans, and praline layer cakes. The store is open daily 9:30am to 10pm (Fri–Sat until 11pm). 225 E. River St. www.savannahcandy.com. © **912/233-8411.**

Cookware

Paula Deen Retail Store ★ The indomitable Paula Deen opened her eponymous store in 2007 next to her restaurant (p. 129). The store is just as popular, selling Deen's cookbooks and her signature bakeware, cookware, cutlery, dinnerware, glassware, souvenir mugs, aprons, and even pots of her house seasoning. It's open Monday to Thursday 10am to 9pm, Friday and Saturday 10am to 10pm, and Sunday 10am to 5pm. 108 W. Congress St. www.pauladeenretailstore.com. © **912/232-1579.**

Jewelry & Silver

Levy Jewelers ★   This local family jewelers opened in 1900 and still offers high-quality diamonds, watches, jewelry, and giftware. It's open Monday to Saturday 10am to 5:30pm. 2 E. Broughton St. www.levyjewelers.com. ✆ **912/233-1163.**

ShopSCAD ★★   Boutique that exclusively features the artwork and designs created by Savannah College of Art and Design artists (SCAD opened the store in 2003). The store is open Monday to Friday 9am to 5:30pm, Saturday 10am to 6pm, and Sunday noon–5pm. 340 Bull St., Madison Sq. www.shopscad.com. ✆ **912/525-5180.**

ENTERTAINMENT & NIGHTLIFE

River Street, along the Savannah River, is the major after-dark venue. Many night owls stroll the waterfront until they hear the sound of music they like, then follow their ears inside. In summer, concerts of jazz, Big Band, and Dixieland music fill downtown **Johnson Square** with lots of foot-tapping sounds that thrill both locals and visitors. Some of Savannah's finest musicians perform regularly on this historic site. *Note:* Almost uniquely in the U.S., you are permitted to drink alcohol in the streets in open cups in Savannah.

Bars, Clubs & Pubs

American Legion Post 135 ★★   Built in 1913 for the Chatham Artillery, this vaguely fortress-like structure was purchased by the American Legion in 1946. Today the no-frills but incredibly hip bar is open to everyone, not just war veterans, with the added attraction of free pool, darts, and Betty Bombers on the premises (p. 133). Wednesday features line dancing at 7pm, Thursday is ladies night (4pm–midnight) featuring $1 beers, while Fridays men get $1 beers from 6 to 8pm. Open Monday to Wednesday 4pm to midnight, Thursday to Saturday 4pm to 2am. 1108 Bull St. www.alpost135.com. ✆ **912/233-9277.**

The Distillery ★★   Congenial gastropub with over 100 craft beers on offer, including a selection of 21 rotating microbrews on tap. The premises were built in 1904 for the Kentucky Distilling Co., converting to Freich's Pharmacy during prohibition. The current pub opened in 2008, and though it contains an antique copper still, no beer is currently made here. It's open Monday to Thursday 11am to 11pm, Friday and Saturday 11am to midnight, and Sunday noon to 10pm. 416 W. Liberty St. www.distillerysavannah.com. ✆ **912/236-1772.**

Hang Fire Bar ★★★   This casual Whitaker Street bar and club has a reputation for being a hipster hangout, but it's a relaxed, fun place to have a few drinks. Monday is happy hour all night (buy one, get the next drink for $1), while the Wednesday trivia night (9pm) is wildly popular, and Thursday is karaoke night. Fridays and Saturdays the DJs come out and it's more like a club. Try the "scorpion tea," a bourbon cocktail ($5). It's open Monday to Saturday 5pm to 3am. 37 Whitaker St. ✆ **912/443-9956.**

Kevin Barry's Pub ★   No-nonsense Irish public house since 1980 offering cold Guinness. It's always great fun, and becomes the epicenter of St. Patrick's Day shenanigans in Savannah. Kevin Barry's serves traditional Irish and American pub food, and every night at 8pm you can hear live Irish and American folk music. They have a generous happy hour Sunday to Thursday noon to 4pm. The pub is open Monday to Saturday 11am to 3am and Sunday 12:30pm to 2am. 117 W. River St. www.kevinbarrys.com. ✆ **912/233-9626.**

Moon River Brewing Co ★★   Savannah's only real brew pub, where you can watch the ales and stouts being made on site. Moon's second best feature is its 5,400-square-foot outdoor Beer Garden, the perfect place to spend a sunny afternoon or warm evening. Beers on tap include the tasty Swamp Fox (IPA), The Bomb (dry Irish stout), and Sauvage Saison (Belgian farmhouse ale), while the menu includes burgers, ribs, sandwiches, and steaks. Open daily 11am to 11pm (Fri–Sat until midnight). 21 W. Bay St. www.moonriverbrewing.com. ✆ **912/447-0943.**

Rocks on the Roof ★★   Try and visit this fashionable cocktail bar high atop the Bohemian Hotel at least once. The views of the Talmadge Bridge, container boats, and River Street crowds are magnificent, and you can order tapas-style snacks to go with the drinks. Lounge on stylish sofas under palmetto palms, or perch on stools around the designer fire pit, with a glamorous, primarily local, crowd. The bar is open Wednesday 7 to 11pm, Thursday to Saturday 9pm to 1am, and Sunday 6 to 10pm. 102 W. Bay St. www.bohemianhotelsavannah.com/dining. ✆ **912/721-3800.**

17 Hundred 90 Lounge   Atmospheric lounge bar next to the lauded restaurant (p. 129), with an excellent wine and cocktail list catering to a primarily professional crowd. Like the restaurant, the lounge recalls an old brick-and-beams tavern, with worn bar stools and wooden counter top. Look out for one of Savannah's many ghosts here: the spirit of Anna Powers, who killed herself by jumping out of the third-floor window, is said to patrol the premises. Happy hour with hors d'oeuvres runs daily 4 to 7pm. The lounge is open daily 11am to midnight. 307 E. President St. www.17hundred90.com. ✆ **912/236-7122.**

Live Music

Jazz'd Tapas Bar ★★   This underground jazz bar lies just south of Ellis Square, a stylish spot to see quality live acts (blues, swing, jazz, or classical), enhanced with exuberant contemporary art, industrial chic furnishings, and an eye-popping bar display (bottles of wine in giant tubes on the wall). The food here is exceptional also, with creative small plates (and soups, salads, and tacos) washed down with punchy martinis. Open Sunday to Thursday 4 to 10pm, and Friday and Saturday 4pm to midnight (no live music Mon). 52 Barnard St. www.jazzdtapasbar.com. ✆ **912/236-7777.**

The Jinx ★★★   One of the city's most popular live venues, with a laid-back indie vibe, vaguely Gothic decor, cool bartenders, and an eclectic roster of acts that includes rock, metal, alternative, country, and even hip hop. Order a Pabst beer, grab some popcorn, and enjoy. It's open Monday to Saturday 5pm to 3am. 127 W. Congress St. ✆ **912/236-2281.**

Wormhole ★★   Popular local live music venue and bar, south of downtown in the area known as the Starland Design District. Most of the bands here are loosely described as "alternative," but there's a lot of variety, from folk and acoustic to bluegrass and grungy rock. The venue also hosts popular Comedy Planet Shows, featuring comedians from all over the country, every first Saturday of the month (8 and 10:30pm). The bar is open Monday to Saturday 7pm to 3am, with most performances Thursday to Saturday. 2307 Bull St., btw. 39th and 40th sts. www.wormholebar.com. ✆ **912/349-6770.**

The Performing Arts

Formed in 2009, the **Savannah Philharmonic Orchestra** (✆ **912/232-6002;** www.savannahphilharmonic.org) presents a full range of concerts each season (Sept–May), from classics to pops. It often performs with the **Savannah Philharmonic Chorus** in the **Lucas Theatre** (www.lucastheatre.com), the Cathedral of St. John the Baptist (p. 136), and other venues around Savannah. Visit the website for the latest schedule. Regular tickets usually range from $16 to $70.

Savannah Civic Center's **Johnny Mercer Theater,** on the corner of Liberty and Montgomery streets, at Orleans Square (✆ **912/651-6556;** www.savannahcivic.com), hosts touring ballets, musicals, and Broadway shows. The Center's **Martin Luther King Arena** hosts major concerts and events. Visit the website to find out what's being presented at the time of your visit. Tickets range from $15 to $100.

Savannah Theatre, Chippewa Square (✆ **912/233-7764;** www.savannahtheatre. com), presents contemporary plays. Tickets are usually $35 for adults, and $17 for children 17 and under.

Late September brings the 5-day **Savannah Jazz Festival** (http://savannahjazz festival.org), with nationally known musicians appearing around the city, while the eclectic **Savannah Music Festival** (www.savannahmusicfestival.org) runs late March into April.

SIDE TRIPS FROM SAVANNAH

S avannah makes an excellent base for journeys further along the Georgia and South Carolina coasts, returning to your lodging after local excursions, or transferring from the city to nearby points of interest.

To the north lies the quaint Southern town of **Beaufort** and **Hilton Head Island,** both part of South Carolina's Lowcountry, where much of the romance, beauty, and graciousness of the Old South survives. Broad white-sand beaches are warmed by the Gulf Stream and fringed with palm trees and rolling dunes. Graceful sea oats, anchoring the beaches, wave in the wind. The subtropical climate makes all this beauty the ideal setting for golf and for some of the Southeast's finest saltwater fishing.

To the south, Georgia's barrier islands extend along the Atlantic coast from Ossabaw Island near Savannah all the way down to Cumberland Island, near Florida. Although some have been developed, others, such as Cumberland and Little St. Simons, still linger in the 19th century. Some are accessible only by boat. This 150-mile-long stretch of coast is semitropical and richly historic. The scenic Georgia portion of U.S. 17 goes past broad sandy beaches, creeks and rivers, and the ruins of antebellum plantations. The major highlights are the **"Golden Isles"**—principally Jekyll Island, Sea Island, and St. Simons Island.

The islands became world famous for their Sea Island cotton, grown on huge plantations supported mainly by slave labor. The last slaver, the Wanderer, (illegally) landed its cargo of Africans on Jekyll Island as late as 1858. The plantations languished and finally disappeared in the post–Civil War period. Today the Golden Isles are ideal for naturalists, with miles and miles of private secluded beaches, plus acres of ancient forests, and a temperature and climate that make the islands a year-round destination.

COCKSPUR ISLAND ★★

14 miles east of Downtown Savannah

This small island in the south channel of the Savannah River is chiefly notable as the site of **Fort Pulaski** and the **Cockspur Island Lighthouse,** now both part of a well-maintained national monument. This was also the place where Methodist founder **John Wesley** first landed in America in 1736, before going on to preach in Savannah itself. A small monument commemorates the event.

A 10-minute drive across the river from downtown Savannah takes you into the wild, even though you can see the city's industrial and port complexes in the background. The **Savannah National Wildlife Refuge** ★ (© **912/652-4415;** www.fws.gov/savannah), which over-flows into South Carolina, was the site of rice plantations in the 1800s and is now a wide expanse of woodland and marsh—ideal for a scenic drive, a canoe ride, a picnic, and most definitely a look at a variety of animals.

From Savannah, get on U.S. Hwy. 17A, crossing the Talmadge Bridge. It's about 8 miles to the intersection of highways 17 and 17A, where you turn left toward the airport. You'll see the refuge entrance, marked LAUREL HILL WILDLIFE DRIVE, after going some 2 miles. Inside the gate to the refuge is a visitor center (Mon–Sat 9am–4:30pm) that dis-tributes maps and leaflets.

Laurel Hill Wildlife Drive goes on for 4 miles or so. It's possible to bike along this trail. People come here mainly to spy on the alligators, and sightings are almost guaranteed. However, other creatures in the wild abound, including bald eagles and otters. Hikers can veer off the drive and go along Cistern Trail, leading to Recess Island. Because the trail is marked, there's little danger of getting lost.

Nearly 40 miles of dikes are open to birders and backpackers. Canoeists float along tidal creeks, which are fingers of the Savannah River. Fishing and hunting are allowed under special conditions and in certain seasons. Deer and squir-rels are commonplace; less common is the feral hog known along coastal Geor-gia and South Carolina. You can visit the refuge daily from sunrise to sunset. Admission is free.

Essentials

The island and Fort Pulaski is an easy and clearly signposted drive from Savannah. Take U.S. 80 East all the way to Fort Pulaski Road, which marks the entrance to the National Monument; a bridge here connects the island to the mainland. There is no public transport.

Exploring Cockspur Island

The **Fort Pulaski National Monument** ★★ (© **912/786-5787;** www.nps.gov/fopu) preserves one of several Civil War fortifications used to defend Savannah from Union forces, though it is chiefly notable for the manner of its defeat: the Union army used its new rifled cannon to compel the Confederate garrison inside to surrender in 1862, marking a landmark in the history of military siege tactics. The effectiveness of rifled cannon (firing a heavier, bullet-shaped projectile with great accuracy at longer range) was clearly demonstrated. The fort had been considered invincible, and the new Union weapon marked the end of the era of masonry fortifications.

Preparations on what would become Fort Pulaski began in 1827, when Robert E. Lee, the future Confederate general, was in charge of designing the first series of canals and earthworks on the island. Construction on the massive two-story fort, with walls 7½-feet thick, was intermittent between 1829 and 1847, when it was finally finished. Later in the Civil War Fort Pulaski was used as a Union prison, infamously holding more than 500 Confederate prisoners (aka "the immortal 600") during the winter of 1864. Some 13 prisoners died during their 5-month stay, mostly of dehydration due to dysentery.

Today you can explore the pentagon-shaped fort, with its galleries and drawbridges crossing the moat. You can still see shells from 1862 embedded in the walls. There are exhibits of the fort's history in the visitor center. The site is open daily 9am to 5pm, with extended hours to 6pm June through August. Admission is $5 (ages 16 and over), with free admission for children 15 and under.

TYBEE ISLAND ★★

18 miles E of Downtown Savannah

For more than 150 years, **Tybee Island** has lured travelers who enjoy swimming, sailing, fishing, and picnicking. Pronounced *Tie*-bee, an Euchee Native American word for salt, the island offers 5 miles of unspoiled sandy beaches, just a short drive from Savannah.

Essentials

GETTING THERE

From Savannah, take U.S. 80 until you reach the ocean. The **Savannah-Tybee Beach Shuttle** (© **866/543-6744**) is a minibus that runs from Savannah Visitor Center (p. 114) to Tybee Island Friday to Sunday at 10am, noon, 2, and 5pm. On Tybee it stops at the Tybrisa/Strand Roundabout (30–40 min.), then Tybee Lighthouse (45 min. from Savannah). Return journeys begin approximately 45 minutes after the outward trip. Fares are $3 one-way (exact change required). Taxis from Savannah Airport (p. 114) charge a fixed-rate of $53.

VISITOR INFORMATION

The **Tybee Island Visitor Center** (© **877/344-3361;** www.tybeevisit.com), 802 1st St., at the corner of Hwy. 80 and Campbell Avenue, provides complete information if you plan to spend more than a day on the island. It's open daily 9am to 5:30pm.

Exploring Tybee Island

Covering just 5 square miles, Tybee was once called the "playground of the southeast," hosting millions of beach-loving visitors from across the country. Built in 1891, **Tybrisa Pavilion,** on the island's south end, became one of the major summer entertainment pavilions in the South. Benny Goodman, Guy Lombardo, Tommy Dorsey, and Cab Calloway all played here. It burned down in 1967 and was rebuilt in 1996.

Over Tybee's salt marshes and sand dunes have flown the flags of pirates and Spaniards, the English and the French, and the Confederate States of America. A path on the island leads to a clear pasture where **John Wesley,** founder of the Methodist Church, knelt and declared his faith in the new land.

Fort Screven, on the northern strip, began as a coastal artillery station in the 1890s and evolved into a training camp for countless troops in both world wars. Remnants of wartime installations can still be seen. The **Tybee Island Museum** is housed in what was one of the fort's batteries. Displayed is a collection of photographs, memorabilia, art, and dioramas depicting Tybee from the time the Native Americans inhabited the island through World War II. Across the street at 30 Meddin Ave. is the **Tybee Lighthouse** (www.tybeelighthouse.org), established in 1742 and the third-oldest lighthouse in America (though it's been rebuilt many times; what you see today dates from the post–Civil War period). It's 154 feet tall, and if you're fit, you can climb 178 steps to the top. From the panoramic deck you get a sense of the broad and beautiful marshes.

For information about the museum and lighthouse, call ℂ **912/786-5801.** Both are open Wednesday to Monday 9am to 5:30pm. Admission is $9 for adults and $7 for seniors 62 and older and for children 6 to 17. Kids 5 and under enter free. The site has picnic tables, and access to the beach is easy.

Tybee Island Marine Science Center, 1509 Strand St., off the 14th Street parking lot, next to the pier (ℂ **912/786-5917;** www.tybeemarinescience.org), has displays on species indigenous to the coast of southern Georgia, a tidal pool touch tank that little ones will enjoy, and a small aquarium, often temporarily home to injured fish and turtles. Hours are daily 10am to 5pm. Admission is $4 for ages 4 and over; free for children 3 and under. Enlightening guided "Walks, Talks & Treks" along the coast are each an hour long and cost $10 per person (kids 4 and under are free). Reserve in advance.

Where to Stay

If you're interested in daily or weekly rentals of a condo or beach house (one or two bedrooms), contact **Tybee Beach Vacation Rentals** (ℂ **800/967-4433** or 912/786-0100; www.renttybee.com). Otherwise, avoid the chain hotels and opt for one of the island's delightful B&Bs.

Surf Song Bed & Breakfast ★★★ If you like B&Bs you'll love this circa 1898 beach house, completely renovated in 2013, with maple hardwood floors, soaring coffered tin ceilings, and Victorian furnishings blended with modern amenities. You can lounge on the wraparound veranda, or take a dip in the small but enticing pool. The beach is a 2-minute walk away. The owners (sisters Cindy and Sherry) and the manager (Patty) are super friendly, and extremely helpful—if you don't have a car they'll set you up with transfers and rides from Savannah and anywhere you'd like to go. The breakfasts do not disappoint either, with anything from mouth-watering southern biscuits and gravy to French toast with peaches and cream on offer. Every afternoon fresh-baked cookies and cakes are served to guests.

21 Officers Row, Tybee Island, GA 31328. www.tybeesurfsong.com. ℂ **912/472-1040.** 5 units. $179–$299 double. Free parking. **Amenities:** Breakfast room; swimming pool; free Wi-Fi.

Tybee Island Inn ★★★ Another beguiling B&B close to the beach, shrouded in lush gardens studded with live oaks and classical statues. Each room is comfy and well-equipped with cable TV and designer linens. Owners Cathy and Lloyd are great hosts, while Gary is the maestro in the kitchen: his deliciously creative breakfasts are truly special, with fresh fruit, juice, casseroles, and filled croissants. Each day in the afternoon homemade brownies, cakes, and other delicacies (think chocolate-dipped pretzels) are served to guests, and teas, coffee, and other drinks are available at any hour.

24 Van Horn Ave., Tybee Island, GA 31328. www.tybeeislandinn.com. ℂ **912/786-9255.** 7 units. $189–$269 double. Free parking. **Amenities:** Breakfast room; free Wi-Fi.

Where to Dine

The Breakfast Club ★ AMERICAN This is one of the more famous diners on the island, and though it definitely trades on its reputation (it's not *that* good), the island decor is quaint, the location near the beach is chilled out, and the food is usually pretty good—go for the experience, accept the lines outside, and enjoy accordingly.

The much eulogized pecan waffle ($6), and half-pound Chicago bear burger ($12), are both worth ordering, but the menu covers six pages and offers something for everyone. Portions are always large and filling.

1500 Butler Ave. www.thebreakfastclubtybee.com. (*) **912/786-5984.** Main courses $6–$13. Daily 7am–1pm. Closed Christmas.

The Crab Shack ★★ SEAFOOD   No-frills barbecue and seafood in a kitschy, atmospheric beach shack that looks like something out of TV show *True Blood* (Merlotte's, anyone?). This is not an undiscovered gem, however, and it's an established tourist haunt. The food is tasty and fresh, though: the Lowcountry boil comes with a huge mound of shrimp, mussels, crab legs, snow crab claws, corn, potatoes, and sausage. The shrimp is going to be some of the best you've ever tasted, seriously. Most of the seating is outdoors, and wildlife that is not on the menu includes crocodiles (safely contained, and which you can feed), and a plethora of feral cats (wandering around, very definitely not contained).

40 Estill Hammock Rd. www.thecrabshack.com. (*) **912/786-9857.** Main courses $8–$25. Daily 11:30am–10pm.

Sundae Cafe ★★★ NEW SOUTHERN   From the outside it appears to be an ordinary strip-mall diner, so this is probably the last place you'd expect to discover creative, haute cuisine, but believe it; seafood cheesecake, anyone? Once inside, the decor is cool and contemporary, and the food is amazing. Southern-style pecan–fried chicken (accompanied by delicate butterbean and sweet-corn succotash), and the jambalaya pasta are standouts, but don't skip the salads, souped up with chopped nuts, sesame sticks, and sunflower seeds. End with the key lime pie and you'll sleep happy. Reservations are crucial on weekdays, but none are taken on weekends, so get here early.

304 First St. www.sundaecafe.com. (*) **912/786-7694.** Main courses $18–$29. Mon–Sat 11am–3pm and 5–9pm.

HILTON HEAD ISLAND ★★

30 miles NE of Downtown Savannah

The largest sea island between New Jersey and Florida and one of America's great resort meccas, **Hilton Head Island** is surrounded by the South Carolina **Lowcountry.** Palms mingle with live oaks, dogwood, and pines, and everything is draped in Spanish moss. Far more sophisticated and upscale than Myrtle Beach and the Grand Strand, Hilton Head's "plantations" (as most resort areas here call themselves) offer visitors something of the traditional leisurely lifestyle that's always held sway here.

Although it covers only 42 square miles (it's 12 miles long and 5 miles wide at its broadest point), Hilton Head feels spacious, thanks to judicious planning from the beginning of its development in 1952. And that's a blessing, because about 2.5 million resort guests visit annually (the permanent population is about 35,000). The expansive beaches on its ocean side; sea marshes on the sound; and natural wooded areas of live- and water-oak, pine, bay, and palmetto trees in between have all been carefully preserved amid commercial explosion. This lovely setting attracts artists, writers, musicians, theater groups, and craftspeople. The only city (of sorts) is Harbour Town, at Sea Pines Resort, a Mediterranean-style cluster of shops and restaurants.

The island's recorded origins go back to visits from Spanish sailors in 1521, and its later "discovery" by an English sea captain, William Hilton, in 1663. By 1860, it

Festive Hilton Head

Hilton Head has plenty of festivals for such a small island. Scattered cultural events in February, including basket-weaving classes, art exhibitions, and storytelling, showcase the island's Gullah heritage (see box, p. 161) as part of the annual **Gullah Celebration.** For more information, call (℃ **843/689-9314** or visit www.gullahcelebration.com.

During the first week of March, the Hilton Head Hospitality Association sponsors **Winefest** ((℃ **800/424-3387;** www.hiltonheadwineandfood.com), an annual outdoor wine tasting—the largest of its kind on the East Coast—that transforms even the most devoted beer drinkers into oenophiles and connoisseurs.

In mid-April, outstanding PGA golfers descend on the island for the **PGA Tour and Tournament** at the Harbour Town Golf Links at the Sea Island Resort ((℃ **800/243-1107;** www.pgatour.com).

To herald fall, the **Hilton Head Celebrity Golf Tournament** ((℃ **843/842-7711;** www.hhcelebritygolf.com) is held on Labor Day weekend at various island golf courses.

For 1 week straddling Halloween, Hilton Head's **Concours d'Elegance and Motoring Festival** ((℃ **843/785-7469;** www.hhiconcours.com) provides a venue for some of the most sought-after antique automobiles in the world.

boasted 24 plantations, most of them cultivating long-stem Sea Island cotton as well as indigo, rice, and sugar cane. On November 7, 1861, Hilton Head became the scene of the largest naval battle ever fought in American waters. More than 12,000 Union soldiers and marines invaded the island as part of a plan to blockade shipping in and out of nearby Charleston and Savannah. After the Civil War, and with the subsequent destruction of its cotton crops by the boll weevil, Hilton Head slid into obscurity, inhabited mostly by descendants of former slaves, who survived on small farms and as hunters and fishermen. An unusual result of the island's obscurity involved the survival of their language and culture, Gullah.

In 1956, Charles Fraser, son of one of the families that owned the island, embarked on an ambitious plan to develop it as a modern resort and residential community. Under Fraser, the Sea Pines Plantation (today the **Sea Pines Resort**) became a much-studied prototype of an ecologically desirable resort community, and was copied worldwide.

Essentials
GETTING THERE
It's easy to fly into Savannah, rent a car, and drive to Hilton Head. From Savannah, take I-95 N. to U.S. 278 E., which leads directly into Hilton Head. If you're driving from other points south or north, take I-95 to reach the island (exit 28 off I-95 S., exit 5 off I-95 N.). U.S. 278 leads over the bridge to the island. The **K-Shuttle** ((℃ **877/243-2050;** www.kshuttle.com) is a minivan service that runs between Savannah airport and the major resorts on the island, daily 10am to 11:45pm every 1 to 2 hours. Rates are $45 one-way or $80 round-trip. Taxis from Savannah airport (p. 114) charge a fixed-rate of $80 to $85.

VISITOR INFORMATION
The official **Welcome Center** of Hilton Head Island, 524 Independence Blvd. (exit 8 off I-95) in Hardeeville ((℃ **800/523-3373** or 843/785-3673; www.hhiwelcomecenter.

The Gullah Heritage of Hilton Head

Tours that take a journey back in time are offered through **Gullah Heritage Trail Tours** (www.gullaheritage.com). Arrangements can be made by calling ℂ **843/681-7066.** Gullah culture is a West African–based system of traditions, art forms, customs, and beliefs. A 2-hour narrated tour takes you through the hidden paths of Hilton Head, where you'll meet fourth-generation Gullah family members, relating firsthand stories of their traditions and even speaking Gullah for you. The tour also takes you to ruins or remnants of Hilton Head of yesterday, including a visit to a one-room schoolhouse, plantation tabby ruins, and a historic marker of the First Freedom Village. Tours depart at 10am and 2pm Tuesday to Saturday and at noon on Sunday, costing $32 for adults and $15 for children 11 and under. Tours depart from the Coastal Discovery Museum at 70 Honey Horn Dr.

com), is open daily 10am to 7pm. You can pick up free vacation guides (or order them from the website) and free maps of the area. The staff can assist you in finding places of interest and activities. For hotel reservations call ℂ **888/741-7666.**

GETTING AROUND

U.S. 278 is the divided highway that runs the length of the island. **Yellow Cab** (ℂ **843/686-6666;** www.yellowcabhhi.net) has two-passenger flat fares determined by zone ($18–$28), with an extra $2 charge for each additional person. You can rent a towncar for $55/hour (3-hr. minimum).

Exploring Hilton Head Island

You can have an active vacation here any time of year; Hilton Head's subtropical climate ranges in temperature from the 50s (teens Celsius) in winter to the mid-80s (around 30 Celsius) in the summer. And if you've had your fill of historic sights in Savannah or Charleston, don't worry—the attractions on Hilton Head mainly consist of nature preserves, beaches, and other places to play.

The **Coastal Discovery Museum,** 70 Honey Horn Dr. (ℂ **843/689-6767;** www. coastaldiscovery.org), provides a concentrated dose of information about the Lowcountry's ecology, history, and sociology. In 1990, the Town of Hilton Head bought 68 acres of landlocked flatlands ("Honey Horn"), historically used to grow cash crops such as rice and indigo, as a means of protecting it from development as a shopping center. The museum site contains about a dozen historic buildings, a few of them from before the Civil War. Guided tours go along island beaches and salt marshes or stop at Native American sites and the ruins of old forts or long-gone plantations. Children can search for sharks' teeth with an identification chart. The nature, beach, and history tours generally cost $10 for adults and $5 for children 4 to 12. The dolphin and nature cruise costs $19 per adult and $13 per child (1–12), and a kayak tour goes for $32 per adult and $28 per child (5–12). Museum hours are Monday to Saturday 9am to 4:30pm and Sunday 11am to 3pm.

Hilton Head's **beaches ★★★** are consistently ranked among the most beautiful in the world. Hilton Head Island's official beach season is April 1st through September 30th of each year. The sands are extremely firm, providing a sound surface for biking, hiking, jogging, and beach games. In the summer, watch for the endangered **loggerhead**

turtles that lumber ashore at night to bury their eggs. All beaches on Hilton Head are public, but much of the land bordering the beaches (and therefore access to it), is private property. Most beaches are safe, although there's sometimes an undertow at the northern end of the island. At only the major beaches, lifeguards are posted, concessions are available, and you can rent beach chairs, umbrellas, and watersports equipment.

Most frequently used are **North** and **South Forest** beaches, adjacent to Coligny Circle (enter from Pope Ave. across from Lagoon Rd.). You can park in the lot opposite the Holiday Inn; the daily parking fee is $4. The adjacent beach park has toilets and a changing area, as well as showers, vending machines, and phones. It's a family favorite.

There are a number of public-access sites to popular beach areas. **Coligny Beach Park** at Coligny Circle at Pope Avenue and South Forest Beach Drive (free street parking) is the island's busiest strip of sand with toilets, sand showers, a playground, and changing rooms. **Alder Lane,** entered along South Forest Beach Road at Alder Lane, offers parking and is less crowded (metered parking 25¢ for 15 min.). Toilets are also found here. Off the William Hilton Parkway, **Dreissen Beach Park** (metered parking 25¢ for 30 min.) at Bradley Beach Road has toilets, sand showers, and plenty of parking as well as a playground and picnic tables. Of the beaches on the island's north, I prefer **Folly Field Beach** (metered parking 25¢ for 15 min.). Toilets, changing facilities, and parking are available.

The **Audubon-Newhall Preserve** ★★, Palmetto Bay Rd. (www.hiltonheadaudubon.org), is a 50-acre preserve on the south end of Hilton Head Island. Here you can walk along marked trails to observe wildlife in its native habitat. Guided tours are available when plants are in bloom. Except for a scattered handful of public toilets, there are no amenities. The preserve is open from sunrise to sunset; admission is free, and it's likely that your entire time within these laissez-faire acres will be unsupervised.

Also on the south end of the island is **Sea Pines Forest Preserve** ★★, at the Sea Pines Resort, 32 Greenwood Dr. (✆ **843/363-4530;** www.seapines.com), a 605-acre public wilderness area with marked walking trails. Nearly all the birds and animals known to live on Hilton Head can be seen here. Yes, there are alligators, but there are also less fearsome creatures, such as egrets, herons, osprey, and white-tailed deer. All trails lead to public picnic areas in the center of the forest. The preserve is open from sunrise to sunset year-round. Maps and toilets are available.

A little further afield, **Pinckney Island National Wildlife Refuge** ★★ (✆ **912/652-4415;** www.fws.gov/pinckneyisland) is protected land with 115 prehistoric and historic sites. French and Spanish settlers inhabited Pinckney Island in the 1500s, with the first permanent settlement formed in 1708. The island is named for General Charles Cotesworth Pinckney, a signer of the U.S. Constitution. By 1818, more than 200 slaves were used to harvest sea-island cotton here. In 1975, the refuge was donated to the U.S. Fish and Wildlife Service. Today, it comprises four islands, including Corn, Little Harry, Big Harry, and Pinckney, the latter the largest of the islands with 1,200 acres. The islands are riddled with hiking and biking trails, and are home to large concentrations of white ibis, herons, and egrets; you may even spot osprey nests. Two of the island's freshwater ponds were ranked among the top-20 wading-bird colony sites of South Carolina's coastal plain. Alligators are also a common sight. To get here, take I-95 to S.C. exit 8; go east on Hwy. 278 toward Hilton Head for 18 miles to the refuge entrance. From Hilton Head itself, exit the island via Hwy. 278 west. The refuge, which can be visited during daylight hours (free admission), will be on your right after a 30-minute drive.

Outdoor Activities

BIKING Hilton Head boasts 25 miles of bicycle paths. There are even bike paths running parallel to U.S. 278. Beaches are firm enough to support wheels, and every year, cyclists delight in dodging the waves or racing fast-swimming dolphins in the nearby water. Most hotels and resorts rent bikes to guests. If yours doesn't, try **Hilton Head Bicycle Company,** off Sea Pines Circle at 112 Arrow Rd. (© **800/995-4319;** www.hiltonheadbicycle.com). The cost starts at $24 per week, or $16 for 3 days. Baskets, child carriers, locks, and headgear are supplied for additional cost. The inventory includes cruisers, BMXs, mountain bikes, tandems, and bikes for kids. Hours are daily 9am to 5pm. The company also offers free delivery and pickup.

Another rental place is **Peddling Pelican** (© **843/785-3546**), offering beach cruisers, tandems, child carriers, and bikes for kids. There's free delivery to any area hotel or resort. Cost is $21 for a full day or $25 for 3 days. Hours are daily 9am to 6pm.

CRUISES & TOURS To explore Hilton Head's waters, contact Captain Mark's Dolphin Cruises, Shelter Cove Harbour, Harbour Dock C, located behind condominium building Harbourside II (© **843/785-4558;** www.captmarksdolphincruises.com). Outings include a 1¾-hour dolphin-watch cruise, which costs adults $16 to $18 and children $8 to $9.

Another outfitter, **Drifter Excursions,** 232 S. Sea Pines Dr., South Beach Marina (© **843/363-2900;** www.hiltonheadboattours.com), takes passengers on dolphin watches, sightseeing cruises, and nature cruises. Call for information on what's happening at the time of your visit. Fishing trips range from $58 to $68 per person.

FISHING Fishing licenses are needed for saltwater and freshwater fishing for anyone 16 years or older. The season for fishing offshore is April through October. Rates for non-residents are $11 for 14 days and $35 for a year.

Off Hilton Head, you can go deep-sea fishing for amberjack, barracuda, shark, and king mackerel. Many rentals are available; I've recommended only those with the best track records. **Drifter Excursions** (see above) features a 50-passenger, 60-foot drifter vessel that offers 3- to 5-hour offshore and inshore fishing excursions ranging in price from $58 to $68. The 32-foot *Boomerang* fishing boat is available for private offshore and inshore custom fishing charters lasting up to 8 hours ($10–$15).

GOLF With more than 20 highly challenging golf courses on the island itself, and an additional 16 within a 30-minute drive, Hilton Head is heaven for both professional and novice golfers. Some of golf's most celebrated architects—including George and Tom Fazio, Robert Trent Jones, Pete Dye, and Jack Nicklaus—have designed championship courses on the island. Wide, scenic fairways and rolling greens have earned Hilton Head the reputation of being the resort with the most courses on any number of the "world's best" lists. For additional information about golf on Hilton Head, go to **www.golfisland.com** or **www.hiltonheadgolf.net**.

Most of Hilton Head's championship courses are open to the public, including those at the **Palmetto Dunes Oceanfront Resort** (© **866/380-1778;** www.palmettodunes. com). Its **George Fazio Course ★,** an 18-hole, 6,534-yard, par-70 course that *Golf Digest* ranked among the top-75 U.S. resort courses, has been cited for its combined length and keen accuracy. Greens fees (with cart) are $89 to $129 for 18 holes. Its **Robert Trent Jones Oceanfront Course** is an 18-hole, 6,122-yard, par-72, with greens fees (with cart) of $105 to $159 for 18 holes. Hours are daily from 7am to 6pm.

On Highway 278, 1 mile west of the bridge leading to Hilton Head, is **Old South Golf Links ★★★**, 50 Buckingham Plantation Dr., Bluffton (© **800/257-8997** or

843/785-5353; www.oldsouthgolf.com). This 18-hole, 6,772-yard, par-72 course was recognized as one of the "Top 10 New Public Courses" by *Golf Digest,* which cited its panoramic views and settings that range from an oak forest to tidal salt marshes. Greens fees are $55 to $95, and it's open daily from 7:30am to 7pm.

Also on Highway 278 is the **Hilton Head National Golf Club,** 60 Hilton Head National Dr., Bluffton (✆ **843/842-5900;** www.golfhiltonheadnational.com), designed by Gary Player. The 27-hole, 6,779-yard, par-72 course has gorgeous scenery that evokes Scotland. Facilities include a full-service pro shop, driving range, and a grill. Greens fees range from $50 to $100, and it's open daily from 7am to 6pm.

Further west on Highway 278 is **Island West Golf Club,** 40 Island West Dr., Bluffton (✆ **843/689-6660;** www.islandwestgolf.net). With its backdrop of oaks, elevated tees, and rolling fairways, it's a challenging but playable 18-hole, 6,803-yard, par-72 course. Green fees are $35 to $49, and it's open daily from 7am to 6pm.

HORSEBACK RIDING   Riding through beautiful maritime forests and nature preserves is reason enough to visit Hilton Head. I like Lawton Stables, 190 Greenwood Dr., Sea Pines Resort (✆ **843/671-2586;** www.lawtonstables.com), which offers trail rides for adults and children through the Sea Pines Forest Preserve (daily 9am, 11am, 2pm, and 4pm). It costs $55 to $65 per person for a ride that lasts a bit over an hour. Riders must weigh under 250 pounds; kids 7 and under ride ponies instead of horses. The stables are open Monday to Saturday from 7:30am to 5:30pm. Reservations are necessary.

KAYAK TOURS   Kayaking is one of the few ways to get an up-close view of the flora and fauna of the salt marshes. Outside Hilton Head (✆ **800/686-6996** or 843/686-6996; www.outsidehiltonhead.com) offers well-orchestrated kayak tours of various Lowcountry waterways and salt marshes from at least two locations on the island. Its busiest location is at 32 Shelter Cove Lane, near the Shelter Cove Marina. The 2-hour guided nature tour costs $40 for adults, and $20 for children 12 and under. After getting instructions on how to control your boat, you'll travel through the salt-marsh creeks of the Calibogue Sound or Pinckney Island National Wildlife Refuge.

A worthy competitor is **Marshgrass Adventures** (✆ **843/684-3296;** www.marsh grassadventures.com), featuring sailing and kayaking tours from a base at Broad Creek Marina. Every day between April and October, an experienced guide takes participants out on 2-hour kayak tours ($60) to see egrets, herons, fish, crabs, and various crawling critters. There's even the occasional dolphin. Three-hour tours are $75; kayak rentals are $20/hour.

SAILING & WATERSPORTS   Hilton Head Island Sailing, Palmetto Bay Marina (✆ **843/686-2582;** www.hiltonheadislandsailing.com), is a two-catamaran charter operator piloted by Captain John and his mate Jeanne. You can pack a picnic lunch and bring your cooler aboard for a 2½-hour trip—which departs at 10am, 2pm, and at sunset throughout the year. The cost for an excursion aboard the 53-foot-long *Pau Hana* is $40 for adults and $20 for children 11 and under. *Flying Circus,* measuring 30 feet in length, offers private 2-hour trips for up to six people priced at $300.

H2O Sports, Harbour Town Marina, 149 Lighthouse Rd. (✆ **877/290-4386;** www. h2osports.com), offers powerboat rentals ($250/2 hr.), jet-skiing ($109/hr.), kayak tours ($40), parasailing ($69), paddleboarding (rentals $30/hr.), and water-skiing ($325/2 hr.).

TENNIS   With more than 300 courts—ideal for beginner, intermediate, and advanced players—Hilton Head boasts an extremely high concentration of tennis

Hilton Head has preserved more of its wildlife than almost any other resort destination on the East Coast.

Hilton Head Island's **alligators** are a prosperous lot, and, in fact, the South Carolina Department of Wildlife and Marine Resources uses the island as a resource for repopulating state parks and preserves in which alligators' numbers have greatly diminished. The creatures represent no danger if you stay at a respectful distance.

Many of the large **water birds** that regularly grace the pages of nature magazines are natives of the island. The island's Audubon Society reports around 200 species of birds every year in its annual bird count, and more than 350 species have been sighted on the island during the past decades. The snowy egret, the large blue heron, and the osprey are among the most noticeable.

Other animals include **deer, bobcat, otter, mink,** and a few **wild boars.** At the Sea Pines Resort, on the southern end of the island, the planners set aside areas for a deer habitat back in the 1950s.

The **loggerhead turtle,** an endangered species, nests extensively along Hilton Head's 12 miles of wide, sandy beaches. Because the turtles choose the darkest hours of the night to crawl ashore and bury their eggs in the soft sand, few visitors meet these 200-pound giants.

Ever present is the **bottle-nosed dolphin.** The water off Port Royal Plantation, adjacent to Port Royal Sound, is a good place to meet up with the playful dolphins, as are Palmetto Dunes, Forest Beach, and all other oceanfront locations. Barring that, consider participating in either of the kayak tours as described under "Kayak Tours," above.

facilities. Of its 19 tennis clubs, 7 are open to the public. A wide variety of tennis clinics and daily lessons are also available.

Sea Pines Racquet Club ★★★, Sea Pines Resort, 5 Lighthouse Lane (🕐 **843/363-4495;** www.seapinestennisresort.com), has been the site of more nationally televised tennis events than any other location. It has 21 clay courts, 4 lit for night play. Hotel guests get 2 hours of complimentary tennis time; after that, it costs $27 per hour. After hours (daily 8am–5pm), courts are free. Note that proper clay court tennis shoes are required.

The closest competitor to Sea Pines is **Van Der Meer Tennis,** 116 Shipyard Dr. (🕐 **800/845-6138** or 843/785-8388; www.vandermeertennis.com). It has about the same number of courts, equivalent prices, and well-respected teachers.

Palmetto Dunes Tennis Center, Palmetto Dunes Resort (🕐 **843/785-1152;** www. palmettodunes.com), is another reliable option with 23 clay courts and 2 hard courts (6 lit for night play). Hotel guests get 2 hours free per day; otherwise, the charge is $30 per hour, or $20 (walk-on only) between noon and 4pm.

Where to Stay

Hilton Head tends to specialize in high-end rentals—mostly of upscale, ocean-fronting luxury homes and villas, with higher prices than what's available in less-desirable parts of South Carolina. But in recent years, the island's roster of lodgings has expanded to include some simple economy lodgings as well. Most facilities offer discount rates between November and March, and golf and tennis packages are available year-round.

VILLA RENTALS

The **Vacation Company** (℃ **800/845-7018;** www.hiltonheadvacationrentals.com) has been in business for almost a quarter-century and specializes in the rental of homes and villas throughout the region. Its leading competitors include **Beach Properties of Hilton Head** (℃ **800/671-5155** or 843/671-5155; www.beach-property.com), and **Hilton Head Vacation Rentals** (℃ **800/232-2463;** www.800beachme.com). The primary condo development on the island the **Sea Pines Resort** (℃ **866/561-8802;** www. seapines.com), sprawling across 5,500 acres at the southern tip of the island, with everything from one- to four-bedroom villas to lavish private homes available for rent when the owners are away.

EXPENSIVE

Hilton Head Island Beach and Tennis Resort ★★   The key word in the name of this resort is "tennis." It is renowned around the island and beyond for its excellent tennis programs, which include packages for adults, teenagers, and private instruction. The tennis pro here is Eric Wammock, who has over 25 years experience in the business. All accommodation is in villas, with varying views (some of the ocean). Serious aficionados may wish to stay in the Tennis Villas, which are located close to the courts and nestled around a lovely fishing lagoon. The resort also boasts three pools, including one just for children.

40 Folly Field Rd., Hilton Head Island, SC 29928. www.hhibeachandtennis.com.℃ **843/842-4402.** 162 units. $129–$219 double. Free parking. **Amenities:** Restaurants; bar; bike rentals; fitness club; room service; tennis courts; 3 pools; free Wi-Fi.

Hilton Head Marriott Resort & Spa ★★   Even though this hotel is a little worn around the edges, it boasts hundreds of glorious yards of beach access. It also has several pools, both indoor and outdoor, an extra large whirlpool hot tub, and a lovely cabana that's the perfect place to grab a drink at sundown. Rooms are comfy if standard Marriott fare, and you can call ahead to arrange an ocean view. Overall, it's a good place to stay for easy and quick access to the beach—golfers will appreciate the on site Palmetto Dunes Golf Club.

1 Hotel Circle (in the Palmetto Dunes Oceanfront Resort), Hilton Head Island, SC 29928. www. marriott.com. ℃ **800/228-9290.** 513 units. $199–$329 double. Free parking (valet parking $19). **Amenities:** Restaurant; 2 bars; babysitting; coffee shop; three 18-hole golf courses; health club; room service; 25 tennis courts; free Wi-Fi.

The Inn at Harbour Town ★★★   Gorgeous boutique-style hotel nestled within the massive 5,000-acre Sea Pines Resort. Some of the highlights include butler service, a real pianist in the lobby, and a myriad of fresh-cut flowers throughout. The rooms are lavishly decorated and spacious, there's gourmet coffee and tea service every morning, complimentary shoe shine, and a big soaking tub. The pool overlooking the golf course is especially enticing (with travertine stone deck, and poolside food and beverage service), and guests can use the complimentary bikes for a ride along the beach.

7 Lighthouse Lane (in the Sea Pines Resort), Hilton Head Island, SC 29928. www.seapines.com. ℃ **800/732-7463.** 60 units. $269–$399 double. Free parking. **Amenities:** Bike rentals; concierge; exercise room; outdoor pool; room service; spa; 23 tennis courts (5 lit); free Wi-Fi.

Westin Hilton Head Island Resort & Spa ★★   A renewed spirit of hospitality has blown through this very expansive Westin Resort in the form of a recent $30-million renovation. Located on a private-white sand beach, the beautiful lobby (stop by for a sip of complementary fruit-infused water), an activities club for children, specialized maps for runners, and a golf and racquet club make for an entertaining stay. The resort has five classes of rooms, beginning with the standard Resort View room with a king and a single sofa bed. All rooms have been jazzed up with a contemporary Southern theme, rain forest showers, iHome, and a private balcony. Dogs are also welcome.

2 Grasslawn Ave., Hilton Head Island, SC 29928. www.westinhiltonheadisland.com. ✆ **800/937-8461** or 843/681-4000. 416 units. $245–$380 double. Children 17 and under stay free in parent's room. **Amenities:** 3 restaurants; bar; three 18-hole golf courses; Jacuzzi; room service; free Wi-Fi.

INEXPENSIVE

Days Inn ★   The quest for budget lodging on Hilton Head is a challenging one, and it essentially comes down to the motel chains. This Days Inn has some of the cheapest rates around, with an excellent location in the heart of the island. Rooms are basic but adequate and clean (with air conditioning, fridge, and microwave), and guests also have access to an outdoor pool (seasonal), and a basic fitness center. In the morning, a no-frills continental breakfast is served in the main lobby.

9 Marina Side Dr. (Hwy. 278), Hilton Head Island, SC 29928. ✆ **800/329-7466** or 843/842-4800. 119 units. $85 double. Kids 17 and under stay free with an adult. Rates include continental breakfast. Free parking. **Amenities:** Breakfast room; outdoor pool; free Wi-Fi.

South Beach Inn ★   For couples and small groups, the South Beach Inn at the southern tip of the island is an ideal, low-key place to overnight. The feel is much more cozy that the larger resorts and it's part of a larger waterfront complex that includes a range of restaurants, including the very popular Salty Dog Cafe. Rooms come with all the basic amenities, and some have a loft area with an additional bedroom. The rooms are all grouped around a common patio that offers guests a pleasant spot to have lunch, make drinks, and just relax. The real draw here is the action outside, though: fishing, walking, biking, and boating outlets are all nearby.

232 S. Sea Pines Dr. (in the Sea Pines Resort), Hilton Head Island, SC 29928. www.sbinn.com. ✆ **800/367-3909** or 843/671-6498. 17 units. $75–$196 double. Free parking. **Amenities:** Outdoor pool; free Wi-Fi.

Where to Dine

Hilton Head has the dubious distinction of having the most expensive restaurants in South Carolina. What on the island might be ranked as moderate would be considered very expensive in other parts of the state. The good news is that quality is high and the options are varied, though, as you'd expect, fresh seafood, Southern, and Lowcountry cuisine tend to dominate.

EXPENSIVE

Charlie's L'Etoile Verte ★★ INTERNATIONAL   Rustic, French-inspired bistro with an elegant dining room that resembles the parlor of a French country house. Charlie's "Green Star" is the only restaurant on Hilton Head that changes its menu daily based on the local catch of the day. You might find grilled snapper, local cobia, or tilapia among the 14 types of fresh fish usually on offer, along with rack of lamb, and filet mignon. The wine list specializes in California Cabernet, Oregon Pinot Noir, the Rhone Valley, and Bordeaux, while the bar features a popular happy hour (Mon–Sat 5–7pm; half-off wines by the glass, $5 house liquor, $3 domestics). Try one of the signature Belgian chocolate martinis.

8 New Orleans Rd. www.charliesgreenstar.com. ✆ **843/785-9277.** Main courses $9–$16 lunch, $26–$42 dinner. Mon–Fri 11:30am–2pm, Mon–Sat 5:30–10pm.

The Jazz Corner ★★★ AMERICAN/SOUTHERN   This dinner and jazz combo is one of the most popular joints on the island, for good reason. With live performances from some of the best performers in the country most nights at 8pm (you can view the latest line-up on the website), this is really a jazz club that also does amazing food. Start with a classic she-crab soup before sampling the Creole–seafood fettuccine, pistachio-encrusted tilapia, or marmalade duck breast, served with lemon-infused Yukon gold mash and sautéed spring vegetables. Save room for the signature "Old Fashioned Pecan Pie," or the addictive apple-and-cinnamon bread pudding.

The Village at Wexford, 1000 William Hilton Pkwy. www.thejazzcorner.com. ✆ **843/842-8620.** Main courses $19–$29. Daily 6–11pm.

Michael Anthony's Cucina Italiana ★★★ ITALIAN   Since 2002 the Fazzini family has been creating outstanding Italian food, virtually the equivalent of eating at a genuine trattoria in Rome (they even have their own cookbook, *A Taste of Italy in the Lowcountry,* which you can buy on-site). The interior boasts a more contemporary look, however, with a stylish marble-top bar, designer lighting, and simple decor. Menus change seasonally, but standouts include the Spaghetti con Granchio (spaghetti with fresh lump crab, sautéed with white wine), and perfectly cooked seafood that might include salmon, scallops, or red grouper, a moist delight served in a scrumptious sauce with pine nuts and raisins. It's also the best place to drink real espresso on the island. The three-course early dining menu is a steal at just $20 (5:15–5:45pm only).

Orleans Plaza, 37 New Orleans Rd. ✆ **843/785-6272.** Main courses $17–$38. Mon–Sat 5:15–10pm.

Red Fish ★★ LOWCOUNTRY/INTERNATIONAL   This spot is a top choice for a romantic evening out, with a huge wine list (over 1000 bottles), and lavish entrees. The restaurant comprises several dining rooms decked out in a simple contemporary style, with one room surrounded by racks of wine and a private room in the wine cellar itself. The operation is overseen by head chef Chaun Bescos, who grew up on an organic farm in Hawaii. Here he works closely with local growers, the Hilton Head Farmer's Market, and home-grown produce from Bear Island Farms to put together a range of seasonal offerings. Menus change but dinner might include a chorizo-crusted local flounder, crab cakes, or Lowcountry shrimp and grits with fried okra and kale. There's also a retail wine store on the premises, and a local jazz trio plays every Wednesday at 7:30pm.

8 Archer Rd. www.redfishofhiltonhead.com. ✆ **843/686-3388.** Main courses $8–$13 lunch, $24–$37 dinner. Mon–Sat 11:30am–2pm; daily 5–10pm.

Vine Bistro & Wine Bar ★★★ INTERNATIONAL/ITALIAN   This intimate, European-style bistro is small and incredibly popular—make a reservation or get here early. The menu is inspired by California's Napa and Sonoma valleys, with farm-to-table produce sourced from local farms, fresh fish, and an eclectic range of dishes from the Mediterranean, France, and Italy created by award-winning Chef Olivier Allain. The main menu is divided into "Dirt Candy" (from the fields), with a range of vegetables; "Grains" (featuring dishes such as the house lasagna and salmon pasta); "Mau'ka" (the sea), featuring line-caught crispy black grouper; and "Ma'kai" (the land), which might include Allain's fabulous osso buco. Candles and black and white movies in the background enhance the mood.

1 North Forest Beach Dr., Ste. 202, Coligny Plaza. ✆ **843/686-3900.** Main courses $18–$31. Mon–Sat 5–10pm.

MODERATE

Bomboras Grille ★ SOUTHERN/SEAFOOD   Stylish restaurant and bar just off Coligny Beach, with a bright outdoor seating area and a smaller interior featuring distressed metal pillars and a bold, marmalade color scheme. Start off with "Southern popcorn"—fried black-eyed peas with cajun seasoning, or the tasty fried garlic pickles. For entrees the menu is based around the concept of "social plates" meant to be shared between two or thre people. Standouts include the pan-roasted mussels, and the black-eyed pea cakes with a curry mayo drizzle. There's also a well-curated wine list, and beer drinkers will appreciate the sixteen drafts on tap, which range from Allagash Yakuza to the extra strong Belgian ale, Kwak.

101 A/B Pope Ave. www.bomborasgrille.com. *C* **843/689-2662.** Main courses $9–$12 lunch, $13–$38 dinner. Daily 11:30am–10pm.

Palmetto Bay Sunrise Cafe Breakfast ★ AMERICAN   One of the best spots to have breakfast on the island, a friendly, no-frills diner with an open porch overlooking the water. Early risers can take advantage of the "Eggs All Ways" special ($6), served from 6am to 8am, which features two eggs (prepared any way), with bacon or sausage and hash browns or grits. Otherwise everything is good and hearty; the Hamptons Brunch ($14) is a real treat—two eggs with a New York strip steak. The menu is fun to read (breakfast trivia is scattered throughout), the outdoor seating is a bonus, and there is also a full bar for those life-saving Bloody Mary's.

86 Helmsman Way. www.palmettobaysunrisecafe.com. *C* **843/686-3232.** Main courses $5–$14. Mon–Fri 6am–2pm, Sat–Sun 6am–3pm.

Skillets Café & Grill ★ LOWCOUNTRY/SEAFOOD   Though it's now open all day, Skillets is still best known for its excellent home-style breakfasts (served until 4:30pm). The seafood is especially good, with favorites including the crab cake benedict, served with an extra flaky biscuit. The French toast is also a winner, with a caramelized crust and a surfeit of cinnamon on top. Dinner menus are also heavy on seafood: crab cakes, scallops, fish tacos, and shrimps usually feature. Come before 6pm and you can order the $17 set menu. Happy hour (Mon–Fri 4–6pm) sees $1 off all glasses of wine, bottled and draft beers, while Sundays see the special prime-rib dinner served 5 to 9pm ($19).

1 N. Forest Beach Dr., Ste. 225. www.skilletscafe.com. *C* **843/785-3131.** Main courses $6–$12. Daily 7am–9pm.

Skull Creek Boathouse ★★ SEAFOOD   Loud, raucous, and lots of fun. The seafood is fresh and the waterfront views are spectacular at sunset, but it's the live music (mostly local rock, folk, and country), and lively atmosphere that pulls in the crowds. Step outside to check out the Dive Bar, a raw bar featuring excellent sushi and elaborate seafood platters of lobster, shucked oysters, little-neck clams, and other shellfish ($34). More unusually, there is a small sake menu, with such gems as a bottle of Fudo Myoo Pearl for $10. Come early to get the best seats for the sunset, and swing by on Tuesdays to hear local troubadour Luke Mitchell.

397 Squire Pope Rd. www.skullcreekboathouse.com. *C* **843/681-3663.** Lunch items $7–$18; dinner main courses $16–$28. Mon–Fri 11:30am–10pm, Sat 10am–11pm, Sun 10am–10pm. Closed Christmas Day.

The Smokehouse ★★ BARBECUE   With a bevy of televisions, 12 beers on tap, and Friday night jam sessions featuring pop-rock bands like Taco Donkey and La Bodega, the Smokehouse is the busiest and best barbecue joint on the island. Opt for the meats coming out of the smoker: standouts include chicken and ribs, and the pork BBQ plate. It's also worth sampling the appetizers, which include grilled shrimp and a superb onion loaf, a blend of thinly sliced, sweet onions served with a tangy dipping sauce. It also boasts one of the better Sunday brunches on the island, complete with a delectable filet benedict, beef tenderloin medallions served with sautéed mushrooms.

34 Palmetto Bay Rd. www.smokehousehhi.com. ✆ **843/842-4227.** Main courses $13–$26. Mon–Sat 11:30am–10pm, Sun 10am–10pm.

INEXPENSIVE

Annie O's Southern Eats ★★ SOUTHERN Though it doesn't look like much from the outside, Annie O's is a friendly little Southern diner, serving up solid comfort food at reasonable prices. You can expect the usual range of staples, from fried chicken, catfish, and meatloaf, to homemade crab cakes, biscuits, mac and cheese, collard greens, and shrimp and grits. The desserts here are extra special, though, and they include a splendid coconut cream pie ($5). There is also a full bar, and plenty of iced tea.

124 Arrow Rd. ✆ **843/341-2664.** Main courses $8–$15. Mon–Sat 11am–9pm.

Harold's Diner ★★ SOUTHERN This is a classic, no-frills, loud Southern diner, serving cholesterol-laden but irresistible cheeseburgers, butter-slathered omelets, and cheesesteaks. The burgers are the standouts, but they also have a modest offering of breakfast items, with pancakes hard to resist. Expect service with plenty of banter and sarcasm (staff are known for adding a rubber rat to plates of food, just to see the reaction). New Yorkers take note: the restaurant is also an old-fashioned, Yankees hating, Red Sox hangout (and they don't like Obama much, either).

641 William Hilton Pkwy. ✆ **843/301-0895.** Main courses $5–$9. Mon–Sat 7am–2pm.

Kenny B's Cajun Seafood Hut ★★ CAJUN/SOUTHERN Decked out in purple, green, and gold and a smattering of New Orleans street-scene murals, this casual diner channels the culinary spirit of the Big Easy. Breakfast features those tasty beignets ($3) and a hefty po-boy that includes ham, bacon, grilled shrimp, or sausage. The theme continues for lunch and dinner, with highlights including the BBQ shrimp and fried green tomato salad, and kettles of boiled crawfish ($9). Come early for the Sunday brunch buffet ($10) as it is extremely popular—it includes over 25 items, including beignets, gumbo, shrimp and grits, and biscuits and gravy.

70A Pope Ave. www.eatatkennybs.com. ✆ **843/785-3315.** Main courses $7–$14. Mon 11am–9pm, Tues–Sat 8:30am–9pm, Sun 8am–8pm (hours change seasonally, call ahead or check website).

Mi Tierra ★★ MEXICAN Brightly colored sunflowers adorn the interior of this casual but authentic Mexican restaurant, a solid choice for a relaxing lunch or dinner. The homemade guacamole is good, fresh and loaded with cilantro. The fish tacos and chicken burritos ($7) are standouts, the latter laced with a tangy barbecue sauce and grilled peppers. The tamales are especially authentic, and this is one place that actually makes decent *moles*. It's also worth sampling one of the 14 specialty margaritas. This is a great place to watch soccer—at least one TV always seems to be tuned to a game.

130 Arrow Rd. ✆ **843/342-3409.** Main courses $6–$12. Sun–Thurs 11am–9pm, Fri–Sat 11am–10pm.

Signe's Heaven Bound Bakery & Café ★★ SANDWICHES/PAS-TRIES Lemon squares, key lime pie, pound cake, and a slew of brownies are the big draws at this Hilton Head institution, which is approaching its fourth decade in business. In addition to the delicious pastries, it knocks out decent frittatas ($10) and whole-wheat waffles ($8). There are smaller portions for kids, including a waffle with sprinkles for just $5, topped with fresh fruit. Those on the go will appreciate "Signe's Goes to the Beach" package of sandwich, pasta or fruit, soda, Zapp's potato chips, and a cookie for $12.

93 Arrow Rd. www.signesbakery.com. ✆ **843/785-9118.** Main items $3–$12. Mon–Fri 8am–4pm, Sat–Sun 8am–2pm; Dec–Feb closes 3pm Mon–Fri and all day Sun.

Steamer Seafood ★★ SEAFOOD/LOWCOUNTRY   Founded in 1991, this is one of the best places to chow down on fairly priced, right-out-of-the-water seafood, with a 70-seat raw bar, a 160-seat dining room, and around 175 chairs outside on two newly renovated decks. Stick to the basics and you can't go wrong: the huge Seafood Platter, king crab legs, buckets of steamed oysters, fried shrimp, or the signature "Bull Bites." The beer menu is massive—250 choices and counting—with locals opting for pitchers of Stumpy's Morphine or Mississippi Molasses. Local entertainer Todd Cowart plays every night except Tuesday (see www.toddcowart.com).

28 Coligny Plaza (next to the Piggly Wiggly grocery store), 1 N. Forest Beach Dr. www.steamersea food.com. ✆ **843/785-2070.** Main courses $10–$39. Daily 11:30am–10pm.

The Urban Vegan VEGAN/VEGETARIAN   Vegans and gluten-free eaters can rejoice: the Urban Vegan has got you covered. It might seem a bit odd that's it located within Captain Fishy's Seafood Restaurant, but this is the real deal, with a bevy of excellent salads, wraps, and seasonal vegetables. Their salad creations are especially good, with the BanaRama salad ($10) comprising kale, carrots, coconut, walnuts, raisins, and agave-curry dressing. For entrees, try the lima-bean burgers with creamy garlic sauce, or the cranberry quinoa burger plate. Soups and eight different sides fill out the menu; don't skip the fried spinach or the apricot-almond coleslaw (both $3).

86 Helmsman Way. www.urbanveganhhi.com. ✆ **843/671-3474.** Main courses $9–$13. Daily 11am–8:30pm.

Entertainment & Nightlife

Hilton Head doesn't have Myrtle Beach's nightlife (see p. 112), but there's plenty to keep you entertained—much of it located in hotels and resorts. Casual dress (but not swimming attire) is acceptable in most clubs. See p. 168 for the Jazz Corner.

Cultural interest focuses on the **Arts Center of Coastal Carolina,** in the Self Family Arts Center, 14 Shelter Cove Lane (✆ **888/860-2787** or 843/842-2787; www.art shhi.com), which enjoys one of the best theatrical reputations in the Southeast. The Elizabeth Wallace Theater, a 350-seat, state-of-the-art theater, was added to the multiplex in 1996. The older Dunnagan's Alley Theater is located in a renovated warehouse. A wide range of musicals, contemporary comedies, and classic dramas are presented. Showtimes are 8pm Tuesday to Saturday, with a Sunday matinee at 2pm. Adult ticket prices range from $45 for a musical to $75 for a play. Tickets for children 16 and under range $18 to $37. The box office is open Monday to Friday 10am to 5pm, and on performance days it's open 10am to curtain time.

The **Quarterdeck** (✆ **843/842-1999;** www.seapines.com), at the base of the Harbour Town Lighthouse, is always a solid bet for a good night out. This waterfront lounge is open daily 11:30am to 9pm with nightly entertainment 5 to 9pm (later in high season).

The island abounds in sports bars, far too many to document here. I recommend **Callahan's,** 49 New Orleans Rd. (✆ **843/686-7665;** www.callahanssportsbar.com),

The Triangle & How Not to Get Lost Within It

Hilton Head's hottest nightlife spot goes by many names—the Triangle, the Golden Triangle, the Barmuda Triangle, and most officially of all, **Hilton Head Plaza.** Set beside Greenwood Drive, very close to the Sea Pines traffic roundabout, the area resembles a shopping center without any shops. Instead, it contains the busiest and best nightclub venues and bars on Hilton Head.

Relying on word-of-mouth buzz for their ongoing success, these bars and restaurants include **Reilley's Grill & Bar** ★★★ (✆ 843/842-4414; www.reilley shiltonhead.com), open daily 11am to 2am; the island's Green Bay Packers headquarters **Jump & Phil's Bar & Grill** ★★ (✆ 843/785-9070; www.jumpand philshhi.com), open daily 11:30am to 10pm; and **One Hot Mama's** ★★

(✆ **843/682-6262;** www.onehotmamas. com), open daily 11:30am to 1am. In a close tie for the least formal establishments and best places to drink beer are South Carolina's first microbrewery, the **Hilton Head Brewing Company** (✆ **843/785-3900;** www.hhbrewingco. com), and the **Lodge** (✆ **843/842-8966;** www.hiltonheadlodge.com), another craft beer specialist. Of these two, I prefer the Lodge with its pool tables. But they're all so close together that if one place isn't to your liking, you can just move on to the next one. The Brewing Company is open daily from 11:30am to 2am, while the Lodge is a nighttime-only affair, open daily from 7pm 'til sometime after midnight every night. None of these bars begin to get busy until after dark.

and **Casey's Sports Bar & Grill,** 37 New Orleans Rd. (✆ **843/785-2255;** www. caseyshhi.com).

DAUFUSKIE ISLAND ★★

1 nautical mile W of Hilton Head

Rich in legend, lore, and history, **Daufuskie Island** is relatively cut off from the world. Lying between Hilton Head and Savannah and accessible only by boat, its heyday came in the mid–19th century when Southern plantations here produced the famous Sea Island cotton—until the boll weevil put an end to that industry. The island was the setting for Pat Conroy's autobiographical book *The Water Is Wide* (1972), and also featured in *Conrack,* the movie version filmed 2 years later, starring Jon Voight.

The island, just 5 miles long and 2½ miles wide, was originally inhabited by the Cusabo and later the Yamacraw Indians. Indian pottery, some of the oldest in America, has been found on Daufuskie, dating back 9,000 years. English settlers eventually took over the island and converted it into a series of plantations, focusing on indigo as its main export. Indigo eventually yielded to cotton plantations. After the boll weevil, an oyster-canning industry took over until it was forced out of business by the pollution of the Savannah River in 1951.

Today half of the island is essentially a nature retreat, with thick, ancient live oaks and angel oaks along with ospreys, egrets, and other waterfowl living among the reeds and rushes. In the 1980s, the other half was developed into private golf courses and elegant "plantations," where people live in condos. The island is now home to about 450 permanent residents, though its **Gullah** population, descendants of slaves freed after the Civil War, has virtually disappeared. **Haig Point** is the private, residential community on the northern end of the island, containing several historic landmarks. The **historic district** comprises much of the southern end of Daufuskie, containing a smattering of homes, artisan studios, and art galleries, as well as the First Union African Baptist Church. The **Webb Tract,** at around 600 acres, is the formal name, for the wild, undeveloped section of Daufuskie, while the modern Melrose, Oak Ridge and Bloody Point communities share the eastern half of the island. You can visit the island by guided tour, or explore independently by golf cart, visiting sights such as the Silver Dew Winery, First Union African Baptist Church, and Mary Fields School, where Pat Conroy taught in the late 1960s.

Essentials
GETTING THERE
There is only one way to Daufuskie Island, and that's by boat. The **Daufuskie Island Ferry** runs between Broad Creek Marina, 18 Simmons Rd., Hilton Head Island, and Freeport Marina on Daufuskie. The ferry is operated by **Calibogue Cruises** (✆ **843/342-8687;** www.daufuskiefreeport.com), and normally runs twice a day, Monday to Saturday. Round-trip tickets are $33; add lunch or dinner at the Old Daufuskie Crab Company, and either a golf-cart rental (map included) or a guided historical tour (see below), and the cost is $64. You can also opt to pay for the bus tour separately (Tues–Thurs; $30), or rent golf carts independently (map included): $60 for 2½ hours or $100 per day (6 hr.).

There are also several private companies that provide high-speed water taxi services to the island.

CRUISES & TOURS
Several companies offer guided tours to Daufuskie. **Calibogue Cruises** (see above) runs a 2-hour bus tour taking in all the main sights, and a crab meal, for $64 (including the ferry). Tours depart once a day Tuesday to Thursday (call ahead to reserve). Calibogue can also set you up in a basic cabin for $100 per night if you'd like to stay longer.

Outside Hilton Head offers tours to Daufuskie by golf cart, guided by interpretive historians (✆ **800/686-6996** or 843/686-6996; www.outsidehiltonhead.com or www.outsidedaufuskie.com). The Daufuskie Island History and Artisans Tour, lasting 4½ hours, is $85 per person (includes boat shuttle, golf cart, and guide).

Exploring Daufuskie Island
Most of the island's attractions can be seen by following the so-called **Rob Kennedy Trail;** maps are available on arrival or can be downloaded from www.daufuskieisland historicalfoundation.org.

Freeport Marina, where the ferry docks, is on the west side of the island near Melrose Landing and the Old Daufuskie Crab Company Restaurant (p. 174). The handy **Freeport Marina General Store** is open Monday to Friday 8am to 5pm, and Saturday and Sunday 10am to 7:30pm.

To the northeast is the **Haig Point Club** and **Mt. Carmel Baptist Church No. 2,** the latter built by the Cooper River community around 1940. In 2001 the Daufuskie Island Historical Foundation (www.daufuskieislandhistoricalfoundation.org) restored the by-now abandoned building, and opened the **Billie Burn Museum** inside (named after long-time resident and island historian, Billie Burn). Among the museum's fascinating collection is a copy of the original land grant from King George II to Dave and Francis Mongin in 1735, an early-19th-century bible, a restored 1890s organ, and even an 11-foot stuffed alligator. It's open Tuesday to Saturday 12:30 to 3:30pm (free admission). Next door is the historic **Jane Hamilton School,** now the home of the Gullah Learning Center and the Daufuskie Island Community Library (same hours as the museum).

The **Haig Point Lighthouse** lies within the Haig Point development but remains a major island landmark (the club uses it as a hotel, but private tours are sometimes possible). The lighthouse was built in 1882, but was retired in the late 1930s. The privately owned **Bloody Point Lighthouse** (www.bloodypoint.com), 146 Beach Rd., dates back to 1872 and was also retired in the late 1930s. The small outbuildings on the property were later transformed into the infamous **Silver Dew Winery** by the legendary Pappy Burn (check out the Bloody Point website to learn about his story). Today the **Silver Dew Winery and Gift Shop** commemorates the old man's venture. Established by Pappy's grandson, Lancy, the **Silver Dew Pottery** (© 843/842-6419) is open May to October, Tuesday to Friday 9am to 4pm, to display the beautifully simple and wholly functional pottery created by him and his wife Emily.

The other galleries on the island are also worth seeking out. The **Iron Fish Art Gallery** (© 843/842-9448; www.ironfishart.com) is the base of acclaimed folk artist Chase Allen, who designs and creates unique metal fish and aquatic sculptures at his historic Gullah cottage. The gallery is always open, even if Chase is not around. He also sells jars of freshly made honey.

The most significant historic landmark on Daufuskie Island is the **First Union African Baptist Church,** built in 1884 on land donated by a former plantation owner (the first church was constructed in 1881, but burnt down). Largely unchanged since the 1880s, it is still in use today as a place of worship. A replica of a traditional Gullah **Praise House** is located behind the building.

Finally, the **Mary Fields School** was built in 1933 for the education of local Gullah children; this is where author Pat Conroy taught during the 1969–70 academic year. The school closed in 1995, but the building still stands.

Where to Stay & Dine

It is possible to arrange private accommodation on the island, or rent a cabin (p. 236), but the most comfortable option is the **Melrose Inn** ★★ (© 888/851-4971; www.melroseonthebeach.com), 47 Ave. of Oaks. The hotel was being comprehensively renovated at the time of research but will eventually feature 52 luxurious guestrooms, private cottages, and even safari-like tents.

There are several places to eat on the island, including the fabulous **Old Daufuskie Crab Company** ★★★ at Freeport Marina (© 843/785-6652), which serves freshly caught shrimp, fish, and, of course, deviled crab (dinner entrée $18). It also fires up excellent steaks and allows you to shuck oysters right off the roasting pit. The outdoor section is perfect for viewing the sunset. The restaurant is usually open Tuesday to Sunday 11:30am to 9:30pm, offering a delicious Gullah/Lowcountry buffet Tuesday to Friday from 11am to 2pm.

Marshside Mama's Café ★★, 15 Haig Point Rd., at the County Dock (© 843/785-4755; www.marshsidemamas.com) is another tranquil, low-key island diner featuring Lowcountry favorites such as shrimp and grits, gumbo, and grouper sandwiches. Call to check opening times (usually Tues–Sat noon–3pm and 6–10pm, Sun noon–6pm), and to make reservations for dinner (recommended in summer).

Despite the deep appeal of the South Carolina coastline, history buffs might want a more enlightening morning's diversion. If that's the case, consider a few hours' excursion to a 19th-century riverfront community in Lowcountry that time has almost passed by: historic **Bluffton ★★**, a town perched on the South Carolina mainland within a short drive of Hilton Head.

Bluffton's historic core remains about the way it looked in 1901. Be warned in advance not to expect palatial, aristocratic homes open to the public. Some of those were burned in 1863 during the Civil War. Most of the ones that remain are private, closed to the public, and relatively small, collectively reflecting the mercantile society of river traders who occupied them. The most impressive of the buildings is the much-weathered **Gothic Episcopal Church of the Cross,** 110 Calhoun St., at the edge of the May River.

Calhoun Street has the community's densest concentration of historic homes. But for a deeper insight into just how slow and sleepy this town really is, drop into the **Heyward House Historic Center,** 70 Boundary St. at the corner of Bridge Street (🕾 **843/757-6293;** www. heywardhouse.org). The low-slung design of the house, originally built in 1840 and later enlarged prior to 1900, was inspired by earlier planters' homes in the British West Indies. It's open for 30-minute guided tours Monday through Friday from 10am to 5pm, and Saturday 10am to 4pm. House tours cost $8 for adults and $2 for students (children 9 and under get in free), but additional donations to the upkeep of the house are appreciated. A caretaker here will also give you a free map for a self-guided walking tour of the town as well. If you want a guided tour of town, they're available by appointment Monday to Friday for $18 (students $12). Depending on the season, there may or may not be a kitschy collection of battered memorabilia for sale somewhere along the length of Calhoun Street.

For more information about sleepy Bluffton, contact the **Old Town Bluffton Merchant Society** at 🕾 **843/815-9522** or visit www.oldtownbluffton.com.

BEAUFORT ★★

41miles NE of Downtown Savannah

Full of old-fashioned inns, rustic pubs, and tiny stores along the Henry C. Chambers Waterfront Park, **Beaufort** (Lowcountry pronunciation: *Bew*-fort) is an old seaport with narrow streets shaded by huge live oaks and lined with 18th-century homes. Officially founded by the British in 1711, the oldest house remaining (at Port Republic and New streets) was built in 1717, though the town's history goes back much further. This was actually the second area in North America discovered by the Spanish (1520), the site of the first fort on the continent (1525), and the first attempted settlement (1562). Several redoubts have been excavated, dating from 1566 and 1577. In more recent times this quaint town was the inspiration for the setting of Pat Conroy's novel *The Prince of Tides* (1986). In fact, parts of the 1991 film were shot here, as were certain scenes from *Forest Gump* and *The Big Chill.* Conroy himself still lives in Beaufort, and actor Tom Berenger has a home here. Unbeknown to most hip-hop fans, DJ Jazzy Jay was actually born here in 1961, his Gullah family moving to New York City soon after.

Today not just tourism but the military keeps the city going: Beaufort's military bases employ thousands of locals (directly and indirectly), and pump millions of dollars into the local economy.

Essentials

GETTING THERE

If you're traveling from the north, take I-95 to exit 33; then follow the signs to the center of Beaufort. If you're leaving from Charleston, take U.S. 17 S.; then head left on U.S. 21, and follow signs to Beaufort. From Hilton Head, go on U.S. 278 W.; after it turns into 278 Alt, exit onto S.C. 170. Follow S.C. 170 into Beaufort.

Greyhound (www.greyhound.com) runs **buses** twice daily between Beaufort and Savannah (55 min.); for Charleston you have to take a bus to Orangeburg and change there. The bus stop is at Coastal Travel (© **843/524-4646**), 3659 Trask Pkwy, on the outskirts of town (U.S. 21).

Palmetto Breeze (© **843/757-5782;** www.palmettobreezetransit.com) runs local buses between central Beaufort, Hilton Head Island, and Bluffton, with fares just $2.

VISITOR INFORMATION

Beaufort Chamber of Commerce Visitor Center, 713 Craven St. (© **800/638-3525** or 843/525-8500; www.beaufortsc.org), has information and self-guided tours of this historic town. It's open Monday to Saturday 9am to 5pm, and Sunday noon to 5pm.

ORGANIZED TOURS

If you're planning to visit Beaufort in early to mid-October, contact the **Historic Beaufort Foundation** (© **843/379-3331;** www.historicbeaufort.org), for dates and details regarding its 3-day **Fall Festival of Houses and Gardens,** when several private antebellum houses and gardens open to the public.

A walking tour by the **Spirit of Old Beaufort,** 103 West St. (© **843/525-0459;** www.thespiritofoldbeaufort.com), takes you on a journey through the old town, exploring local history, architecture, horticulture, and Lowcountry life. You'll see houses that are not accessible on other tours. Your host, clad in period costume, will guide you for 2 hours Monday to Saturday at 10am and 2pm. The cost is $18 for adults and $9 for children 7 to 12. Tours depart from just behind the John Mark Verdier House Museum.

Exploring Beaufort

Remnants of the original English colonial settlement of Beaufort are preserved in the **historic district** downtown, designated a National Historic Landmark. The **John Mark Verdier House Museum,** 801 Bay St. (© **843/379-6335;** www.historicbeaufort.org/verdier-house.php), is a restored 1804 house partially furnished to depict the life of the prosperous merchant who lived here until 1825. An excellent example of a Federal-style home, it was once known as the Lafayette Building because the Marquis de Lafayette is said to have spoken here in 1825. It's open Monday to Saturday 10am to 4pm. Admission is $10; children 6 and under are admitted free. A scale model **diorama** of 1863 Bay Street is displayed on the ground floor of the house; this exhibit is free (same hours).

St. Helena's Episcopal Church, 505 Church St. (© **843/522-1712;** www.sthelenas1712.org), traces its origin back to 1712, though the current church was built around 1724. Visitors, admitted free Monday to Saturday from 10am to 4pm, can see its classic interior and visit the graveyard, where tombstones served as operating tables during the Civil War.

A worthwhile excursion from Beaufort is the 15-mile drive to the state park at **Hunting Island** ★★★, 2555 Sea Island Pkwy. (📞 843/838-2011; www.huntingisland.com), a lush island where the Vietnam battle scenes from *Forrest Gump* were filmed. Long a layover for sailors and pirates, including Blackbeard, the island was once a base for hunting deer. With 3 miles of natural sandy beaches—some of the most beautiful coastline in South Carolina—this 5,000-acre park is now a nature and wildlife refuge. There are showers and dressing rooms on the beach, a 200-site campground, plus cabins, a boardwalk, and nature trails, as well as a fishing pier and boat landing.

In the center of the park stands the 132-foot historic **Hunting Island Lighthouse.** The lighthouse was rebuilt in 1875 after it was destroyed in the Civil War; you can climb the 167 steps to the top for spectacular views March through October daily 10am to 4:45pm (Nov–Feb closes 3:45pm). Admission is $2.

The park collects an entry fee of $5 for adults, $3 for seniors and kids ages 6 to 15. The park is open daily from 6am to 6pm. **The Visitors Center** is open Monday to Friday 9am to 5pm and Saturday and Sunday 11am to 5pm.

Where to Stay

Beaufort Inn ★★   This luxurious option in the Historic District combines the intimacy of a B&B with the amenities of a posh hotel. Built as a summer retreat for his family by attorney and Congressman William Sidney Smith in 1897, the handsome Victorian features all the heart-pine floors, real fireplaces, claw-foot soaking tubs, lush gardens, courtyards, porches, verandas, and balconies you'd expect, but also an on-site spa, modern bathrooms, and free Wi-Fi. Food is another draw, with breakfasts crafted by renowned Chef Christopher Hewitt, and homemade scones and jams served to guests in the afternoons.

809 Port Republic St., Beaufort, SC 29902. www.beaufortinn.com. 📞 **888/522-0250.** 21 units. $159–$229 double. Rates include full gourmet breakfast. No children 7 and under. **Amenities:** Room service; spa; free Wi-Fi.

Cuthbert House Inn ★★   This is a classic old Southern beauty, an all-white clapboard Federal-style mansion built around 1790 and now a wonderful B&B. Built by the Cuthbert family, successful indigo and cotton planters, General Sherman actually stayed here after capturing the city in the Civil War. Rooms are faithfully decked out in period style, some with four-posters, working gas fireplaces, and soaking claw foot tubs or whirlpool tubs. Rates include a sumptuous Southern-style breakfast, plus complimentary sunset hors d'oeuvres and refreshments on the veranda.

1203 Bay St., Beaufort, SC 29902. www.cuthberthouseinn.com. 📞 **800/327-9275** or 843/521-1315. 7 units. $150–$259 double. Rates include full breakfast and afternoon tea or refreshments. Free parking. **Amenities:** Breakfast room; bike rentals; free Wi-Fi.

Rhett House Inn ★★★   Beaufort's trifecta of gorgeous historic inns is rounded out by this romantic, award-winning hotel, a Greek Revival masterpiece built by Thomas Smith Rhett in the 1820s (the cottage dates from 1864, and once served as a store for freed slaves). Though the interior retains much of the historic ambience, this is no chintzy B&B—rooms are a blend of antiques and oriental rugs with fresh orchids and contemporary style with flatscreens on the wall. Tea, lemonade, and tempting homemade cookies are available throughout the day.

1009 Craven St., Beaufort, SC 29902. www.rhetthouseinn.com. 📞 **888/480-9530** or 843/524-9030. 17 units. $169–$299 double. Rates include full breakfast, afternoon tea, and evening hors d'oeuvres. Free parking. No children 4 and under. **Amenities:** Restaurant; free bikes; free Wi-Fi.

Where to Dine

Blackstone's Café AMERICAN   No frills-breakfast institution, popular with locals since opening in 1991. Shrimp is big here: shrimp and grits or shrimp omelets for breakfast, and flavorful homemade soups with shrimp-salad sandwich for lunch, but there are plenty of other options, including pancakes, French toast, bagels and traditional egg breakfasts.

205 Scott St. www.blackstonescafe.com. ℂ **843/524-4330.** Breakfast $6–$10; sandwiches $7–$10. Mon–Sat 7:30am–2:30pm, Sun 7:30am–2pm.

Emily's INTERNATIONAL   Appealing restaurant and tapas bar, with exceptional seafood: bake grouper, crab-cake dinners, and the seafood platters are all outstanding. However, the artfully prepared tapas plates can also make a meal here—order several to share. My favorites include the tangy garlic shrimp, the stuffed mushrooms, the Italian sausage, sautéed with sweet pepper and onions, and for a real treat, the lobster ravioli.

906 Port Republic St. www.emilysrestaurantandtapasbar.com. ℂ **843/522-1866.** Tapas $9–$12; main courses $16–$28. Daily 4–10pm (main courses served starting at 6pm).

Old Bull Tavern ★★★ GASTROPUB   Justly popular gastropub in the heart of the Historic District, featuring a changing menu based on farm-to-table produce and European comfort foods, washed down with innovative cocktails and craft beers. Since opening in 2012, this has fast become the foodie destination in town—reservations are essential, though there is a community table for walk-ins, under the watchful gaze of an actual bull's head (stuffed on the wall). The soft-shell crab sandwich alone is a work of art, but everything is good—a lot of work has gone into the cocktail menu, too. Check out the new brick-oven-fired pizzas.

205 West St. ℂ **843/379-2855.** Main courses $10–$18. Tues–Sat 5pm–midnight.

SAPELO ISLAND ★

72 miles S of Downtown Savannah

The fourth largest of Georgia's barrier islands, **Sapelo Island** is filled with the diverse wildlife of the forested uplands as well as a salt marsh and a complex beach-and-dunes system. The island is reached by boat from the Sapelo ferry dock, 8 miles northeast of Darien off Ga. 99. Educational **tours** of this undeveloped barrier island are conducted year-round by the Georgia Department of Natural Resources.

Taking in everything from maritime forests to marshes, the **R. J. Reynolds State Wildlife Refuge** encompasses 8,240 acres. Some 5,900 of these acres have been designated as the **Sapelo Island National Estuarine Research Reserve.**

Guale Indians, Spanish missionaries, English freebooters, and French royalists called this island home before Thomas Spalding purchased the south end of the island in 1802. In the antebellum years, Spalding (1802–51) refined the Georgia Sea Island cotton and sugar industries, and designed and constructed an octagonal tabby sugar mill in 1809 (Tabby is a mixture of equal parts of oyster shell, sand, water, and lime.)

In 1912, Howard E. Coffin purchased the island from Spalding's heirs. Coffin undertook a complete rebuilding of **South End House,** Spalding's plantation mansion, which dated from 1810. By 1928, the house was ready to entertain President and Mrs. Coolidge, and later President and Mrs. Hoover in 1932. In February 1929, Charles A. Lindbergh landed on the island and visited the Coffins. The house was purchased in 1934 by the tobacco heir Richard J. Reynolds. Twenty years later, Reynolds donated the dairy complex of the farm to the University of Georgia for use as a marine research laboratory. Jimmy Carter used the mansion during his administration in 1980.

Today the island has some 400 acres of private property, concentrated in a hamlet known as **Hog Hammock,** whose residents are descended from slaves from Spalding's plantation days. Interpretive programs include marsh and beach walks, bird and wildlife observation, and special historical tours. Salt-marsh vegetation includes needlerush, sea oxeye, salt grass, glasswort, and cordgrass. You'll see osprey feeding in the Duplin River and hear the call of the clapper rail, a marsh bird. The island is inhabited by such species as raccoons, feral cows, white-tailed deer, and a variety of snakes, including the eastern diamondback rattler and the cottonmouth. Chachalacas, a Mexican species of bird introduced to the island as a game bird, might also be spotted.

A 30-minute ferryboat ride from the mainland aboard the *Sapelo Queen* takes visitors to the island. Guides accompany guests on the half-day **bus tour,** including a marsh walk. The ferry leaves Wednesday at 8:30am, returning at 12:30pm; and Saturday at 9am, returning at 1pm, throughout the year, and also Friday 8:30am to 12:30pm June through Labor Day. March to October, an extended tour is conducted the last Tuesday of each month from 8:30am to 3pm. The tour costs $15 for adults and $10 for children 6 to 12, including the boat ride (free for kids 5 and under). Reservations are required. To make a reservation, contact the **Sapelo Visitors Center,** Landing Road, in Meridian, Georgia, just outside of Darien, Georgia (📞 **912/437-3224;** www.sapelo nerr.org). The center is open Tuesday to Friday 7:30am to 5:30pm and Saturday 8am to 5:30pm.

BRUNSWICK

75 miles S of Savannah

The gateway to the Golden Isles is a sleepy town not quite awake to the tourism potential of its antique houses, palms, flowering shrubs, and moss-draped live oaks. **Brunswick** has always been an important port, with a natural harbor that can handle oceangoing ships. In World War II, with Nazi U-boats prowling the Atlantic, Brunswick's shipyard began to construct "Liberty Ships," stronger, larger cargo vessels. Beginning in 1943, these 447-foot vessels slipped down the ways at the feverish rate of some four a month. Today, instead of Liberty Ships, you'll find a large fleet of **shrimp boats**—the town bills itself as the "shrimp capital of the world."

At some point, you'll want to sample **Brunswick stew** in the town of its origin (although the citizens of Brunswick County, Virginia, would beg to differ). It is made basically with a combination of meats and flavored with an array of vegetables such as tomatoes, potatoes, okra, lima beans, and corn. In the old days, cooks would make it with squirrel, rabbit, or what virtually amounted to roadkill, all simmering in the same pot—but preparations are less exotic today. A good time to sample the versions is during the **Brunswick Stewbilee,** a Brunswick stew cook-off held here the second Saturday in October from 11:30am to 3pm.

Essentials

GETTING THERE   From Savannah, head west, following the signs to I-95; you'll take the highway south until the Brunswick turnoff.

Six miles north of downtown, **Brunswick Golden Isles Airport** (© **912/264-9200;** www.flygcairports.com) is served by **Delta Connection** (© **800/221-1212** or 912/267-1325; www.delta.com). It offers flights to Brunswick from Atlanta (37 min.) several times daily. At the small airport, car rental agencies are available, including **Avis** (© **912/638-2232;** www.avis.com) and **Hertz** (© **912/265-3645;** www.hertz.com). Shuttle service into town is provided by Sea Island (© **912/638-3611**) and FLETC (© **912/267-2100**).

VISITOR INFORMATION The **Golden Isles Convention & Visitors Bureau** operates a welcome center located at I-95 southbound, between exits 42 and 38 (© **912/264-0202;** www.goldenisles.com), open Monday to Saturday 9am to 5pm and Sunday 1 to 5pm.

Exploring Brunswick

The welcome center will provide you with a free map indicating the main points of interest, which include the waterfront off Bay Street, with its bustling docks and fleet of shrimp boats. Oceangoing freighters are often seen here.

The **Lanier Oak,** along U.S. 17, off Lanier Boulevard, is said to be the tree where the Georgia poet Sidney Lanier was inspired to write "The Marshes of Glynn." Another tree, the 9-century-old **Lover's Oak,** at Albany and Prince streets, is also a source of pride for the town.

After dark, the big attractions are the dinner and casino cruises aboard the *Emerald Princess* (© **800/842-0115;** www.emeraldprincesscasino.com). Bookings can be made at the **Golden Isles Cruise Lines,** 1 St. Andrews Court in Brunswick (© **912/265-3558**). This 200-foot luxury cruiser offers dining, dancing, and live entertainment on one level, and a full casino with slot machines, poker, blackjack, craps, and roulette on another level. After departure, the ship sails out past the 3-mile limit, where the casino then opens for business. Cruises depart from Gisco Point, conveniently located at the southern end of the Sidney Lanier Bridge.

Reservations are not required, but you should make them anyway just to be on the safe side. The rate is $10 per person. Cruise hours are Monday to Thursday 7pm to midnight, Friday and Saturday 7pm to 1am, and Sunday 1 to 6pm. A special Saturday-morning departure leaves at 11am and returns at 4pm. All cruises offer a full meal at sea, with music, dancing, and games such as scavenger hunts. Call ahead for special summer deals.

Where to Dine

Gary Lee's Market ★★★ BARBECUE   The best barbecue in town and perhaps on the whole coast; an old-fashioned, unassuming place that serves sandwiches or plate lunches, but also cuts of beef or sausages by the pound to take home. The pulled pork is especially good, very smoky and bursting with flavor (they smoke over pecan and oak here), and they also serve smoked brisket, sausage, chicken, ribs, smoky baked beans, and even cheeseburgers. Finish off with a slice of pie or cake, all made locally.

3636 U.S. 82 (just outside town). © **912/265-1925.** Main courses $6–$11. Tues–Sat 11am–6pm.

Indigo Coastal Shanty ★★ LOWCOUNTRY/INTERNATIONAL   Another simple, unassuming place that doesn't look like much from the outside, Indigo Coastal is actually one of the best restaurants in town. Chef Kate Buchanan has developed a playful menu that blends local produce and Lowcountry flavors with a host of international dishes. Signature plates include Bahamian chicken curry and Pasta Veracruz (sauté of chicken, roasted tomatoes, seared corn, caramelized onions, and linguine in a creamy tequila-chipotle pan sauce), as well as sesame-crusted catfish and classic meatloaf.

1402 Reynolds St. www.indigocoastalshanty.com. ℂ **912/265-2007.** Main courses $13–$17. Tues–Fri 11am–3pm, Fri–Sat 5–10pm.

ST. SIMONS ISLAND ★★

83 miles S of Downtown Savannah

The largest of the Golden Isles (just over 16 sq. miles), **St. Simons Island** is also the most popular for its beaches, golf courses, scenery, and numerous tennis courts. Through tunnels of ancient oaks, you can bike and drive the length of St. Simons, finding treasures at every turn. It's a vacation haven for families.

The early inhabitants of the island are thought to have been the Timucuan people, with a Native American presence going back at least 2,000 years. **Fort Frederica** was built by James Oglethorpe here between 1736 and 1748 to protect the southern boundary of the British colony of Georgia from Spanish raids. In the 1742 battles of **Bloody Marsh** and **Gully Hole Creek,** Oglethorpe's forces trounced Spanish invading troops. Like most of the islands on this stretch of coast, St. Simons later became a center of production for Sea Island cotton. The huge numbers of African slaves who worked these plantations eventually created the unique Gullah culture, though little remains of their presence today. Since the early-20th century the island has been transformed into a resort community, though much of it remains untrammeled marsh and woodland.

Essentials

GETTING THERE   Take I-95 to Ga. 25 (the Island Pkwy.) or U.S. 17 to Brunswick, where signs direct visitors across the F. J. Torras Causeway to St. Simons Island.

VISITOR INFORMATION   The Golden Isles Convention & Visitors Bureau runs a **Visitors Center** on the island in the Old Casino Building, 550 Beachview Dr. (ℂ **912/638-9014;** www.goldenisles.com), open daily 10am to 5pm.

Exploring St. Simons Island

The best way to introduce yourself to the island is via **St. Simons Trolley Island Tours** (ℂ **912/638-8954;** www.stsimonstours.com), 649 Dellwood Ave., which acquaints you with 400 years of history and folklore, taking 1½ hours and costing $23 for adults and $10 for children 4 to 12; tours for children 3 and under are free. Tours depart daily at 11am and 1pm in April, June, and July, and daily at 11am the rest of the year. Buses depart from the big oak tree at the pier in Pier Village, near 117 Mallery St.

The island's chief attraction is **Fort Frederica National Monument** (ℂ **912/638-3639;** www.nps.gov/fofr), on the northwest end of the island (signposted). Go first to the **Visitor Center,** where a film and displays explain the role of the fort and the town that grew up around it. There isn't much left; about all you'll see of the original construction is a small portion of the magazine and the barracks tower, but archaeological excavations have unearthed many foundations. The fort and town were established in 1736 by General James Oglethorpe, the founder of Savannah, and served as a key base during the crucial battles of 1742. By 1749 the Spanish were no longer a threat, and the fort was abandoned; the town clung on for a few more years, but a fire in 1758 destroyed what was left. On the grounds is a gift shop, and walking tours can be arranged. Admission is $3 per person, free for children 15 and under. It's open daily from 9am to 5pm.

Christ Church (© **912/638-8683;** www.christchurchfrederica.org), 6329 Frederica Rd., at the north end of the island, was built in 1820. It was virtually destroyed when Union troops camped here during the Civil War, burning the pews for firewood and butchering cattle in the chapel. In the 1880s, Reverend Anson Greene Phelps Dodge, Jr., restored the church as a memorial to his first wife, who had died on their honeymoon. The serene white building nestled under huge old oaks is open Tuesday to Sunday from 2 to 5pm. There's no admission charge.

St. Simons Island Lighthouse Museum, 101 12th St. (© **912/638-4666;** www. saintsimonslighthouse.org), is a restored lightkeeper's house from 1872. You can climb its 129 steps for a panoramic view of the Golden Isles. Inside are exhibits devoted not only to the lighthouse, but also to the Golden Isles in general. But you go more for the view than the nautical exhibits. Admission is $10 for adults, $5 for children 6 to 11, and free for children 5 and under. Hours are Monday to Saturday 10am to 5pm and Sunday 1:30 to 5pm.

Scattered from end to end on St. Simons are ruins of the plantation era: the **Hampton Plantation** (where Aaron Burr spent a month after his duel with Alexander Hamilton) and **Cannon's Point** on the north; **West Point, Pines Bluff,** and **Hamilton Plantations** on the west along the Frederica River; **Harrington Hall** and **Mulberry Grove** in the interior; **Lawrence, St. Clair, Black Banks,** the **Village,** and **Kelvyn Grove** on the east; and the **Retreat Plantation** on the south end. There's a restored chapel on West Point Plantation made of tabby, with mortar turned pink from an unusual lichen. Locals say it reflects blood on the hands of Dr. Thomas Hazzard, who killed a neighbor in a land dispute and built the chapel after being so ostracized that he would not attend Christ Church.

Outdoor Activities

St. Simons not only attracts families looking for a beach, but it's also heaven for golfers. Jet-skiing, charter fishing, scuba diving, and cruising can also be arranged at **Morning Star Marinas at Golden Isles,** 206 Marina Dr. (© **912/634-1128;** www. morningstarmarinas.com/golden-isles), on the F. J. Torras Causeway.

BEACHES You'll find two white-sand public beaches here, foremost of which is East Beach at Massingale Park, 1350 Ocean Blvd. (© **912/265-0620**). This county-maintained beach contains a picnic area and a bathhouse. It's open daily 6am to 10:30pm; a lifeguard is on duty June 1 to Labor Day, daily from 11am to 4pm. Parking is free in designated areas, and drinking is allowed on the beach but only from plastic containers (no glass). Fishing is free from the beach but allowed only from 4 to 10pm.

Another public beach is the **Coast Guard Station Beach,** East Beach Causeway, also family oriented, with a bathhouse and showers (this section of East Beach is often referred to as just "First Street Beach Access," or just "Coast Guard Station"). Lifeguards are also on duty from June 1 to the Labor Day weekend, daily from 11am to 4pm. Parking is free in designated areas, and fishing is permitted during non-swimming hours from 4:30 to 10pm. Drinking is allowed on the beach from plastic containers only.

BIKE RENTALS **Ocean Motion,** 1300 Ocean Blvd. (© **800/669-5215** or 912/638-5225), suggests that you explore St. Simons by bike and will provide detailed instructions about the best routes. The island is relatively flat, so biking is easy. Beach cruisers are available for men, women, and kids, with infant seats and helmets. Bike rentals cost $12 for 4 hours and $16 for a full day.

FISHING   Your best bet is **Golden Isles Charter Fishing,** 104 Marina Dr., Golden Isles Marina Village (© **912/638-7673;** www.goldenislesfishing.com), which offers deep-sea fishing and both offshore and inshore fishing. Captain Mark Noble is your guide.

GOLF   It's golf—not tennis—that makes St. Simons Island a star attraction. Foremost among the courses is the for-guest-use-only **Sea Island Golf Club ★★★**, 100 Retreat Ave. (© **912/638-5118;** www.seaisland.com), owned by the Cloister of Sea Island. At the end of the "Avenue of Oaks" at historic Retreat Plantation, the club consists of three 18-hole courses: the Retreat Course, the Plantation Course, and the Seaside Course.

The club opened in 1927 and offers dramatic ocean views, adding a measure of excitement to the game. Its greatest fans mention it with the same reverence as St. Andrews, Pebble Beach, or Ballybunion. Former president George H. W. Bush liked the courses so much that he once played 36 holes a day. Seaside, host of the PGA Tour's McGladrey Classic, is definitely the most famous of all—known for the 414-yard no. 7. *Golf Digest* has called this hole one of the best in golf and among the toughest in Georgia. A drive has to clear a marsh-lined stream and avoid a gaping fairway bunker.

Greens fees range from $90 in December to $295 March through May, with the cart and the caddie fee included. The state-of-the-art **Golf Learning Center** (www.sea islandglc.com) on the grounds can help improve even an experienced golfer's game. Also on the grounds are a pro shop, clubhouse, and restaurant. Courses are open daily from 8am to 6pm.

Sea Palms Golf & Tennis Resort, 5445 Frederica Rd. (© **800/841-6268** or 912/638-3351; www.seapalms.com), offers outstanding golf on its Tall Pines/Great Oaks (18 holes, 6,500 yd., par 72), and Sea Palms West (9 holes, 2,500 yd., par 72) courses. Some holes nestle alongside scenic marshes and meandering tidal creeks. Reserved tee times are recommended, and cart use is required. The courses are open daily 7am to 7pm, charging greens fees of $84, with cart rental included.

NATURE TOURS   **Ocean Motion Surf Co,** 1300 Ocean Blvd. (© **912/638-5225;** www.stsimonskayaking.com), offers nature tours by kayak of the island's marsh creeks and secluded beaches. Featured are a 2-hour dolphin nature tour for $45.

SAILBOAT RENTALS   **Ocean Motion Surf Co** (see above), also arranges hourly, half-day, or full-day Hobie Cat sailboat rentals ($75/hr.), along with sailing lessons (by experienced instructors) and sailboat rides ($95/hr.).

Where to Stay

In addition to the accommodations listed below, private cottages are available for weekly or monthly rental on St. Simons. You can get more information from **Parker-Kaufman Realtors,** 22 Beachway Dr., Jekyll Island, GA 31527 (© **888/453-5955;** www.parker-kaufman.com). The office is open Monday to Friday 9am to 5pm and on Saturday 9am to 1pm. Vacation rental cottages can range from one to four bedrooms. Rentals begin at $625 per week in summer, lowered to as little as $490 per week off season.

King and Prince Beach & Golf Resort ★   Plush, modern beachfront resort, with five sparkling oceanfront pools, spas, tennis courts, and plenty of golf. It's a family-friendly spot, with two kiddie pools, children's menus, special activities for kids, and two-bedroom suites to five-bedroom beach houses to accommodate groups. The resort actually has its roots in a dance club that opened here in 1935, but it's been completely renovated many times since then and rooms feature an elegant, classic design with wooden beds, rosewood furnishings, and all the amenities.

201 Arnold Rd., St. Simons Island, GA 31522. www.kingandprince.com. © **800/342-0212** or 912/638-3631. 188 units. $159–$349 double, $351–$919 villa. **Amenities:** Restaurant; bar; babysitting; exercise room; 5 pools (1 indoor); room service; 2 tennis courts; free Wi-Fi.

The Lodge at Sea Island Golf Club ★★ Truly luxurious digs, with rooms decked out in an elegant South-meets-English manor house style. It's a relatively tranquil getaway, with expansive ocean views, and justly popular with golfers given the courses that surround it (see Golf, above). The old-world experience is rounded out by the 24-hour butler service, dining at Colt & Alison and The Oak Room, and, the pièce de résistance, a real bagpiper to serenade the setting sun.

100 Retreat Ave. www.seaisland.com. © **912/634-4300.** $337–$750 double. 40 units **Amenities:** 4 restaurants; 2 bars; babysitting; three 18-hole golf courses; exercise room; Jacuzzi; room service; sauna; spa; free Wi-Fi.

Saint Simons Inn by the Lighthouse ★★ Pleasant, low-key B&B alternative to the big resorts, with friendly staff, homey decor, and a relaxed vibe. Most rooms are simple but cozy, with modern fittings, spacious bathrooms, and basic cable TV. Weekend bookings require a 2-night minimum stay. And, yes, it really does stand right next to the Lighthouse, within easy walking distance of the downtown area.

609 Beachview Dr., St. Simons Island, GA 31522. www.stsimonsinn.com. © **912/638-1101.** 34 units. $139–$159 double. Rates include continental breakfast. **Amenities:** Outdoor pool; free Wi-Fi.

Where to Dine

Bennie's Red Barn ★ STEAKS/SEAFOOD This is a fun, family place to eat good, wholesome food, though the red barn itself looks like it's been transported from Pennsylvania Dutch Country. Established in 1954, founder Bennie Gentile was indeed inspired by the barns he saw in Germany in World War II. The menu is fairly straightforward, with a big selection of steaks (cooked over a wood fire), and seafood, all served with the traditional house salad, baked potato, or French fries. End your evening with the locally infamous "Raccoon Frozen Cocktail" for dessert (a spiked milkshake).

5514 Frederica Rd. www.benniesredbarn.com. © **912/638-2844.** Main courses $12–$32. Daily 5:30–10pm.

Delaney's Bistro ★★ MODERN AMERICAN Chef Tom Delaney has been delighting locals and visitors alike at this bistro since 1994, with cozy corner booths, soft lighting, and black-and-white photos of the island on the walls. Among a variety of fresh seafood and especially game dishes, his signatures include a grilled magret duck breast, with a Thai peanut sauce ($29), and the charred fresh foie gras verjus, served over baby greens with a sour grape sauce ($21). Alternatively, you can sit at the bar and order from the tapas menu of sliders, peppered shrimp, salads, *tinga*, and double-stuffed mushrooms.

3415 Frederica Rd. www.delaneysbistro.com. © **912/638-1330.** Main courses $9–$12 lunch, $18–$35 dinner. Tues–Sat 11am–2pm and 6–10pm.

Southern Soul Barbeque ★★ BARBECUE   Top BBQ joint on the island, with all the classics done exceptionally well. In addition to plates of pulled pork, ribs, brisket, and turkey breast, the sandwiches are especially good, with ribs, pork knuckle, and burnt ends all crammed within a toasted bun, and topped with pickles and a dollop of 'slaw. All the meats are available by the pound, and the sides menu is substantial, featuring Brunswick Stew ($4–$7), mac and cheese, and fried okra.

2020 Demere Rd. www.southernsoulbbq.com. ☏ **912/638-7685.** Main plates $10–$15. Daily 11am–10pm.

LITTLE ST. SIMONS ISLAND ★

20-min. boat ride from St. Simons Island

The ideal place to savor the wild beauty of Georgia's coast is still untouched by commercial development. Reached only by boat, **Little St. Simons Island**—6 miles long and 2- to 3-miles wide—remains one of the last privately owned islands off the Georgia coast. The Berolzheimer family used the island as a private retreat from 1908 to 1978, when they opened it to the general public, with only a few accommodations and a maximum of 32 people per night. To visit you'll have to be one of them and stay the night at the pricey Lodge, or opt for a much cheaper, if not quite as romantic, **day-trip.** These include a guided island tour and interpretive program led by an experienced naturalist, and a lunch of Lowcountry specialties. The cost is $95 per person, and includes the ferry.

The island is a haven for naturalists and for those seeking a secluded getaway. (But be warned that mosquitoes are a serious problem in summer.) Activities on Little St. Simons include shelling, swimming, and sunbathing along 7 miles of secluded beaches; hiking (watch out for snakes); and horseback riding through acres of ancient forest. There are also canoeing and fishing in the island's many rivers and creeks, plus bird-watching of at least 200 species. Guests can learn about the local ecosystems by joining naturalists on explorations.

Essentials

GETTING THERE   Take I-95 to Ga. 25 (the Island Pkwy.) or U.S. 17 to Brunswick, where signs direct visitors across the F. J. Torras Causeway to St. Simons Island. Once on the island, follow the signs to the Hampton River Club Marina. At the marina, on the north end of St. Simons, a ferryboat departs daily at 10:30am and returns at 4:30pm. It's privately owned, so unless you're a guest, you are not even allowed to ride the ferry. Day visitors must make advance reservations (☏ **888/733-5774**).

VISITOR INFORMATION   All information is supplied directly by the lodge (see below).

Where to Stay & Dine

The Lodge on Little St. Simons Island ★   Accommodation on the island comprises six rustic but comfy cottages, tucked beneath the oaks inside the main lodge compound (all fully air-conditioned with real fireplaces for the winter). Rates include three full meals daily, all snacks and beverages, unlimited use of activities and recreation gear, and the boat transfer to/from the island. The most historic cottages are the Hunting Lodge, dating back to 1917, with exposed wood walls and floors, and rustic timber beds, and Helen House, a tabby structure built in 1928, with plantation-style rooms featuring exposed beams, antique beds, and period furnishings.

1000 Hampton Point Dr., Little St. Simons Island, GA 31522. www.littlestsimonsisland.com. © **888/733-5774** or 912/638-7472. 15 units. $600–$725 double. Rates include all meals and beverages. **Amenities:** Restaurant; bar; bikes; outdoor pool; free Wi-Fi.

SEA ISLAND ★★

86 miles S of Downtown Savannah

Just 3 miles east of St. Simons Island, across the Blackbank River, **Sea Island** was purchased back in 1926 by Howard Coffin, who built a causeway from St. Simons to reach the 5-mile-long barrier island. His world-famous resort, the **Cloister,** opened in October 1928 and is still the main attraction here. It owns the entire piece of land, which can be visited on a day trip from Savannah if you don't want to stay overnight; just allow about 1½ hours to get there. When you arrive, take a scenic drive along **Sea Island Drive,** also called "Millionaire's Row." Today, in addition to the hotel, the island is home to some of the most elegant villas and mansions in the Southeast. Many of Sea Island's residences are second homes to CEOs and other wealthy folks. Some can be rented if you can afford it. Call **Sea Island Cottage Rentals** (© **877/732-4752;** www.seaisland.com), but be prepared for very high prices.

The Cloister combines 10,000 acres of forest, lawn, and marshland, plus 5 miles of beachfront. It has impressed everybody from Margaret Thatcher to Queen Juliana of the Netherlands, plus four U.S. presidents, including George H. W. Bush, who honeymooned here with his wife Barbara in the 1940s.

Essentials
GETTING THERE
From Brunswick, take the F.J. Torras Causeway to St. Simons Island and follow Sea Island Road to Sea Island.

Where to Stay & Dine
The Cloister ★★★   Despite numerous renovations, the main building that dominates the Cloister resort retains a magnificent Mediterranean/Spanish Revival facade, inspired by the 1928 original. Scattered around the complex are luxury accommodations, the Sea Island Yacht Club, the Cloister Spa, the Cloister Beach Club, and four excellent restaurants, including the renowned Georgian Room. All rooms come with wood furnishings, exposed beam ceilings, overstuffed chairs, hardwood floors, and handmade Turkish rugs.

100 Cloister Dr., Sea Island, GA 31561. www.seaisland.com. © **912/638-3611.** $460–$750 double. Golf, tennis, and honeymoon packages available. **Amenities:** 4 restaurants; 2 bars; babysitting; exercise club; three 18-hole golf courses; room service; spa; 8 tennis courts (4 lit); free Wi-Fi.

JEKYLL ISLAND ★★★

94 miles S of Downtown Savannah

Once a winter playground for the Rockefellers, Pulitzers, Goulds, Morgans, and Cranes, **Jekyll Island** is the smallest of the state's coastal islands, with 5,600 acres of highlands and 10,000 acres of marshlands. Today it's no longer the exclusive enclave it once was, and is open to all those attracted by its miles of beautiful white-sand

Atlantic beaches and holes of championship golf. It also has far better tennis complexes than St. Simons Island. Families primarily come here for a wealth of outdoor activities.

Essentials

GETTING THERE   From Brunswick, take U.S. 17 South to the turnoff for Jekyll Island. Head east across the Jekyll Island Causeway, paying a daily **parking fee** of $6 per vehicle to enter the island at the Guest Information Center (weekly pass $28).

VISITOR INFORMATION   The **Jekyll Island Guest Information Center,** located about 4 miles down the Causeway, 901 Jekyll Island Causeway (© **912/635-3636;** www.jekyllisland.com), is open daily from 9am to 5pm, dispensing maps, brochures, and other helpful information.

Exploring Jekyll Island

The best way to see the **Historic District ★★**—the former enclave of the millionaires of America's Gilded Age, who built what they called "cottages" here—is to take a guided historical tram tour departing daily at 11am, 1pm, and 3pm from the **Jekyll Island Museum** (© **912/635-4036**), 100 Stable Rd. The tour lasts 1½ hours, costing $16 for adults, $7 for children 7 to 15, and free for children 6 and under (no tours in Dec). Highlights of the tour include **Indian Mound** (or Rockefeller) **Cottage** dating from 1892, and the **du Bignon Cottage** from 1884. The museum itself is free and open daily 9am to 5pm.

On your own, you can view the 1906 Goodyear Cottage on Riverview Drive, housing the **Jekyll Island Arts Association** (© **912/635-3920;** www.jekyllartsassociation. org)—with a gift shop and a free monthly exhibition. Admission is free, and it's open daily noon to 4pm. Also in the historic district, the Dutch Colonial Revival–style **Mistletoe Cottage,** 341 Riverview Dr., was built in 1900 by businessman and Congressman Henry Kirke Porter, one of the first members of the Jekyll Island Club.

Jekyll Island is also home to **Horton's Brewery Site,** Georgia's first brewery, signposted on the northwest end of the island. It was started by General Oglethorpe, who evidently knew how to put first things first for his settlers. This two-story ruin, dating from 1742, is one of the oldest standing structures in the state. It was mainly constructed of tabby, a building material made of crushed oyster shells that is native to coastal Georgia. Very near the brewery stand the ruins of **Horton House,** built in 1738 by William Horton, one of Oglethorpe's captains and the first Englishman to obtain property on Jekyll Island. In the summer (usually June and July), Jekyll Island Museum runs illuminating guided tours of the site (Sat 10am and 2pm; adults $16, children 7–15 for $7, free for ages 6 and under). Reserve at © **912/635-4036.**

Kids will enjoy the **Georgia Sea Turtle Center,** 214 Stable Rd. (© **912/635-4444;** www.gstc.jekyllisland.com), a hospital for ill and injured sea turtles. The center is open to the general public and offers an interactive exhibit gallery and Rehabilitation Pavilion, with a number of viewable, and very cute, sea turtle patients. Adult admission is $7; seniors over 65 pay $6, and children 4 to 12 pay $5.

Kids will also enjoy the **Summer Waves Water Park,** 210 S. Riverview Dr. (© **912/635-2074;** www.jekyllisland.com/summer-waves), offering 11 acres of watersports with more than a million gallons of water. It features rides and attractions ranging from a totally enclosed speed flume that jets riders over three breathtaking humps, to a ride over the rolling waves in the Frantic Atlantic wave pool. You can also hang on around the twisting turns of the Hurricane Tornado and Force 3 slides. For toddlers,

OUTDOOR pursuits AT JEKYLL ISLAND

If you have a car, take the South Jekyll Loop to survey the scene before concentrating on specifics. Drive south on North Beachview Drive to view some of the island's 10 miles of public beaches with public bathhouses and picnic areas. Your loop around the island's southern end will include the **South Dunes Picnic Area.** Continue around onto South Riverview Drive, passing **Summer Waves** and the **Jekyll Harbor Marina,** until you return to Fortson Parkway.

BEACHES There are three public beaches on the island, all open daily round-the-clock and free to the public. Those choosing to swim off Jekyll Island do so at their own risk, as there are no lifeguards on duty. The **St. Andrew Picnic Area,** reached beyond Summer Waves, the water park along South Riverview Drive, is one of the best beaches at the southeastern tip of the island. It has an adjacent picnic area, but no

bathhouse or showers available. **South Dunes Beach,** with a picnic area and showers, is north of St. Andrew and is reached along South Beach Drive. Farther along, **Central Dunes** has showers but no picnic area. Saltwater fishing is allowed on the public beaches, and no license is required.

BIKING Because of its flatness, Jekyll Island is relatively easy to explore by bike. Rentals are available from **Jekyll Island Club Hotel** (see below). Bikes rent for $10 for a half day and $18 for a full day.

GOLF Three championship 18-hole courses await golfers on Jekyll Island, plus one historic 9-hole course. The **Great Dunes Golf Course,** Beach View Drive (© 912/635-2170), is a small 9-hole course patterned after the course at St. Andrews, Scotland. It offers some holes that were part of the original course laid out in 1898 when only millionaires played golf here. The

there's the Pee Wee Puddle—fun in only a foot of water. Admission is $20 for those 48 inches or taller, and $16 for children under that height. Children 3 and under enter free. Open the weekend before Memorial Day to December 31, Sunday to Thursday 10am to 6pm and Friday and Saturday 10am to 8pm.

Where to Stay

Jekyll Island cottage rentals are available through **Parker-Kaufman Realtors,** 22 Beachview Dr. (© **888/453-5955** or 912/635-2512; www.parker-kaufman.com). The realtor offers over 100 individual properties ranging from a small one-bedroom apartment to a six-bedroom home. Rental prices start at $750 per week in winter, rising to over $5,000 per week in the busy summer months. Reservations for summer rentals are accepted as early as December 1. The office is open Monday to Saturday 9am to 5pm.

The landmark island hotel is the luxurious **Jekyll Island Club Hotel ★★★**, 371 Riverview Dr. (© **800/535-9547** or 912/635-2600; www.jekyllclub.com), which comes loaded with amenities, pools, restaurants, and golf courses. The original clubhouse opened in 1888, thereafter hosting some of the giants of the Gilded Age. Rooms range $189 to $309.

Jekyll Island Campground, North Beachview Drive (© 866/658-3021 or 912/635-3021; www.jekyllisland.com), is managed by the Jekyll Island Authority and is the only island campground in the Golden Isles. On its 18 wooded acres are 206 sites, nestled among live oaks and pines. The facilities include bathhouses, showers, laundry course was remodeled as an authentic links course in the 1920s by Walter J. Travis. A 3,023-yard, par-36 course, it's open daily from 7am to 6pm. There is a small pro shop and a clubhouse on the grounds. Greens fees are $18 to $25.

Jekyll Island Golf Club, 322 Captain Wylly Dr. (© **912/635-2368;** www.golf jekyllisland.com), consists of three separate courses: **Oleander** (18 holes, 6,241 yd., par 72), **Pine Lake** (18 holes, 6,760 yd., par 72), and **Indian Mound** (18 holes, 6,282 yd., par 72). Dick Wilson's Oleander is consistently ranked among the state's best courses, and the *Atlanta Constitution* called its 12th hole "the most demanding par 4 of any daily fee course in the state." Pine Lakes was designed by Clyde Johnson and is the longest and tightest layout on Jekyll Island. Tree-lined fairways dogleg both left and right as they wind through the island's interior. Indian Mound was

designed by Joe Lee with wide fairways and large, sloping greens.

All courses prefer that you reserve tee times, and charge $17 to $45 for greens fee, depending on time of day and season. Play is daily from 7am to 6pm for all three courses. A clubhouse, restaurant, and pro shop are on the grounds.

TENNIS   Jekyll Island Tennis Center ★★, 400 Captain Wylly Dr. (© **912/635-3154**), boasts 13 clay courts, seven of them lighted for night play, all of them favored because of low-impact conditions and cooler court temperatures. The center is open daily 9am to 6pm. Ball machines can be rented for $12 per hour, and the court fee is $6 per person, per session. Professional instruction is available for $25 per hour. There's a pro shop on the grounds, plus a restaurant and showers.

facilities, camping equipment, pure tap water, a grocery store, garbage pickup, propane, and bike rentals. Tent sites cost $23, with hook-up sites available for $28 to $37.

Where to Dine

The Grand Dining Room ★★ SOUTHERN/INTERNATIONAL   The island's finest dining certainly evokes the Gilded Age. It's an elegant-but-restrained Victorian parlor replete with Ionic columns, real fireplaces, candlelight, and piano music. The food here is continental haute cuisine, albeit with Southern touches. Dinner might start with Jekyll Club crab cakes, lemon-peach marmalade, and pistachio-crusted rack of lamb or a deluxe version of shrimp and grits, sautéed with garlic butter, scallions, Andouille sausage and herbs, and finished with wine and cream. The Sunday brunch is a local institution, and a relatively good deal at $30 for adults and $15 for children 11 and under.

In the Jekyll Island Club Hotel, 371 Riverview Dr. © **912/635-2600.** Jacket preferred for men. Main courses $25–$35. Mon–Sat 7am–2pm and 6–9pm, Sun 10:45am–2pm (brunch) and 6–9pm; Victorian tea daily 4–5:30pm.

Latitude 31 Restaurant & Rah Bar ★★ SEAFOOD/INTERNATIONAL   The location couldn't be better, right on the historic wharf, perfect for sunset viewing. The main restaurant serves up fresh seafood and delicious steaks, as well creative riffs on seafood pastas and good-old shrimp and grits. The Rah Bar is the more-relaxed beach shack next door, serving no-frills, wild Georgia shrimp, oysters, Dungeness crab legs, and Lowcountry boils. Wash it all down with their Rah Margaritas or Rum Smash cocktails.

Jekyll Wharf. www.latitude31jekyllisland.com. © **912/635-3800.** Main courses $19–$35; Rah Bar $8–$23. Restaurant daily 11am–2pm and 5–10:30pm; Rah Bar 11am–11pm.

CUMBERLAND ISLAND ★

7 miles NE of St. Marys

Nowhere else on the East Coast are peace and unspoiled natural surroundings so perfectly preserved as at **Cumberland Island.** Since 1972, most of this island has been a National Seashore administered by the National Park Service.

Cumberland Island reached the peak of its prestige in the Gilded Age. In the 1880s, Thomas M. Carnegie, brother of steel magnate Andrew Carnegie, bought land on Cumberland for a winter retreat. Their lavish home, dubbed Dungeness, burned to the ground in 1959 and only ruins remain. Most of the other major buildings were built by the Carnegie family: Classical Revival **Plum Orchard,** completed in 1898, is still standing, and managed by the National Park Service; **Greyfield,** built in 1900, now a private hotel (p. 191); and the **Stafford Mansion,** built for Lucy Carnegie in 1901, and still privately owned by one of the descendants of the family. Not only the Carnegies wielded power here, but also the Rockefellers and even the Candlers of Atlanta (founders of Coca-Cola). The island was also the top-secret site of the 1996 wedding of John Kennedy, Jr., and Carolyn Bessette. After the publicity generated in the aftermath of that wedding, Cumberland became famous around the world.

To visit Cumberland Island, just 16 miles long and 3 miles across at its widest point, is to step into a wilderness of maritime forest, salt marshes alive with waving grasses, sand dunes arranged by wind and tide into a double line of defense against erosion, and wide, gleaming sand beaches. It is to enter a world teeming with animal life, where alligators wallow in marshes, white-tailed deer bound through the trees, wild pigs snuffle in the undergrowth, armadillos and wild turkeys roam freely about, more than 300 species of birds wheel overhead, and wild horses canter in herds.

Essentials

GETTING THERE   The only public transportation to the island is via the ferry from St. Marys on the mainland. (Get to St. Marys on Ga. 40 from I-95 or U.S. 17.) You must reserve passage on the ferry; contact the National Park Service, **Cumberland Island National Seashore** (© 912/882-4335; www.nps.gov/cuis). There are two trips daily from March through November every day at 9am and 11:45am, returning 10:15am and 4:45pm; there is also an additional departure at 2:45pm Wednesday through Saturday up to September 30. December to February the ferry departs 9am and 11:45am Thursday through Monday, returning at 10:15am and 4:45pm. In summer, book as far in advance as possible. The fare is $20 for adults, $18 for seniors, and $14 for children 12. These fees are in addition to the **island admission fee,** which is $4 for ages 16 and above (good for 7 days).

Bike rentals are first-come first-served and are beach cruiser–type bikes. Rentals are $16 per day, or $20 if keeping the bike over night. Camping is $4 per night, or $2 for backcountry camping.

If you plan to stay overnight in the hotel, the best way to reach Cumberland is by the Greyfield Inn ferry, the *Lucy R. Ferguson,* which maintains a regular schedule to

Fernandina Beach, Florida. Reservations are necessary and must be made through the Greyfield Inn (see below).

VISITOR INFORMATION   Information is available from the Greyfield Inn (see below), or from the National Park website.

Exploring Cumberland Island

Don't look for a swimming pool, tennis courts, or a golf course—Cumberland's attractions are a different sort, straight out of *The Prince of Tides*. The inn is just a short walk from those high sand dunes and a wild, undeveloped beach. Beachcombing, swimming, shelling, fishing, and exploring the island are high on the list of activities.

No signs are left of the Native Americans who lived here beginning some 4,000 years ago, nor of the Franciscan missionaries who came to convert them during the 1500s. No ruins exist of the forts built at each end of the island by Gen. James Oglethorpe in the 1700s. What you will find as you poke around this island are the ruins of the Carnegie's massive mansion, **Dungeness;** the **Greene-Miller cemetery,** which still holds inhabitants from Revolutionary War times through the Civil War era; and the **Stafford plantation house.** Down the lane a bit is **Plum Orchard,** another Carnegie mansion, fully furnished but unoccupied and now the property of the U.S. Park Service. Visitors can tour the home (free) when volunteer caretakers are in residence. Ask at the Sea Camp Ranger Station for details.

Where to Stay & Dine

The main place to stay and eat on the island is the historic **Greyfield Inn** ★★ (ⓒ **866/401-8581** or 904/261-6408; www.greyfieldinn.com). The house was built by Thomas and Lucy Carnegie for their daughter, Margaret Ricketson, in 1900, and was converted to a hotel in 1962. Rates are $425 to $595 for doubles, but this includes the ferry and all meals, tours, use of bikes, snacks, and non-alcoholic drinks. Even the smallest rooms are dressed with family heirlooms, antique beds, and period antiques, with the larger suites boasting window seats and vintage mahogany king beds. Lunches are usually provided in picnic form (homemade potato salad, sandwiches, and the like), while dinners are more elaborate sit-down affairs, served around a communal table (guests usually dress up), featuring contemporary Southern and international dishes; fresh seafood is a staple, with organic vegetables and herbs supplied from their gardens. Note that there is no Internet and no TV at the inn.

ST. AUGUSTINE

When driving South into Florida, many people make the grave mistake of speeding through the Northeast without as much as a single stop beyond the Cracker Barrels, Denny's, and gas stations lining the highways. Thankfully, Juan Ponce de León made the *fortunate* mistake of discovering just how magnificent the northeast part of the state is. You would do well to follow in his footsteps.

The entire state of Florida owes a lot to the wandering de León, whose misguided quest for the Fountain of Youth landed him somewhere between present-day Jacksonville and Cape Canaveral. (He was a bit off course—he meant to land in what is now Bimini—but who can blame a guy who didn't have GPS?) Observing the land's lush foliage, he named it *La Florida,* or "the flowery land."

In 1565, the Spanish established a colony at St. Augustine, the country's oldest continuously inhabited European settlement. Not much, if anything at all, has changed in St. Augustine (in a wonderful way). The streets of the restored Old City look much as they did in Spanish times. Unlike neighbors in Central Florida, however, this is no Epcot. St. Augustine is real, living history.

Not everything in these parts is antiquated, however. To the south, there's the "Space Coast," where rockets blast off from the Kennedy Space Center at Cape Canaveral. In Cocoa Beach, you can watch surfers riding the rather sizable waves.

Up near the state line, cross a bridge to Amelia Island, where you'll discover exclusive resorts that take advantage of 13 miles of beautiful beaches. Amelia's Victorian-era town, Fernandina Beach, is another throwback to the past, helping to further render the northeast region a fascinating juxtaposition of the old, the new, and somewhere in between.

ST. AUGUSTINE: AMERICA'S FIRST CITY ★★

105 miles NE of Orlando; 302 miles N of Miami; 39 miles S of Jacksonville

America's oldest permanent European settlement, St. Augustine draws history buffs and romantics to its **Colonial Spanish Quarter** and 18th-century buildings. With its *coquina* buildings and sprawling, moss-draped live oaks, visitors can do more than just museum hop. St. Augustine encourages guests to sit down for a while, and to drink in scenes from the past along with a chilled glass of sweet tea.

Tourism is St. Augustine's main industry these days. However, despite the number of visitors, it's an exceptionally charming town, with good restaurants, a small-town nightlife, and shopping bargains. Give yourself 2 days to tour the magnolia-lined streets of old St. Augustine, longer to fully savor this historic gem.

ESSENTIALS

Arriving

BY PLANE The **Daytona Beach International Airport** is about an hour's drive south of St. Augustine, but service is more frequent—and fares usually lower—at **Jacksonville International Airport** (p. 232), about the same distance north.

BY CAR The drive is a straight shot on 1-95.

BY TRAIN The nearest **Amtrak** (*©* **800/872-7245;** www.amtrak.com) is at **Palatka,** 220 N. 11th St. (platform only), though this is still 29 miles southwest of downtown St. Augustine. Buses sometimes make the connection, but you must check in advance.

BY BUS Greyhound connects St. Augustine with the Amtrak train station at Palatka (45 min.) twice a day; and Daytona Beach, Orlando, and even Savannah (1 daily; 5 hr.), via Brunswick. Buses drop off at 1 Castillo Dr., right in the heart of St. Augustine.

Visitor Information

TOURIST OFFICES Before you go, contact the **St. Augustine, Ponte Vedra & The Beaches Visitors and Convention Bureau,** 88 Riberia St., Ste. 400, St. Augustine, FL 32084 (*©* **800/653-2489** or 904/829-1711; www.floridashistoriccoast.com). Request the *Visitor's Guide,* which details attractions, events, restaurants, accommodations, shopping, and more.

The **St. Augustine Visitor Information Center** is at W. Castillo Drive and Cordova Street, just off U.S. 1 and near the Castillo de San Marcos National Monument (*©* **904/825-1000;** www.staugustinegovernment.com). There are numerous ways to see the city, depending on your interests and schedule; this makes a good first stop. Once you've looked through the extensive information and made plans, you can buy tickets for the sightseeing trains and trolleys, which include discounted admissions to the attractions (see "Organized Tours," p. 208). The center is open daily from 8:30am to 5:30pm.

City Layout

The oldest city isn't exactly the largest. At just 12 square miles, St. Augustine is like a CliffsNotes version of history, with everything compacted in the city's pride and joy—the **historic district.** St. George Street, from King Street north to the Old City Gate (at Orange St.), is the heart of the historic district. Lined with restaurants and boutiques selling everything from T-shirts to antiques, these 4 blocks get the lion's share of the town's tourists. You'll have much less company if you poke around the narrow streets of the primarily residential neighborhood south of King Street. Most of the town's attractions do not have guided tours, but many do have docents on hand to answer questions.

Getting Around

Once you've parked at the visitor center (cost is $10, but worth it because parking is a premium here), you can walk or take one of the sightseeing **trolleys, trains,** or horse-drawn carriages around the historic district. The trolleys and trains follow 7-mile routes, stopping at the visitor center and at or near most attractions daily between 8:30am and 5pm. You can get off at any stop, visit the attraction, and step aboard the next vehicle that comes along (about every 20 min.). If you don't get off at any attractions, it takes about 1 hour and 10 minutes to complete the tour. The vehicles don't all go to the same sights, so speak with their agents at the visitor center in order to pick the right one for you. You can buy tickets, as well as discounted tickets to some attractions, at the visitor center or from the drivers. See "Organized Tours," p. 208.

BY BUS   The **Sunshine Bus Company** (© **904/823-4816;** www.sunshinebus.net) operates public bus routes Monday through Saturday from 6am to 7pm. The line runs between the St. Augustine Airport on U.S. 1 and the historic district via San Marco Avenue and the Greyhound bus terminal on Malaga Street. Rides cost $1 per person. All-day tickets are $3 for adults and $1.50 for seniors. Call for the schedule.

BY TAXI   For a taxi, call **Yellow Cab** (© **904/824-6888**).

BY BIKE OR SCOOTER   **Solano Cycle,** 61 San Marco Ave., at Locust Avenue, 2 blocks north of the visitor center (© **904/825-6766;** www.solanocycle.com), rents bicycles and scooters. Bikes cost $18 a day, while scooters are $75 for a single passenger and $80 for two. Open daily 10am to 6pm.

[FastFACTS] ST. AUGUSTINE

Dentists   For same-day emergency dentist appointments, try **St. John's Family Dentistry,** 2225 A1A S. (© **904/471-7300;** www.staugustinedentist.com). Another place to try for same-day care **is St. Augustine Family Dentistry,** 1980 A1A S. (© **904/829-2082;** www.staugustinedentistry.com).

Doctors & Hospitals   For a physician referral or 24-hour emergency-room treatment, contact

Flagler Hospital, 400 Health Park Blvd. (© **904/819-5155;** www.flaglerhospital.org), or **St. Augustine Health** (www.staugustinehealth.com/dir/primary_care_clinics) for the names of local walk-in clinics.

Emergencies   In an emergency, dial © **911.** If the situation isn't life threatening, call © **904/825-1099** for the fire department and © **904/825-1074** for the police.

Pharmacies   Try **CVS Pharmacy,** 2703 N. Ponce de Leon (© **904/824-2838**), open 24 hours. For four other CVS locations, go to www.cvs.com/stores/cvs-pharmacy-locations/Florida/Saint-Augustine.

Post Office   The St. Augustine Post Office in the historic district is at 99 King St. (© **904/825-0628**), open Monday to Friday 9am to 6pm and Sat 9am to 2pm.

ST. AUGUSTINE HOTELS

There are plenty of moderate and inexpensive motels and hotels in St. Augustine, but the most popular are the B&Bs, of which there are plenty charming choices. Then there are the chains. Most convenient to the historic district is the 40-room **Best Western Spanish Quarter Inn,** 6 Castillo Dr. (© **800/528-1234** or 904/824-4457; www.staugustinebestwestern.com), directly across from the visitor center. It's completely surrounded by an asphalt parking lot, but it does have a pool and hot tub.

Another nice spot on the beach is **La Fiesta Ocean Inn & Suites,** 810 A1A Beach Blvd. (© **800/852-6390** or 904/471-2220; www.lafiestainn.com), a Green-certified

Where to Stay in St. Augustine

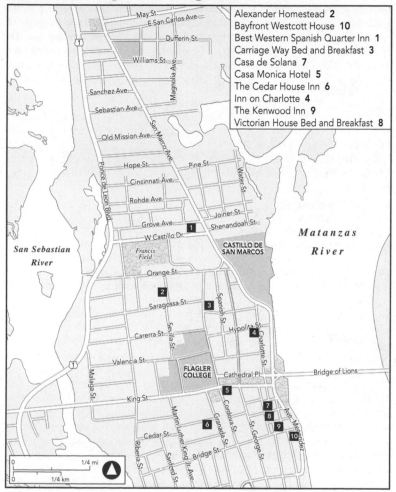

Alexander Homestead **2**
Bayfront Westcott House **10**
Best Western Spanish Quarter Inn **1**
Carriage Way Bed and Breakfast **3**
Casa de Solana **7**
Casa Monica Hotel **5**
The Cedar House Inn **6**
Inn on Charlotte **4**
The Kenwood Inn **9**
Victorian House Bed and Breakfast **8**

hotel that has won awards for its beautiful landscaping, and there's a heated pool and gardens. Best of all, guests enjoy a daily complimentary breakfast, delivered to your room, with fresh-baked scones and muffins, bagels and cream cheese, yogurt, and fruit cup. Rates start at $85 in the winter and $139 in the summer.

La Fiesta's sister property, the oceanfront Beachfront Bed & Breakfast, 1 F St. (*C* **800/370-6036** or 904/461-8727; www.beachfrontbandb.com), is exclusively for grown-ups and features delicious breakfasts, heated pool, outdoor Jacuzzi, and 25-foot beamed ceilings in the ocean-view great room, all within 10 minutes of the historic district. Rates start at $150 in the winter and $190 in the summer.

Once a ramshackle fishing camp, the **Devil's Elbow Fishing Resort,** 7507 A1A South (*C* **904/471-0398;** www.devilselbowfishingresort.com), offers 10 brand-new resort-style waterfront rental cottages built in the classic Old Florida style with covered porches, tin roofs, roof-top cupolas, and hardwood floors. It's an ideal place for family reunions or just some good old-fashioned R&R. Rates start at $175 a night.

If you're coming on a weekend, expect the higher end of the listed rates—almost all accommodations increase their prices on weekends, when the town is most crowded with visitors. St. Johns County charges a 10% tax on hotel bills (4% bed tax plus 6% state tax).

RECOMMENDED AGENCIES

The companies below are especially recommended.

AirBnB (www.airbnb.com) offers hundreds of properties in and around St. Augustine. The San Francisco-based Internet venture connects private property owners with travelers at a variety of price points.

Couchsurfing (www.couchsurfing.org) is another website connecting travelers with folks willing to rent a house, room, or apartment. It offers plentiful options in and around St. Augustine.

Bed & Breakfasts

Alexander Homestead ★★ B&B   Tucked away on one of St. Augustine's intriguing little side streets, the Alexander Homestead is separated from the buzz of the historic district, but close enough to get there by foot when you want to. An immaculate, six-room B&B, the Alexander Homestead, in all its Victorian glory, is the real deal. Owner Bonnie is on-hand to make sure all is well inside this bucolic little world that dates back to the 1800s. While the building may be historic, it is by no means ancient or outdated, fusing fabulously to the modern world with creature comforts like surprisingly large bathrooms with whirlpool tubs or rain showers. Each room (in keeping with the history of the era from which the building dates, they're referred to as "bedchambers") has its own distinct personality. I highly recommend those in the front of the house, which have porches overlooking the property's yard. For even more privacy, check into the Hideaway Suite, which is just that, over the garage with its own private entrance. The Hideaway Suite is also the only accommodation that allows (and is big enough for) children. Homemade breakfast, fresh-brewed coffee every morning, and a communal fridge with complimentary water, sodas, and red and white wine are just added bonuses. Ask Bonnie for recommendations on area sites and tours and her insider tips. Weekends have 2-night minimum stays in each room, while major holidays may require up to a 3-night stay in each room. Small dogs are permitted in certain rooms, with crate only.

14 Sevilla St., St. Augustine, FL 32084. www.alexanderhomestead.com. (C) **888/292-4147** or 904/826-4147. 6 units. $150–$269 double. **Amenities:** Full breakfast; complimentary soda and wine; free Wi-Fi.

Bayfront Westcott House ★★ B&B   Joy and Andrew Warren have major experience in the luxury hotel business, coming from storied careers at swanky stays in Southern California. They don't just know hospitality, they live it. And you will too when you stay at their fantastic bay-front B&B. It's hard to decide which of the 15 rooms to choose from. They're all immaculate, with decor in varying themes, like the feminine, pastel Abigail, or the masculine, classic Minorcan. One thing all the accommodations have in common is incredibly comfortable beds. Most rooms have electric fireplaces, and many on the second floor have private balconies. Food at the Bayfront Westcott House is no joke, beginning with a hot entrée every morning, and continuing through the day with varying snacks and hors d'oeuvres. There is always something sweet available in the dining room. Even sweeter is the "Fact or Folklore" social hour every Monday and Wednesday from 6 to 7pm, hosted by a professional storyteller from Ancient City Tours. If and when you do decide to leave the property—and it's not so easy to tear yourself away—you're just a short walk from the historic district.

146 Avenida Menendez, St. Augustine, FL 32084. www.westcotthouse.com. ☎ **800/513-9814** or 904/825-4602. 15 units. $189–$319 double. **Amenities:** Full breakfast, social hour; free Wi-Fi.

Carriage Way Bed and Breakfast ★★ B&B   After over 2 decades in the nurturing hands of the Johnson family, an emotional decision was made to pass the torch and sell this 130-year-old Victorian jewel box to Michaele O'Neill. The former owners couldn't have chosen a more passionate innkeeper to breathe new life into the B&B. It's easy to tell that O'Neill, a mother of three and a yoga teacher, was meant to do this. Greeting each guest by name, she makes you truly feel at home, more like family than a guest. A hot gourmet breakfast presented tableside is served every morning from 8:30 to 10am. There are freshly baked sweets every afternoon and complimentary wine, sodas, coffee, tea, and bottled water. If you need Wi-Fi, it's available in the parlor. The main house has 11 rooms, each furnished simply, yet immaculately and comfortably. They all have decanters of sherry for that warm, old-fashioned, spirited touch. I recommend the Masters Room (renovated in 2013), located upstairs and featuring a king-size oak bed, or the Pittman Room (also renovated in 2013), with its electric fireplace and king-size cherry-wood bed. For couples, larger groups, and families with kids 13 and under, **The Cottage,** down the street, is an 1885 clapboard house with a living room, mini-kitchen, and a two-person Jacuzzi. The B&B's location in the heart of the historic district is a major plus, and even better is the free use of bicycles, which makes it easy to tool around and explore the city.

70 Cuna St., St. Augustine, FL 32084. ☎ **800/908-9832** or 904/829-2467. 12 units. $150–$319 double. **Amenities:** Full breakfast; complimentary drinks and desserts; free bikes; free Wi-Fi.

Casa de Solana ★★ B&B   Let me just cut to the chase—this B&B is said to be haunted. Whether you believe it or not, you need to know that the Montejurra room has guests who can check out any time they like, but they can never leave. Some folks go for this; others have panic attacks over it. Just beware that the manager says that on occasion people staying in the Montejurra have reported having their shoulders shaken in the middle of the night. Plus the floors creak, which some find charming, while others just book rooms on the upper floor, where the footing is more solid. Beyond the paranormal, this 250-year-old, seventh-oldest house in St. Augustine is full of worldly charm. The 10-room B&B may have spirits, but it also has the scent of cinnamon raisin soufflé, apple harvest pancakes, or something else equally delicious emanating from the kitchen. Rooms have been uniquely decorated by the owners. The first-floor Mary Mitchell (a pet-friendly room) has tinges of blue and a stellar Sleep Number bed. Just outside the room is a pergola with rocking chairs. The renovated Cielo room is located at the end of the hall on the second floor and features a jetted Jacuzzi tub and a private balcony overlooking the courtyard. It's no wonder ghosts like it here.

21 Aviles St., St. Augustine, FL 32084. www.casadesolana.com. ☎ **877/824-3555** or 904/824-3555. 10 units. $159–$279 double. **Amenities:** Full breakfast; early evening social hour; free bikes; free Wi-Fi.

The Cedar House Inn ★★★ B&B   A Victorian home dating back to 1893, the seven-room Cedar House Inn features 10-foot ceilings and polished pine floors. Unlike many of the area's Spanish-style B&Bs, it also features old-Florida decor, which is almost as rare as a Florida native. Your day at The Cedar House begins with a two-course gourmet breakfast served on crystal and china at individual linen-lined tables. Throughout the day there are wine, port, sodas, bottled water, and fresh baked goods available. A sublime wrap-around porch and sun deck are made for lingering, but for travelers bitten by the exploration bug, it's just a 3-minute walk to the center of town. Rooms are small in size, but huge in charm. They're spotless, too. Many have private porches. I particularly like the Vizcayan room, with its dark wood floors and two-person tiled shower. Let innkeeper Cyndi know what you're looking for and she will go out of her way to get it for you. A game room with chess, checkers, puzzles, and board games will keep you entertained should the indoors beckon. And it will. Trust me. There's a 2-night minimum on weekends.

79 Cedar St., St. Augustine, FL 32084. www.cedarhouseinn.com. (*) **800/845-0012** or 904/829-0079. 7 units. $169–$299 double. **Amenities:** Breakfast; complimentary wine port, bottled water, and soft drinks; reserved on-site parking; free Wi-Fi.

Inn on Charlotte ★★ B&B   Built in 1913, the eight-room Inn on Charlotte is a newbie compared to most of its neighbors, which came along in the previous century. The rooms are done up in varying styles of antiques; seven have whirlpool tubs while the eighth has a huge double shower. Beds in all can only be described as dreamy. Mary Lily's suite is styled with a 1920s French influence and features a queen bed and a two-person Jacuzzi. One of the most requested accommodations is Marjorie K. Rawling's bungalow—no, it didn't belong to "The Yearling" author, that's just its name—with its private courtyard, electric fireplace, and two-person Jacuzzi tub/shower. And then there's breakfast. Served daily at 9:15am, a morning meal could include poached pear with almond-cream sauce, followed by Belgian waffles with bananas, pecans, and a homemade praline sauce. Sip lemonade from the front porch during the day, or wine at the inn's nightly social hour. Owners Rodney, Ann, Jerry, and Ginny make guests feel like friends and family, and go above and beyond to make sure your stay is nothing short of spectacular. Make sure you don't miss breakfast here, because the innkeepers (and I) would consider that criminal. No one under 21 and no pets are allowed.

52 Charlotte St., St. Augustine, FL 32084. www.innoncharlotte.com. (*) **800/355-5508** or 904/829-3819. 8 units. $129–$299 double. No one under 21 allowed. **Amenities:** Breakfast; wine social hour, complimentary soft drinks; one reserved parking spot per room; free Wi-Fi.

The Kenwood Inn ★★★ B&B   This three-story, 13-room Queen Victorian stunner is the oldest continuously operating inn in St. Augustine. Common areas are inviting and cozy, with a little help from the fireplaces, sweeping bay windows, and a baby grand piano that guests are welcome to play. Innkeepers Pat and Ted Dobosz, seasoned hospitality execs, have renovated several rooms, adding refreshed decorations and furniture. Décor runs the gamut from contemporary to classic, with carpets, fireplaces, hardwood floors, Jacuzzis, and, in some rooms, balconies with hammocks. A third-floor suite has a huge living room and balcony with magnificent views of the bay. A new deck overlooking a koi pond is command central for the outstanding breakfasts served daily—ham, grits, lox, bagels, eggs Benedict, and fresh baked pastries, among other temptations. On weekends there's a delicious buffet and make-your-own Bloody Marys and mimosas. There's also a wine social every evening, and a guest pantry stocked with teas, coffees, and lemonade. The inn's residential location makes it a perfect starting point to blend in and act like a local. Explore the area by foot or borrow one of the house bikes. Children over 8 are welcome, and there are a few dog-friendly rooms.

38 Marine St., St. Augustine, FL 32084. www.thekenwoodinn.com. © **800/824-8151** or 904/824-2116. 13 units. $139–$269 double. **Amenities:** Breakfast; wine social hour; complimentary tea, coffee, and soft drinks; free off-street parking lot; free bikes; pool; free Wi-Fi.

Victorian House Bed and Breakfast ★★ B&B   History buffs love this place because it's located between the United States' allegedly two oldest streets. Food fans love it because of the breakfast, which some say is Food Network-quality. Innkeepers Anthony and Marilyn Sexton could quit their day jobs and just open a breakfast restaurant, but thankfully they manage to fuse food with fantastic hospitality at this 1895 charmer. There are five rooms in the main house and six in the carriage house, each tastefully touched up with American country antiques. All have private bathrooms and some include double Jacuzzi tubs, fireplaces, and private porches. The B&B's newest room, The Sea Mist, is tiny, but dolled up with an ocean theme and an antique iron queen bed. Speaking of the ocean, local trolleys pull up here to take you to the beach. Make sure to buy discounted trolley tickets at the inn.

11 Cadiz St., St. Augustine, FL 32084. www.victorianhousebnb.com. © **904/824-7990.** 11 units. $119–$219 double. **Amenities:** Breakfast, complimentary coffees and teas; free parking at off-site lot; free Wi-Fi.

Hotel

Casa Monica Hotel ★★★ HOTEL   If you're not a B&B kind of person, then Casa Monica is the place to stay in St. Augustine. The hotel was taken over by Marriott in 2010, joining the chain's swankier Autograph Collection. This is not your typical cookie-cutter Marriott, that's for sure. The building was constructed in the Moorish Revival style, the interiors highlighted by antique furnishings, Moorish columns, and original artwork. Red velvet headboards in the guest rooms (some say they aren't quite true to the age of the hotel) make this anything but a typical Marriott. Upper floors have views of the pool, while rooms along the main street have park views. Bathrooms are large, with high-end toiletries, and showers or tub/shower combos. High rollers should consider one of the seven suites in the hotel's towers and central turret, which will have anyone feeling like the king or queen of the castle. A bar and the highly regarded 95 Cordova restaurant make this centrally located stay a point of interest in its own right. As historic as the building may be, it's far from a plastic-on-the-couch kind of place; in fact, pets are allowed for a non-refundable $150 fee.

95 Cordova St., St. Augustine, FL 32084. www.casamonica.com. © **800/648-1888** or 904/827-1888. 138 units. $179–$319 double. **Amenities:** Breakfast; complimentary wine, port, bottled water, and soft drinks; reserved on-site parking; free Wi-Fi.

WHERE TO DINE

Spicy food lovers, St. Augustine has something special for you: the Datil, one of the hottest peppers you'll ever find. Restaurants across town add whole and ground Datils to their menus. **Hot Stuff Mon** sells an assortment of Datil delicacies you can take home with you. Those who prefer things on the less spicy side will find plenty to eat in town; I especially love the retro-modern menu and feel at **GAS Full Service Restaurant,** a converted station where fuel is food and the name's other implications may hold true, perhaps, if you indulge in their potent jalapeno popper burger.

Caps on the Water ★ SEAFOOD   Location, location, location, as they say. The reason you go to Cap's is for its stunning waterfront, front garden canopy, and its own beach, shaded by an ancient Florida cedar tree. This is Old Florida finery at its best.

The food's okay, but the views are better. Standard seafood selections are joined by some quintessential Floridian ones, like deep-fried gator tail in citrus sauce. The staff is great, but again, the scenery is better. While outdoors is the preferred dining spot, there's also a separate indoor restaurant, decked out in, of all things, Indonesian antiques, and a cozy oyster bar in case the weather is iffy. If it is iffy, though, I'd save the visit for a day or night when the weather is better and head here for drinks and appetizers during sunset. Cap's is very kid-friendly, as little ones especially love playing on the beach, and don't seem to mind that they're not welcome in the indoor dining room or the bars. A January 2014 renovation spruced the place up and provided a bit of an overhaul.

4325 Myrtle St. www.capsonthewater.com. ℂ **904/824-8794.** Main courses $13–$35. Mon–Thurs 4–9pm, Fri–Sun 11:30am–10pm.

Catch 27 ★★ SEAFOOD   This place is named Catch for several reasons, one being the obvious—it's a seafood spot—and another because if you walk too fast, you may miss it. Then there's the Joseph Heller reference: Serving only fresh seafood bought locally on a daily basis, Catch 27 creates ordering dilemmas, offering on any given day temptations that range from a stellar Minorcan clam chowder in a smoky, spicy broth, to a simply seasoned blackened Florida triggerfish. Fish tacos with a side of black beans and rice are a favorite here, too, kicked up several notches with the local datil-pepper hot sauce. Non-fish eaters needn't steer clear, as the pork bowl—filled with juicy seasoned chunks of meat—is a hearty, tasty dish. Boozers beware: Catch 27 is BYOB, although there's a wine shop around the corner and the restaurant doesn't charge a corkage fee. With just a few tables inside the clean and modern dining room and on the cozy little patio outside, reservations are strongly encouraged.

17 Hypolita St. www.facebook.com/Catch27. ℂ **904/217-8190.** Sun–Mon and Wed–Thurs 11:30am–8:30pm, Fri–Sat 11:30am–9:30pm.

Collage Restaurant ★★ AMERICAN   Quaint and romantic, in a tiny house reminiscent of something you'd find after getting lost on a cobblestoned European street, Collage is aptly named for its multifaceted menu of high-end fare. If you want a "nice dinner" to celebrate a special occasion, this place would be it. The tablecloths, candles, and flowers certainly help set a relaxed, romantic mood, but the food can make you want to disrupt that calm with inappropriately ecstatic cries. A little bit old school, but with some modern American touches, the menu has several consistent favorites, including a divine wheel of brie baked in phyllo and served with a caramelized onion and apple chutney, and a datil-pepper carrot bisque with Havarti cheese and bacon that should not be missed. Homemade lobster ravioli is magnificent, pillowy and overloaded with fresh chunks of lobster. There are also fine cuts of meat and daily specials. The wine list is impressive, and service is exceptional, thanks to an experienced staff that genuinely seems to know and love food.

60 Hypolita St. http://dev.collagestaug.com. ℂ **904/829-0055.** Main courses $28–$45. Nightly from 5:30pm.

The Floridian ★★★ SOUTHERN   As hard as it is to find a native Floridian, it's even harder to find a restaurant that's wholly devoted to the cuisine and ingredients of the state. Enter the appropriately named The Floridian, which takes its moniker very seriously, right down to using purveyors that source from northeast and north-central Florida. Menus are seasonal and change often; a dinner might include small plates of pickled pepper shrimps in local datil-pepper brine, fried green tomato bruschetta,

Where to Dine in St. Augustine

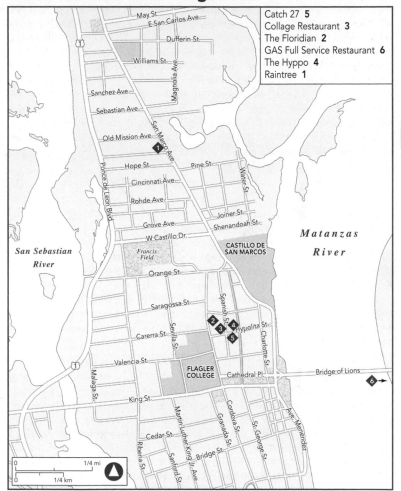

Catch 27 **5**
Collage Restaurant **3**
The Floridian **2**
GAS Full Service Restaurant **6**
The Hyppo **4**
Raintree **1**

pan-fried polenta cakes, and cornbread panzanella with your choice of grilled catch of the day, shrimp, or tempeh. Or maybe the house will be serving the kitschy-named Kitchen Sink Cobb, with house-smoked bacon, black-eyed pea Southern "caviar," datil-deviled eggs, and pickled sweet onions. Local and regional organic craft beers and biodynamic wines are also on the menu. Everything here really is farm-fresh and fully Floridian, a match for the kooky, Floridian country-style decor, which is both rustic and kind of nuts, complete with a canoe hanging upside down from the ceiling. The no-reservations policy makes The Floridian even more of a hot ticket, but if you call in advance you may be able to snag what they call "priority seating."

39 Cordova St. www.thefloridianstaug.com. © **904/829-0655.** Main courses $9–$21. Mon, Wed–Thurs, Sun 11am–3pm and 5–9pm, Fri–Sat 11am–3pm and 5–10pm.

GAS Full Service Station ★★ AMERICAN   Despite the dubious name and all its implications, GAS is a hip, retro-modern, reasonably priced hot spot favored by the locals. It's worlds away from touristy historic district spots in so many ways. The retro theme may be kitschy and cheeky, but the menu is modern, updating comfort food with an emphasis on burgers. Not for the faint of heart or calories, GAS's Jalapeño Popper Burger is a specialty, a hearty serving of two beef patties stuffed with cheddar cheese, cream cheese, and fresh jalapeños, then grilled and panko-breaded and deep fried. Just describing it spiked my cholesterol, but it's oh, so very good. The meatloaf, pork chops, and espresso-rubbed rib-eye are also pretty irresistible. For those looking to be a little better in the health department, there's some divine tofu, marinated in mojo and grilled. As with most hipster spots these days, there's a very worthy craft beer list here. The mod interior leans heavily on old-fashioned gas pumps and comes complete with a sign that reads "THANK YOU FOR NOT PASSING GAS."

9 Anastasia Blvd. www.facebook.com/gasfullservice. ℰ **904/217-0326.** Main courses $7–$15. Tues–Thurs 11am–9pm, Fri–Sat 11am–10pm.

The Hyppo ★★ COMFORT FOOD   This cute little Popsicle stand serves some of the most gourmet-quality frozen treats you'll ever eat, from Mexican hot chocolate and datil strawberry, to mango-habanero-and-pistachio rosewater pops. It's no coincidence that you have to say "hip" when mentioning The Hyppo. It's more than a passing fad, though, and much more than a pop shop. There are also gourmet sandwiches: Roast pork with fig preserves, Gorgonzola, and sprouts on sourdough bread, or perhaps The Elvis is more your speed, with crunchy peanut butter, local honey, fresh banana, and bacon on multigrain bread. The place is so popular that in addition to Charlotte Street there's also The Hyppo Hut on St. George Street and two other locations as well.

48 Charlotte St. www.facebook.com/gasfullservice. ℰ **904/217-7853.** Pops and sandwiches $4–$8. Daily 11am–11pm.

Purple Olive ★★ AMERICAN   Family owned and operated, Purple Olive prides itself on supporting local farmers and purveyors. The restaurant is known for its mix-and-match, make-your-own meals, in which diners choose from all sorts of entrées, sauces, condiments, and side dishes. For those who'd rather leave it in the expert hands of chef/owner Peter Kenney, I highly recommend the "datil seafood fra diablo." When in St. Augustine, you may as well embrace the unofficial flower—er, hot pepper, the datil—which adds a sensational current of spice to the fra diablo's sea of seafood and marinara sauce. Other highlights include the espresso-rubbed, Gorgonzola-crusted pork loin, or, out of left field, the Thai vegetable curry. An early bird menu has some stellar specials such as beef tips tossed in truffle-Gorgonzola sauce. Chef Kenny used to be a saucier, so he knows his sauce. The menu may be all over the place, but you don't need a theme to indulge in what tastes good. Don't be put off by the strip-mall location and the no-frills inside, with its partially purple walls and purple tablecloths. What Purple Olive lacks in ambience is made up for in the cuisine.

4255 A1A South. www.purple-olive.com. ℰ **904/461-1250.** Main courses $15–$31. Tues–Thurs 5–9pm, Fri–Sat 5–10pm.

Raintree ★★ AMERICAN   Raintree, housed in an 1879 Key West–style Victorian house, is a definite special-occasion spot. It has a menu (and, oftentimes, a clientele) to match, with signatures like crisp roasted half duckling in a raspberry demi-glace, beef Wellington, and a rack of New Zealand lamb. But it's not all textbook cuisine. Some necessary modernizing has been done to the menu, which now also ticks off everything from Kobe beef and black bean burgers to grilled pita-bread pizzas and ahi tuna carpaccio. A tiki torch-lit outdoor patio with a fire pit makes for a magnificent setting, especially at night, or during the popular Sunday brunches. Indoor dining is a bit more, shall I say, "antebellum" (in less historic terms, outdated). Sit outside when you can.

102 San Marco Ave. www.raintreerestaurant.com. (📞) **904/824-7211.** Main courses $13–$30. Daily 5–10pm, Sun brunch 10am–2pm.

EXPLORING ST. AUGUSTINE

St. George Street, from King Street north to the Old City Gate (at Orange St.), is the heart of the historic district. Lined with restaurants and boutiques selling everything from T-shirts to antiques, these 4 blocks get the lion's share of the town's tourists. You'll have much less company if you poke around the narrow streets of the primarily residential neighborhood south of King Street. Most of the town's attractions do not have guided tours, but many do have docents on hand to answer questions.

Be sure to drive through the parking lot of the Howard Johnson Express Inn, at 137 San Marco Ave., to see a gorgeous and stately **live oak tree** ★★ that is at least 600 years old; then continue east to **Magnolia Avenue** ★★, a spectacularly beautiful street with a lovely canopy of old magnolia trees.

Historic sites top the list in this 16th-century town. The top attractions include the **Castillo de San Marcos,** the recently revamped **Colonial Quarter** where what's old is truly new again, and the amazing **Lightner Museum,** a Victorian-era mansion packed with all kinds of curios and memorabilia.

Authentic Old Jail ★ MUSEUM   Satisfying some people's morbid curiosities is this 1891 jail, built by railroad magnate Henry Flagler and placed on the National Register of Historic Places in 1987. Yes, there's history here—the Old Jail served as the county jail until 1953—but there's also cheese, and lots of it. Tour guides fronting as comedians are a turn-off to many people who just want to hear the cold hard facts of old-world incarceration. At times during some of these tours, you, too, may feel incarcerated. If you can get past the tackiness, there's some truly fascinating history in here and, for fans of the paranormal, allegedly some ghostly jailbirds as well.

167 San Marco Ave. www.staugustineattractions.net. (📞) **904/829-3800.** Admission $9 adults, $5 children 6–12. Daily 8:30am–4:30pm

Castillo de San Marcos ★ HISTORIC SITE   Should you ever wish to build an authentic fort, take notes at Castillo de San Marcos, America's oldest and best-preserved masonry fortification. The structure represents the quintessence of the bastion system of fortification. It took 23 years to build, and sprawls over a 20½-acre complex that includes a double drawbridge entrance (the only way in or out) that spans a 40-foot dry moat. There's also a reconstructed section of the walled defense line that surrounded St. Augustine, incorporating the city's original gate. The Castillo was never captured in battle, and its *coquina* (limestone made from broken seashells and corals) walls did not crumble when pounded by enemy artillery or violent storms for over 300 years. Today, the old bombproof storerooms surrounding the central plaza have exhibits about the history of the fort, a national monument since 1924. You can tour the vaulted powder magazine, a dank prison cell (supposedly haunted), the chapel, and the guard rooms. Climb the stairs to get a photo op-worthy view of Matanzas Bay. A self-guided tour map and brochure are provided at the ticket booth. If available, the 20- to 30-minute ranger talks are well worth attending. Popular torchlight tours of the fort are offered in winter, and special evening events and historical reenactments take place often. Check the website for more information and schedules. Visits here take an average of 1 to 2 hours.

1 S. Castillo Dr. www.nps.gov/casa. *C* **904/829-6506.** Admission $7 adults, free children 15 and under. Daily 8:45am–5:15pm; closed Christmas Day.

Colonial Quarter ★ HISTORIC SITE   Opened in 2013, Colonial Quarter in downtown St. Augustine is a 2-acre trip back in time, spanning several centuries of the city's colorful history via interactive attractions and exhibits. Pat Croce, owner of the next-door St. Augustine and Treasure Museum, partnered with the University of Florida to spruce up the former Colonial Quarter Spanish Museum, infusing it not just with cash but with authenticity. Stroll through a recreated town plaza, fully operational leather worker's shop, gunsmith shop, and blacksmith shop. You can even participate in a musket drill. Afterwards, stop for a snack at the Spanish tapas restaurant or the old English pub, both of which are populated by staff in period costumes. The food isn't fancy, but it's not centuries-old grub either, and being able to order booze in a theme park is a plus. Guided tours are informative and fun and are included in your admission. It's hard to see everything at once, especially on the tours, so I recommend you break up your visits into the sections you are most interested in. It may not be Colonial Disney, but Colonial Quarter is surprisingly worthy of a few visits.

33 St. George St. www.colonialquarter.com. *C* **904/342-2857.** Admission $13 adults, $7 children 6–12. Daily 9am–6pm.

Fountain of Youth Archaeological Park ★ PARK   For those still looking for that Dorian Gray–agelessness, forget following in Ponce de León's footsteps and get yourself some botox. Just kidding, but really, this clichéd tourist attraction sort of is a joke, a 25-acre park billing itself as North America's first historic site. And while some of that is indeed true(ish)—Smithsonian Institution archaeological digs have established that a Timucuan Indian village existed here some 1,000 years ago—there's still absolutely no evidence that Ponce de León visited the spot during his 1513 voyage. Search for evidence yourselves while walking through the not-so-interesting grounds, but you'll learn more on a 45-minute guided tour or at a planetarium show about 16th-century celestial navigation. Yep, a planetarium. Because nothing says "Fountain of Youth" like a laser show. At any rate, the grounds are lovely—there are peacocks here, burial and excavation sites, a cafe, boathouse, and pretty much everything but evidence of Ponce de León and/or everlasting youth.

11 Magnolia Ave. (at Williams St.). www.fountainofyouthflorida.com. *C* **800/356-8222** or 904/829-3168. Admission $12 adults, $11 seniors, $8 children 6–12, free for children 5 and under. Daily 9am–5pm.

Lightner Museum ★★★ MUSEUM   Once a hotel catering to its era's "one percent," this 1887 structure was bought in 1946 by Chicago publisher Otto Lightner to house his major collection of Victoriana. Much of the stunning Spanish Renaissance Revival structure still exudes that historic-hotel vibe, from the architecture down to the

St. Augustine Attractions

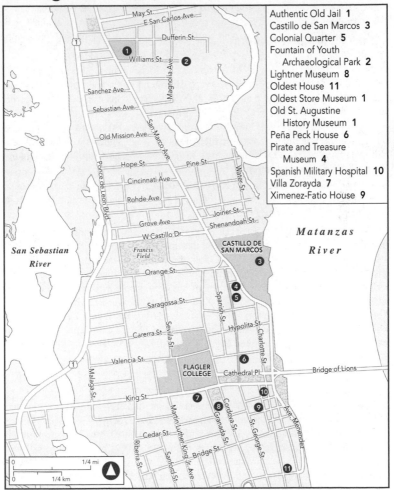

Authentic Old Jail **1**
Castillo de San Marcos **3**
Colonial Quarter **5**
Fountain of Youth
   Archaeological Park **2**
Lightner Museum **8**
Oldest House **11**
Oldest Store Museum **1**
Old St. Augustine
   History Museum **1**
Peña Peck House **6**
Pirate and Treasure
   Museum **4**
Spanish Military Hospital **10**
Villa Zorayda **7**
Ximenez-Fatio House **9**

cafe that's housed in what used to be the hotel's pool (back in 1889 it was the world's largest). The collection is spread out over three floors, featuring an impressive array of relics of America's storied Gilded Age, from costumes and furnishings to mechanical musical instruments that may suddenly break into songs that were popular back in the day. Take advantage of the guided monthly tours by Lightner Museum Curator Barry Myers, who, at 10am on the first Wednesday of each month, leads visitors on intimate encounters with a select few of the Lightner's eclectic relics, including a mummy, shrunken heads, hair art, Russian baths, and a lion that belonged to Winston Churchill. In 2013, Myers took visitors to the museum's private fourth floor, which isn't open to the public, so you never know what you may discover. Best of all, these tours are included in the admission price. Expect to spend at least a couple hours here, and if you have the time, more.

75 King St. www.lightnermuseum.org. ℭ **904/824-2874.** Admission $10 adults, $5 children 12–18. Daily 9am–5pm.

Old St. Augustine History Museum ★ MUSEUM   If you just haven't seen enough of old stuff, you can always spend another 30 minutes wandering through this museum documenting 400 years of Florida's past, focusing on the life of Henry Flagler, the Civil War, and the Seminole Wars. Highlights are a collection of toys and dolls, mostly from the 1870s to the 1920s, and a replica of a Spanish galleon filled with weapons, pottery, and treasures, along with display cases filled with gold, silver, and jewelry recovered by treasure hunters. A typical wattle-and-daub hut of a Timucuan Indian in a forest setting illustrates the lifestyle of St. Augustine's first residents, and a traditional Florida Cracker trading post shows you how shopping was done back in the day. Ideal for a rainy day if need be.

167 San Marco Ave. (at Williams St.). ℭ **904/829-93800.** Admission $6 adults, $5 children 6–12, free for children 5 and under; free admission with purchase of Old Town Trolley Tour, and cheaper at www.trustedtours.com. Daily 8:30am–4:30pm.

Oldest House ★ HISTORIC SITE   Yep, if it's St. Augustine, it must be the oldest something or other—this time, it's a house that's the oldest surviving Spanish Colonial dwelling in Florida. Since the 1600s, the Gonzalez-Alvarez house was influenced by the Spanish, British, and American occupations of St. Augustine. Today, it's part of a larger complex of old stuff that you can tour to see just how people lived back in those truly olden days. Among the sites you will see at the complex: The Manucy Museum, covering over 400 years of Florida's history; the Page L. Edwards Gallery, with various changing exhibits also reflecting St. Augustine's biggest export besides datil peppers—yep, you guessed it, history; the Oldest House Garden, and a detached 18th-century kitchen.

14 Francis St. www.staugustinehistoricalsociety.org. ℭ **904/824-2872.** $18 families, $8 adults, $7 seniors, $4 students, free for children 5 under. Daily 9am–5pm. Guided tours given every half-hour (last one at 4:30pm).

Oldest Store ★ MUSEUM   Where else could one find everything from tonics and elixirs to guns and ammo, bikes, corsets, and worm syrup back in the day—long before Wal-Mart, Kmart, and Target ever existed? The Oldest Store pays homage to retail past, an old country store if you will, with costumed staffers pretending to sell you tractor equipment or a goat-powered washing machine. Inside, there are over 100,000 items on display from the original inventory dating back to the early 1900s. As for it being *the* oldest store, that's debatable, but it's pretty interesting nonetheless.

4 Artillery Lane. ℭ **904/829-9729.** $10 adults, $5 children 6–12 (tickets through www.trolleytours. com/st-augustine/oldest-store.asp). Daily 8:30am–4:30pm.

Peña Peck House ★ HISTORIC SITE   Built in the mid-1700s by order of the King of Spain as the residence of his royal Treasurer, Juan Esteban de Peña, this First Spanish Period home eventually became the property of Connecticut doctor Seth Peck, whose family lived here for 94 years. In 1892, the home became part of the Women's Exchange, which helped down-on-their-luck women get back on their feet. Today you can tour the place and see 18th-century American antiques and hear stories about what it was like to live in the Oldest City when, well, it wasn't so old.

143 St. George St. www.penapeckhouse.com. ℭ **904/829-5064.** Free admission (donations welcome). Guided tours Sun–Fri 12:30–4pm, Sat 10:30am–4pm.

In the Beginning . . .

In 1562, a group of French Huguenots settled near the mouth of the St. Johns River, in present-day Jacksonville. Three years later, a Spanish force under Pedro Menéndez de Avilés arrived, wiped out the Huguenot men (de Avilés spared their women and children), and established a settlement he named St. Augustín. The colony survived a succession of attacks by pirates, Indians, and the British over the next 2 centuries. The Treaty of Paris, ending the French and Indian War, ceded the town to Britain in 1763, but the British gave it back to Spain 20 years later. The United States took control when it acquired Florida from Spain in 1821.

Pirate and Treasure Museum ★★★ MUSEUM   Pat Croce, former owner of the Philadelphia 76ers, is obsessed with pirates. And because he's rich enough from his own loot to play into his obsession, he opened this fantastic homage to all things swashbuckling. St. Augustine, it turns out, was a hotbed for pirates like Sir Francis Drake and Robert Searles. Among the 800 or so artifacts here are an original journal of Captain Kidd's last voyage, the oldest pirate wanted poster, and the world's only authentic pirate treasure chest. New and noteworthy at the museum is a rare burnt-wood remnant from one of two 16th-century ships attributed to Drake that Croce discovered with a team of explorers during an October, 2011 expedition to Panama. Interactive exhibits and cheesy-but-amusing animatronics make for an engaging and entertaining visit. Depending on your level of pirate interest, you can spend anywhere from 30 minutes to over 2 hours here. Kids who are deep into their own pirate phases obviously flip over the place.

12 S. Castillo Dr. www.thepiratemuseum.com. *℡* **877/467-5863.** Admission $12 adults, $6 children 5–12. Daily 10am–8pm.

Spanish Military Hospital ★ MUSEUM   Forget modern medicine and take a stab at this former Second Spanish Colonial Period military hospital where, today, costumed guides explain and at times demonstrate frightening medical procedures that took place on site from 1784 to 1821. Those with fears of doctors may want to sit this one out or at least just visit the museum's apothecary's garden, full of herbs still used in medicine today. A collection of antique surgical instruments may be on the macabre side, but it's all fascinating. Tours last 40 minutes.

3 Aviles St. www.spanishmilitaryhospitalmuseum.com. *℡* **904/342-7730.** Daily 10am–6pm. Admission $7 all ages.

Villa Zorayda ★★★ MUSEUM   The renovated and restored Gilded Age–era winter home of architect Franklin Smith features a sizable collection of antiques, including custom-made bone china, Oriental rugs, and exquisite Egyptian artifacts. The latter is highlighted by the Sacred Cat Rug, a 2,400-year-old tapestry made from the hairs of ancient cats that roamed the Nile. Rumor has it there's a curse waiting for anyone who walks on it. Luckily, you won't be at risk, as the rug is hanging safely on a wall. A 45- to 60-minute guided tour provides an in-depth look at the historical significance of Villa Zorayda, which is a scale copy of a Moorish castle and has, over the years, been everything from a home and a nightclub to a casino and a speakeasy. The docent-led tours are great, but the self-guided audio tour is ideal for those who want to go it alone, with recordings explaining everything in detail. December holiday season is particularly majestic here, as the home is lit up with over 100 candles.

83 King St. www.villazorayda.com. ✆ **904/829-9887.** Self-guided audio tour admission $10 adults, $8 students 13 and over, $4 children 7–12; docent-led tours $15 adults, $7 children 7–12. Mon–Sat 10am–5pm, Sun 11am–4pm.

Ximenez-Fatio House ★★ HISTORIC SITE   The cool thing about St. Augustine is that when they say these are historic houses, they aren't kidding. This one in particular happens to be one of the best preserved of the three-dozen colonial buildings remaining in St. Augustine, dating back to the city's original town plan of 1572. Meticulous restoration and furnishings of period decorative arts and historical objects provide authentic glimpses into territorial life and early statehood in St. Augustine with a focus on the home's role as a boarding house, representing one of the few socially acceptable business ventures for an ambitious 19th-century woman. After a 2002 archaeological dig on the grounds, a cross was discovered that hailed from a hillside town in southeastern Spain; the cross was used to celebrate the end of the plague back in the 17th century. Watch where you're walking here, as you never know what part of history you may be stepping on.

20 Aviles St. www.ximenezfatiohouse.org. ✆ **904/829-3575.** $7 adults; $5 students, seniors, and military; $15 families. Tues–Sat 11am–4pm. Tours given hourly.

Organized Tours

BY TROLLEY   **Old Town Trolley Tours** (✆ 800/213-2474; www.historictours.com) takes you on a 90-minute tour with more than 20 stops at the historic district and its most famous sites. Best of all, you can hop on and off at your leisure all day. Tickets include admission to the St. Augustine History Museum and a beach shuttle that picks up and drops off passengers at various resorts and attractions around town. Tickets are good for 3 consecutive days. The tour costs $26 for adults, $11 for kids 6 to 12. Rates are cheaper online.

BY TRAIN   **Red Train Tours** (✆ 800/226-6545 or 904/824-1606; www.ripleys.com/redtrains) covers the same 20 stops as the trolleys, only its red open-air trains, operated by "Ripley's Believe It or Not," are small enough to go down more of the narrow historic-district streets. Tickets are $20 for adults, $9 for kids 6 to 12, and good for 3 consecutive days. The company also sells package tickets for your convenience, and rates are often cheaper online.

BY HORSE   For water views, **Country Carriages** (✆ 904/826-1982; www.country carriages.net) offers 1-hour guided tours on horseback on St. Augustine's beaches. Tours are $75 per person (minimum of 2 people ages 13 and up) and require advance reservations.

WALKING TOURS   For a tasty tour of St. Augustine, **City Walks Guided Tours** (✆ 904/540-3476; www.staugustinecitywalks.com) has a delicious tour, **The Savory Faire,** a 2½-hour walking tour exploring historical and cultural influences on St. Augustine cuisine from tapas to desserts. Cost is $49 per person and, if you want wine, add on an extra $19. For those who get hopped up on beer, they offer a buzzy Pub Crawl & Beer Tasting Experience, a 2½-hour tour of downtown drinking spots departing nightly at 5pm. The $39-per-person ticket includes beer, wine, ales, and sangria as well as some snacks. For more personalized group excursions, call **Tour Saint Augustine** (✆ 800/797-3778 or 904/825-0087; www.staugustinetours.com), which offers guided walking tours around the historic area. Rates vary based on the number of people in the group.

You can search for old spirits with the nightly **Ghost Tours of St. Augustine** ★★ (© **888/461-1009** or 904/461-1009; www.ghosttoursofstaugustine.com), in which guides in period dress lead you through the historic district or to the St. Augustine Lighthouse. Fans of the show Ghost Hunters will especially dig their "Paranormal Investigations" of area haunts complete with EMF meters to detect those otherworldly types. There are also Paranormal Pub Crawls and an excellent "Ghostly Experience" through the town. Tickets are $15 to $26 per person, depending on the tour. Call for schedules and reservations.

Outdoor Activities

BEACHES There are several places to find sand and sea: **Vilano Beach,** on the north side of St. Augustine Inlet; and **St. Augustine Beach,** on the south side (the inlet dumps the Matanzas and North rivers into the Atlantic). Be aware, however, that erosion has almost swallowed the beach from the inlet as far south as Old Beach Road in St. Augustine Beach. A $14-million sand re-nourishment program in 2012 also ended up eroding, but in the meantime, hotels and homes here have rock seawalls instead of sand bordering the sea.

Erosion has made a less noticeable impact on **Anastasia State Park** ★★, on Anastasia Boulevard (A1A) across the Bridge of Lions and just past the Alligator Farm, where the 4 miles of beach (on which you can drive and park) are still backed by picturesque dunes. On its river side, the area faces a lagoon. Amenities include shaded picnic areas with grills, restrooms, windsurfing, sailing, and canoeing (on a saltwater lagoon), a nature trail, and saltwater fishing (for bluefish, pompano, redfish, and flounder; a license is required for nonresidents). In summer, you can rent chairs, beach umbrellas, and surfboards. There's good bird-watching here, especially in spring and fall; pick up a brochure at the entrance. For history buffs who can't get their minds off the cobblestone, there's even an archaeological site where *coquina* rock was mined to create the Castillo de San Marcos National Monument. The 139 wooded campsites are in high demand year-round; they come with picnic tables, grills, and electricity. Admission to the park is $8 per vehicle, $4 single-occupant vehicle, $2 per bicyclist or pedestrian. Campsites cost $28. For camping reservations, call © **800/326-3521** or go to www.reserveamerica.com. The day-use area is open daily 8am to sunset. You can bring your pets. For more information call © **904/461-2033** or visit www.floridastate parks.org/anastasia.

March through Labor Day, all St. Augustine beaches charge a fee of $8 per nonresident car at official access points; access is free at other times of the year, however, restroom facilities are not available on the beaches at these times and lifeguards are only on duty the first weekend in May through September.

CRUISES The Usina family has been running **St. Augustine Scenic Cruises** (© **904/824-1806;** www.scenic-cruise.com) on Matanzas Bay since the turn of the 20th century. They offer 75-minute narrated tours aboard the double-decker *Victory III,* departing from the Municipal Marina just south of the Bridge of Lions. You can sometimes spot dolphins, brown pelicans, cormorants, and kingfishers. Snacks, soft drinks, beer, and wine are sold onboard. Departures are usually at 11am and 1, 2:45, and 4:30pm daily except Christmas, with an additional tour at 6:15pm April to May 21 and from Labor Day to October 15. From May 22 to Labor Day, there are two additional tours, at 6:45 and 8:30pm. Call ahead—schedules can change during inclement weather. Fares are $17 for adults, $14 for seniors, $8 for children ages 4 to 12. If you're driving, allow time to find parking on the street.

You can also take the free ferry (visitor passes must be obtained at the Visitor Center) to Fort Matanzas on Rattlesnake Island. There are often dolphins in the water as you make the trip, and the fort is interesting. Ferries take off from 8635 Hwy. A1A (follow A1A S. out of St. Augustine for about 15 miles). Call ℭ **904/471-0116** or visit www.nps.gov/foma for more information.

ECO-TOURS   St. Augustine Eco Tours (ℭ **904/377-7245;** www.staugustineeco tours.com), offers several kayak and boat tours through St. Augustine's waterways, including Guana River and Lake, Moultrie Creek, Moses Creek, Washington Oaks, Faver-Dykes, and Six Mile Landing. Prices range from $40 to $50 adults, $30 to $40 kids. They also have a 27-foot catamaran sailing into the remote backwaters, creeks, and estuaries for glimpses of manatees, sea turtles, dolphins, and birds. Cost is $50 for adults, $35 for kids 12 and under.

Ripple Effect Eco Tours (ℭ **904/347-1565;** www.rippleeffectecotours.com) offers tours on vegetable oil-powered eco-explorer boats—they warn passengers not to come hungry as it does smell something like a restaurant. Tours are in conjunction with Marineland Dolphin Adventure and include admission into the park. Rates start at $50 per person.

For the more adventurous types and fans of the History Channel's *Swamp People,* **Adrenaline Alligator Adventures** (ℭ **904/607-6399;** www.gators365.com) is led by a licensed alligator trapper and takes you from swamps to golf course fairways on a mission to subdue and remove nuisance gators. Cost is $475 for a group of up to four people who will get right into the middle of the action as you assist in the snaring, subduing, and taping of the gator's monster jaws. Good luck and, please, send us a picture.

FISHING   You can fish to your heart's content at **Anastasia State Park** (see above). Or you can cast your line off **St. Johns County Fishing Pier,** at the north end of St. Augustine Beach (ℭ **904/461-0119**). The pier is open 24 hours daily and has a bait shop with rental equipment that's open from 6am to 10pm. Admission is $3 ($2 children 11 and under) for fishing, $1 for sightseeing.

For full-day, half-day, and overnight **deep-sea fishing** excursions (for snapper, grouper, porgy, amberjack, sea bass, and other species), contact the **Sea Love Marina,** 250 Vilano Rd. (A1A N.), at the eastern end of the Vilano Beach Bridge (ℭ **904/824-3328;** www.sealovefishing.com). Full-day trips on the party boat *Sea Love II* cost about $80 for adults, $75 for seniors, and $70 for kids 14 and under; half-day trips $60 for adults, $55 for seniors, and $50 for kids 14 and under. No license is required, and rod, reel, bait, and tackle are supplied. Bring your own food and drink.

GOLF   The area's best golf resorts are in Ponte Vedra Beach—a half-hour's drive north on A1A, closer to Jacksonville than St. Augustine.

The **Tournament Players Club Sawgrass** (ℭ **888/421-8555;** www.tpc.com/sawgrass) offers the **Tour Player Experience,** where duffers will be treated like pros and have access to the exclusive wing of the 77,000-square-foot clubhouse where only actual pros, such as Vijay Singh and Jim Furyk, are allowed. You also get a personal caddy wearing a bib with your name on it. The experience also includes a stay at the Sawgrass Marriott Resort and Spa, dinner, spa services, instruction at the Tour Academy, and a golf gift bag that includes balls, marker, and shirt. Packages start at $288 per person, per night.

Passionate golf fans can easily spend a day at the **World Golf Hall of Fame** ★ ((ℂ) **904/940-4000;** www.wgv.com), a state-of-the-art museum honoring professional golf, its great players, and the sport's famous supporters (including comedian Bob Hope and singer Dinah Shore). It's the centerpiece of **World Golf Village,** a complex of hotels, shops, offices, and 18-hole golf courses (at exit 95A off I-95). There's an IMAX screen next door.

Museum admission is $20 for adults, $19 for seniors and students, and $5 for children 4 to 12, and includes a round of golf on the putting green and two shots on the Hall of Fame Challenge Hole. For admission with IMAX ticket, add $5. IMAX tickets without admission range from $9 to $13 for adults, $8 to $12 for seniors and students, and $6 to $10 for children. The museum is open Monday to Saturday 10am to 6pm, and Sunday

noon to 6pm; IMAX film times vary.

The village is built around a lake with a "challenge hole" sitting out in the middle, 132 feet from the shoreline. You can hit balls at it or play a round on the nearby putting course. Admission to the Hall of Fame includes a round on the putting course. The **Walkway of Champions** (whose signatures appear in pavement stones) circles the lake and passes a shopping complex where the main tenant is the two-story **Tour Stop** ((ℂ) **904/940-0422**), offering pricey apparel and equipment.

If you'd like to stay overnight, contact the **World Golf Village Renaissance Resort,** 500 S. Legacy Trail, St. Augustine, FL 32092 (www.worldgolf renaissance.com; (ℂ) **888/740-7020** or 904/940-8000), which offers newly renovated rooms and a free shuttle to downtown St. Augustine.

At **World Golf Village,** 12 miles north of St. Augustine, at exit 95A off I-95 (see "Where Golf Is King," above), the **Slammer & The Squire** and the **King & The Bear** ((ℂ) **904/940-6088;** www.wgv.com) together offer 36 holes amid a wildlife preserve. Locals say they're not as challenging as their greens fees, which start at around $79 and go up—way up—from there. Specials, however, are available off season and off times. For those not schooled in golf history, the "Slammer" is in honor of Sam Sneed, the "Squire" is for Gene Sarazen, the "King" is Arnold Palmer, and the "Bear" is Jack Nicklaus. Palmer and Nicklaus collaborated in designing their course.

Nicklaus had a hand in the stunning course at the **Ocean Hammock Golf Club** ★★ at the Hammock Beach Resort ((ℂ) **386/477-4600;** www.hammockbeach.com), on A1A, in Palm Coast, about halfway between St. Augustine and Daytona Beach. With 6 of its holes skirting the beach, it is the first truly oceanside course built in Florida since the 1920s.

There are only a few courses in St. Augustine, including the **St. Augustine Shores Golf Club,** 707 Shores Blvd., off U.S. 1 ((ℂ) **904/794-4653**), a par-70, 18-hole course with lots of water, a lighted driving range and putting green, and a restaurant and lounge. Greens fees usually are $31, including cart.

For more course information, go to www.golf.com or www.floridagolfing.com, or call the **Florida Sports Foundation** ((ℂ) **850/488-8347**) or **Florida Golfing** ((ℂ) **866/833-2663**).

WATERSPORTS Jet skis and equipment for surfing and windsurfing can be rented at **Surf Station,** 1020 Anastasia Blvd. (A1A), a block south of the Alligator Farm

(© **904/471-9463;** www.surf-station.com); and at **Raging Water Sports,** at the Conch House Marina Resort, 57 Comares Ave. (© **904/829-5001;** www.ragingwatersports. com), off Anastasia Avenue (A1A) halfway between the Bridge of Lions and the Alligator Farm.

Especially for Kids

Without emphasizing the scholarly, historic aspect of old St. Augustine, the city truly is a kid's dream come true and not just because the Fountain of Youth allegedly exists here, but for so many reasons, one being the **St. Augustine Pirate and Treasure Museum** (p. 207), where kids can channel their inner swashbuckler amongst artifacts including the original journal of Captain Kidd's last voyage; get a taste of old world Scared Straight by visiting the **Authentic Old Jail** (p. 203); and see how the real old folks did it way back when at the **Colonial Quarter** (p. 204) where history is alive, well, and actually kinda, sorta cool. Throw in some **beaches** (p. 209) and, for those seeking a bit of a thrill, **Adrenaline Alligator Adventures** (p. 210), and you've got a theme park without the park, the lines (if you're lucky), and most of all without those creepy animatronic figures. This is the real deal, kids—welcome to your awesome history lesson!

SHOPPING

Spanish-influenced home decor and furniture fill the antique shops and galleries in the historic district. Glossy oak tables, Mediterranean-style tiles, and silver bric-a-brac fill display windows along **Aviles Street** and **St. George Street.**

The winding streets of the historic district are home to dozens of **antiques stores** and **galleries** stocked full of original paintings, sculptures, bric-a-brac, fine furnishings, china, and other treasures. Brick-lined **Aviles Street,** a block from the river, has an especially good mix of shops for browsing, as does **St. George Street** south of the visitor center, and the Uptown area on **San Marco Avenue** a few blocks north of the center. Check at the visitor center for lists of art galleries and antiques shops, or contact the **Antique Dealers Association of St. Augustine,** 60 Cuna St., St. Augustine, FL 32084 (no phone).

Experience chocolate heaven at **Whetstone Chocolates,** 2 Coke Rd. (Fla. 312), between U.S. 1 and the Mickler O'Connell Bridge (© **904/825-1700;** www.whet stonechocolates.com). Free self-guided tours of the store and factory usually take place Monday through Saturday from 10am to 5pm, but call ahead to confirm the schedule. Whetstone has a retail outlet at 42 St. George St., in the historic district.

ENTERTAINMENT & NIGHTLIFE

Despite its reputation as a place where old reigns, St. Augustine has a pretty vibrant, young scene, especially on weekends when the Old Town is full of strollers and partiers making the rounds of dozens of bars, clubs, and restaurants. For up-to-date details on what's happening in town, check the local daily, the *St. Augustine Record* (**www. staugustine.com**), or the irreverent *Folio Weekly* (**www.folioweekly.com**). Another nighttime activity is taking one of the many ghost tours—the pub crawls are particularly, er, spirited.

The best-looking and rowdiest crowd in town can be found at the **A1A Ale Works**, 1 King St. (© **904/829-2977;** www.a1aaleworks.com). Twenty-something hipsters and middle-aged partiers mingle at this New Orleans–style microbrewery and restaurant.

You'll find live music Thursday through Saturday at the bar—usually light rock and R&B tunes. Monday through Thursday they're open until 10:30pm, Friday through Sunday until 11pm.

Ann O'Malley's Deli & Pub, 23 Orange St., near the Old City Gate (𝄋 **904/825-4040;** www.annomalleys.com), is an Irish pub that's open until 1am, but its tagline speaks volumes: "You Can't Drink *All* Day If You Don't Start Early." There's always something happening in here, from sports telecasts and open-mic nights to live music and, almost always, beer specials. There's no hard liquor here, just beer and wine, but they get pretty creative with both. Besides the selection of ales, stouts, and drafts, this is one of the only spots where you can grab a late-night snack.

Also popular with locals, **Mill Top Tavern and Listening Room,** 19½ St. George St., at the Fort (𝄋 **904/829-2329;** www.milltop.com), is a warm and rustic tavern in a 19th-century mill building (the water wheel is still outside). Weather permitting, it's an open-air space. There's an eclectic range of music here every day from 1pm to 1am. For those traveling with little ones who can't experience the place at night, Mill Top is family friendly during the day and worth a stop by for an adult beverage with your views.

Scarlett O'Hara's, 70 Hypolita St., at Cordova Street (𝄋 **904/824-6535;** www.scarlettoharas.net), a catacomb of cozy rooms with working fireplaces in a rambling, 19th-century wood-frame house, is the setting for everything from DJs and karaoke to live music (everything from bluegrass to 1980s hits). Ask for a tour of the second floor "Ghost Bar," if you're into those kind of spirits. Sporting events are aired on a large-screen TV; and, if you're hungry, check out the Southern-fried chicken. Hours vary on weeknights, but they're usually open till 1am; Friday and Saturday they keep things going to 2am (weeknights until they decide to close). For more *Gone With the Wind*–inspired nightlife, head next door to Scarlett's other half, **Rhett's Piano Bar & Brasserie.**

For a fusion of old and new worlds, the retro-rustic **Cellar 6,** 6 Aviles St. (𝄋 **904/827-9055;** www.cellar6staugustine.com) or C6 as it's known by area hipsters, offers over 100 bottles of wine, specialty martinis, cocktails, and over 35 beers from around the world, plus live entertainment and tapas. It's open until midnight during the week and until 2am Fridays and Saturdays.

THE SPACE COAST

46 miles SE of Orlando; 186 miles N of Miami; 65 miles S of Daytona

The "Space Coast," the area around Cape Canaveral, was once a sleepy place where city dwellers escaped the urban centers of Miami and Jacksonville. But then came NASA. Today the region produces and accommodates its own crowds, including the hordes who come to visit the Kennedy Space Center and enjoy the area's 72 miles of beaches (this is the closest beach to Orlando's mega-attractions), as well as excellent fishing, surfing, and golfing. And although the shuttle program is history, the area isn't completely kaput. In fact, in May of 2014, NASA announced plans to convert the old Kennedy Space Center space shuttle landing strip into a commercial spaceport for vehicles that takeoff and land like aircraft as part of a drive to convert KSC to a combo government and private spaceport.

Also thanks to NASA, this is a prime destination for nature lovers. The space agency originally took over much more land than it needed to launch rockets. Rather than sell off the unused portions, it turned them over to the **Canaveral National Seashore** and the **Merritt Island National Wildlife Refuge** (www.nbbd.com/godo/minwr), which have preserved these areas in their pristine natural states.

A handful of Caribbean-bound cruise ships also depart from Port Canaveral. The south side of the port is lined with seafood restaurants and marinas, which serve as home base for gambling ships and the area's deep-sea charter and group fishing boats.

Essentials

GETTING THERE

The nearest airport is **Melbourne International Airport** (✆ **321/723-6227;** www. mlbair.com), 22 miles south of Cocoa Beach, served by **Continental** and **Delta.** Orlando International Airport, about 35 miles to the west, is a much larger hub with many more flight options and generally less expensive fares. It's an easy 45-minute drive from the Orlando Airport to the beaches via the Bee Line Expressway (Fla. 528, a toll road)—it can take almost that long from the Melbourne Airport, where **Avis, Budget, Hertz,** and **National** all have car-rental desks. The **Melbourne Airport Shuttle** (✆ **321/724-1600**) will take you from the Melbourne Airport to most local destinations for about $10 to $30 per person. Driving distance from St. Augustine to Kennedy Space Center is 115 miles, mostly down 1-95.

VISITOR INFORMATION

For information on the area, contact the **Florida's Space Coast Office of Tourism,** 430 Brevard Ave., Ste. 150, Cocoa Village, FL 32922 (✆ **877/572-3224** or 321/433-4470; www.visitspacecoast.com).

GETTING AROUND

A car is essential in this area. If you're not coming by car, you can rent one at the airport. **Space Coast Area Transit** (✆ **321/633-1878;** www.ridescat.com) operates buses ($1.25 adults, 60¢ seniors and students), but routes tend to be circuitous and extremely time-consuming.

Attractions

In addition to the attractions below, Eastern Florida State College's **Planetarium and Observatory,** 1519 Clearlake Rd., Cocoa Beach (✆ **321/634-3732;** www.eastern florida.edu/community-resources/planetarium), south of Florida 528, is home to one of the largest public telescopes in Florida—a 24" Ritchey-Chretien reflector. And from high-tech to high-camp, the place is also known for its far-out sound-and-light shows. Call or check the website for schedules and prices.

Brevard Zoo ★★ ZOO   This small-yet-substantial 75-acre zoo houses over 880 animals, including giraffes, white rhinos, red kangaroos, cheetahs, alligators, siamang gibbons, giant anteaters, jaguars, wallabies, crocodiles, bald eagles, red wolves, and river otters. The Zoo's mission of wildlife conservation is taken one step further by contributing 25¢ of each admission to assorted conservation projects. Enjoy a 10-minute train tour of the grounds ($3); hand-feed gentle giraffes in Expedition Africa and lorikeets in a free-flight aviary; get friendly with the wildlife at the Paws On play area, featuring a 22,000-gallon aquarium, water play, and petting zone; and kayak around an animal exhibit ($6) or paddle boat through a 22-acre restored wetlands for $15 per person. For an up-close-and-personal view of the animals, try a rhino encounter, offered daily from noon to 1pm for $15 per person. Plan to spend 1 to 4 hours here.

8225 N. Wickham Rd., Melbourne (just east of I-95 exit 191/Wickham Rd.). www.brevardzoo.org.
✆ **321/254-9453.** Admission $16 adults, $15 seniors, $12 children 3–12, free for children 2 and under. Daily 9:30am–5pm (last admission 4:15pm).

John F. Kennedy Space Center ★★★ ICON   Whether or not you're a space buff, you'll appreciate the sheer grandeur of the facilities and technological achievements displayed at NASA's primary space-launch facility. Astronauts departed Earth from here in 1969 en route to the most famous "small step" in history—the first moon walk—and space shuttles lifted off from here on missions to the International Space Station. Today, military and commercial rockets regularly launch from Cape Canaveral Air Force Station.

Because all roads other than State Road 405 and State Road 3 are closed to the public in the Space Center, you must begin your visit at **Kennedy Space Center Visitor Complex.** A bit like an amusement theme park, this privately operated complex continuously receives renovations, so check beforehand to see if tours and exhibits have changed since this was written. Call ahead to see what's happening the day you intend to be here and arrive early. You'll need at least 2 hours to see the Space Center's highlights on the bus tour, up to 5 hours if you linger at stops along the way, and a full day to see and do everything. Buy a copy of the *Official Tour Book,* and you can take it home as a colorful souvenir (though the bus tours are narrated and the exhibits have good descriptions).

The Visitor Complex has real NASA rockets and the actual Mercury Mission Control Room from the 1960s. Exhibits portray space exploration in its early days and where it's going in the new millennium. There are hands-on activities for kids, a daily "encounter" with a real astronaut, dining venues, and a shop selling space memorabilia. IMAX movies shown on five-and-a-half-story-high screens are both informative and entertaining.

While you could spend an entire day at the Visitor Complex, you must take a **KSC Tour** to get a behind-the-scenes glimpse of Kennedy Space Center. Buses depart every 15 minutes or so, and you can re-board as you wish. They stop at the Apollo/Saturn V Center, a tribute to the Apollo moon program, which includes artifacts, shows, photos, interactive exhibits, and the 363-foot-tall *Saturn V,* the most powerful rocket ever launched by the United States.

Don't miss the **Astronaut Memorial.** Dedicated in 1991, the memorial honors the U.S. astronauts who gave their lives for space exploration. The 43×50-foot "Space Mirror" brilliantly illuminates the names cut through the monument's black granite surface.

Today, the U.S. Air Force operates Cape Canaveral Air Force Station on Cape Canaveral, the barrier island east of the Banana River, where military and commercial rockets are launched. Launch days are great days to visit the Visitor Complex. Rocket launches taking place during operating hours can be viewed from the main Visitor Complex with the regular admission price of $50 plus tax per adult and $40 plus tax per child (ages 3–11).

For an out-of-this-world experience, do **Lunch With an Astronaut,** a once-in-a-lifetime opportunity available every day ($30 plus tax for adults, $16 plus tax for kids ages 3–11, in addition to Visitor Complex admission). Astronauts who have participated in the past include some of the greatest, such as Jim Lovell, Al Worden, Story Musgrave, and Jon McBride. Seating is limited; call ⓒ **877/313-2610** to make a reservation. They also offer a 30-minute **Astronaut Encounter** featuring Q&A sessions with bona-fide astronauts who have been there, done that.

Kennedy Space Center Visitor Complex also offers the **Astronaut Training Experience,** a combination of hands-on training and preparation for the rigors of spaceflight. You'll hear first-hand from veteran astronauts as you progress through an authentic half-day of mission simulation and exploration and even get to check out true-to-training simulator exercises. Due to the program's highly interactive nature, ATX crews are small and advance reservations are required. Cost is $145 per person; call ℂ **877/313-2610** to make a reservation.

In 2014, KSC introduced the exceptional Space Shuttle Atlantis attraction in which you not only see this spaceworthy marvel up close and personal, rotated 43.21 degrees with payload bay doors open and its Canadarm (robotic arm) extended, as if it has just undocked from the International Space Station, but you can also control the thing with over 60 interactive, touch-screen experiences and high-tech simulators. Train like an astronaut, get inside, float in space, go orbital, take control in the shuttle cockpit, and realize that yes, indeed, this really is rocket science. This brand new, out-of-this-world opportunity for space geeks is part of your regular admission.

Note: Make sure to stop by the **U.S. Astronaut Hall of Fame,** on State Road 405, on your way to Kennedy Space Center Visitor Complex or on your way home. The Hall of Fame, approximately 6 miles west of the main Visitor Complex, is included with regular admission to the Visitor Complex. The Hall of Fame features exhibits and tributes to the heroes of the Mercury, Gemini, Apollo, and Space Shuttle programs. There's also the world's largest collection of personal astronaut memorabilia and a Mercury *Sigma 7* capsule on display. Separate admission to the Hall of Fame only is $20 plus tax adults, and $16 plus tax children 3 to 11.

NASA Pkwy. (Fla. 405), 6 miles east of Titusville, ½ mile west of Fla. 3. www.kennedyspacecenter. com. ℂ **877/313-2610** for general information and reservations. Admission $50 plus tax adults, $46 plus tax seniors 55 and over, $40 plus tax children 3–11, free for children 2 and under. Audio guides $6 plus tax per person. Daily 9am to closing times that vary according to season. Bus tours depart daily beginning at 10am. Closed Christmas Day.

Beaches & Wildlife Refuges

To the north of the Kennedy Space Center, **Canaveral National Seashore ★★★** is a protected 13-mile stretch of barrier-island beach backed by cabbage palms, sea grapes, palmettos, marshes, and Mosquito Lagoon. This is a great area for watching herons, egrets, ibises, willets, sanderlings, turnstones, terns, and other birds. You might also glimpse dolphins and manatees in Mosquito Lagoon. Canoeists can paddle along a marked trail through the marshes of Shipyard Island, and backcountry camping is possible November through April (permits required; see below).

The main **visitor center** is at 7611 S. Atlantic Ave., New Smyrna Beach, FL 32169 (ℂ **321/867-4077,** or 321/867-0677 for recorded information; www.nps.gov/cana), on Apollo Beach, at the north end of the island. The southern access gate to the island is 8 miles east of Titusville on Florida 402, just east of Florida 3. A paved road leads from the gate to undeveloped **Playalinda Beach ★★★**, one of Florida's most beautiful. Though illegal, nude sunbathing has long been a tradition here (at least, for those willing to walk a few miles to the more deserted areas). The beach has toilets, but no running water or other amenities, so bring everything you'll need. There's also a **pontoon boat tour** of the Indian River Lagoon for $20 per person and a turtle-watch program for $14 per person. For those looking for a little more history, The **Eldora Statehouse** is a step back in time, a well-preserved example of earlier life along Mosquito Lagoon. It is in Canaveral National Seashore's Apollo district, and is open year-round. The seashore is open daily 6am to 8pm during daylight saving time, daily 6am to 6pm during standard time. Entry fees are $5 per car or $1 per pedestrian or bicyclist. National Park Service passports are accepted. Backcountry camping permits cost $10 for up to six people per day and $20 for more than six people per day, and must be obtained from the New Smyrna Beach visitor center (📞 386/428-3384, ext. 10). For single-day access to backcountry beaches between Playalinda and Apollo beaches, it's $2 per person each day. For advance information, contact the seashore headquarters at 308 Julia St., Titusville, FL 32796 (📞 321/867-4077 or 321/267-1110; www.nps.gov/cana).

Canaveral National Seashore's neighbor to the south and west is the 140,000-acre **Merritt Island National Wildlife Refuge ★★**, home to hundreds of species of shorebirds, waterfowl, reptiles, alligators, and mammals, many of them endangered. Pick up a map and other information at the visitor center, on Florida 402 about 4 miles east of Titusville (it's on the way to Playalinda Beach). The center has a quarter-mile boardwalk along the edge of the marsh. Displays show the animals you may spot from 6-mile Black Point Wildlife Drive or from one of the nature trails through the hammocks and marshes. The visitor center is open Monday through Saturday from 9am to 4pm; it's closed on Sundays and federal holidays. Entry is free. For more information and a schedule of programs, contact the refuge at P.O. Box 6504, Titusville, FL 32782 (📞 321/861-0667; www.nbbd.com/godo/minwr).

Note: Parts of the national seashore near the Kennedy Space Center and all of the refuge close 4 days before a shuttle launch and usually reopen the day after.

Another good beach area is **Lori Wilson Park,** on Atlantic Avenue at Antigua Drive in Cocoa Beach (📞 321/868-1123), which preserves a stretch of sand backed by a forest of live oaks. It's home to a small but interesting nature center, and restrooms are available. The park is open daily from sunrise to sunset; the nature center is open Monday through Friday 1 to 4pm.

The beach at Cocoa Beach Pier, on Meade Avenue east of A1A (📞 321/783-7549), is a popular spot with surfers, who consider it the East Coast's surfing capital. The rustic pier was built in 1962 and has 842 feet of fishing, shopping, and dining overlooking a wide, sandy beach (see "Where to Dine," below). Because this is not a public park, there are no restrooms other than the ones in restaurants on the pier.

Jetty Park, 400 E. Jetty Rd., at the south entry to Port Canaveral (📞 321/783-7111; www.jettyparkbeachandcampground.com), received a major facelift that debuted in March 2012. The park has a fantastic beach with lifeguards, a fishing pier with bait shop, a playground, a volleyball court, a horseshoe pit, picnic tables, a snack bar, a grocery store, restrooms, changing facilities, the area's only campground, and rentals of chairs, umbrellas, surfboards, and kayaks. From here, you can watch the big cruise ships as they enter and leave the port's narrow passage. The park is open daily from 7:30am to dusk; the pier is open 24 hours for fishing. Admission is $10 per car for nonresidents of Brevard County ($5 for residents), $15 per RV (all cash only). The 150 tent and RV campsites (some of them shady, most with hookups) cost $27 to $49 a night, depending on the location and time of year. There are also 8 brand-new-as-of 2014 cabins for $83 per night, sleeping four and featuring a queen bed and bunk beds, half bathroom, and air conditioning. Linens are available for an additional $10 per night. All areas of the campground have one modern comfort and the antithesis of roughing it—Wi-Fi. Properly immunized pets are allowed in some areas of the park.

Outdoor Activities & Spectator Sports

BASEBALL The **Washington Nationals** play spring-training games at **Space Coast Stadium,** 5800 Stadium Pkwy., Viera (📞 321/633-4487), located south of Cape Canaveral and north of Melbourne. Tickets are $10 to $30. The stadium also hosts minor-league action from the Brevard County Manatees, an affiliate of the Nationals.

Tickets to those games are a bargain, from $6 to $10 and often include the option to upgrade your ticket for $7 extra to include all-you-can-eat hot dogs, nachos, and ice cream for 2 hours at the game.

ECO-TOURS   **Island Boat Lines** (© 800/979-3370; www.islandboatlines.com) offers a variety of wildlife-heavy trips, including daily eco-tours, dinner cruises, fishing expeditions, and private charters around the Kennedy Space Center and Merritt Island National Wildlife Refuge areas. Reservations are required.

FISHING   Head to Port Canaveral for catches such as snapper and grouper. **Jetty Park** (© 321/783-7111), at the south entry to the port, has a fishing pier equipped with a bait shop (see "Beaches & Wildlife Refuges," above). The south bank of the port is lined with charter boats. Try deep-sea fishing on *Miss Cape Canaveral* (© 321/783-5274; www.misscape.com), one of the party boats based here. All-day voyages departing daily at 8am cost $80 adults, $75 seniors, $70 kids 11 to 17; all trips come with parking, a hot meal, unlimited soda, coffee, two cans of cold beer, bait, and tackle. A new nightly shark fishing tour from 7 to 11pm is $40 per person and includes a hot meal, unlimited soda and water, coffee, two draft beers, rod, reel, bait, tackle, license and parking.

GOLF   You can read about Northeast Florida's best courses in the free *Golfer's Guide,* available at the tourist information offices and in many hotel lobbies.

The municipal **Cocoa Beach Country Club,** 500 Tom Warringer Blvd. (© 321/868-3351; www.golfcocoabeach.com), has 27 holes of golf and 10 lighted tennis courts set on acres of natural woodlands, rivers, and lakes. Greens fees (including cart) are $17 to $43, depending on the time and season.

On Merritt Island south of the Kennedy Space Center, the **Savannahs at Sykes Creek,** 3915 Savannahs Trail (© 321/455-1377; www.golfthesavannahs.com), has 18 holes over 6,636 yards bordered by hardwood forests, lakes, and savannas inhabited by a host of wildlife. You'll have to hit over a lake to reach the 7th hole. Fees with a cart are $34 to $55, and $19 to $43 without.

The best nearby course is the Gary Player–designed **Baytree National Golf Club,** 8010 N. Wickham Rd., a half-mile east of I-95 in Melbourne (© 321/259-9060; www. baytreenational.com), where challenging marshy holes are flanked by towering palms. This par-72 course has 7,043 yards with a red-shale waste area. Fees are $25 to $75 depending on the time and season, including cart.

For course information, go to **www.golf.com** or **www.floridagolfing.com**, or call the **Florida Sports Foundation** (© 850/488-8347) or **Florida Golfing** (© 866/833-2663).

KAYAKING   For those who want to see Merritt Island National Wildlife Refuge at night, **A Day Away Kayak Tours** (© 321/268-2655; www.adayawaykayaktours.com) offers guided bioluminescent trips—meaning besides the moon, the only light you'll see on this fabulous tour is that of tiny, illuminated creatures swirling beneath the surface of the water and providing a lanternlike pathway across the water—through the Refuge, Thursday through Monday nights, June through September. Tours start at 7:30pm and last for about 2 hours. Cost is $35 for adults and $27 for children ($39 and $29 on Saturdays). Book early and don't forget the mosquito repellent!

SURFING   Rip through some occasionally awesome waves (by Florida's standards, not California's or Hawaii's) at the **Cocoa Beach Pier** area or down south at **Sebastian Inlet.** Get outfitted at **Ron Jon Surf Shop,** 4151 N. Atlantic Ave. (© 321/799-8888; www.ronjons.com), and then learn how to hang five or ten with

Ron Jon Surf School ★, 150 E. Columbia Lane (© **321/868-1980;** www.cocoa beachsurfingschool.com). The school offers equipment and lessons for beginners and pros at area beaches. Be sure to bring along a towel, flip-flops, sunscreen, and a lot of nerve. Rates range from $50 to $135 depending on how many people are in the group and how many hours of lessons are wanted.

Where to Stay

Most of the hotels listed below are in Cocoa Beach, the closest resort area to the Kennedy Space Center, about a 30-minute drive to the north. (For pop-culture junkies, Cocoa Beach was where the TV show *I Dream of Jeannie* took place.) Closest to the space center and Port Canaveral is the **Radisson Resort at the Port,** 8701 Astronaut Blvd. (A1A), in Cape Canaveral (© **800/333-3333** or 321/784-0000; www.radisson. com). It isn't on the beach, but you can relax in its landscaped courtyard, where a waterfall cascades over fake rocks into a heated pool. Rooms aren't fancy but are clean and comfortable. The hotel caters to business travelers and passengers waiting to board cruise ships (with free transportation to the port and free parking while you cruise); it offers a substantial hot and cold complimentary breakfast.

The usual chain motels in this area are the **Hampton Inn Cocoa Beach,** 3425 Atlantic Blvd. (© **877/492-3224** or 321/799-4099; http://hamptoninncocoabeach. com), and **Courtyard by Marriott,** 3435 Atlantic Blvd. (© **800/321-2211** or 321/784-4800; www.courtyardcocoabeach.com). They stand side by side and access the beach via a pathway through a condominium complex.

The area has a plethora of rental condominiums and cottages. **King Rentals, Inc.,** 102 W. Central Blvd., Cape Canaveral, FL 32920 (© **888/295-0934** or 321/784-5046; www.kingrentals.com), has a wide selection in its inventory.

Given the proximity to Orlando, the generally warm weather year-round, and the business travelers visiting the space complex, there is little, if any, seasonal fluctuation in room rates here. They are highest on weekends, holidays, and during special events, such as space shuttle launches. You'll pay a 5% hotel tax on top of the Florida 6% sales tax here.

Tent and RV camping are available at **Jetty Park,** in Port Canaveral (see "Beaches & Wildlife Refuges," above).

Hilton Cocoa Beach Oceanfront ★

How many hotels can boast that you can view rocket launches from their rooms? Hilton Cocoa Beach can, with views of the Cape Canaveral Air Force Station. The renovated rooms at this seven-story Hilton lack balconies or patios; instead, they have small, sealed windows. Yes, it's a little frustrating, but it's nothing an elevator ride down can't help. While rooms lack an ocean breeze, they are clean and Hilton-haute, if that's not an oxymoron (that is, cookie-cutter, chain chic), within close proximity to the ocean. The oceanfront pool deck has a small heated pool and tiki bar and really, what more can you ask for? There's also an on-site restaurant that's nothing to write home about, but what's really impressive about the place is the staff. Professional, attentive, and accommodating, they almost make up for the lack of balconies. This hotel is popular with pre- and post-cruise passengers and serves as an unofficial hub for Disney Cruise Line passengers, which means kids, lots of them. The hotel is very kid-friendly, so if you're looking for a quiet place from which to experience rockets and fireworks, this isn't it.

1550 N. Atlantic Ave., Cocoa Beach, FL 32931. www.hiltoncocoabeach.com. © **800/445-8667** or 321/799-0003. 296 units. $109–$189 double, $209–$249 suite. **Amenities:** Restaurant; 2 bars; concierge-level rooms; exercise room; heated outdoor pool; limited room service; watersports equipment/rentals; Wi-Fi (for a charge).

The Inn at Cocoa Beach ★★ Cocoa Beach may not be known for luxury or even hip boutique hotels, but this cozy, old-world European-style 50-room inn is the antithesis of the area's bleaker, less personable stays. The inn's owner Karen Simpler has a background in interior decorating and has infused the place with a charming mish mosh of pine, tropical, and French-country pieces. Rooms in the three- and four-story buildings are the largest and have superb ocean views. There are also older, noisier rooms that open onto a courtyard with a dated but nice pool. Puppies and macaws in the lobby, honor bar, library, excellent continental breakfast, and evening wine-and-cheese social hour gives the place a B&B vibe and while kids are welcome here, the Inn's catchphrase is "The Quiet Place," so if that's not a warning enough to keep the more rambunctious tots away from here, I don't know what is. P.S.: The place is also allegedly haunted.

4300 Ocean Blvd., Cocoa Beach, FL 32932. www.theinnatcocoabeach.com. ℂ **800/343-5307** or 321/799-3460. 50 units. $115–$325 double. Rates include continental breakfast and social hour. **Amenities:** Bar; outdoor pool; sauna; free Wi-Fi.

Where to Dine

On the **Cocoa Beach Pier** (www.cocoabeachpier.com), at the beach end of Meade Avenue, you'll get a fine view down the coast to accompany the seafood offerings at **Atlantic Ocean Grille** (ℂ **321/783-7549**) and the mediocre pub fare at **Marlins Good Times Bar & Grill** (same phone). The restaurants may not justify spending an entire evening on the pier, but the outdoor, tin-roofed **Mai Tiki Bar ★**, where live music plays most nights, is a prime spot to have a cold one while watching the surfers or a sunset.

Florida's Fresh Grill ★★ SURF/TURF Although strip-mall doesn't exactly scream fresh seafood, the aptly named Florida's Fresh Grill is one of Cocoa Beach's off-the-beaten path best bets for exactly that. A warm and welcoming interior of copper-plated ceilings, woods, and candles transports you from the saltier spots in town to a casual, yet swankier scene. A menu heavy on sea-to-table fish includes standouts such as buttermilk-dipped pecan-crusted Stealhead trout and a Longfin tilapia topped with lump crab and sautéed in lemon caper butter. Not in the mood for sea fare? Try their cheesy, yet appropriately named Craveable Classic Burger—a hearty, well-seasoned half pound of fresh-ground brisket on a warm knotted brioche bun. Service here is exceptionally friendly and knowledgeable and bartenders take pride in their mixology. There's even a side menu that puts a gourmet twist on the gluten-free diet with dishes such as grilled fresh fish with mango salsa or scallops with jalapeño-bacon cream sauce.

2039 N. Atlantic Ave. Cocoa Beach. www.floridasfreshgrill.com. ℂ **321/613-5649.** Main courses $11–$22. Mon–Sat 5–10pm, Sun 5–9pm.

Rusty's Seafood & Oyster Bar ★ SEAFOOD Water views here may be a dime a dozen, but fresh-shucked oysters—which aren't *that* cheap—in these parts are not. In addition to the shucked-as-you-order oysters, Rusty's serves up some serious seafood, from spicy seafood gumbo to a pot of steamed oysters, clams, shrimp, and crab legs, served with potatoes, and corn on the cob. Check out the cruise ships departing the port from a seat outside on the new deck where there's a tiki bar and live entertainment. Sunsets are particularly stellar from here. Daily happy hour from 3 to 6pm offers two-for-one well drinks, and raw or steamed oysters and spicy Buffalo wings go for 90¢ each. There are also daily early bird specials served at $12 from 11am to

6pm—shrimp scampi, sirloin steak, mahi, and more bring in the crowds during these hours. The place is completely kid-friendly as well—throwing in an ice cream sandwich with every kids' meal. Rusty's is salty, casual, and exactly what it should be. Nothing fancy, just good food, drinks, and even better views.

628 Glen Cheek Dr. (south side of the harbor), Port Canaveral. www.rustysseafood.com. *C* **321/783-2033.** Main courses $12–$26, sandwiches and salads $7–$12. Mon–Thurs 11am–10pm, Fri–Sun 11am–11pm.

The Space Coast After Dark

For a rundown of current performances and exhibits, check out the **Brevard Cultural Alliance** (*C* **321/690-6817;** www.artsbrevard.org). For live music, walk out on the **Cocoa Beach Pier,** on Meade Avenue at the beach, where **Oh Shucks Seafood Bar & Grill** (*C* **321/783-7549**), **Marlins Good Times Bar & Grill** (*C* **321/783-7549**), and the alfresco **Mai Tiki Bar ★** (same phone as Marlins) feature bands on weekends, more often during the summer season. In fact, most places on the water feature entertainment, be it a band or just people-watching in general. You kind of can't go wrong there. For more specific nightlife events, go to **www.brevardnightlife.com**.

AMELIA ISLAND

32 miles NE of Jacksonville; 71 miles NE of St. Augustine; 192 miles NE of Orlando; 372 miles N of Miami

Paradise is found on the northernmost barrier island of Florida. With 13 beautiful miles of beach and a quaint Victorian town, Amelia Island is a charming getaway about an hour and 15 minutes from St. Augustine by car. This skinny barrier island, 18 miles long by 3 miles wide, has more in common with the Lowcountry of Georgia (across Cumberland Sound from here) and South Carolina. In fact, it's more like St. Simons Island in Georgia or Hilton Head Island in South Carolina than other beach resorts in Florida.

Amelia has five distinct personalities. First is its southern end, an exclusive real estate development built in a forest of twisted, moss-laden live oaks. Here you'll find a country-club lifestyle of tennis and golfing at two of Florida's most luxurious resorts. Second is modest **American Beach,** founded in the 1930s so that African Americans would have access to the ocean in this then-segregated part of the country. Today it's a modest, predominantly black community tucked away among all that south-end wealth. Third is the island's middle, a traditional beach community with a mix of affordable motels, cottages, condominiums, and a seaside inn. Fourth is the historic bayside town of **Fernandina Beach ★★★**, which boasts a 50-square-block area of gorgeous Victorian, Queen Anne, and Italianate homes listed on the National Register of Historic Places. And fifth is the unfettered **Fort Clinch State Park,** which keeps developers from turning the island's northern end into more ritzy resorts.

The town of Fernandina Beach dates from the post–Civil War period, when Union soldiers who had occupied Fort Clinch began returning to the island. In the late 19th century, Amelia's timber, phosphate, and naval-stores industries boomed. Back then, the town was an active seaport, with 14 foreign consuls in residence. You'll see (and occasionally smell) the paper mills that still stand near the small seaport here. The island experienced another economic explosion in the 1970s and 1980s, when real estate developers built condominiums, cottages, and two big resorts on the island's southern end. Fernandina Beach has seen another big boom, this time in bed-and-breakfast establishments and, to the dismay of some, Amelia has experienced its own real estate rush, with several new housing developments emerging, from multi-million dollar coastal estates to both mid- and lower-range housing developments.

Essentials

GETTING THERE

The island is served by Jacksonville International Airport, 12 miles north of Jacksonville's downtown and 43 miles from the island. Skirting the Atlantic in places, the scenic drive here from St. Augustine is via A1A and the St. Johns River Ferry. The fast, four-lane way is via I-95 North and the Buccaneer Trail East (A1A).

VISITOR INFORMATION

For information, contact the **Amelia Island–Fernandina Beach–Yulee Chamber of Commerce,** 102 Centre St. (P.O. Box 472), Fernandina Beach, FL 32035 (② **800/226-3542** or 904/277-0717; www.ameliaisland.org). The chamber's visitor center, in the rustic train station at the bay end of Centre Street, is open Monday through Friday from 9am to 5pm, and Saturday from 10am to 2pm.

GETTING AROUND

There's no public transportation on this 13-mile-long island, so you'll need a car. An informative and entertaining way to tour the historic district is a 30-minute ride with **Old Towne Carriage Company** (② **904/277-1555;** www.ameliacarriagetours.com), whose horse-drawn carriages leave from the waterfront on Centre Street between 6:30 and 9pm. Advance reservations are essential. Rides cost $15 for adults and $7 for kids 12 and under; private 30-minute tours are the same but with a minimum of $60 per ride, 1-hour tours with a minimum of $120 per ride. Keep an eye out for $10 discount coupons at local B&Bs, hotels, restaurants, and the Visitor's Center. Reservations are required when these coupons are used and they apply to tours for 2 or more people. The carriage company closes from November to April, when the horses get a much-deserved rest.

Another excellent way to see the town is on a walking tour sponsored by the Amelia Island Museum of History (p. 224).

Hitting the Beach

Thanks to a reclamation project, the widest beaches here are at the exclusive enclave on the island's southern third. Even if you aren't staying at one of the swanky resorts, you can enjoy this section of beach at Peters Point Beach Front Park, on A1A, north of the Ritz-Carlton. The park has picnic shelters and restrooms with indoor and outdoor showers. The **Amelia Island Trail,** a 6.2-mile path for biking and hiking that opened in 2013 starts here too. North of the resort, the beach has public-access points with free parking every quarter-mile or so. The center of activity is Main Beach, at the ocean end of Atlantic Avenue (A1A), with good swimming, volleyball courts, playground, restrooms, picnic shelters, outdoor showers, a casual beach bar and restaurant, and **Fernandina's Putt-Putt,** which serves milk shakes, ice cream, and soft drinks at the beach, and lots of free parking. This area is understandably popular with families.

The beach at **Fort Clinch State Park ★★,** which wraps around the island's heavily forested northern end, is backed by rolling dunes and is filled with shells and driftwood. A jetty and pier jutting into Cumberland Sound are popular with anglers. There are showers and changing rooms at the pier. Elsewhere in the park, you might see an alligator—and certainly some of the 170 species of birds that live here—by hiking the

Willow Pond nature trail. Rangers lead nature tours on the trail, usually beginning at 10:30am on Saturday. There are also 6 miles of off-road bike trails here. Construction on the remarkably well-preserved **Fort Clinch** began in 1847 on the northern tip of the island and was still underway when Union troops occupied it in 1862. The fort was abandoned shortly after the Civil War, except for a brief reactivation in 1898 during the Spanish-American War. Reenactors gather the first full weekend of each month to recreate how the Union soldiers lived in the fort in 1864 (including wearing their wool underwear, even in summer!). Rangers are on duty at the fort year-round, and they lead candlelight tours ($3 per person) on Friday and Saturday evenings during summer, beginning about an hour after sunset. You can arrange guided tours at other times for an extra fee. The park entrance is on Atlantic Avenue near the beach. Entrance fees are $6 per vehicle with up to eight occupants, $2 per pedestrian or bicyclist. Admission to the fort costs $2, free for children 4 and under. The park is open daily from 8am to sunset; the fort, daily from 9am to 5pm. For a schedule of tours and events, contact the park at 2601 Atlantic Ave., Fernandina Beach, FL 32034 (© **904/277-7274;** www. floridastateparks.org/fortclinch).

The park also has 61 **campsites**—some behind the dunes at the beach (no shade out there), most in a forest along the sound side. They cost $26 per night, including tax. You can reserve a site up to 11 months in advance (a very good idea in summer) by calling © **800/326-3521** or going to www.reserveamerica.com.

Pets on leashes are allowed on all of the island's public beaches and in Fort Clinch State Park.

Outdoor Activities

BIKING   Despite the name, Ray and Jody Hetchka's **Kayak Amelia** ★★ (© **888/305-2925** or 904/251-0016; www.kayakamelia.com), based near Talbot Island State Park (technically in Jacksonville) offers bike rentals at $7 an hour or $20 a day.

Bikers and hikers traveling along the 3,000-mile East Coast Greenway connecting major cities from Calais, Maine, to Key West can now take the "Blueway Bypass" thanks to the **Cumberland Sound Ferry Service** (© **877/264-9972;** www.amelia rivercruises.com), which runs privately chartered trips to St. Marys, Georgia. The trip takes approximately 1 hour and features live narration of the region's history, natural features, and wildlife. You'll also get to explore each of the cities. Trip costs $20 round-trip per person with a minimum of 20 passengers or $400 per round trip for a group of less than 20 passengers.

BOATING, FISHING, SAILING & KAYAKING   The **Amelia Island Charter Boat Association** (© **800/229-1682** or 904/261-2870), at Tiger Point Marina on 14th Street, north of the historic district (though the boats dock at Centre St.), can help arrange deep-sea fishing charters, party-boat excursions, and dolphin-watching and sightseeing cruises. Other charter boats also dock at Fernandina Harbor Marina, downtown at the foot of Centre Street.

Windward Sailing School, based at Fernandina Harbor Marina, 3977 First Ave. (© **904/261-9125;** www.windwardsailing.com), will teach you to skipper your boat; it also has charters and boat rentals. Call for details and reservations.

You have to be careful in the currents, but the backwaters here are great for kayaking, whether you're a beginner or a pro. However, you'll have to travel just off the island to do it. **Kayak Amelia** ★★ (© **888/305-2925** or 904/251-0016; www.kayak amelia.com) also offers beginner and advanced-level trips on back bays, creeks, and marshes. Half-day trips go for about $65 for adults and $55 for children. Kayak and canoe rentals go from $35 to $62. Reservations are required.

A fabulous company that takes you along the salt marshes, wilderness beaches, and historic riverbanks of Amelia, Fernandina Beach, and Cumberland Island, Georgia, where wild horses roam the unfettered beaches, **Amelia River Cruises** (𝒞 **877/264-9972;** www.ameliarivercruises.com) offers all sorts of tours including extensive eco-tours of Cumberland Island and Beach Creek and, seasonally, a BYOB evening cruise, ranging from $23 to $26 for adults, $18 to $24 for seniors, and $14 to $20 for children 12 and under. New in June 2014 is a 2-hour catch-and-release eco-shrimping tour of the St. Mary's River Basin using an otter trawl shrimp net. Cost is $27 for adults and $17 for kids.

GOLF If you're not staying in a resort with a golf course (see "Where to Stay," below, and note these courses can be extremely expensive), try the 36-hole **Amelia Links** (𝒞 **904/261-6161;** www.omniameliaislandplantation.com), featuring two signature courses designed by Pete Dye and Bobby Weed at the Omni Amelia Island Plantation, where greens fees range from $125 to $150 per person depending on the time and season. The **Long Point** ★★ course, a mind-blowingly beautiful Tom Fazio–designed 18-holer, has two par-3s in a row bordering the ocean. Fees are highish—from $115 to $200 depending on the time and season. Or play the older and less expensive 27-hole **Fernandina Municipal Golf Course** (𝒞 **904/277-7370;** www.fernandinabeachgolf club.com), where prices are $20 to $41 for 18 holes or $16 to $26 for 9 holes.

For course information go to www.golf.com or www.floridagolfing.com; or you can call the **Florida Sports Foundation** (𝒞 **850/488-8347**) or **Florida Golfing** (𝒞 **866/833-2663**).

HORSEBACK RIDING You can ride on the beach with the **Kelly Seahorse Ranch** (𝒞 **904/491-5166;** www.kellyranchinc.net), on the southernmost tip of Amelia Island within the Amelia Island State Park. The cost is $70 per person for a 1-hour ride; the ranch is open daily from 8am to 6pm. Reservations are required. *Note:* Riders must be 13 or older, at least 4½ feet tall, and weigh less than 230 pounds. No experience is necessary.

SEGWAY TOURS Kayak Amelia also provides 1- and 2-hour eco tours on Segways through upland tree hammocks, Spanish moss, Fort Clinch State Park, Fort George Island, Kingsley Plantation, the Timucuan Preserve, and all that makes this area one of the most scenic and diverse ecosystems in the country. Tours are $75 to $95 per person. Riders must be 14 or older and under 265 pounds. A short lesson on how to ride the Segway will precede the tour.

TENNIS Ranked among the nation's top-50 by *Tennis* magazine, the Omni Amelia Island Plantation's **Racquet Park** (𝒞 **904/261-6161;** www.aipfl.com/Tennis/tennis. htm), with 23 Har-Tru tennis courts (naturally shaded by a canopy of gorgeous trees), hosts many professional tournaments, and is home to the renowned Cliff Drysdale Tennis program.

An Old Jail Turned Historic Museum

Amelia Island Museum of History ★ MUSEUM The only time you'll ever want to spend some time in a county jail may be at this uber-cool museum, housed in the old Nassau County jail and full of fascinating facts, factoids and artifacts about Amelia Island. Even cooler is the fact that this museum is the state's first spoken history museum that prides itself on perpetuating their story-telling tradition with a slew of tours catering to all sorts of ages and interests. Permanent exhibits include a replica of a typical Timucuan Village of Amelia Island circa 4000 years ago, a children's exhibit on an old ship, and assorted artifacts and stories of the area from the Spanish Mission Period and the Civil War until present day.

The museum also offers fun and fascinating **walking tours** of historic Centre Street on Thursday and Friday from September to June. These depart at 3pm from the chamber of commerce (p. 222) and cost $10 for adults, $5 for students. You can't make a reservation—just show up. Longer tours of the 50-square-block historic district can be arranged with 24-hour notice; these cost $10 per person with a minimum of four persons required. I especially recommend the ghost tour at 6pm every Friday beginning in the cemetery behind St. Peters Episcopal Church at 801 Atlantic Ave. ($10 adults, $5 students), or the pub crawl that leaves Thursday evenings at 5:30pm to tour four of the small town's most popular, notorious, or otherwise historic pubs and bars. Cost is $25 per person (21 and over only) and reservations for this one are a must.

233 S. 3rd St. (btw. Beech and Cedar sts.). www.ameliamuseum.org. ✆ **904/261-7378.** Admission $7 adults, $4 students; tours $10 adults, $5 students. Mon–Sat 10am–4pm. Tours Mon–Sat 11am and 2pm.

Where to Stay

More than two-dozen of the town's charming Victorian and Queen Anne houses have been restored and turned into B&Bs. For a complete list, contact the chamber of commerce (p. 222) or the **Amelia Island Bed & Breakfast Association** (✆ **888/277-0218;** www.ameliaislandinns.com). You can tour all the B&Bs during an island-wide open house the first weekend in December. Your best camping option here is **Fort Clinch State Park** (p. 222). *Note:* Rates are subject to an 11% hotel tax (7% sales tax, 4% bed tax).

Elizabeth Pointe Lodge ★★   A whole lot of Nantucket-style charm exists on a magnificent piece of Amelia Island beachfront thanks to this three-story shingled stunner. Although the Lodge's original owners have sold and some say it's not as comfy-cozy and personal, others disagree and say the new owners have added a bit of much-needed modernity via updated, coastal furnishings. What hasn't changed are the views through big-paned windows looking out to the sea, be it from a plush couch in the library or from a table in the bright and airy breakfast room. A dreamy front porch is an alluring spot from which to just breathe in the sea air, but then again, you are sitting right on an unparalleled beachfront so you may want to get up and head into the surf. Or not. Antiques, reproductions, and other touches lend the 20 rooms in the main building a turn-of-the-20th-century beach-cottage vibe. All have oversize tubs. The recently restored Ocean House next door has four large guest rooms in a West Indies motif, and the two-bedroom, two-bathroom Miller Cottage is great for small groups. You'll never go hungry here, either. In addition to the breakfast, there are snacks throughout the day, a wine and hors d'oeuvres hour, and changing menus of light meals, snacks, and desserts available 24 hours a day.

98 S. Fletcher Ave. (just south of Atlantic Ave.), Fernandina Beach, FL 32034. www.elizabeth pointelodge.com. ✆ **800/772-3359** or 904/277-4851. 25 units, including 1 cottage. $185–$395 double, $450 cottage. Rates include full seaside buffet breakfast, parking, and wine hour. Packages available. **Amenities:** Bike rentals; room service; free Wi-Fi.

Fairbanks House ★★   What used to be known as Fairbanks's Folly because of its circa 1885-ostentatious decor is currently one of Amelia Island's most romantic standouts. Rooms here are each decorated differently, but they have one thing in common: they're *very* Victorian, though the Country French Room is more Laura Ashley than Laura Ingalls. Many rooms and all of the cottages offer private entrances for guests who prefer not to walk through the main house. The two-bedroom Grand Tower Suite, occupying the entire top floor, sleeps up to four people, has 360-degree views and its own whirlpool tub, and exudes a bit of Brady Bunch vibe with wood paneling and whatnot. Five other units here have whirlpool tubs as well. The Fairbanks also has a great pool. As old as the place is, it is entirely modern in thinking, with all landscaping renovated to eco-friendly standards and boasting a fluttery little butterfly garden. Creative packages including "Girls Just Wanna Have Fun" and a variety of very popular romance packages.

227 S. 7th St. (btw. Beech and Cedar sts.), Fernandina Beach, Amelia Island, FL 32034. www.fair bankshouse.com. (℘ **888/891-9882** or 904/277-0500. 12 units, including 3 cottages. $185–$230 double, $230–$395 cottage, $265–$450 suites. Rates include full breakfast and evening social hour (beverages and hors d'oeuvres). Packages available. No children 11 and under. **Amenities:** Free use of bikes; outdoor pool; free Wi-Fi.

Florida House Inn ★
Name droppers and history buffs love this place. Among those who have stayed here: Ulysses S. Grant, Henry Ford, Laurel & Hardy, Mary Pickford, José Martí, The Carnegies, and the Rockefellers. And while no Kardashians have yet to lay their heiry heads here, Florida House Inn, the state's oldest-operating hotel, is a charming throwback to simpler times. Each of the 17 rooms and suites offer varying color schemes and antiques but also have the modern comforts of flatscreen TVs and Wi-Fi. Enjoy fried chicken and champagne in Leddy's, the inn's dining room, serving lunch and dinner, followed by a thoroughly modern cocktail (cucumber, lime juice, jalapeño, and tequila, anyone?) at The Mermaid Bar located on the downstairs level. If a few of those don't leave you spinning, consider rocking away on the two gingerbread-trimmed front verandas or on a back porch overlooking a brick courtyard shaded by a huge oak tree just like they did in the good ol' days. *Note:* Children 13 and under are allowed "at the proprietor's discretion," but I'll save you the sizing up and say that this is not a place for kids at all.

22 S. 3rd St. (btw. Centre and Ash sts.), Fernandina Beach, FL 32034. www.floridahouseinn.com. (℘ **800/258-3301** or 904/261-3300. 17 units. $110–$240 double. Rates include parking, full breakfast, and happy hour. **Amenities:** Restaurant; bar; free Wi-Fi.

Hampton Inn & Suites Amelia Island ★★
Not every Hampton Inn is cookie-cutter sterile. Well, maybe most are, but the one here overlooking the Fernandina Beach Marina and within walking distance to shops and restaurants happens to be the chain's crown jewel, at least in Florida anyway. The outside of the hotel looks—dare I say vaguely Portofinoqesue, with different structures, all in the styles and sherbet hues of the Victorian storefronts lining Centre Street. Wooden floors taken from an old Jacksonville church, slatted door panels straight off of a 19th-century schooner, and a lobby with grand staircase, fireplace, and ceiling clock add to the place's charm. Half the rooms have king-size beds, gas fireplaces, and two-person whirlpool tubs. Standard suites are large enough for families, and the other rooms are adequately equipped for business travelers. About a third of the units have balconies. Those higher up on the west side have fine views over the river and marshes. Trains slowly rumble by the west side a few times a day, but somehow that only adds to the place's charm. This is not your roadside Hampton Inn—not even close.

29 S. 2nd St. (btw. Centre and Ash sts.), Fernandina Beach, FL 32034. www.hamptoninnandsuites ameliaisland.com. (℘ **800/426-7866** or 904/491-4911. 122 units. $119–$319 double. Rates include extensive hot breakfast buffet. **Amenities:** Fitness room; Jacuzzi; pool; free Wi-Fi.

Omni Amelia Island Plantation ★★ You have to give Omni credit for calling their $85-million revamp of the island's largest resort a "re-imagination." And while whatever you call it boils down to semantics, I call it amazing. And huge. With over 1,350 lush beachfront acres of manicured golf greens, bike trails, and a breathtaking coastal wilderness of marshes and lagoons, this massive resort is so spread out that a free tram runs around the grounds every 15 minutes. Or you can just wander and get lost. That's half the charm. For the athletic types, there's serious golf, tennis, and two fitness centers, one with a 20-yard-heated indoor lap pool. For those who prefer to lay back and be pampered, a 16-room, all-natural spa also features a meditation garden, plus nontoxic, paraben-free products and services. There are two amazing pools here—one is an adults-only infinity pool and the other a sprawling family-friendly one complete with splash park for the tiniest sunbathers. There are 404 oceanfront hotel rooms here, all spruced up in minimalistic, modern Omni-style. For larger accommodations, **The Villas of Amelia Island Plantation Resort** offer one-, two-, and three-bedroom stays reminiscent of someone's apartment. I prefer the hotel because you are smack in the middle of everything. Speaking of everything, there are 9 different dining options here, but I favor the pub-style Falcon's Nest and its build-your-own-burger option. There's also a pizza place, a seafood spot, and Southern-inspired restaurant. Kids love it here for so many reasons, among them, Camp Amelia for kids ages 4 to 12 and a nature center that plays host to all kinds of critters and conducts cool tours such as the Crab Grab in which you go fishing the old fashioned way—with your hands. *Note:* You can Segway your way around the massive resort. Prices for Segway transportation devices range from $40 for a 30-minute kids' excursion to $80 for a 1½-hour seaside tour of the property. All tours include orientation, coaching, and tour guides.

6800 First Coast Hwy., Amelia Island, FL 32034-3000. www.omniameliaislandplantation.com. ⓒ **800/834-4900** or 904/261-6161. 404 units $99–$419 double, $169–$459 villa. Packages available. Valet parking $15, free self-parking. **Amenities:** 9 restaurants; 5 bars; babysitting; bike rental; age-specific youth programs; concierge; 3 championship golf courses; health club; Jacuzzi; heated indoor pool and 2 outdoor pools (1 heated); limited room service; sauna; spa; 23 tennis courts Wi-Fi (charge).

Ritz-Carlton Amelia Island ★★★ While nearby Omni is sprawling, massive, and thoroughly modern, the Ritz is glitzier and smaller, but no less impressive. While there is a great kids' program here, I still recommend the Omni for kids over this place. The Ritz is more for couples looking to retreat into luxury and to bask in its beachy glow or, perhaps, make use of the extensive recreational facilities, including a beautiful 18-hole championship golf course. The rooms—all with oceanfront or oceanview balconies or patios—are large and typical Ritz with marble bathrooms and fancy bath products. The swanky **Salt** ★★★, the longest-running AAA Five Diamond restaurant in Florida, features a modern American menu heavy on steaks and seafood (the Florida snapper with black garlic pasta is to go gaga for); the restaurant is named after the 30-plus international salts the kitchen collects. You could easily plan your stay around one of their fantastic, hands-on cooking classes or the chef's nightly changing "Chef's Adventure" menus. Check the website for dates. There's a beautiful outdoor pool with all sorts of Ritzy amenities—spritz of Evian on your face perhaps? And an indoor heated pool for chillier temps. While chairs at the pristine beach are free, umbrellas will set you back $25. There's also a state-of-the-art spa with a sublime, adults-only spa pool.

4750 Amelia Island Pkwy., Amelia Island, FL 32034. www.ritzcarlton.com. ⓒ **800/241-3333** or 904/277-1100. 446 units. $199–$439 double, 389–$829 suite. Golf, tennis, and other packages available. Valet parking $20. **Amenities:** 5 restaurants; 3 bars; babysitting; bike rental; children's programs; concierge; concierge-level rooms; golf course; fitness center; heated indoor and out-door pools; room service; spa; 9 tennis courts; watersports equipment rentals; Wi-Fi (charge).

Where to Dine

You'll find several restaurants, pubs, and snack shops along Centre Street, between the bay and 8th Street (A1A), in Fernandina Beach's old town. Two good dining options stand opposite the Hampton Inn & Suites on South 2nd Street, between Centre and Ash streets: the hip **Joe's 2nd Street Bistro** (✆ 904/321-2558; www.joesbistro.com) and the more formal but still relaxed **Le Clos** (✆ 904/261-8100; www.leclos.com). Joe's serves fine international fare in an old store, while Le Clos provides provincial French fare in a charming old house. Joe's serves lunch and dinner while Le Clos serves dinner only; reservations are recommended. Drop by during the day for a look at the menus posted outside each.

And don't forget **Salt** at the Ritz-Carlton Amelia Island (see above); a world-class four-course "Chef's Adventure" menu is worth the $95 per-person price tag ($140 per person paired with wines).

Brett's Waterway Cafe ★ SEAFOOD/STEAK   When it comes to location, Brett's wins as the only place in town where you can eat and drink while watching the boats come and go on the river and the sun set over the marshes. And the food's pretty good too. One of the best dishes is the shrimp and grits, served with collard greens and Vidalia onion threads. Another good one is the low country boil with expertly cooked crawfish, clams, and shrimp. Don't come expecting a fancy seafood spot. This is as Lowcountry as it gets on Amelia Island.

1 S. Front St. (at Centre St. on the water), Fernandina Beach. ✆ **904/261-2660.** Main courses $15–$30. Mon–Sat 11:30am–2:30pm and 5:30–9:30pm, Sun 5:30–9:30pm.

Joe's 2nd Street Bistro ★★★ NEW AMERICAN   While I don't think the phrase "Eat at Joe's" started here, it could easily be applied here—it's an unpretentious spot that locals call home and where visitors must go. With a brick fireplace inside and a more tropical vibe outside on the patio, Joe's is the destination for things you won't find else-where—chicken and Andouille wontons; grouper filet grilled in a cornhusk wrapper with roasted jalapeño; and a phenomenal flat-iron pork steak topped with caramelized onion gravy, a sunny side up egg, and grits. On Fridays, Saturdays, and Sundays, Joe's serves up stellar slow-roasted prime rib. Joe's rocks. Don't miss it. Eat at Joe's.

14 S. 2nd St. (at Front St.), Fernandina Beach. www.joesbistro.com. ✆ **904/321-2558.** Reserva-tions recommended. Main courses $24–$32. Mon, Wed–Sun 11am–3pm and 5:30–9pm; closed Tues.

The Marina Restaurant ★ AMERICAN   A quaint red-brick building with red-and-white–striped awning houses this locals' Lowcountry mainstay serving Southern specials such as pan-fried pork cube steak, fried crab cakes, Salisbury steak with spicy dirty rice, and smothered chicken with white-cream gravy. While there's little to write home about in terms of its downhome, diner-like ambience, The Marina is the quintes-sence of a comfort-food joint. They speak Southern Fried (fried beer-battered broc-coli!) and they speak it fluently.

101 Centre St. (at Front St.), Fernandina Beach. ✆ **904/261-5310.** Main courses $9–$30. Daily 11am–9pm.

29 South ★★★ NEW AMERICAN   Chef Scotty Schwartz has cooked at The James Beard House and received numerous accolades, but all that is just on paper.

What matters is what's on his plate and it's all pretty outstanding and out of the ordinary for these parts. Signature items include lobster corn dogs with spicy horseradish ketchup spiked with Ketel One vodka, sweet tea–brined DelKat Family Farm pork chop on macaroni gratin with warm blackberry preserves, and grilled heart of romaine salad with Maytag blue vinaigrette with bacon and toasted walnuts. Best of all, Schwartz, part of the Slow Food Movement (as ironic as that sounds with his quick, au courant menu), procures as much as he can from local purveyors. The restaurant also has its own chef's garden from which it plucks fresh herbs and veggies. Best of all, it's not a trendy, snobby spot but a casual eatery in a converted house reminiscent of something out of Key West. This place manages to turn everything into something extraordinary. Even coffee and doughnuts are served here—as glazed doughnut bread pudding with butterscotch drizzle and mocha ice cream. Book early because this place fills up fast.

29 S. 3rd St., Fernandina Beach. www.29southrestaurant.com. ⓒ **904/277-7919.** Reservations strongly suggested. Main courses $18–$30. Sun 10am–2pm, Tues–Sat 11:30am–2:30pm, Mon–Thurs 5:30–9:30pm, Fri–Sat 5:30–10pm.

After Dark

Palace Saloon ★ AMERICAN   The state's oldest continuously operating (legal) drinking establishment, the Palace Saloon is a must before or after dinner if but for a drink and to drink in the ambience of inlaid mosaic floors, embossed tin ceiling, and murals depicting scenes from Shakespeare to Dickens. While the Saloon used to serve food, they now only cater to, as they say, "those on a liquid diet." Nightly entertainment from DJs to live bands is good, but not nearly as enthralling as the history of the place. It was originally constructed as a haberdashery in 1878 until 1903, when hats were replaced with booze, even on the very last night before Prohibition, when the Saloon was the last to close, staying open until midnight and grossing $60,000 in a single day. Incidentally, the Saloon was also the first hard liquor bar to begin serving Coca-Cola, around 1905. If you're lucky, you'll get a bartender who knows the history of the place and he or she can regale you with fascinating spirited stories to go with your cocktails.

117 Centre St. (at Front St.), Fernandina Beach. www.thepalacesaloon.com. ⓒ **904/491-3332.** Daily noon–2am.

SIDE TRIPS
Ocala, Florida's Horse Country

Just 78 miles west of Daytona Beach is **Ocala,** a different world that is more Kentucky than Central Florida. Known for its rolling hills, cow pastures, and Derby-caliber horse farms, Ocala is a nature-lover's paradise and home to the stunning **Ocala National Forest ★** (ⓒ 877/445-3352; www.floridatrail.org), with 600 lakes, 23 spring-fed streams, and two rivers and lakes, including **Lake George,** the second-largest lake in Florida, whose west side is encompassed within the forest and features springs and an impressive variety of wildlife and fish, including Atlantic stingray, mullet, striped bass, and blue crab. In fact, there's so much blue crab in Lake George that it supports a local fishery, making it one of the few freshwater blue crab fisheries in the world. Designated a National Scenic Trail in 1983, the forest's Florida Trail features the remains of homesteads made famous by Marjorie Kinnan Rawlings's classic *The Yearling.* Speaking of, located next door to the **Marjorie Kinnan Rawlings Historic State Park,**

18700 S. County Rd. 325 (℗ **352/466-3672;** www.floridastateparks.org/marjorie kinnanrawlings), in which you can walk through the restored Cracker-style home in which she wrote the book, is a restaurant of the same name. **The Yearling,** 14531 E. County Rd. 325 (℗ **352/466-3999;** www.yearlingrestaurant.net) serves venison, sour-orange pie, frog legs, catfish, and cheese grits and features antique outboard motors, old guns, and other authentic memorabilia. Entrees range from $15 to $23. Admission to the park and Rawlings' home is $3 per car, and for a tour $3 adults, $2 children ages 6 to 12.

Just outside of Ocala is **Silver Springs,** 5656 E. Silver Springs Blvd. (℗ **352/236-2121;** www.silversprings.com), a 350-acre natural theme park whose main attraction is the country's largest collection of artisan springs. The park is listed on the National Register of Historic Landmarks and features wild animal displays, glass-bottom boat rides, a jungle cruise, and a jeep safari. Ocala, in Marion County, which has been called the "Horse Capital of the World," also has a quaint, historic downtown district, with renovated Victorian homes and buildings, boutiques, antiques shops, restaurants, and cafes. While Ocala isn't necessarily somewhere to spend a week, it is worth exploring the **Heart of Florida Scenic Trail** (www.floridaseden.org), which comprises the college town of Gainesville, the horse country of Ocala, Old Florida towns including the very Victorian McIntosh and Micanopy, and the scenic Rainbow River (www.therainbowriver.com). For more information on the area, contact the **Marion County Visitors and Convention Bureau,** 2102 SW 20th Place (℗ **888/356-2252;** www.ocalamarion.com).

Paynes Prairie Preserve

Just 40 minutes north from Ocala is **Micanopy** (www.welcometomicanopy.com), Florida's oldest inland settlement that's full of great antiques shops and home to the **Paynes Prairie Preserve State Park,** 100 Savannah Blvd. (℗ **352/466-3397;** www. floridastateparks.org/paynesprairie), a bird-watcher's dream, featuring more than 270 species, as well as alligators and bison. Exhibits and an audiovisual program at the visitor center explain the area's natural and cultural history. A 50-foot-high observation tower near the visitor center provides a panoramic view of the preserve. Eight trails provide opportunities for hiking, horseback riding, and bicycling. November through April, ranger-led activities are offered on weekends. Admission is $6 per vehicle with up to eight people, $4 single-occupant vehicle, and $2 pedestrians. From I-75 South, take exit 374 (the Micanopy exit) and turn right at the end of the exit ramp. You will then be traveling east on C.R. 234. Stay on this road 1¼ miles until it intersects with U.S. 441. Turn left onto 441 and go about ⅔ mile to Paynes Prairie Preserve State Park.

PLANNING YOUR TRIP

A s with any trip, a little preparation is essential before you start your journey. This chapter provides a variety of planning tools, including information on how to get there, how to get around within the city once there, and when to come. And then, in a mainly alphabetical listing, we deal with the dozens of miscellaneous resources and organizations that you can turn to for help. If you do your homework on special events, pick the right season, and pack for the climate, preparing for a trip to Charleston, Savannah, and St. Augustine should be pleasant and uncomplicated.

9

GETTING THERE
By Plane
TO CHARLESTON

American Airlines and **American Eagle** (✆ 800/433-7300; www. aa.com), **Delta** and **Delta Connection** (✆ 800/221-1212; www.delta.com), **Jet Blue Airways** (✆ 801/449-2525; www.jetblue.com), **Southwest Airlines** (✆ 800/435-9792; www.southwest.com), and **United Express** (✆ 800/241-6522; www.united.com) all serve **Charleston International Airport** (www.chs-airport.com) from points all over the East Coast and Mid-West. Jet Blue offers especially good deals from Boston, New York-JFK, and Washington-National. Flying from the West Coast, Canada, or other international locations you will have to change planes at least once (usually in Atlanta). Note that there are no commercial flights between Charleston and Savannah—most visitors drive or take a bus. For information on getting to central Charleston from the airport, see p. 43.

TO SAVANNAH

American Eagle, Delta Airlines/Delta Connection, Jet Blue Airways, and **United Express** all serve **Savannah/Hilton Head International Airport** (www.savannahairport.com). Delta and Jet Blue fly non-stop from New York, while Jet Blue flies non-stop from Boston, and United flies non-stop from Chicago and Houston. As with Charleston, most other flights to Savannah involve a change in Atlanta (there are no direct flights from the West Coast, Canada, or international locations). There are no flights between Savannah and Charleston. For information on getting to central Savannah from the airport, see p. 113.

SAVING money ON AIRFARES

Sad but true, airfares are going up and up and up, thanks to the merger of the airlines. But there are still some savvy trips you can use to save—a hair—on airfares.

1. **Search smartly:** By which we mean don't just rely on the "name brand" sites when you're looking for good fares. A relatively new type of airfare site called "consolidators" now search itineraries without selling them (they get a commission if a fare is bought) which means by looking at them you get a much broader search. They not only scan such online travel agencies as Orbitz and Expedia, they also search the airline sites directly as well as some of the lesser-known discount sites. The ones we would recommend are **Momondo.com** (you'll find them on the Frommers.com website), **Kayak.com,** and **DoHop.com.**

2. **Go when no one else is:** And that doesn't just mean flying in the off-season (though that can be a big money-saver). Recent studies of airline booking data have shown that passengers who depart on a Wednesday (the cheapest day of the week to fly to most destinations) pay on average $40 less than those who fly on Sundays (the priciest day of the week).

3. **Book at the right time:** Perhaps it's because consumers have more time to search for airfares on the weekends, but those who book then end up paying significantly more than those who book during the week. As well, according to a study from the Airline Reporting Corporation (the company that acts as the middleman between airlines and travel agents) those who book 6 weeks in advance for a domestic ticket statistically spend the least amount of money.

TO ST. AUGUSTINE

St Augustine actually has its own airport, the **Northeast Florida Regional Airport** (www.flynfra.com), 4796 U.S. Hwy. 1 (4 miles north of the center), but the only scheduled flight there at present is the Frontier Airlines (www.flyfrontier.com) service from Trenton, New Jersey. The nearest major airport is **Jacksonville International Airport** (www.flyjacksonville.com) 50 miles and 55 minutes drive to the north, with connections to major cities all over the U.S.

By Car

I-95 enters South Carolina from the north near Dillon and runs straight through the state to Hardeeville on the Georgia border. The major artery into **Charleston** itself is I-26, running southeast from Columbia (115 miles), crossing I-95, and dropping you smack in the center of the city. U.S. 17 is the sleepier coastal road—northeast lies Myrtle Beach (95 miles), while Savannah lies 105 miles to the southwest.

In South Carolina, vehicles must use headlights when windshield wipers are in use as a result of inclement weather. Remember that drivers and front-seat passengers must wear seat belts.

I-95 runs north-south along the Eastern Seaboard of Georgia, conveniently skirting the suburbs of **Savannah** itself. I-16 runs into the heart of the city; it's also the major route west to Macon (166 miles) and Atlanta (250 miles). Jacksonville lies 140 miles south on I-95, with **St. Augustine** 40 miles farther south along the same highway.

By Train

Charleston and Savannah both lie on the **Amtrak** (© **800/872-7245;** www.amtrak.com) "Silver Service" line from New York to Miami and Tampa. Amtrak offers tour packages including hotel, breakfast, and historic-site tours in both cities. Be sure to ask about discount fares or any other current fare specials. Amtrak also offers attractively priced rail/drive packages in the Carolinas and Georgia. It's also possible to travel between Charleston and Savannah by Amtrak train. For more information on getting to Charleston by train, see p. 44; for Savannah, see p. 114.

The nearest Amtrak station to St. Augustine is at **Palatka,** 220 N. 11th St. (platform only), though this is still 29 miles southwest of downtown St. Augustine. Buses sometimes make the connection, but you must check in advance. Greyhound (see below) runs between the two twice a day (40 min.), departing Palatka at 6:05am and 5:10pm.

By Bus

Greyhound (© **800/231-2222;** www.greyhound.com) and **Southeastern Stages** (© **404/591-2750;** www.southeasternstages.com) link Charleston and Savannah with each other and with major destinations in South Carolina and Georgia, though for long distances the bus is not recommended. If you book far enough in advance, domestic flights are not that much more expensive, and are far more convenient. International visitors can obtain information about the **Greyhound North American Discovery Pass.** The pass can be obtained from foreign travel agents or through www.discoverypass.com for unlimited travel and stopovers in the U.S. and Canada. For more information on getting to Charleston by bus, see p. 44; for Savannah, see p. 114.

Greyhound connects **St. Augustine** with the Amtrak train station at Palatka (see above), Jacksonville (45 min.) twice a day, and Daytona Beach, Orlando, and even Savannah (1 daily; 5 hr.), via Brunswick. Buses drop off at 1 Castillo Drive, right in the heart of St. Augustine.

GETTING AROUND

When it comes to getting around Charleston, Savannah, and St. Augustine, the best advice is to park your car and forget about it for the rest of your stay. The Historic Districts of all three cities are easily—and most enjoyably—explored **on foot,** and if you get tired, local buses are either cheap or completely free. We've included details about **renting bikes** in the relevant chapters.

By Car

Whilst **driving** around central Charleston, Savannah, or St. Augustine is neither necessary or recommended, having a car will be extremely useful if you plan to explore sights on the outskirts or further out of town. Public transport is minimal beyond the city limits, and in any case, you'll have a lot more freedom with your own wheels.

RENTING A CAR

Renting cars is easy at local airports, as well as within the cities themselves. Alamo (www.alamo.com), Avis (www.avis.com), Budget (www.budget.com), Dollar (www.dollar.com), Enterprise Rent-a-Car (www.enterprise.com), Hertz (www.hertz.com), National (www.nationalcar.com), and Thrifty (www.thrifty.com) are all represented. Rates are typically cheaper if booked online.

Drivers are supposed to have held their licenses for at least 1 year, and folks under 25 may encounter problems or restrictions when renting (there is usually a surcharge of of $10–$25 a day). If you're under 25, always call ahead. If you're under 21, you will not be able to rent a car at all. United Kingdom, Canadian, most European, Australian, and New Zealand nationals can drive in the U.S. provided they have a full driving license from their home country.

Car rental companies will also expect you to have a credit card; if you don't have one, they may charge you a hefty deposit (at least $300–$500), but it's highly unlikely you'll be able to rent.

If you intend to pick up the car in Charleston and drop it off in Savannah (or vice versa) check if there are any drop-off or one-way fees—Budget, for example, generally doesn't charge extra for this.

Loss Damage Waiver (LDW) is a form of insurance that often isn't included in the initial rental charge, and without it you're liable for every scratch to the car, regardless of who was at fault. LDW can cost anything from $12 to $25 per day in addition to rental charges, depending on the type of car rented, although some credit card companies offer automatic LDW coverage to anyone using their card to pay in full for the rental.

PARKING

Parking in the Historic Districts of Charleston, Savannah, and St. Augustine can be a nightmare, even for the locals. Almost every hotel will have some kind of parking arrangement for guests, though only a handful offer free parking. We've included parking prices in the relevant accommodation sections.

The **City of Savannah** operates over 3,000 metered parking spaces, five public parking garages, and six surface lots in downtown Savannah. The cost for parking meters range from 30¢ per hour to $1 per hour depending on the location. Parking meter rates in the three **River Street parking lots** are $1 per hour. Tourists may purchase a 2-day **parking pass** for $12, or a 1-day pass for $7 (get them at the Visitor Center). Meters are in force Monday through Friday, 8am to 5pm; you can park for free outside of these times. For more on parking in Savannah, see p. 115.

Charleston offers a similar blend of lots, garages, and parking meters, with metered rates starting at 5¢ for 4 minutes, and up to 25¢ for 20 minutes. Meters are in force Monday through Saturday, 8am to 6pm; you can park for free outside of these times. For more on parking in Charleston, see p. 46.

In **St. Augustine,** parking lots are located throughout the downtown area and on-street parking is also available: some spots require payment via pay-stations and others

9

PLANNING YOUR TRIP | Getting Around

via traditional meters. Rules are enforced Monday to Saturday 8am to 5pm; you can park for free outside of these times (apart from around the Castillo San Marcos, where rules are enforced 7 days a week). Rates are normally $1.50 per hour, with a 3- to 4-hour limit. The best place to park is the **Historic Downtown Parking Facility,** located adjacent to the Visitors Information Center (see p. 193); there is a $10 flat rate daily.

Note that parking regulations are strictly enforced in all three cities—always check with a local or your hotel if you are unsure about your parking spot. Getting towed or "booted" by the authorities is a depressingly common (and expensive) occurrence.

By Bus

Though all three cities boast efficient **public bus systems,** you are unlikely to need to use them when exploring the respective Historic Districts. If you do get tired, Charleston and Savannah offer excellent **free bus services:** the **Downtown Area Shuttle** in Charleston (p. 46), and the **"dot" Express Shuttle** in Savannah (p. 116).

For exploring the surrounding areas, we recommend renting a car.

ENTRY REQUIREMENTS
ESTA & Visas

Under the **Visa Waiver Program (VWP),** citizens of Australia, Ireland, New Zealand, most European countries, and the U.K. do not require visas for visits of 90 days or less to the U.S. You will, however, need to obtain **Electronic System for Travel Authorization (ESTA)** online before you fly at **https://esta.cbp.dhs.gov/esta**, which involves completing a basic immigration form in advance, on the computer. There is a processing fee of $4, and a further $10 authorization fee once your ESTA has been approved (all paid via credit card online). Once received, authorizations are valid for multiple entries into the U.S. for 2 years—submit an ESTA application as soon as you fix your travel plans (in most cases the ESTA will be granted immediately, but it can sometimes take up to 72 hr.). You will need to present a machine-readable passport to Immigration upon arrival in the U.S. Canadians now require a passport to cross the border, but can travel in the U.S. for up to a year without a visa or visa waiver. If you do not hold a passport from one of the 38 countries included in the ESTA program, you will need to apply for a **tourist visa** before you visit the U.S., usually at your nearest U.S. Embassy, and pay at least $160 in application fees. Visit **www.travel.state.gov** for the latest details.

Medical Requirements

Unless you're arriving from an area known to be suffering from an epidemic, inoculations or vaccinations are not required for entry into the United States. If you have a medical condition that requires **syringe-administered medications** or treatment with **narcotics,** you should carry documented proof with you.

Customs
WHAT YOU CAN BRING INTO THE U.S.

Every visitor more than 21 years of age may bring in, free of duty, the following: (1) 1 liter of wine or hard liquor; (2) 200 cigarettes, 100 cigars (but not from Cuba), or 3 pounds of smoking tobacco; and (3) $100 worth of gifts. These exemptions are offered to travelers who spend at least 72 hours in the United States and who have not claimed them within the preceding 6 months. It is forbidden to bring almost any meat products (including canned, fresh, and dried meat products such as bouillon, soup mixes, and so on). Generally, condiments including vinegars, oils, spices, coffee, tea, and some cheeses and baked goods are permitted. Avoid rice products, as rice can often harbor insects. Bringing fruits and vegetables is not advised, though not prohibited. Customs will allow produce depending on where you got it and where you're going after you arrive in the U.S. Foreign tourists may carry in or out up to $10,000 in U.S. or foreign currency with no formalities; larger sums must be declared to U.S. Customs on entering or leaving, which includes filing form CM 4790. For details regarding U.S. Customs and Border Protection, consult your nearest U.S. embassy or consulate, or **U.S. Customs** (www.cbp.gov).

LODGINGS

Throughout this guide, we've tried to steer you to the types of hotels that will really offer you a great experience of the destination. But we won't sugarcoat the ugly truth about hotel pricing, which has been skyrocketing in recent years. If you'd like to save money on lodgings, consider the following strategies:

o **Buy a money-saving package deal.** A travel package that combines your airfare and your hotel stay for one price may just be the best bargain of all. In some cases, you'll get airfare, accommodations, transportation to and from the airport, plus extras—maybe an afternoon sightseeing tour or restaurant and shopping discount coupons—for less than the hotel alone would have cost had you booked it yourself. Most airlines and many travel agents, as well as the usual booking websites (Priceline, Travelocity, Expedia) offer good packages.

o **Choose a chain.** With some exceptions, we have not listed mass-volume chain hotels in this book, as they tend to lack the character and local feel that most independently run hotels have. And it's that feel, we believe, that is so much a part of the travel experience. Still, when you're looking for a deal, they can be a good option. That's because you can also pull out all the stops for discounts at a budget chain, from reward points to senior status to corporate rates. Most chain hotels let the kids stay with parents for free.

o **Avoid excess charges and hidden costs.** Use your own cellphone instead of dialing direct from hotel phones, which usually incur exorbitant rates. And don't be tempted by minibar offerings: Most hotels charge through the nose for water, soda, and snacks. Finally, ask about local taxes and service charges, which can increase the cost of a room by 15% or more. If a hotel insists upon tacking on an "energy surcharge" that wasn't mentioned at check-in, you can often make a case for getting it removed.

o **Make multiple reservations.** This strategy is only necessary in high season. But often then, as the date of the stay approaches, hotels start to play "chicken" with one another, dropping the price a bit one day to try and lure customers away from a nearby competitor. Making this strategy work takes vigilance and persistence, but since your credit card won't be charged until 24 hours before check-in, little risk is involved.

o **Use the right online sites.** Such websites as Booking.com, HotelsCombined.com, and Trivago.com often beat the rest because they cast a broader net when quoting prices. In the case of the latter two, that means that you'll see choices from a number of discounters, some less well-known but all reliable. Booking.com works a bit

New Year's Day: January 1

Martin Luther King, Jr's Birthday: Third Monday in January

Presidents' Day: Third Monday in February

Memorial Day: Last Monday in May

Independence Day: July 4

Labor Day: First Monday in September

Columbus Day: Second Monday in October

Veterans' Day: November 11

Thanksgiving Day: Fourth Thursday in November

Christmas Day: December 25

differently, but it has become known for making side deals with the small mom-and-pop hotels that many of the bigger travel agency sites skip.

o **Book Blind.** If you just want a place to sleep, consider paying before you know the name of the hotel for big savings. You can do so on either **Priceline.com** or **Hotwire.com**, and there is a way to "scoop" the system. A site called BetterBidding. com allows travelers to post how much they bid on a hotel room and which hotel they got. You'll be amazed both at how often the same hotels come up; and by the quality of these hotels (both sites only deal with major chains so you're pretty much assured that you won't be lodged in a dump).

o **Book Last Minute.** An unused bed is inventory lost for a hotelier, so many are willing to play "let's make a deal" in the few days prior to a stay. And many play that game with the app **HotelTonight,** which can only be used on the day of travel. If you have the courage to wait that long, you can often get discounts of up to 70% on hotel rooms.

o **Try an Alternative Accommodation.** Strange but true, it's sometimes cheaper to rent an entire apartment, complete with a kitchen and living room, than it is to stay in a hotel room. On AirBnB, for example, you can rent a complete apartment in the historic district for just $141 per night. If you're willing to just rent a room in an apartment (an informal B&B arrangement), you can pay as little as $45/night in that city. Other sources that rent either full apartments and homes or rooms in private homes include **Wimdu.com, HomeAway.com, Rentalo.com, VRBO.com** and **FlipKey.com.**

[FastFACTS] CHARLESTON, SAVANNAH & ST. AUGUSTINE

Area Codes   It's **843** for Charleston and the South Carolina coast; the area code for Savannah is **912;** and **904** for St. Augustine.

Business Hours, Banks & ATMs   The following are general open hours; specific establishments may vary. **Banks:** Monday to Friday 9am to 3pm (some are also open Sat 9am–noon). Most banks and other outlets offer 24-hour access to automated teller machines (**ATMs**). **Offices:** Monday to Friday 9am to 5pm. **Stores:** Monday to Saturday 10am to 6pm, and some also on Sunday from noon to 5pm. Malls usually stay open until 9pm Monday to Saturday, and department stores are usually open until 9pm at least 1 day a week.

As in the rest of the United States, the easiest

and best way to get cash in Charleston, Savannah, or St. Augustine is from an ATM, sometimes referred to as a "cash machine" or "cashpoint." Be sure you know your personal identification number (PIN) and daily withdrawal limit before you depart. International travelers should confirm their cards are valid for U.S. withdrawals. Look for ATMs with the **Cirrus** (© **800/424-7787;** www.mastercard.com) or **PLUS** (www.visa.com) network symbols, as these are more likely to accept foreign-issued cards.

Dentists For information about dentists in Charleston, see p. 47; for Savannah, see p. 116 for St. Augustine, see p. 194.

Disabled Travelers Many hotels and restaurants in Charleston, Savannah, and St. Augustine provide easy access for persons with disabilities. However, it's always a good idea to call ahead to make sure. South Carolina has numerous agencies that assist people with disabilities. For an updated list, call **Sciway** (© **843/795-3951;** www.sciway.net/med/disabilities.html). Primary agencies include **Protection & Advocacy for the Handicapped** (© **803/782-0639;** www.pandasc.org), the **South Carolina Commission for the Blind** (© **800/922-2222;** www.sccb.state.sc.us), and the **Disabilities Board of Charleston County** (© **843/805-5800;** www.dsncc.com). For transportation within South Carolina or

Georgia, individuals with disabilities can contact **Wheelchair Getaways, Inc.** (© **800/642-2042;** www.wheelchairgetaways.com).

The **Georgia Council of Developmental Disabilities** (© **888/275-4233;** www.gcdd.org) may also be of help.

Note that in all three cities, historic homes and house museums are generally not wheelchair accessible, beyond their gardens. Exceptions in Charleston include the Nathaniel Russell House Museum (p. 71), and the Aiken-Rhett House Museum (p. 66). Wheelchair access also varies at the churches. In Charleston, the Unitarian Church (p. 74), and the French Protestant Church (p. 70), are both accessible, as is Christ Church Episcopal (p. 136) in Savannah. Fort Sumter is wheelchair accessible, but call in advance (p. 78). The museums in all three cities are generally accessible. In Savannah, the only easy way for wheelchair users to pass between River Street/the riverfront and the Historic District proper is to go to the Hyatt hotel and take the elevator. Try and view a copy of the Savannah Accessibility Guide (www.savannahga.gov/DocumentCenter/View/3283) before you go.

In St. Augustine, **Old Town Trolley Tours** have buses that can accommodate handicapped travellers, but it's best to contact them in advance (see p. 208).

Drinking Laws The minimum drinking age in the

Unites States is 21; proof of age is required and often requested at bars, nightclubs, and restaurants, so it's always a good idea to bring ID when you go out.

In Charleston (unlike the rest of South Carolina), in-store beer and wine sales are allowed 24 hours a day, 7 days a week. However, the retail sale of liquor is only permitted Monday to Saturday, from 9am to 7pm. Liquor sales are also banned in Savannah on Sundays, but retailers can sell beer and wine from 12:30 to 11:30pm.

In Savannah's Historic District (but NOT in Charleston's), you are allowed to drink in the street (one alcoholic beverage at a time, in an open plastic container of not more than 16 ounces).

In St. Augustine, Florida Law prohibits the possession of open containers of alcoholic beverages by the driver and passengers of most motor vehicles. In the city itself you can drink in public in certain areas only: notably the Visitor Center, and the greenspace located south of the Center between the Canos de San Francisco Fountain and the Zero Mile Marker. Liquor sales are permitted on Sundays, after 1pm. Don't even think about driving anywhere while intoxicated.

Doctors & Hospitals For information about hospitals in Charleston see p. 47; for Savannah, see p. 116; for St. Augustine, see p. 194.

Electricity Like Canada, the United States uses 110–120 volts AC (60 cycles), compared to 220–240 volts AC (50 cycles) in most of Europe, Australia, and New Zealand. Most mobile phones, cameras, MP3 players, and laptops are dual voltage these days (older hair-dryers are the most common problem for travelers).

Emergencies Dial ℂ **911** for police, ambulance, paramedics, and the fire department. This is a nationwide toll-free call (no coins are required at a public telephone).

Family Travel The American South is a family-oriented society. Most restaurants are set up to handle small kids (many offer discounts and special menus), and there are plenty of family-friendly attractions. Having said that, Charleston and Savannah have developed a reputation as romantic destinations for couples in recent years: many of the best hotels and B&Bs in both historic districts have minimum age requirements, sometimes as high as 21 and above (these are noted in reviews). For attractions specifically for kids in Charleston, see p. 82; for Savannah, see p. 149; for St. Augustine see p. 212.

Health For up-to-date health-related travel advice in the U.S., go to the **Centers for Disease Control and Prevention** website at **wwwnc.cdc.gov/travel**.

You'll have little trouble finding hospitals and doctors in the South Carolina, Georgia, and Florida—in fact, the region has some of the most highly regarded medical centers and teaching facilities in the country (for Charleston see p. 47; for Savannah see p. 116; for St. Augustine see p. 194).

If you suffer from a chronic illness, consult your doctor before your departure. Pack **prescription medications** in your carry-on luggage, and carry them in their original containers, with pharmacy labels—otherwise, they won't make it through airport security. Visitors from outside the U.S. should carry generic names of prescription drugs.

There are no health issues specific to Charleston, Savannah, or St. Augustine. If you do get sick or have an accident, things can get incredibly expensive. It will cost more than $100 to simply see a doctor or dentist, and prescription drugs can be very pricey. For U.S. travelers, most reliable healthcare plans provide coverage if you get sick away from home. Foreign visitors will have to cough up the money and make a claim later. Most hotels will have links to a local practice or doctor for minor illnesses. Should you be in a serious accident, an ambulance will pick you up and charge later. Note that basic emergency care will cost at least $250, ranging to several thousand dollars for serious trauma—that's in addition to fees for drugs, appliances, supplies and the attendant physician, who will charge separately.

Insurance Foreign travelers should definitely invest in **travel insurance** when visiting the U.S. A typical policy provides cover for the loss of baggage, tickets, and—up to a certain limit—cash or checks, as well as cancellation or delay of your journey. Sickness and accident benefits are often extra, but given the cost of healthcare in the U.S, well worth investing in. Note that some all-risks home-insurance policies may cover your possessions when overseas, and many private medical schemes include cover when abroad.

Internet Access As in most parts of the United States, **Wi-Fi** (wireless Internet) is king in Charleston, Savannah, and St. Augustine and internet cafes are becoming a rarity. Most **hotels, coffee shops,** and **public libraries** offer free Wi-Fi access, though not always computer terminals for those without a Wi-Fi–enabled device.

The **Charleston** free Wi-Fi network (www.charleston freewifi.com) provides free Wi-Fi access throughout Marion Square Park (just connect your device to the wireless network named "CharlestonFreeWiFi".) Thanks to Google, free Wi-Fi is also available at Waterfront Park. In **Savannah,** free Wi-Fi is usually available along the Martin Luther King, Jr. Boulevard corridor, River Street, Ellis Square, the south end of Forsyth Park, and in Johnson Square. For the latest list of Wi-Fi hotspots in Savannah, visit www.savannahwifi.com. In **St. Augustine,** numerous cafes offer free Wi-Fi, as does the Barnes & Noble on U.S. 1, and the six local St. Johns County libraries.

Legal Aid While driving, if you are pulled over for a minor infraction (such as speeding), never attempt to pay the fine directly to a police officer; this could be construed as attempted bribery, a much more serious crime. Pay fines by mail, or directly into the hands of the clerk of the court. If accused of a more serious offense, say and do nothing before consulting a lawyer. In the U.S., the burden is on the state to prove a person's guilt beyond a reasonable doubt, and everyone has the right to remain silent, whether he or she is suspected of a crime or actually arrested. Once arrested, a person can make one telephone call to a party of his or her choice. The international visitor should call his or her embassy or consulate.

LGBT Travelers

Though Bible-belt Georgia and South Carolina are generally conservative states, and not especially welcoming for outwardly gay travelers, Charleston and Savannah are a little different. Savannah especially has a fairly tolerant reputation, with numerous gay-owned B&B's, and a decent selection of gay and lesbian bars (especially on River Street). After all, John Berendt, author of *Midnight in the Garden of Good and Evil*, is gay, as are several key characters in "The Book,"

notably The Lady Chablis. The **Savannah Pride Festival** usually takes place in Forsyth Park in September (www.savpride.com). For the latest listings visit **www. gaysavannah.com**.

Though not quite as open, even Charleston has a healthy gay community and several gay-friendly establishments. **Charleston Pride Festival** takes place in August (www.charleston-pride.com). Visit **www. gaycharlestononline.com** for the latest. Lesbians might also want to contact the **Charleston Social Club** (www.charlestonsocialclub. com).

Though northern Florida is not yet as gay-friendly as the southern part of the state, St. Augustine is relatively liberal, and even has a few gay-friendly bars (try St. George Tavern). **At Journey's End Bed & Breakfast** (✆ **904/829-0076;** www. atjourneysend.com) is a gay-friendly inn.

Mail & Postage Ordinary mail within the US costs 49¢ for letters weighing up to an ounce, and 34¢ for postcards; addresses must include a zip code (postal code) and a return address in the upper left corner of the envelope. International mail costs $1.15 for letters and postcards. To find a post office or check up-to-date rates, see www.usps.com or call ✆ **800/275-8777.** For information about **post offices** in Charleston see p. 47; for Savannah, see p. 117; for St. Augustine, see p. 194.

Mobile Phones International visitors who want to use their mobile phones or tablets in Charleston, Savannah, and St. Augustine will need to check with their phone provider at home to make sure they will work in the U.S., and what the charges will be. Unless you have a tri-band device, it is unlikely that a mobile bought for use outside the U.S. or Canada will work inside the United States (all iPhones should work fine).

Assuming your phone does work, beware of roaming charges, especially for data, which can be extortionate; even checking voicemail can result in an expensive phone bill. If you have a compatible (and unlocked) GSM phone and intend to use it a lot, it can be much cheaper to buy a U.S. SIM card ($10 or less) to use during your stay (you can also buy a micro-SIM for iPhone 4, 4S, or any compatible smartphone, or a nano-SIM for iPhone 5). **AT&T** (www.att.com) is usually the most convenient option. Some networks also sell basic phones (with minutes) for as little as $15 (no paperwork or ID required).

Public telephones are becoming harder to find due to the popularity of mobile phones. The cost of a local call is usually 25¢ for 3 or 4 minutes, depending on the carrier (each phone company runs its own booths). Calls elsewhere within the U.S. are usually 25¢ for one minute; international long-distance rates are pricier, and you're better off using a prepaid calling card ($5, $10, and $20), which you can buy at most grocery stores and newsstands.

Money & Costs

Credit cards are the most widely used form of payment in the United States: **Visa, MasterCard, American Express, Diners Club,** and **Discover.** You can withdraw cash advances from your credit cards at banks or ATMs, provided you know your PIN, though most banks will charge fees of up to $3 for the service. Visitors from outside the U.S. should inquire whether their bank assesses an additional fee on charges incurred abroad.

It's highly recommended that you travel with at least one major credit card. You must have one to rent a car, and hotels and airlines usually require a credit card imprint as a deposit against expenses.

The value of the U.S. dollar tends to vary considerably against other currencies. At press time, one dollar was worth 0.59 British pounds (£), 0.72 euros (€), 1.10 Canadian dollars (Can$), 1.07 Australian dollars (Aus$), 1.17 New Zealand dollars (NZ$), and 10.5 South African Rand (R). For current exchange rates, check **www.xe.com**.

Packing The most important item in your suitcase will be a pair of very, very comfortable shoes, because your dogs are gonna be barking! These

are walking cities, and what with getting from place to place and trudging through the historic homes, a springy, supportive pair of shoes is essential (you may want to bring two pairs to increase your feet ease). Other than that, fill your suitcase with what pleases you most at home: Very few actual Southerners dress up during the day and unless you plan on going to a very fancy restaurant, casual clothes should suffice.

Dressing appropriately for the weather is also key, so be sure to check the chart on p. 39 for the average temperatures at various times of the year.

Passports To enter the United States by air, international visitors must have a valid passport that expires at least 6 months later than the scheduled end of your visit.

Note: Canadian citizens entering the U.S. at land and sea ports of entry from within the western hemisphere must now also present a passport or other documents compliant with the Western Hemisphere Travel Initiative (WHTI; see **www.getyouhome.gov** for details).

Pharmacies For information about pharmacies in Charleston see p. 47; for Savannah, see p. 117; for St. Augustine see p. 194.

Safety Although tourist areas are generally safe in the South, crime can occur anywhere, and U.S. urban areas tend to be less safe than those in western

Europe or Japan. This is true of parts of Savannah, Charleston, and St. Augustine. Avoid deserted areas at night. Don't go into any city park at night unless there's an event that attracts crowds. Generally speaking, you can feel safe in areas where there are many people and open establishments.

Remember also that hotels are open to the public, and security may not be able to screen everyone who enters. Always lock your room door.

Downtown Charleston is well-lit and patrolled throughout the night to ensure public safety. People can generally walk around downtown at night without fear of violence. Central St. Augustine is similarly well policed and generally safe at all hours.

In Savannah, though it's reasonably safe to explore the Historic and Victorian districts during the day, the situation changes at night. The clubs along the riverfront, both bars and restaurants, report very little crime. But muggings and drug dealing are common in Savannah's poorer neighborhoods.

Senior Travel The National Park Service (NPS) offers a **Senior Pass** (formerly the **Golden Age Passport**), which gives seniors 62 years or older (U.S. citizens or permanent residents only) lifetime entrance to all properties administered by the NPS— national parks, monuments, historic sites, recreation areas, and national wildlife refuges—for a one-time processing fee of $10. The pass must be purchased in person at any NPS facility that charges an entrance fee. For more information, go to www.nps.gov/findapark/passes.htm.

Many attractions in Charleston, Savannah, and St. Augustine offer discounted admission for seniors—we've noted these throughout.

Nearly all major U.S. hotel and motel chains now offer seniors a discount, so ask for the reduction when you make the reservation; there may be restrictions during peak days. Then be sure to carry proof of your age (driver's license, passport, and so on) when you check in. Among the chains that offer the best discounts are **Marriott Hotels** (✆ **800/228-9290**) for those 62 and older, and **La Quinta Inns** (✆ **800/531-5900**) for ages 55 and older.

Members of **AARP,** 601 E St. NW, Washington, DC 20049 (✆ **888/687-7277;** www.aarp.org), get discounts on hotels, airfares, and car rentals but be sure to surf the internet before accepting their "bargains." Sometimes they're undercut, and undercut deeply, by the prices that discounters can get nowadays.

Smoking Since 2011 smoking has been prohibited in all public places and workplaces in Savannah, and you may not smoke cigarettes in any bar or restaurant. A similar ban has been in force in Charleston since 2012 (though North Charleston still allows smoking in some bars). In 2013 the smoking ban was extended to public sidewalks and streets in the downtown hospital district (the area around the Medical University of South Carolina and Roper St. Francis). Florida's enclosed workplaces, including restaurants and public places, have been smoke-free since 2003, though bars and hotels are exempt and the issue has become quite contentious in recent years. For now smoking is permitted in designated areas in clubs, bars, and hotels in St. Augustine.

Student Travel Almost every attraction in Charleston, Savannah, and St. Augustine offers student discounts on admission; we've noted these throughout. Sadly, youth hostels are rare in these cities.

Taxes South Carolina levies a 6% sales tax; Charleston County adds another 2.5% for a total 8.5% on most purchases. Charleston hotels charge a total 13.5% accommodations tax. Savannah has a 7% sales tax. It also tacks a 6% accommodations tax (a room or occupancy tax) on your hotel bill. In St. Augustine you'll pay a 6% local sales tax. The United States has no value-added tax (VAT) or other indirect tax at the national level. Please note that taxes will not appear on price tags.

Tipping Tipping, in a restaurant, bar, taxi cab, or hotel lobby, on a guided tour, and even in some washrooms, is a part of life in the Unites States. In restaurants in particular, it's unthinkable not to leave the minimum (15% of the bill or double the tax)—even if you disliked the service. It's normal to tip bar staff at least $1 per drink and a coatcheck attendant $1 per coat.

What are other tips you should give? Thoughtful people leave $2 a day for the chambermaid and tip $1 per bag to the bellboy who sees them to their room. For taxis, the accepted tip is 15% of the fare.

Time Charleston, Savannah, and St. Augustine are on Eastern Standard Time (EST), which is 5 hours behind Greenwich Mean Time (GMT), 3 hours ahead of Pacific Standard Time, 14 to 16 hours behind East Coast Australia (variations for Daylight Savings) and 16 to 18 hours behind New Zealand (variations for Daylight Savings).

Toilets These are available throughout the downtown **Charleston** area, including at Broad and Meeting streets, at Queen and Church streets, on Market Street between Meeting and Church streets, and at other clearly marked strategic points in the historic and downtown districts. In **Savannah** you'll find public restroom facilities at the Bryan Street Garage, 100 E. Bryan St., at the Visitor Center on MLK Boulevard, at the Liberty Street Garage, and at the Visitor Center on River Street. In **St. Augustine** there are public restrooms at the Visitor Center, on St. George Street near the Spanish Bakery.

Visas   The U.S. State Department has a **Visa Waiver Program (VWP)** allowing citizens of the following countries to enter the United States without a visa for stays of up to 90 days: Andorra, Australia, Austria, Belgium, Brunei, Czech Republic, Denmark, Estonia, Finland, France, Germany, Greece, Hungary, Iceland, Ireland, Italy, Japan, Latvia, Liechtenstein, Lithuania, Luxembourg, Malta, Monaco, the Netherlands, New Zealand, Norway, Portugal, San Marino, Singapore, Slovakia, Slovenia, South Korea, Spain, Sweden, Switzerland, and the United Kingdom. (**Note:** This list was accurate at press time; for the most up-to-date list of countries in the VWP, consult http://travel.state.gov/visa.) Even though a visa isn't

necessary, in an effort to help U.S. officials check travelers against terror watch lists before they arrive at U.S. borders, visitors from VWP countries must register online through the Electronic System for Travel Authorization (ESTA) before boarding a plane or a boat to the U.S. Travelers must complete an electronic application providing basic personal and travel eligibility information. The Department of Homeland Security recommends filling out the form at least 3 days before traveling. Authorizations will be valid for up to 2 years or until the traveler's passport expires, whichever comes first. Currently, there is a US$14 fee for the online application. Existing ESTA registrations remain valid through their expiration dates. **Note:** Any passport issued on or after October 26, 2006, by a VWP country must be an **e-Passport** for VWP travelers to be eligible to enter the U.S. without a visa. Citizens of these nations also need to present a round-trip air or cruise ticket upon arrival. E-Passports contain computer chips capable of storing

biometric information, such as the required digital photograph of the holder. If your passport doesn't have this feature, you can still travel without a visa if the valid passport was issued before October 26, 2005, and includes a machine-readable zone; or if the valid passport was issued between October 26, 2005, and October 25, 2006, and includes a digital photograph. For more information, go to **http://travel. state.gov/visa**. Canadian citizens may enter the United States without visas, but will need to show passports and proof of residence.

Citizens of all other countries must have (1) a valid passport that expires at least 6 months later than the scheduled end of their visit to the U.S.; and (2) a tourist visa.

For information about U.S. visas go to **http:// travel.state.gov** and click on "Visas."

Water   The water in your hotel, or at public drinking fountains, is safe to drink.

Index

Restaurants